Although sometimes religion and sexuality are treated as an aberrant theme in American literary and religious history, American writers from Nathaniel Hawthorne to John Updike have been fascinated with the connection between religious and sexual experience. Through the voice of American fiction, *Religion and Sexuality in American Literature* examines the relations of body and spirit (religion and sexuality) by asking two basic questions: How have American novelists handled the interaction between religious and sexual experience? Are there instructive similarities and differences in how male and female authors write about religion and sexuality? Using both canonical and noncanonical fiction, Ann-Janine Morey examines novels dealing with the ministry as the medium wherein so many of the tensions of religion and sexuality are dramatized and then moves to contemporary novels that deal with moral and religious issues through metaphor. Based upon a sophisticated and selective application of metaphor theory, deconstruction, and feminist postmodernism, Morey argues that while American fiction has replicated many traditional animosities, there are also some rather surprising resources here for commonality between men and women if we acknowledge and understand the intimate relationship between language and physical life.

CAMBRIDGE STUDIES IN AMERICAN LITERATURE AND CULTURE

Editor:

Eric Sundquist, *University of California, Los Angeles*

Advisory Board
Nina Baym, *University of Illinois, Champaign-Urbana*
Sacvan Bercovitch, *Harvard University*
Albert Gelpi, *Stanford University*
Myra Jehlen, *University of Pennsylvania*
Carolyn Porter, *University of California, Berkeley*
Robert Stepto, *Yale University*
Tony Tanner, *King's College, Cambridge University*

Continued on pages following the Index

CAMBRIDGE STUDIES IN AMERICAN LITERATURE
AND CULTURE

Religion and Sexuality in American Literature

Religion and Sexuality in American Literature

ANN-JANINE MOREY
Southern Illinois University at Carbondale

CAMBRIDGE
UNIVERSITY PRESS

Published by the Press Syndicate of the University of Cambridge
The Pitt Building, Trumpington Street, Cambridge CB2 1RP
40 West 20th Street, New York, NY 10011-4211, USA
10 Stamford Road, Oakleigh, Melbourne 3166, Australia

First Published 1992

Printed in the United States of America

Library of Congress Cataloging-in-Publication Data
Morey, Ann-Janine.
Religion and sexuality in American literature / Ann-Janine Morey.
p.   cm. – (Cambridge studies in American literature and
culture 57)
Includes bibliographical references (p.) and index.
ISBN 0-521-41676-0 (hc)
1. American literature–History and criticism.   2. Religion and
literature.   3. Sex–Religious aspects.   4. Sex in literature.
I. Title.   II. Series.
RC685.V2P56   1992
616.1'25–dc20   91-46465
                                                                    CIP

A Catalog record for this book is available from the British Library.

ISBN 0-521-41676-0   hardback

For Robert Detweiler and Todd Hedinger

Language is like shot silk; so much depends upon the angle at which it is held.
—John Fowles, *The French Lieutenant's Woman*

Contents

vii

Acknowledgments

During the process of writing this book, I became a devoted reader of acknowledgments pages, for as solitary an endeavor as this has been, my appreciation for the company of friendly minds who contribute to the making of any book has greatly deepened. Before I ever began writing, George McClure generously gave me numerous opportunities for conversation, and his lively interest in my subject was vital early encouragement. Robert Detweiler read so many versions of the entire manuscript and commented so generously at every stage, that no amount of documenting could account for his contribution to this book. Lee Person and Bill Doty also made extensive comments on the entire manuscript, each supplying just the right critical perspective needed to produce effective revisions. Nina Baym offered helpful comments on Chapter 4, James Nelson and Ralph McCoy lent their friendly readership to Chapter 1, and I have Margaret Winters to thank for translating John Updike's frisky French for Chapter 3. The late Alan Cohn of Morris Library's Humanities Division, Southern Illinois University at Carbondale (SIUC), saw me through more researching blunders than I care to recall, while Angela Rubin, also of Morris Library's Humanities Division, was indefatigable in locating the obscure writers and novels that occupy Chapters 4 and 5. In addition, I owe thanks to the anonymous readers of Cambridge University Press and series editor Albert Gelpi for asking the right hard questions.

A 1983 summer stipend from the National Endowment for the Humanities helped me open up my materials for Chapter 2, and I am grateful to SIUC for my sabbatical year of 1987, during which I finally was able to begin writing. Rebecca Flannagan did a great job confirming or unearthing all manner of pesky bibliographic details during one sultry southern Illinois summer. Robert Jensen, associate dean of SIU's College of Liberal Arts, and Seymour Bryson, executive assistant to the president, collaborated financially to provide me with research support for more than one important phase of writing. I am immensely appreciative of their support of my work and their goodwill toward humanities scholarship during a time of financial famine at SIUC. In addition, my chair, Richard Peterson, and John Jackson, dean of the College of Liberal Arts, made it possible for me to transfer my tenure to the Department of English, thereby giving me a secure and friendly academic environment in which to complete my work. I will always be grateful for their willingness to listen and act upon my behalf.

Small portions of the book were first tested in different contexts. The comparison between Updike and Frederic (Chapter 2) is adapted from "Embodiment and the American Imagination," *Modern American Cultural Criticism* (NEH: Proceedings of the Conference, March 1983): 39–45; the discussion in Chapter 6 comparing Updike, Percy, and Gass is expanded from "Religion and Sexuality in Walker Percy, William Gass and John Updike: Metaphors of Embodiment in the Androcentric Imagination," *Journal of the American Academy of Religion* LI/4 (December 1983): 595–609; and the discussion of "in/out" in Chapter 8 is drawn from "The Old In/Out," in *The Daemonic Imagination: Biblical Text and Secular Story*, ed. Robert Detweiler and William Doty (Atlanta, Ga.: Scholars Press, 1991), pp. 169–79. A version of Chapter 5 first appeared as "The Reverend Idol and Other Parsonage Secrets: Women Write Romances about Ministers, 1880–1950," *Journal of Feminist Studies in Religion* 6 (Spring 1990): 87–103. My thanks for the permissions granted from all these sources. I would also like to thank Joyce Carol Oates and Raymond I. Smith, the owners of "Open Air" by Carolyn Plochmann, for their permission to reproduce the painting on the dust jacket.

Finally, this book is dedicated to two people, my friend and colleague Robert Detweiler and my friend and husband, Todd Hedinger. Back in what I think of as my dark days, Robert took for granted that I would write and that it would be worth reading, and I can probably never adequately express my appreciation for that gift of confidence. To Todd, of course, belongs all the rest, for what Robert helped me begin, Todd helped me complete by making the future a magical, present reality.

Introduction

While I was writing this book, I was invited to speak to a church women's group. Upon what topic, it was inquired, might I address the gathering?

"My research deals with religion and sexuality in American fiction," I replied.

"Oh!" (punctuated with a noncomedic pause). "We'll have to tone that down a bit," responded the respectable female on the other end of the line. "This is a serious group of people, and the men will want to join the women for the lecture."

I was amused by the idea that in the 1980s putting "religion" and "sexuality" in the same sentence could produce a minor consternation, for my research was clearly indicating that, historically speaking, Americans have long been familiar with the partnership of religion and sexuality, even if it is professed to be a dangerous public topic for an audience of mixed sex.

There is nothing intrinsically antagonistic about religion and sexuality except insomuch as a particular culture defines the two experiences as conflictual. Hinduism, for example, is structured by the forcefield of sacred sexuality, and many Native American and African religions similarly incorporate the mystery and power of human sexuality as expressions of carefully controlled sacred energy. Cultural realms dominated by monotheism (in this book, the monotheism is Christianity), however, treat religion and sexuality as a binary opposition – a tensive pairing in which "religion" is the dominant term, "sexuality" the lesser term. Twentieth-century wisdom, then, operates upon a reluctant and uneasy acknowledgment of a relationship between religion and sexuality.

The response of twentieth-century writers, readers, and critics to the intersection of religion and sexuality is periodically continuous with nineteenth-century treatment. For all their reputation for repression, nineteenth-century citizens were at least as aware as we are, if not more so, of the fascinating, combustible possibilities of religion and sexuality.

1

The lore of camp meetings and revivals, after all, was that at events of such prodigal emotionality "more souls were made than saved," and "one old timer remarked that the encampments at Rock Spring in Lincoln County, North Carolina, 'had been mating grounds for that state for fifty years.'"[1] During that period of millennialism, numerous sectarian groups flourished whose goal was to facilitate earthly perfection by realizing purity in community living. Three of these experiments – by the Shakers, the Oneida community, and the Mormons – sought to inaugurate the kingdom by perfecting sexual relations here on earth. That the Shakers are known for their celibacy, the Mormons for polygamy and reproductive abundance, and the Oneidans for free love and eugenics does not indicate their marginality, but rather the fact that each group surfaced something that can be traced right back to the heart of respectable, middle-class culture – the partnership of religious and sexual experience.[2]

The mutuality of religion and sexuality is not just a novelty of nineteenth-century circumstance. Harold Frederic's comment about his contemporaries' views of sexual appetite can be applied to twentieth-century fastidiousness toward religiosexual connections: "Most people regard it as something so sacred they cannot bring themselves to discuss the conditions attending it – hence our present muddle."[3] Certainly, twentieth-century arts and letters suffer from no lack of sexually explicit material, but we have yet to cultivate a responsible public conversation about the intertwining of these two basic human passions.

An overabundance of religious energy is commonly dismissed as "nothing but" repressed sexuality, but as Chapter 1 demonstrates, this reductive move violates the integrity of religious experience without enhancing the reputation of sexuality. At the same time, the persistent tendency of religious persons to subordinate and control sexual energy under the guise of this or that doctrinal authority works a similar scornful devaluation upon the integrity of sexual experience. Suppose the values were reversed, and we revered sexuality while regarding religious behavior with suspicion and disdain. What if sexual people sought to reg-

---

1 Bernard A. Weisberger, *They Gathered at the River: The Story of the Great Revivalists and Their Impact upon Religion in America* (Boston: Little, Brown, 1958), 36; Charles A. Johnson, *The Frontier Camp Meeting: Religion's Harvest Time* (Dallas: Southern Methodist University Press, 1955), 209.

2 For two excellent and complementary studies, see Lawrence Foster, *Religion and Sexuality: Three American Communal Experiments of the Nineteenth Century* (New York: Oxford University Press, 1981); and Louis J. Kern, *An Ordered Love: Sex Roles and Sexuality in Victorian Utopias – the Shakers, the Mormons and the Oneida Community* (Chapel Hill: University of North Carolina Press, 1981). Kern takes a psychological approach to his material, whereas Foster examines these communities in more sociological terms.

3 A Saunterer in the Labyrinth [Harold Frederic], "Musings on the Question of the Hour," *Pall Mall Budget* 33 (August 13, 1885): 12.

ulate the activities of religious people and claimed that religion could
occur only in private, but those activities would be subject to public
modification and scrutiny regardless of the will of the individuals involved; that certain religious aids and symbols (crosses with dead bodies
hanging on them, for example) were prohibited as antithetical to human
decency? Religious book vendors would be regularly prosecuted as community menaces, and churches and ministers would periodically be
brought to court as dangerous to the healthy expression of physical
pleasure, love, and public well-being.

Indeed, several of the outspoken critics of religious institutions writing
in the first half of the twentieth century (Chapter 1) championed the
ascendancy of healthy sexuality over the morbidity of religious denial,
so this is not such an outlandish proposition. In its exaggeration through
reversal, however, we recognize that religious institutions have a powerful investment in regulating human sexuality while proclaiming and
preserving the distance between the spiritual and carnal portions of human beings. The determined application of so-called higher religious
values to issues of public and private sexual morality – especially where
the sovereignty of women's bodies is concerned – makes understanding
the relation between religious and sexual energy ever more pressing.

In Western Christian theology, the intimate connection between religion
and sexual experience has its basis in Incarnation theology – the Word
made flesh, the spirit joined with the body – and the promise that humans
participate in this divine conjunction. Western theology polarizes this
condition, however, seeing the sexual body as an unreliable container
for a captive spirit. I refer to this unreconciled relation of body and spirit
as "embodiment," and I am interested in how the doubled resonance of
this term (theological, biological) forces one to reflect on the mutuality
of body and language in the tradition of American writing.

I am also interested in how such matters of body and spirit are defined
in terms of male and female. As we know, in the Western tradition
women symbolize carnality and fallen humanity, men symbolize spirituality and redemptive possibility. Presumably the language and thought
issuing from the male body is more objective, rational, and literarily
creative than that produced by the female, for the culturally authoritative
male voice has always assumed the deleterious effect of the female body
upon a woman's mind and spirit. No such harmful correspondence is
assumed between the male body and mind, however. This sense of
superior male mind and body is one reason why the culturally dominant
male has presented himself as the linguistic and experiential norm of
humanity, when, in fact, the very claim itself is proof that the male mind
is no more or less influenced by the physiology of the male body than

is the female mind by the female body. It is intellectually dishonest to argue that we should transcend the specifics of language in order to recognize a universal ground of religious experience (as traditional commentators do quite often) and yet use androcentric metaphors and symbols so consistently that we cannot but be persuaded that the specifics of the language are part of the definition. Male and female sexuality are not symmetrical, exchangeable values in the cultural-theological world. Often they are not even complementary. The androcentrism of the traditional metaphors of embodiment is an essential ingredient in the language of religion and sexuality, and *our* present muddle stems in part from the persistent conflation of language with the thing itself.

Two basic questions, then, have shaped my work. First, how have American novelists handled the interaction between religious and sexual experience? Second, are there instructive similarities and differences in how male and female authors write about embodiment? The originating terms of my study, "religion and sexuality," are shaped by the Western theological tradition as it has been expressed by the white male author writing in nineteenth- and twentieth-century Protestant America. Although this represents a relatively narrow base when considered against the diversity of American culture, white males are the ones responsible for shaping and defining our received sense of literary heritage. That this definition of our literary culture is in need of renovation is without question, but such a reassessment should begin with these originating voices.

As one of several steps toward renovation, I have selected canonical *and* noncanonical novels for study, specifically, those that use the Protestant church and clergy as definitive players, or novels that dramatize theological perplexity about embodied life without any particular reference to churches or clergy. My *general* focus on Protestantism as an institutional and cultural force is both a practical and historically grounded decision. First, I needed to establish some manageable limits to my reading. Second, I take seriously the spirit of H. R. Niebuhr's affirmation that "both history and religious consensus support the statement that Protestantism is America's only national religion and to ignore that fact is to view the country from a false angle."[4] That said, however, I have entertained no absolute rule in this regard. Catholics and Protestants share many a generalized presupposition about the sexual body and religious experience, and, moreover, I am much less interested in institutional history than I am in the diffused cultural history of Christian

4 H. R. Niebuhr, *The Kingdom of God in America* (New York: Harper Torchbook, 1959), 17.

ideas about religion and sexuality as seen through the literary vision of white male writers.

Paired with these male-authored novels are novels written by nineteenth- and twentieth-century white women, most of which are not recognized as classic documents of American literary history. These woman-authored works set in motion my second question: Are there instructive differences in the ways in which men and women have written about embodiment? Indeed, this second question greatly complicates the first, for by consulting women-authored texts as equal authorities on such matters, the very terms of the question – "religion" and "sexuality" – are jeopardized, along with all the traditional language of embodiment called forth in the male-authored texts. Writing as persons circumscribed and marginalized by the master narrative, women both challenge and confirm traditional language in ways that displace, but do not destroy, the boundaries of androcentric language.

Unfortunately for intellectual orderliness, however, sex-dividing fiction does not produce a tidy arrangement of gender allegiance, a messy reality that forces my second question back upon itself. As I began my writing, it was my intention to use "androcentric" and "gynocentric" to refer to how writers situate gender in fictional worlds without automatically assuming that the sex of the writer would determine the gender-centrism of his or her vision. Theoretically, not all male authors are androcentric; not all female authors are gynocentric. My intentions for this terminology have proved more noble in the abstract than in practice, however, because all the male authors I discuss are androcentric (with the interesting exception of one or two nineteenth-century writers), whereas women writers are far more divided in their point of view. The women writers in Chapter 5, for example, are distinctly male-identified in their outlook whereas the women writing from the context of feminist activism of the late twentieth century are much closer to a gynocentric vision. The variety of gender vision found in women authors is a function of how much women may be divided against themselves as females in a male-dominated culture, a dilemma taken up in Chapter 7.

What I do here, then, is create a temporary order by assuming that biological/cultural identity is sufficiently related and enough of a cultural factor to look for a male- and female-identified language in male and female authors, respectively, while offering part-time acknowledgment of a difference between biological sex and the cultural constructions of gender through a necessarily inconsistent usage of terms like "androcentric" and "gynocentric." Ironically, in order to challenge the androcentric use of male universality, I have had to rely on another problematic universal, that of "woman." Current feminist discussion renders this an equally troublesome structural move on at least two fronts. First, it moves my position uncomfortably close to essentialism, which seems to me to be a useful stage in terms of the continuing discussion of differences between women and men, but is also reductive of women (and men) to an anatomical, albeit mystical, destiny. Second, some women have suggested that the construct "woman" replicates the hegemony of white male in the form of the white, feminist female who, having denounced the male oppressor as a false universalizer, proclaims herself as a universal voice. In the interests of preserving the cultural and racial integrity of their experience, African-American womanists do not want to be classified with white women, for example, and lesbian women have articulated a similar separatist outlook. "Woman," in other words, may no longer be used uncritically to cover the diversity of female culture any more than "male" may be used to cover the diversity of the culture at large.

One idea I have found helpful in thinking through my problematic use of "woman" comes from Margaret Homans's discussion of the uniqueness of women's writing as "(ambiguously) nonhegemonic," a description of the equivocal position women hold relative to normative androcentrism. When novelists are writing self-consciously as women, "they have more in common with '(ambiguously) nonhegemonic' women of the ruling class and race than with nonhegemonic men, and that, speaking descriptively, complicity with an oppressive male authority is a shared woman's experience."[5] Or, as Carolyn Heilbrun puts it, "the sense of being oppressed and stigmatized by the male world (even if one sleeps with it) is something that unites women"[6] beyond racial difference or sexual preference. In this study I concentrate on the white female authors who were in most immediate and intimate conversation with their white male peers. I do not take their viewpoint as unilaterally representative for *all* women; I do take their viewpoint as pertinent to women in general. As Susan Bordo comments, "while it is imperative to struggle continually against racism and ethnocentrism in all its forms, it is impossible to be 'politically correct,' for all ideas (no matter how 'liberatory' in some contexts or for some purposes) are condemned to be haunted by a voice from the margins . . . awakening us to what has

---

5 Margaret Homans, " 'Her Very Own Howl': The Ambiguities of Representation in Recent Women's Fiction," *Signs* 9 (Winter 1983): 200. Homans borrows this term from Rachel Blau duPlessis and the members of Workshop 9, "For the Etruscans: Sexual Difference and Artistic Production – the Debate over a Female Aesthetic," in *The Future of Difference*, ed. Hester Eisenstein and Alice Jardine (New Brunswick, N.J.: Rutgers University Press, 1985), 128–56.
6 Carolyn Heilbrun, "A Response to Writing and Sexual Difference," in *Writing and Sexual Difference*, ed. Elizabeth Abel (Chicago: University of Chicago Press, 1982), 297.

been excluded, effaced, damaged."[7] As we will see, the very terms guiding this study, "religion" and "sexuality," are so closely shaped by white male constructs, that even introducing white women writers into the conversation challenges the terminology. Indeed, such terms are largely inappropriate and irrelevant for black and other non-Anglo writers who record a much different experience of bodily and spiritual integrity. For that reason, I introduce nonwhite writers only in the last chapter on contemporary women's voices, where I discuss writers who are beginning that crucial move away from white Protestant cultural definition toward rethinking the whole.

Some scholars and activists may question my interest in locating commonality, or a "whole" at all, and obviously, a study that still entertains "universal," "woman," or even "human" as viable analytic categories will have little to offer to those who celebrate cultural worlds as irrevocably and justly divided by difference. My position is that somehow we must assume some goodwill of common ground, even as we are suspicious of unexamined claims to universalism, and as long as we do not take our expansive pronouncements to be some sort of absolute cultural template. My approach is much like that of Sandra Gilbert and Susan Gubar in their revisionist literary history of American cultural canons. As they describe their critical process, "once we reimagine the author as a gendered human being whose text reflects key cultural conditions, we can conflate and collate individual literary narratives, so that they constitute one possible metastory."[8] I think of the process as "synoptic," a term I've appropriated from the tradition of biblical interpretation, a reading together of thematically similar sources in search of a common story. My study depends on the reader's acceptance of the aerial view of culture gained by a synoptic reading of many stories, a process that could not proceed without the sure footing provided by close textual readings from other scholars.

I assume, then, a fiction of a common "woman's experience" in order to explore the ways in which women's writing about embodiment registers differences or similarities relative to the androcentric narrative. It is my goal to contribute an expansive look at gender and embodiment issues through the use of informed universals, while keeping in mind that generalizations about "male" and "female" must be continually and implicitly critiqued by the pluralities excluded by the limitations of this study. Thus, Chapters 3 to 7 are sex-segregated in order to distinguish the unique contributions of the male and female narrative voice.

7 Susan Bordo, "Feminism, Postmodernism, and Gender-Skepticism," in *Feminism/Postmodernism,* ed. Linda J. Nicholson (New York: Routledge, 1990), 138.
8 Sandra Gilbert and Susan Gubar, *The War of the Words, No Man's Land,* vol. 1 (New Haven, Conn.: Yale University Press, 1988), xiv.

I am writing in a time when theoretical discourse about literature far overshadows critical discussion of fiction, and it would be imprudent to launch a book of literary criticism without some word in this direction. Generally speaking, feminist critics, myself included, are undecided about what stance to take regarding the theoretical gamesmanship that so occupies academics.[9] Sometimes scholarly prose is necessarily difficult and should not be dismissed just because it is intense and exacting of the reader's highest capabilities. On the other hand, a good deal of theory strays too often into an extremely provincial in-house discussion. Indeed, more than one resisting female reader has pointed out how much the obscurities of contemporary theory seem to constitute a hidden agenda designed to circumvent feminist criticism by creating a critical language of such technical virtuosity as to include only the chosen initiates (read: white, male).[10]

Being not especially theoretically minded even under favorable conditions, but realizing the utility of theory at the same time, I have taken a clue from Judith Martin's advice about silk underwear and academic titles. What good is a Ph.D. if no one knows you have one? asks a reader. Miss Manners replies, "You are in the position of a woman who has invested in silk underwear. She must derive her satisfaction from knowing she has it on, and perhaps the knowledge of an intimate or two. To let everyone know cheapens the effect."[11] Theory, in other words, ought to be worn just as graciously as silk underwear: sensed rather than seen, an essential, elegant foundation, not something to be vulgarly flourished in an attempt to outdo the next person. There are numerous places, for example, where I might have discussed postmodernist theory, and sometimes in footnotes I alert the interested reader to such opportunities. Indeed, the entire book could have been constructed around critical and theoretical postmodern debates about representation and the authority of linguistic sexual charge. But I want to focus on fiction itself, and not the fictions of criticism, for it seems to me that fiction is far richer in its representations of embodied life and existential ambiguity than theories of fiction have yet managed to account for. Thus, although I will certainly have more than one occasion to advise the reader about my theoretical

9 Elizabeth Meese discusses strategies in *Crossing the Double-Cross: The Practice of Feminist Criticism* (Chapel Hill: University of North Carolina Press, 1986), esp. 135–50.
10 On this point, see Annette Kolodny, "Dancing between Left and Right: Feminism and the Academic Minefield in the 1980's," *Feminist Studies* 14 (Fall 1988): 453–66 and Gilbert and Gubar, *The War of the Words*, vol. 1, 262–5. The reference to the "resisting" critic comes from Judith Fetterly's *The Resisting Reader: A Feminist Approach to American Fiction* (Bloomington: Indiana University Press, 1978).
11 Judith Martin, *Miss Manners' Guide to Excruciatingly Correct Behavior* (New York: Atheneum, 1982), 73.

approach, I try not to let such things intrude more frequently than is
necessary.

In addition to my synoptic method and feminist outlook, my approach
to my topic can be described as phenomenological, therapeutic, and
metaphoric. Beyond asking certain questions of my texts, which in itself
unavoidably begins to shape an answer, I have tried to listen with as
little bias as possible. It is this simple method – simple only in the saying,
and not the doing – to which I refer from the tradition of phenomenology.
It is a practice that advises the cultural analyst to cultivate a state of alert
vulnerability in order to let the other speak as itself through the imaginative ear of the reader.

My use of the term "therapeutic" helps me expand what it means to
listen in this manner. According to one kind of thinking, a good therapist
acts much like a good translator. You cannot eliminate all of yourself in
the hearing, but the goal is to translate the psychological text of the client
back to him or her in ways that give the client a new perspective. Obviously, texts are not persons and there is a big difference between the
spoken and printed word, but literary critics do act in some sense as
cultural therapists, and the kind of respectful listening posited by this
therapeutic model is a valuable checkpoint. By outlining a therapeutic
model of criticism, I am not advocating that we relinquish our privilege
to commentary. There is no such thing as value-free listening, but in the
interest of intellectual honesty there is a utility in keeping before us the
ideal. Every translation or description implies a normative stance, and
all literary critics have an investment in judgment that is no less political
for being denied or unmarked. My work as a crisis intervention counselor
has taught me that the kind of listening I have described here as therapeutic is extremely difficult, and I have often thought that if more literary
critics were required to undertake some training in the listening skills
counseling entails, the gaps between theory, experience, and self-
knowledge that mar so much academic work might be narrowed to good
effect.

My loosely invoked therapeutic model also reminds me of the human
personality of the printed materials that so engage me. At several points
in the book I initiate discussion of religion and sexuality with a personal
narrative drawn from real life because a cultural study such as this one
should not be so diffuse – ever a hazard with the kind of wide-ranging
analysis I attempt here – that we lose touch with the finely spun threads
of individual lives that help create the larger weave of cultural meaning.
The kind of questions raised by religion and sexuality are at once intensely
personal and extensively cultural, and without too much ostentatious

pointing I hope to keep before us the interlocking drama between persons, institutions, and culture.

Listening – attentiveness to textual sound and silence – is one key metaphoric paradigm that emerges from my study of religion and sexuality in American fiction. My appreciation of metaphor as a structure of reciprocity shapes the structure, style, and approach to my texts. For those more comfortable with traditional discursive analysis, this approach may be unsatisfying. But I take seriously the idea that metaphor is not only a rich analytic resource, but often the only way we have to speak truthfully of difficult things that cannot be said directly or literally. Understanding and respecting the function of metaphor relative to religious language might help extinguish the simple-minded and dangerous literalisms that govern large portions of American religious belief and practice. Thus, Chapter 1 takes up the question of religious language and sexual bodies, first by examining the religious-materialist debate that flourished in the first half of the twentieth century. Then, building on the terms of that debate as they clarify attitudes about embodiment, I move to a consideration of metaphor and theological language, arguing that metaphor is a key resource for understanding the connections we make between religious words about bodies and bodies themselves.

Chapter 2 establishes some tentative universals in the language of religion and sexuality used by nineteenth-century American novelists, and this exploration of our allegedly repressed literary ancestors underscores a major theme of the chapters that follow: to take seriously the claims of the physical body. Sound and silence emerge as a series of key metaphoric devices about passion used by nineteenth-century writers to observe the boundaries between public and private domains while saying what could not be said literally.

The stubborn density of desire – what nineteenth-century writers called passion – is the enigmatic universal that empowers all metaphoric strategies in nineteenth- and twentieth-century fiction, and the work in Chapter 2 forms the gateway to the sex-segregated fiction at the heart of the book (in Chapters 3–7). First, I focus on the ministry as the vocational theater wherein so many of the pressures of embodiment are initiated and exposed. I would emphasize, however, that although I remind the reader of this institutional context in my text selections, commentary, and footnotes, I am interested in the literary and cultural sense of this experience, and not in the specifics of institutional history as such.[12]

12 The history of institutional management of religion and sexuality demands a separate consideration, as studies in Puritan religious life or the dynamics of revivals so richly testify. In addition to works already cited, and for some tantalizing clues to the largely untapped possibilities in an institutional and historical approach, see, for example, Troy

Chapters 3, 4, and 5 deal with novels *about* the ministry *written by* men and women. Chapter 3, which examines novels about the ministry written by men, uncovers key dilemmas for the male officeholder, including various aesthetic temptations and the prolonged, religiously enforced adolescence of the male minister. The theatrics of the office are sustained by theological emphasis on the masculine dispensation of the Word, revealing an intricate relation between women and words in the sexually achieved preaching performance.

Women writing about the ministry from the mid-nineteenth to the mid-twentieth century contest the exclusively male ministerial office, however. Barred from preaching, they seized the novel as a homiletic platform, and Chapter 4 investigates how the homiletic writers recreate the disdained female body through novelistic testimony to their purifying suffering. In their quest for embodied perfection, they violate conventional boundaries between natural and supernatural, mind and body, head and heart – our first clue to the importance of boundary for women's writing about passion. In Chapters 3 and 4, the writers are engaged in a war of words over whose body – male or female – will be the administrator and beneficiary of the empowerment of words or the Word. The romance writers of Chapter 5 join the lists with the androcentric imagination, writing in mirror image of their homiletic sisters. These female writers of the little-known parsonage romances reinforce the traditional, sexually charged theological formulas about women and men. In particular, this chapter explains how the literary formula for romance in the parsonage romance exposes a series of parallel relationships: the theological relationship between God and the sinner, the minister and his female congregant, and the male hero and his submissive female lover.

Through the fictional treatment of ministers, Chapters 3–5 explore the institutional setting wherein many of the tensions of religion and sexuality are played out. Chapters 6 and 7 move beyond the institutional frame to plumb the deep structures of language about religion and sexuality by comparing metaphoric accounts of embodiment by contemporary male and female authors. My reasons for this shift from institutional culture to metaphoric culture emanate from the fiction itself. Although,

D. Abell, *Better Felt Than Said: The Holiness Pentecostal Experience in Southern Appalachia* (Waco, Tex.: Markham, 1982); Ann Douglas, *The Feminization of American Culture* (New York: Alfred A. Knopf, 1977); Peter Gardella, *Innocent Ecstasy: How Christianity Gave America an Ethic of Sexual Pleasure* (New York: Oxford University Press, 1985); Edmund Leites, *The Puritan Conscience and Modern Sexuality* (New Haven, Conn.: Yale University Press, 1986); Sandra S. Sizer, *Gospel Hymns and Social Religion: The Rhetoric of Nineteenth Century Revivalism* (Philadelphia: Temple University Press, 1978); Jeff Todd Titon, *Powerhouse for God: Speech, Chant and Song in an Appalachian Baptist Church* (Austin: University of Texas Press, 1988); and Barbara Welter, *Dimity Convictions: The American Woman in the Nineteenth Century* (Athens: Ohio University Press, 1976).

as we will see, some contemporary male writers do continue to use male clergy to represent embodied distress, these clergy operate in a peculiarly deinstitutionalized setting. For example, William Gass's Jethro Furber (*Omensetter's Luck*) does have a church assignment, but the action of the novel takes place largely in his head, and, as a result, the church setting is hallucinatory, not realistic or documentary. We need only compare this treatment with the institutionally precise location of Harold Frederic's Theron Ware (*The Damnation of Theron Ware*) to be immediately apprised of the shift in emphasis. Similarly, the theological dis-ease expressed in contemporary fiction is, by and large, discernible in no particular institution or doctrine but persists as part of a diffused, troubled cultural voice, which is why the contemporary male writer need not use the clergy or the church to depict recognizable theological distress. Thus, despite the obvious doctrinal and church-centered themes in John Updike's Rabbit novels, for instance, the appeal of the novels stems from their articulation of recognizable but deinstitutionalized theological distress in the life of an ordinary working American.

It is an important premise of this study that religious dogma about sexuality is part of the deep structure of our cultural imagination, an influence that operates well beyond the immediacy of institutional life and the ministerial vocation. Perhaps admitting the presence of women writers makes this even clearer, for with the exception of the romance writers, women cease worrying about institutional and ministerial misogyny somewhere in the early twentieth century.[13] Contemporary women writers display little interest in the clergy or the church, yet they are clearly interested in engaging the ongoing cultural and theological conversation about gendered embodiment.[14] The best way to compare male and female voices, then, is to bring the metaphoric structure of contemporary narratives into the foreground and allow the original ministerial and institutional frame for the question to recede.

Accordingly, Chapter 6 discusses the crisis and enclosure metaphors of four male authors that convey the simultaneous terror and rapture of embodiment and the insufficiency of language to express this experience of captivity and flight. Making metaphoric connections between words, water, and women, the androcentric writer shows us that women are experienced as iconic containers of life water. In this universe defined by the male gaze women are creatures comfortable with death and chaos, although relatively untouched by the surge of mortal passion within and

---

13 I suspect this shift occurs as an authentic woman's voice gains recognition outside and apart from the religious institution that provided her only approved access to audible public discourse, but also denied her any actual institutional power. Simply put, other, less equivocal forms of institutional and cultural power become available to her.

14 Novelist Mary Gordon is the notable exception here.

around them. Words, then, become a substitute for the life water the male creature cannot control; the raft and rope of language may give the (drowning) male spirit some fragile barrier against death and the mindless engulfment of female-as-life. In the androcentric universe, words about women become as real and as powerful as women themselves.

Concerns about language, water, and the fragility of flesh are not exclusive to the androcentric writer, however. Chapter 7 investigates the metaphors of flight and water through which the contemporary woman writer expresses her ambivalence toward the androcentric culture whose language both imprisons and enlists her in the ongoing narrative construction of cultural stability. In particular, we see that women, too, have difficulty working out a satisfactory relationship with the iconic female body. There is a common language, although the male writer concentrates on the fact and fury of his imprisonment by life water and the iconic female, whereas women writers challenge traditional institutional and theological boundaries, violating the polarized territories of natural/ supernatural, body/spirit, and religion/sexuality. The boundaries he clings to as support (and yet prison) of the male spirit are the boundaries she dissolves as a false reality (and yet comfort) for the female spirit.

As long as discussion focuses on androcentric authors, the central question of this book maintains contact with the physical facts of sexual experience as that experience interacts with religious beliefs and institutional life. But the gynocentric voice takes us past literal and traditional significations into the embodiment of the boundaries of human passion as they are experienced by women and men. Chapter 8 brings the discussion to a conclusion by reflecting on the nature of boundary as it is experienced in metaphor and the human body, noting that the reciprocity of metaphor causes terms like "religion" and "sexuality" to disappear. Indeed, the moment of boundary dissolution in women's fiction offers a rare moment of rapprochement between the gender-polarized world of male and female, for women writers do not set up reversals in the wake of dissolving traditional authority. That is, unlike the understandable tendency of feminist theory and theology to replace god with goddess, or patriarchy with matriarchy, women's fiction itself stages a far more complex discussion by refusing to polarize or conclude. And in that margin of dissolution, question, and waiting, we are invited to consider fragile commonalities. What is left between women and men is the risky experience of physical love and human life, the troublesome meaning of the female body, and a passionately shared, monumental defiance lodged against the inevitable dissolution of the loving life-body.

In this study I have re-read some traditionally revered materials of American literature, and I have put them in touch with literary voices rarely heard, often denied. That is what it means to adopt a metaphoric style and structure: putting seemingly unlike things side by side, knowing that "language is like shot silk; so much depends upon the angle at which it is held," the light in which it is perceived, "the company we keep."[15] That contact must change the story we tell about embodied life as American women and men, and I hope that the sex-alternated chapters will generate more dialogic resonances for the reader than I can enumerate. As Annette Kolodny has said, feminist literary criticism

> has never simply been about decoding the gender and racial biases in literary history or deconstructing the gender, race and class assumptions in literature and criticism, nor even about recuperating individual women writers and entire female traditions. Within the academy, it is and always has been a moral and ethical stance that seeks to change the structures of knowledge and, with that, the institutional structures in which knowledge gets made and codified.[16]

The dysfunctional partnership of religion and sexuality as they have been traditionally defined is apparent, but perhaps studies such as this one may contribute to a renovation of body language, so that we may find better ways to imagine and embody the love of the precious flesh we share together.

15 John Fowles, *The French Lieutenant's Woman* (New York: NAL, 1969), 358; Wayne C. Booth, *The Company We Keep: An Ethics of Fiction* (Berkeley: University of California Press, 1988).
16 Kolodny, "Dancing between Left and Right," 464.

1

Body Language: Religion, Sexuality, and the Bioluminescence of Metaphor

In his now classic study of the sexual and pornographic underside of Victorian culture in *The Other Victorians,* Steven Marcus quotes physician William Acton, who noted that cases of extreme masturbation and insanity "chiefly occur in members of families of strict religious education. . . . Those who from this cause have become insane have generally . . . been of strictly moral life, and recognized as persons who paid much attention to the forms of religion. . . . In the acute attacks resulting from this cause . . . religion forms a noted subject of conversation or delusion." Marcus goes on to note that somehow religion seems connected with masturbation and insanity in Acton's observation, but "the connection goes unexplored – which can only lead us to conclude that the process by which causality is ascribed is often highly selective and tendentious."[1]

Marcus, who is not especially concerned with the religiosexual connection, does not pursue the question of causality, and so we are left to ask, what, specifically, is selective or biased about Acton's observation – the connections between masturbation and insanity, or the larger relationship proposed between religion, sexual repression, and insanity? What trapdoor lurks beneath this glancing observation about the intertwining of religion and sexuality? Marcus's study was one of the first of a new generation of studies in the cultural history of sexuality, and the kinds of questions it raised are essentially the questions of this book. We will find, however, more plainly marked entrances and exits than trapdoors, and many more explicit statements of connection than those first postulated by Marcus.

The question of religion and sexuality has been problematic for religious persons in every Christian era, and to link religion, sexuality, pornography, and insanity is to throw the discussion to the outer mar-

---

1 Steven Marcus, *The Other Victorians: A Study of Sexuality and Pornography in Mid-Nineteenth Century England* (New York: Basic Books, 1964), 21.

gins of credible conversation for most religious persons. In addition, nineteenth-century observers are themselves an enigmatic emblem of outlandish connections, combining as they did some remarkably acute medical and social observations with an inherited backlog of pious sentimentality and biological misinformation. More recent studies in the cultural history of sexuality – Peter Gay's ongoing work in *The Bourgeois Experience: Victoria to Freud,* volumes 1 and 2, is an outstanding example – have deepened our understanding of our own attitudes toward human sexuality and made it significantly more difficult for us to isolate nineteenth-century attitudes as simply dysfunctional or aberrant. And lest the connection between religion, sexuality, and pornography seem too comfortably located in the past, here is Susan Sontag to make short work of such comfort. In the following quotation, she discusses the relationship between sexual drive, religious ecstasy, and the verbal torrent we find converging in twentieth-century pornography.

> In some respects, the use of sexual obsessions as a subject for literature resembles the use of a literary subject whose validity far fewer people would contest: religious obsessions. So compared, the familiar fact of pornography's definite, aggressive impact upon its readers looks somewhat different. Its celebrated intention of sexually stimulating readers is really a species of proselytizing. Pornography that is serious literature aims to "excite" in the same way that books which render an extreme form of religious experience aim to "convert." ... Of course, the pornographic imagination is hardly the only form of consciousness that proposes a total universe. ... Certain of the well-known states of religious imagination ... operate in the same cannibalistic way, engorging all materials available to them for retranslation into phenomena saturated with the religious polarities.[2]

The resemblances between religious literature and pornography are these: abundance, aggression, incitement to action, and totalitarian obsession. This list might also be regarded as characteristic of extremes. Yet that gruesome word, "cannibalism," should stalk the thoughtful reader beyond the passing remark, because it works back through savagery, aggression, appetite, and food (all of which are expressions for sexual experience), from margin to center and normality. In appetite and food, if not also in aggression and savagery, we meet acceptable religious practices and belief – a brutal death translated into a liturgical feast, expressive of the fear of the body and a hunger for the reliable, blissful experience of eternal life.[3] As this and the next chapter demonstrate,

2 Susan Sontag, *Styles of Radical Will* (New York: Farrar, Straus & Giroux, 1966), 47, 67.
3 For an involving, metaphoric analysis of religion, violence, and pornography, see Susan Griffin, *Pornography and Silence: Culture's Revenge against Nature* (New York: Harper & Row, 1981), esp. "Sacred Images," 8–80. For an equally engrossing discussion of the

nineteenth-century observers, many of whom were students in the growing investigations into sexual culture, noted much the same thing – the
fascinating (from their point of view) and disturbing (from the believer's
point of view) convergence of religious and sexual energy within ordinary
lives. Indeed, many nineteenth-century observers seemed more resigned
to than horrified at the sexual tonality of religious experience, as though
it were a fact of life with which they were thoroughly familiar.

Once we cut through predictable public expressions of sentiment regarding such matters, we, too, become thoroughly familiar with the
relationship of religion and sexuality. Furthermore, the linkage is not
simply visible under extreme or unusual circumstances, but, as I will
argue throughout this book, the mutuality of religion and sexuality is a
natural outcome of ordinary human existence. In the sections that follow
I trace both the ordinary manifestations of religion and sexuality by taking
testimony from an "average" individual and the extraordinary problems
of religion and sexuality by reviewing the ferment of cultural debate that
surrounded turn-of-the-century studies of sexology. I use the clues of
individual narrative to locate and identify the key issues of religion and
sexuality that are the focus of this book: (1) the compelling, disturbing
presence of the sexual body in religious life, and (2) the centrality of
language as the instrument of communication, expression, and control
between religious and sexual experience.

Religion and Sexuality

By her own account, Myrtle Cummings Ballew was a vain and
fun-loving girl who loved to dress up in pretty clothing and with her
childhood chum, Lillian, once skipped Sunday School to ride the merry-
go-round.[4] When she was a teenager, her father was stricken with the
kidney disease that eventually killed him, and to facilitate his care, he
was moved to the parlor during the final months of his illness. In the
evening, the local Free Methodists would call upon him for prayer and
hymn singing, all earnest efforts on behalf of his salvation. One hymn
offered the stricken man the dubious consolatory refrain, "Let me die!"
During such visits, Myrtle and Lillian eavesdropped outside the parlor
doors, giggling at the dolorous proceedings and singing in counterpoint,
"Let me live!"

Myrtle Cummings Ballew tells this story of her youthful frivolity in
order to contrast it with the overwhelming experience of her conversion

---

use of food as an erotic religious symbol, see Caroline Walker Bynum, *Holy Feast and
Holy Fast: The Religious Significance of Food to Medieval Women* (Berkeley: University of
California Press, 1987).
4 Interviews with Myrtle Cummings Ballew (b. October 28, 1893) in August 1980 in
Atlanta, Georgia, and April 1987 in Orlando, Florida. She is my maternal grandmother.

to that same Free Methodist sect. With a timing that any Freudian would appreciate, she was claimed by the Lord at a camp meeting that concluded the Easter celebration of April 10, 1910, only three months after the death of her father. She was sixteen years old, and she had been captivated by one of the most rigid of the primitive fundamentalist groups operating in turn-of-the-century north Georgia. She would never again be permitted to take delight in her long, glossy hair, for believers were forbidden all worldly vanity and adornment and these strictures were especially directed toward women whose fleshly weaknesses seemed to provide such inviting opportunities for the devil's activities. Upon her first encounter with Jesus, Myrtle vowed never to wear red again because it was the color of harlots.

She experienced a renewal of her commitment several years later. Married to a Free Methodist minister, she was tending three sick children one Sunday morning. As was often the case among this peripatetic and impecunious sect, her family was quartered in several small rooms directly above the sanctuary. She could feel the floor vibrating under her feet first from the voices of the singing congregation and then from her husband, who was preaching "under deep anointing." The voices seemed to enfold her. She remained in a trancelike state for several hours, for she was "getting promises." That is, the Lord was sending her Bible verses that were to be regarded as spiritual keepsakes. She received these promises: from the Song of Solomon 4:7, "Thou art all fair my love, there's no spot in thee," and from Psalms 45:13, "The King's daughter is all glorious within." She took care to make sure I had the proper understanding of these verses: "Now mind, some evil-minded folks try to twist these scriptures. They refer to the spiritual relationship between Jesus Christ and his redeemed bride, the Church."

Myrtle Cummings Ballew was ninety-seven in 1991, and she has always considered herself a bride of Christ. At no point in her long and religiously devoted life has she allowed herself to ignore the utter seriousness of the body. She was so scrupulous in her devotion to the physical restraints of her religion that even her feet could become an item of spiritual concern. Years of poverty and ill-fitting shoes had left knots of distressed flesh upon her feet so that most conventional shoes were quite uncomfortable to wear. But among the Free Methodists the wearing of open-toed shoes was proscribed, so Myrtle took it to the Lord in prayer. She was advised by her Mighty Counselor that to purchase new shoes with open toes, which might be construed as seductive or fashionable, would be sinful, but she might cut out the toes and sides of the shoes she already owned. Thus might she accommodate her aching feet without seriously compromising her status among the sanctified.

Feet are not usually regarded by the Western world as a great resource for evil, so this podiatric predicament emphasizes how seriously and respectfully the temptations of the sensual world may be regarded. Red is a dangerous color, and sound can be a persuasive environment for meditation and inspiration. Flesh can either be a resource for evil or testimony to the presence of sanctification, but either way, the body is the essential if unwilling crucible for spiritual achievement. Finally, in ironic confirmation of the uneasy entwining of things physical with things spiritual, the marriage metaphors of scriptural love poetry provide the language of a religion that practices great hostility toward literal matters of the flesh.

In this brief witness, then, we see a number of elements that make up the larger story of religion and sexuality: the utter, commanding seriousness of the body; the power of sensual experience such as color and sound (words, music); and the specific gravity of the female body. Finally, lurking within the crevices of even a brief testimony such as this one, is the shadow of death. No narrative of religion and sexuality would be complete without it. In this case, the death of her father sends Myrtle Cummings Ballew hurtling toward Jesus and a religious system that seeks to smother the luxuriance of the body in this life in order to enjoy a nonbodied life in some eternal future. Many Christians have tried to live as though physical life were a dress rehearsal for "real" life beyond. Apparently the way to do this is to replace the physical script we are born to with a divine script and live by word alone.

Enthusiasts with various remedies for corralling the call of the flesh have flourished in every age, and Myrtle Ballew's own religious passion can be seen as part of this larger pattern. But it is also important to note that she came to girlhood during an unusual period of scientific optimism and religious skepticism, and the landscape of her mature religious commitment was studded with acrimonious battles between modernists and fundamentalists over the nature and destiny of human life. The spectacular public symbol of these battles was the Scopes trial, which was not simply about a theory of creation, but called into question the entire moral universe of the religious devotee. Scientific investigations into religious claims were not confined to the accuracy of biblical biology or geology. As part of a wide-ranging investigation of the biological basis of the human mind, various scientists and philosophers documented the fact that, in plain English, religious ecstasy often looks suspiciously like sexual ecstasy in both physical and linguistic realms. Thus, the modernists, or "medical materialists," to use William James's designation, were, among other things, also interested in the utter seriousness of the body, but for a much different purpose. While Myrtle Ballew and other purists sought ways to subdue and discipline the call of the flesh, scientific enthusiasts around her investigated the source of religious passion in the cool, dispassionate manner of their discipline in order to release the flesh for erotic healthiness.

Representative of the Freudian and Darwinian attitudes of the late nineteenth and early twentieth century on the American scene was Theodore A. Schroeder (1864–1953), who examined the question of religious passion and its relationship to sexual impulses.[5] Schroeder was a lawyer and freethinker who began his career by speaking out against religious intolerance, first on behalf of Mormons in Utah, and then *against* Mormonism when he came to perceive that religious system as inimical to a free society. Having been charged by Mormons with "obscenity," Schroeder turned his attention to free-speech issues, which soon occupied the bulk of his voluminous writings. He acted as counsel for various legal cases involving free speech, and there are indications that his work contributed to the defense in the Scopes trial.

In addition to his efforts on behalf of civil liberties, he pursued his interest in religion. Building upon work by sexologists such as Havelock Ellis, Richard Krafft-Ebing, and Henry Maudsley, and drawing upon his early experiences with Mormonism, Schroeder collected cross-cultural descriptions from historians, medical experts, anthropologists, psychoanalysts, and novelists and poets testifying to the similarity between religious and sexual experience. He studied "The Psychic Eroticism of a Negro Revival," "Shaker Celibacy and Salacity," medieval accounts of spirituality that worked toward "Converting Sex to Religiosity," and in a fascinating psychological-theological analysis, he contemplated "Divinity in the Semen."[6]

One study records his observations of a black female religious ecstatic. Noting that she had been sexually abused, Schroeder is sympathetic

---

5 Biographical information on Theodore Schroeder is drawn from *Theodore Schroeder, A Cold Enthusiast. A Bibliography,* compiled by Ralph McCoy, "Biographical Sketch" by Dennis L. Domanyer, and "Impressions" by Arnold Maddaloni (Carbondale: Southern Illinois University Press, 1973). Published materials by Schroeder were made available to me through the courtesy of Special Collections, Morris Library, Southern Illinois University at Carbondale.

 For a broader sense of the American psychoanalytic conversation and Schroeder's place therein, see Nathan G. Hale, *Freud and the Americans: The Beginnings of Psychoanalysis in the United States, 1876–1917, Freud in America,* vol. 1 (New York: Oxford University Press, 1971). For a recent survey of Schroeder's erotogenetic theory of religion, see Anne Coughlin, "A Unique Heathen: The Sexual Dogmatics of Theodore Schroeder" (Ph.D. diss., Fuller Theological Seminary, 1986, University Microfilms).

6 Theodore A. Schroeder, "Revivals, Sex and Holy Ghost: Being a Description of the Psychic Eroticism of a Negro Revival," *Journal of Abnormal Psychology* 14 (April–July 1919): 34–47; "Shaker Celibacy and Salacity Psychologically Interpreted," *New York Medical Journal* 113 (June 1, 1921), 800–5; "Converting Sex into Religiosity," *Medical Review of Reviews* 39 (September 1933): 407–15; and "Divinity in the Semen," *Journal of Nervous and Mental Disease* 76 (1932): 110–27.

toward her turn to religion. In addition, he comments that white treatment of the black race has contributed to the black person's lack of self-worth, and religion may provide a comforting refuge. He copied down key phrases from her ecstatic utterances and then pieced them together to form a synthetic sermon. She was given the sermon to edit or correct, and then he submitted the sermon to a "mystical journal," whose editor praised the essay for its "profoundly mystical ideas . . . which are so exact to Eastern philosophy." Schroeder's Durkheimian-style conclusion was that "education serves only to supply a more cultured rationalization for the unconsciously determined needs and experiences."[7] In other words, all religious forms have evolved from the same basic needs and instincts, which, in our time, are dressed up in the deceptive garb of civilization.

From this kind of expansive and eclectic evidence Schroeder developed his theory of "the erotogenesis of religion," a designation first used by him. Schroeder wrote several articles entitled "The Erotogenesis of Religion," or some variation thereof, distinguished primarily by subtitle. In one such essay he develops "A Working Hypothesis," and in another he considers "Its Opponents Reviewed." "According to the erotogenetic theory of religion, out of certain personal sexual experiences coming into consciousness there grew the idea of the sacredness of the sexual organs and later their worship. . . . This sex essence of the later religious complex sometimes does not even come to the surface of consciousness, though always present as an essential of religion." Thus, the

> differential essence of religion is always reducible to a sex ecstacy [sic]. When frankly avowed as such, then the apotheosis of sex results in some form of phallic worship. When not recognized as a sex ecstacy, or not frankly avowed as such, the erotic origin of religion is revealed by an extravagant overvaluation of the sacredness or sinfulness of some sex manifestations.

Schroeder concludes that far from having lost touch with its "sexual character," modern religion demonstrates its erotic origins through its denial of that origin, which "leads to genuine phobias against normal sexuality."[8]

Although much of Schroeder's material is drawn from extravagant or exotic religious activity, he argues that the mutuality of religion and sexuality is not merely a feature of abnormal religious experience but is also true of the experience of "perfectly healthy religionists."[9] One article

7 Theodore A. Schroeder, "A 'Living God' Incarnate," *Psychoanalytic Review* 19 (January 1932): 44.
8 Theodore A. Schroeder, "The Erotogenetic Interpretation of Religion: Its Opponents Reviewed," *Journal of Religious Psychology* 7 (January 1914): 30, 23, 31.
9 Theodore A. Schroeder, "The Erotogenesis of Religion: Developing a Working Hypothesis," *Alienist and Neurologist* 34 (November 1913): 31–2.

compiles discussions from clergy who have observed the intermingling of "religion and lust," indicating clearly that religious leaders have recognized and struggled with the tangle of religion and sexuality. Schroeder regards their testimony as especially efficacious for his own cause because "their whole interest has been to support religion, and their admission are [sic] all against that interest."[10] That is, to identify an erotic source for religious behavior and belief was to undermine that belief, and Schroeder hoped that his work would persuade people to reexamine their religious prejudices. The anticipated outcome of this examination would "deny to moral sentimentalism its present super-rational sanctions and thus clear the ethical field of its perverted consciousness and prepare the field for a sane and scientific sexual morality which we have scarcely dared to contemplate as a possibility."[11] Like many scientific enthusiasts of his time, Schroeder was certain that once the sexual, biological origins of religious belief and behavior were understood, rational people could divest themselves of the primitive morality engendered by religious systems. Logic and reason could then be applied toward creating a healthy moral system based upon fact and understanding rather than fear, guilt, and bodily alienation.

Not surprisingly, pietists were offended by the idea that religion was reducible to misdirected carnality. William James, identified by Schroeder as "the best known American critic of the erotogenetic theory," defended the efficacy of personal belief and experience against the invasions of the materialists. In *The Varieties of Religious Experience* (1902), James protests the "reinterpretation of religion as perverted sexuality." Using a bodily origin to discredit a state of mind is a common ploy, but as soon as one investigates the "immediate content of religious consciousness . . . one sees how wholly disconnected it is in the main from the content of sexual consciousness." We might as well "call religion an aberration of the digestive function," for "language drawn from eating and drinking is probably as common in religious literature as language drawn from the sexual life."[12]

James cites gustatory examples of how "religious language clothes itself in such poor symbols as our life affords." Unfortunately, nearly all of his references display the believer as the infant, suckling the milk from the breast of the mother, such as this description of the *New England Primer*: "Spiritual milk for American babes, drawn from the breasts of

10 Theodore A. Schroeder, "Religion and Sensualism as Connected by Clergymen," *American Journal of Religious Psychology* 3 (May 1908): 17.
11 Schroeder, "Opponents Reviewed," 44.
12 William James, *The Varieties of Religious Experience. A Study in Human Nature* (New York: Modern Library, 1902), 11–14.

both testaments."[13] Theodore Schroeder pounces upon this familiar image of divine nurturance, his retort an extended and witty exposition that anticipates both feminist and structuralist literary criticism. He agrees that, indeed, religious language relies upon symbols, but affirms that it is valid to ask why we choose the symbols we do. If food and hunger are the only motivation for such symbolic language, then why not describe the hunger of the New England believer as being satisfied by "a spiritual ham sandwich from both quarters of God's word? In New England ham was just as important an element of diet as mother's milk." Schroeder reminds us that the author of such phraseology is not the mother herself, for the activity is described from the point of view of the infant, nor is the author literally a greedy, blissful infant. The symbolist is an adult male thinking about women's breasts, and it is certainly appropriate to "discover what force or craving compelled an adult man, writing a primer which imparts 'spiritual food,' to conceive of this as 'milk from the breasts of both Testaments.'" Schroeder finds, then, that "Prof. James' refutation of the erotogenetic theory of religion becomes a confirmation thereof."[14]

For his part, James does not deny that religion and sexuality sometimes appear together, but he finds the claims of the materialists reductive, "evaporating into a vague general assertion of the dependence, *somehow*, of the mind upon the body." As a sympathetic observer, if not participant, in the religious experience, James writes to demonstrate that the effects of religious experience, especially as seen in the exalted, mystical experience, have their source in a real cause – the Divine. "We know that whatever be our organism's peculiarities, our mental states have their substantive value as revelations of the living truth."[15] That is, common sense tells the believer that bodily states may affect the psyche and so this need not be a determinative observation about the efficacy of religious experience.

James takes a dignified high road in disassociating religious from bodily, and more specifically, sexual, states. Commentators with a more explicitly Christian agenda who sought to accept the advance of modern knowledge without compromising their Judeo-Christian framework adopted a similar posture. They acknowledged the convergence of religion and sexuality, especially as it appeared under abnormal conditions, and then offered an antidote in the form of a spiritualized sexuality in which biological function serves religious purposes for a purified communion between the sexes. In his discussion of *Christianity and Sex Prob-*

13 Ibid., 12.
14 Schroeder, "Opponents Reviewed," 35–7.
15 James, *Varieties*, 14.

lems (1916), for example, Hugh Northcote opens, "It is not fanciful to recognize, between the various human ecstasies or raptures, prophetic, religious, or erotic, a close connection and powerful interaction. Religious literature and love literature may reach a mystic point at which they blend." He concludes his study of these interactions thus: "Well, obviously, the sexual instinct must be spiritualized."[16]

Other religious participants, however, can provide a more doctrinally satisfying account. Whenever religious ecstasy is confounded with sexual passion, the devil is involved. Myrtle C. Ballew is quite well aware that religious and sexual experience may become entangled, but this happens when "evil-minded folks" try to twist the sacred word. For her this is a sign that the devil is at work, for he is the Great Deceiver. Jonathan Edwards, whose discourse on religious affections and the Great Awakenings is an important source for both William James and Theodore Schroeder, observed exactly the same thing when he recorded the wondrous work of the spirit during the Great Awakenings.

In *Some Thoughts Concerning the Present Revival in New England* (1743), Edwards painstakingly distinguished the authentic religious experience from the inauthentic, arguing that even when persons are deceived about the origin of their religious commitment, the integrity of divine truth still prevails. He warmly defends the blessings of the revival, even in its more lavish physical manifestations, arguing that, given the unutterable power of God, the descent of the Spirit might well be expected to be "violent" in some of its manifestations. But, although God may send blessings that may seem to "exceed the capacity of the vessel," the extravagance of affections may all be seen as part of a larger, benevolent purpose.

Edwards also notes that the defenders of the revival experience are often as immoderate in their claims as those who attack the revivals, and his *Thoughts Concerning the Revival* is an example of his conscientious practice of his own advice toward moderation. In the latter part of the essay, he delineates errors that may not be imputed to God's glory, but that are to be taken as a warning that "the Devil has many advantages against us." In particular, the ever-prescient Edwards discusses the role of spiritual pride, which leads to a "degeneracy of experiences, because it grieves and quenches the Spirit of the Lamb of God, and so kills the spiritual part; and it cherishes the natural part; it inflames the carnal affections, and heats the imagination." The prideful person, however, takes the total violence of his experience to be sanctified, and so commingles "common affection" with love for God:

16 Northcote, *Christianity and Sex Problems* (Philadelphia: F. A. Davis Co., 1916), 23, 458.

> So zeal, that at first might be in great part spiritual ... may degenerate more and more into human and proud passion. ... And so love to the brethren may by degrees come to little else but fondness and zeal for a party; yea, through a mixture of a natural love to the opposite sex, may degenerate more and more, till it issues in that which is criminal and gross. ... Certainly the mutual embraces and kisses of persons of different sexes under the notion of Christian love and holy kisses, are utterly to be disallowed and abominated, as having the most direct tendency quickly to turn Christian love into unclean and brutish lust.

In other words, sexual passion may be mistaken for a religious experience. This, Edwards notes, may be particularly a problem for impressionable "young people of both sexes," who have a tendency to "go to such meetings chiefly for the sake of such an opportunity for company keeping." The devil knows how to excite the "animal spirits," and there have even been some instances of persons being under such an "unaccountable kind of bodily pressure, without any extraordinary view of anything in their minds, or sense of anything upon their hearts" that they have professed profound religious sentiment. In such display, concludes Edwards, we see "the immediate hand of the Devil."[17] The fact that human beings might mistake bodily passions for sanctification did not invalidate the entire religious experience in Edwards's view, nor for many of his dedicated descendants. But all are careful to subordinate the body or otherwise isolate the sexual event from the core religious event.

Some of the materialists assured their readers that it was not their purpose to degrade religion by exposing the sexual origins of religious belief systems. Chapman Cohen, for example, says, "it is not my purpose to prove, nor is it my belief, that religion springs from perverted sexuality, nor that the study of religion is no more than an exercise in pathology. Neither sexuality, no matter how powerful, nor disease, no matter how pronounced, can account for the religious idea."[18] Despite this disclaimer, his evidence argues otherwise. By focusing on "sexual and pathological states," Cohen offers extended examples of displaced sexuality operating as unhealthy religious activity: adolescent conversions, and "religious epidemics" such as crusades, the flagellants, monasticism, and witch persecutions. Similarly, Theodore Schroeder was no particular respecter of the religious experience, and he regarded modern religion as an evolutionary anachronism. While expressing his interest

17 *Some Thoughts Concerning the Present Revival of Religion in New England,* ed. C. C. Goen, vol. 4 of *The Works of Jonathan Edwards,* John E. Smith, general ed. (New Haven: Yale University Press, 1972), 459–69.
18 Chapman Cohen, *Religion and Sex: Studies in the Pathology of Religious Development* (London: T. N. Foulis, 1919), 9.

in a healthy physical and erotic life, he also bases his discussion of religious behavior upon an understanding that to locate the physiological and sexual component in an idea or belief is to undermine that belief. Others, however, did little to disguise their distaste for the religious event. Furthermore, their opprobrium was directed particularly toward Christianity, which was seen as the source of many contemporary sexual dysfunctions. Anthropologist Robert Briffault declared it common knowledge that "religious exaltation such as inspired the founders of Christian moral tradition is a close transformation of sexual appetites." Specifically, the church fathers "dwelt upon sex with an insistence compared to which the Freudians are reticent, and they did not hesitate to proclaim the Freudian doctrine that in one way or another the insidious manifestations of sex pervade human activities." Briffault's conclusion is that "all Christian culture has been sex-obsessed."[19]

The bulk of materialist commentary on religious passion takes for granted that the materialist already has the body firmly under hand, which leaves the devout with the unenviable task of controlling the tricky body in order to thwart the work of the devil. What the religious person takes as a sign of Satanic activity (Edwards) or mere natural coincidence (James) is read by the materialist as a sign of the fraudulent basis of religious practice. All assume, whether consciously or unconsciously, that the bodily origin of spiritual or psychological events somehow reduces the significance and integrity of the religious event. That is, the skeptic and the believer have this in common. They recognize (in varying degrees) the utter seriousness of the body, and the potential for intimacy between religious and sexual spheres. The believer tries to diminish the importance of the body by spiritualizing or dismissing it, or by attributing bodily works to the devil in order to protect the religious experience; the materialist uses that same sense of bodily shame to discredit the religious experience. Both agree that to claim a bodily source for religious passion – to suggest that religious passion and sexual passion may take root together – is to "reduce" the integrity of the religious experience, if not to expose or slander religious experience as a fraud. Because they share the same value system regarding the body, the religious individual has little defense but repression, denial, or spiritualization relative to the claims of the skeptic.

All respond to the enigma of sexual desire and religious ecstasy from the context of Western, rationalist theology. From this position, it is impossible to affirm that there is a sexual component to religious experience without automatically being guilty of degrading religion. Fur-

---

19 Robert Briffault, *Sex and Sin,* introduction by Bertrand Russell (New York: Haskell House, 1973), 57, 56, 120.

thermore, both the materialist and the theologian adopt essentially the
same strategy for distancing and controlling the body – they give the
problem to women.

Assigning the religiosexual tangle to women is the theological (philosophical and scientific) strategy upon which all other strategies are but
variations, and feminist theologians have traced the development of this
phenomenon so thoroughly I need only summarize it here. An elaborate
theological symbolism reserves for men the higher nature of spirit, for
women, the lower nature of body. Any embarrassing intersection of
religion and sexuality can be explained under this scheme, which places
sex and soul in their proper hierarchical status relative to one another.
To speak about religion and sexuality, then, is to be concerned about
what the mechanics of the sexual body have to do with the motions of
the spirit. In this view, women are the sexual body against which the
male spirit struggles. Men have religious experience, women (female
bodies) have religious significance. Unfortunately, that religious significance is largely dark and forbidding. Because of the sin of Eve, women's
sexuality is the direct, and often irresistible, gateway to the death that
comes to all human beings.
   In the case of the materialists, their propensity for an unexamined
biological prejudice is evident from their argument that although the
source of religion is erotogenetic and begins with "man's" worship of
the phallic principle, nonetheless, women are more susceptible to religiosexual confusion. Schroeder doesn't speculate about why this is so,
but his contemporaries rehearse the usual explanations: women, by virtue
of their maternal reproductivity, are more earthy and intuitive, less spiritual, less intellectual, if not simply less intelligent, than men.[20] The fact
that the male body might be obtruding itself upon their perceptions is
not an issue for materialists since, given their intellectual heritage, a male
body is not as much of a body as a female body. Apparently the materialist
has more distance from the body – his and hers – by virtue of his superior,
rational mind. Of course, this is exactly the theological argument relative
to men and women, and a clear example in both instances of how,

20 For example, James Weir, Jr., *Religion and Lust, or the Psychical Correlation of Religious Emotion and Sexual Desire*, 3d ed. (Chicago: Chicago Medical Book Co., 1905); and (from a Christian materialist) George Barton Cutten, *The Psychological Phenomena of Christianity* (New York: Scribner's, 1908). Anthropologist Robert Briffault seems to be the rare exception to materialist misogyny. In *Sex and Sin* he argues that theologically based social systems are largely responsible for inequities between the sexes and suggests that, given a coercive patriarchal system, marriage under these conditions is for women a "heartless seduction," and "the conscience of every clergyman ought to give him no peace on account of the women he has ruined" (180).

unbeknownst to even the presumably enlightened owner, the body directs the mind.

Despite the biological determinism of their views, and despite their artless assumptions about their own objectivity, however, the materialists accurately identified the intersection of religion and sexuality and the consequences of this exchange for the structure of Western moral systems. Furthermore, the insights of early scientific materialism have exerted immeasurable influence on modern culture, from shaping the secular sanctity of the therapeutic couch, to enriching our technical and popular psychological and scientific vocabulary, to reshaping a good deal of literary and academic discourse. Yet the rather astonishing materialist attack on the Christian foundations of Western morality – in particular, the erotogenetic theories of religion – seemingly dissolved before the intransigence of religious institutions.

The conclusion to Theodore Schroeder's life is an ironic symbol of the obstacles inherent in any examination of the erotic inspiration of Western religious life. After his death, two of Schroeder's cousins put in a claim for his estate and used his own writings to break his will, which had included provisions for editing and publishing his collected works. His books and articles were described as "irrational, undisciplined, unscientific, unoriginal and anti-religious," and the judge "handed down a decision invalidating Schroeder's will, stating, 'An examination of the writings of the deceased indicates that there is no social improvement to be had from their publication. . . . On the contrary, they offend religion and extol anti-social ideas.' " Even in appeal, the ruling was upheld: " 'The Law will not declare a trust valid when the object of the trust . . . is to distribute articles which reek of the sewer.' "[21]

Thus, the man who devoted his life to the cause of free speech and release from pious tyranny was censored once he had been silenced by death. Schroeder had not been a man ahead of his time – witness the vigor of the debate on the subject during his lifetime – but he certainly outlived his time. He died in 1953, and the material critique of religion seems by that time to have been safely entombed by the conservatism and complacency that, fairly or unfairly, we associate with the decade of the 1950s. Ten years later, however, a journalist named Betty Friedan published *The Feminine Mystique,* a study of the curious malaise of educated white women in the 1940s and 1950s. One year after that, in 1964, Steven Marcus published *The Other Victorians,* a study of the pornographic underworld of respectable Victorian England. Friedan's book symbolizes the renewal of twentieth-century feminism; Marcus's book

21 Dennis Domayer, "Biographical Sketch," in *Theodore Schroeder, a Cold Enthusiast. A Bibliography,* compiled by Ralph McCoy (Carbondale: Southern Illinois University Press, 1973), 4.

symbolizes a renewal of discussion about the cultural history of sexuality, and both renewed the possibility of exploring the forbidden pathways of religion and sexuality. Both signal the reopening of what has become in our time yet another cultural discussion about human sexuality and Western religious values, a discussion that may very well be reentering the same kind of cultural twilight that condemned Theodore Schroeder and the erotogenetic theory of religion to obscurity once before.

The materialist-religious debate of the first half of the twentieth century reminds us that some of the dilemmas of human life seem quite intractable. It is not that we have failed to see how religion and sexuality coincide. Indeed, the materialist-religious debate provides an impressive record of cross-cultural evidence and historical and self-conscious commentary regarding the partnership of religious and sexual energy. Rather, we seem unable to manage the implications of this "coincidence" beyond the time-bound strategies reviewed here: spiritualize it, blame the messenger, ignore it, or endlessly rediscover that primal connection.

This last response is illustrated in contemporary feminism, which has had to rediscover, if not reinvent, some form of an erotogenetic theory of religion. Building upon the surge of feminist literary criticism of the late 1960s, the feminist critique of Western theological systems takes as its starting point the sexual politics underlying the abstractions of church dogma and the institutional structures. To take but one recent example, Elaine Pagels demonstrates in *Adam, Eve and the Serpent* (1987) that the account of the Fall in the Book of Genesis informs the entire structure of Western moral thought. She argues persuasively that for the first four hundred years of Christian history, Christians associated this account with *freedom,* not enslavement to sin. All this changed with Augustine:

> When we actually compare Augustine's interpretation with those of theologians as diverse as Origen, John Chrysostom, and Pelagius, we can see that Augustine found in Romans 7 what others had not seen there – a sexualized interpretation of sin and a revulsion from "the flesh" based on his own idiosyncratic belief that we contract the disease of sin through the process of conception.[22]

It is Augustine's fear and loathing of the sexual body that has determined the entire course of Christian history, and, Pagels suggests, even his admirers would do well to reassess the felicity of this circumstance. Her conclusion about Augustine reiterates at least fifteen years of feminist readings of the same material and, in much milder form, the views of several of the materialists and sexologists. Fifty years earlier, Robert

22 Elaine Pagels, *Adam, Eve, and the Serpent* (New York: Random House, 1988), 143.

Briffault, for one, had announced the same connection between sex and sin, but with considerably less tact:

> Those delirious obsessions of early Christianity may be regarded as curiosities of cultural history . . . pathological aberrations. But upon those views is founded the moral tradition of Western culture which identifies morality with sexual expression, and sin with sex. [Contemporary sexual morality is the] outcome of a special religious doctrine which arose under particular conditions in a sect of fanatics, mentally abnormal and diseased, who were in favour of castrating themselves and of abolishing procreation, and most of whom would, had they lived at the present day, been removed to asylums for the insane.[23]

Juxtaposing Pagels with Briffault provides yet one more reminder that pointing to the sexual body behind theological and institutional structure does not offer any new insight, but apparently this is something that must be said over and over again. The basis for identifying the androcentric bias of Western religious thought is the understanding that body and language are interactive, and that the word symbols we use to represent the world are constitutive of personal, cultural, and institutional reality. The part of this proposition that says language shapes us and our world is commonly understood, but the suggestion that the body is constitutive of language is far more controversial. That is, it is not simply identifying the *male* body that is problematic, but identifying the body as a source of thought at all.

Ironically, the same issue of objective truth that should have troubled the materialists reappears in the feminist discussion of the sexual basis of cultural form. Although accurately reexposing the male body lurking behind the seemingly disembodied forms of Western thought, feminist thinkers have opened an equivocal and hazardous path to our own bodies. Women have been oppressed by a scornful assessment of the female body, which has been thought to exert a regressive function over the female mind. Is it possible to reclaim the female body in positive terms so that a claim for the interlocking relation of body and mind is not an ingrown and ineradicable liability? Second, assuming the mutual influence of body and mind, in what ways might female-originated thought be as subject to sex-distinctive prejudices as male-originated thought has been? Or are we to think that prejudice and political arrogance are uniquely male attributes and that these qualities, so often productive of racism and sexism, will be eliminated by the triumph of female-embodied thought? The question of female imperfection, or evil, has barely even entered the domain of feminist theological discourse, and one need not be speaking

23 Briffault, *Sex and Sin*, 59, 73.

from a Christian context to recognize the validity of basic questions about the limitations of human goodness.

My own questions indicate how little we understand about the relation of body and mind, and correspondingly, why the joint performance of religion and sexuality continues to be such a traumatic subject. For both the feminist theologian and the feminist literary critic, the crucial battle is canonical and textual – a matter of whose body issues and interprets the language that defines culture. As Robert Detweiler has observed of contemporary fiction, "to the problem of the ineffability of sex and religion is added . . . the problem of the mystery and despair of language."[24]

Body Language

The misuse or misunderstanding of language by Christians is both an ironic and significant development given the Protestant romance with the Word. In the doctrine of Incarnation language bears a direct relationship to the physical world, and yet theologians have built an immense theological system ever more dazzling in its elaborations, and ever more deceived about its embodied origins – a profound betrayal of the very thing the church presumably exists to proclaim. In her books about metaphor and theology, Sallie McFague suggests that we live in an age of literalism, and she is not just referring to fundamentalists who take literal meaning for the thing itself. The disembodied rationalism of Western theology becomes its own kind of literalism, mistaking the form of language for the thing itself, believing its own rhetorical structure of transcendence and detachment. McFague argues that if Western religious forms are to recover any semblance of truthful, life-giving vitality, we will need to understand theological language as metaphoric, and metaphoric language as theological.[25]

With Sallie McFague, I affirm the essentially metaphoric nature of religious, theological language and the implied theological import of metaphoric thought. Where McFague argues that the image making of

---

24 Robert Detweiler, "Updike's *A Month of Sundays* and the Language of the Unconscious," *Journal of the American Academy of Religion* 47 (December 1979): 612.
    Of course, language is not the only way in which we might approach this problem. Visual evidence of religiosexual convergence is an underutilized, but promising avenue. See, for example, Leo Steinberg, *The Sexuality of Christ in Renaissance Art and in Modern Oblivion* (New York: Pantheon, 1983); and my "Gestures: I. Notes on Empowerment, Control and the Consolation of Suffering: Pentecostal Women Talk about the Spirit; II. Notes on Supplication, Sublimation and Surrender: A Photographic Essay on Pentecostal Experience" (with Cedric Chatterley), *Cross Currents* 37 (Winter 1987–88): 427–41.
25 See Sallie McFague, *Metaphorical Theology: Models of God in Religious Language* (Philadelphia: Fortress, 1982), and *Models of God: Theology for an Ecological, Nuclear Age* (Philadelphia: Fortress, 1987).

metaphor is a different but equally valid resource for conceptual thought, however, I claim that metaphor is a basic language resource for all thought, and not just a function of poetic, or nonconceptual language. Metaphor *is* the way we think. To understand metaphor as the basis for human thought is to acknowledge just how much the body and mind are inseparable and mutually interactive. Indeed, metaphor is no more disposable for rational, creative cognition than is the body disposable to the mind. The structure and function of metaphor provide a model for grasping the activity of body and spirit, or, to return to another troubling manifestation of the tensions between body and spirit, religion and sexuality.

Scholarly work on metaphor has become so extensive that I can make no claim to representing a comprehensive discussion of metaphor theory. It would be difficult, however, for any literary critic – and especially one working the territory of religion and literature – to use metaphor as an analytic device without citing the highly influential theories of Jacques Lacan and the structuralist/deconstructive school. Many thinkers such as Ferdinand de Saussure, Roman Jakobson, Roland Barthes, Jacques Derrida, and Julia Kristeva resist classification, nor do I mean to subordinate the complex of contemporary semiotic philosophy to a single person. But for all their determined iconoclasm, these people have in common an understanding about the ways in which texts and sexual bodies share meaning and presence.

Most Lacanian style thought is marked by the Jakobsonian polarization of language that occurs when all language is divided into a series of binary oppositions of which the relationship between metaphor and metonymy is the organizing paradigm for a subsequent series of polarities: continuity/contiguity; poetry/discourse; paradigmatic/syntagmatic; condensation/displacement; abundance/lack; presence/absence.[26] According to Lacan, the desire that drives all language is a metonymically expressed, metaphorically veiled ontological longing for that which is forever absent and unavailable except as it is present as the signifier. We cannot have the thing itself, so language and word become the tangible substitute and expression of our desire. Lacan tries to subvert the rigidity of the binary oppositions that govern our desire by using a tensive model between presence/absence, signifier/signified, yet his reliance upon a "limited number of key psychoanalytic concepts (castration, phallus, Other, Father, Law, etc.)" with which to "account for the 'true meaning' of all

26 For the discussion that identifies the two poles of language as metaphor (romance) and metonymy (realism), see Roman Jakobson and Morris Halle, "Two Aspects of Language and Two Types of Aphasic Disturbances," in *Fundamentals of Language* (The Hague: Mouton, 1956), esp. 76–82.

rhetorical discourse" merely disperses the binary oppositions into their primeval figures – male/female.[27] As Maria Ruegg says,

> What gives the Lacanian analysis its particular force is the fact that it specifies the nature of those symbolic "absences" that determine our desire; and in doing so, provides us with a code, a translation key, in terms of which all discourse can be at last truly understood.
>
> The master symbol of that code – master symbol at once of absence and of desire – is the phallus . . . the signifier of signifiers. . . . As such, it is the symbol that permits Lacan to articulate female desire in terms of penis-envy and male desire in terms of the fear of castration, and in either case, it is the "law of the father" . . . that will determine the future of both. (153)

Lacanian discourse seems to allow for free play – what I would call a full, tensive interaction – between metaphor and metonymy when in fact the range of possible meanings are already circumscribed by the physical/metaphysical universe of traditional philosophical ideas. Contrary to his claims, then, the Lacanian model is no revolution in language at all, but a return to the "comforting security of classical metaphysical idealism" (153). The range of meanings available in the structuralist universe, that is, are all metonymically measured by the thinking, male body, and metonymy becomes "a phallic conceit, the part standing for the whole, standing for the hole."[28] The phallus (which is not supposed to be the same thing as the penis), then, is the pillar of Western civilization. Since the event of phallic significance is loaded in the unconscious (a transaction undetectable and uncontrollable by the victim) and since it appears as language, whose duplicities are well documented (it is never what it seems and certainly never subject to human intention or intervention), then arguing that the phallus is not the crucial linguistic event of Western discourse is rather like arguing about appearances of the Holy Spirit. Deconstructive thought has demonstrated the infinite enfoldings of language with the endless loop capacity of metaphor to create simultaneous betrayals and concealments, transformations and revelations. Ironically enough, however, theorists persist in populating the landscape with phalluses when female genitalia might be an equally appropriate metaphoric resource for how we think about how we think. Indeed, contemplating the dynamics of Lacanian language formation leads Gilbert and Gubar to ask, "Is it possible, then, that the idea that language is in its essence or nature

27 Maria Ruegg, "Metaphor and Metonymy in the Logic of Structuralist Rhetoric," *Glyph* 6 (1979): 147. Subsequent page citations in the text appear in parentheses.
28 Jane Gallop, *The Daughter's Seduction: Feminism and Psychoanalysis* (Ithaca: Cornell University Press, 1982), 20.

patriarchal may be a reaction formation against the linguistic primacy of the mother?"[29] Deconstructive thought recreates a textual/sexual universe that is ideally expansive (all language is some sort of modulated interaction between metaphor and metonymy) yet actually narrow (the function and purpose of all language is signified by the phallus). Perhaps this expansive contractionism is best read as an indication of the essentially metaphoric nature of all language, including metonymy.[30]

It is not my intention to dismiss theories of the unconscious, the duplicity of language and intention, nor even the idea that, at one level, some critics are obsessed with penises. As will be evident, my interpretations often depend upon such insights. However, I would like to take such accounts into consideration without having to accept them as a sufficient, much less absolute, explanation for how we make sense of our world. Correspondingly, I do wish to emphasize, as several have before me, how much the metonymic myopia of traditional Western thought limits and deforms our approach to knowing *human* possibilities – how much, in short, the body is part of the mind as we see androcentric critics demonstrating the centrality of symbolic and real male organs in shaping ontological destiny.

The metonymic thrust of postmodern literary theory suggests one good reason why a feminist critic might prefer to look elsewhere for a theoretical and methodological grounding. Metaphor is not the only language tool one might use in approaching my topic, nor is every succeeding chapter keyed specifically to metaphoric structure. My understanding of metaphor, however, is an essential backlight for the kind of literary criticism I offer here.

One basic definition of metaphor is that it sets up a comparison between unlike domains, thereby creating continuity without yet denying ambiguity. I like this tension model of metaphor, for it affirms uncertainty without cutting out the possibility of resolution, and the circle of ambiguity-possibility-resolution-ambiguity seems to me to be paradigmatic of the volatile, hopeful energies of human life. The tension between unlike things that characterizes metaphor also works to prevent us from

29 Sandra M. Gilbert and Susan Gubar, *The War of the Words, No Man's Land: The Place of the Woman Writer in the Twentieth Century*, vol. 1 (New Haven, Conn.: Yale University Press, 1988), 264.

30 I do not mean from these last remarks to simply reconfirm the polarized and hierarchialized Lacanian universe by linking the female body with one kind of language and the male body with another, although that is one alternative being explored by French feminists such as Helene Cixous and Luce Irigaray. See Toril Moi, *Sexual/Textual Politics: Feminist Literary Theory* (London: Methuen, 1985), esp. 102–49, for a helpful survey of French feminist theory as it seeks to recenter writing and reading for the female person.

mistaking words for the thing itself. Metaphor is a process of thought that resists being flattened into literal or absolute pronouncements, language that gives as it takes away. Metaphor sets up a rhythm between its seemingly incongruous parts, a movement that thwarts the dead hand of absolute interpretation.

I also like this tension model because it replicates our experience of body and spirit, sexuality and religion. I use metaphor as an interpretive lever in order to enhance a language of tensive interaction for matters of body and spirit, and in order to minimize the traditional structures of polarity and hierarchy that have shaped so much of Western discourse. Body and sexuality are seen to represent a domain lesser than, and ultimately removed from, the realm of spirit and religion. The simultaneity of sexuality and religion (body/spirit) enacts an incongruous coupling that the tradition of Western theological wisdom has sought to minimize, deny, or negate. Yet body and spirit would be meaningless without each other. So, too, religion and sexuality. It is the tension set up between these seemingly disparate domains of body and spirit, religion and sexuality, that gives us the enigmatic resonances of thought and event that are so powerfully a part of our world. Body and spirit are not the same thing, and there may be good ontological reasons why our culture has devised a language and a social structure for separating the two ideas. But the dualisms of Western thought cannot be the unarguable conclusion to such matters, else we would be so secure in these dualisms that we would not have to keep putting body back in its place, nor would so much theological energy have to be wasted patrolling the boundaries between religious and sexual experience. Having failed to recognize the essential metaphoric nature of thought and imagination, we are clumsy and reductive when confronted with the persistence of crucial, seemingly disparate domains: body and spirit, religion and sexuality.

Finally, what is most important about my understanding of metaphor is its grounding in concrete physical reality. Metaphor is body language. To say this from a positive stance is to cut directly across the grain of two traditional philosophical agendas. First is the philosophical bias against the body represented in theology as the unreliable female body. Figurative, metaphoric language associated with the subjectivity of the emotional, physical life is correspondingly denigrated by its immanence. Like women, body and body language are fallen – defective, second in the order of creation, first in the disorder of human life. Second is the traditional claim to the exercise of a higher, rational language that can be seen, for example, in the notion that there is a universally recognized, disinterested standard for assessing literary merit, or in the claims of the materialists to an objective perspective on religious folly. This, too, reflects an understanding about the relationship between body and language, although this idea asserts the transcendence of language and thought from the body. Because this rational language is disembodied in some miraculous way, it is reliable, objective, truth-telling in a way that metaphoric language cannot be.

The approach to language, reason, and truth outlined above is what philosopher Mark Johnson, in *The Body in the Mind: The Bodily Basis of Meaning, Imagination, and Reason,* refers to as objectivism. The objectivist position claims that "there is a rational structure to reality, independent of the beliefs of any particular people, and correct reason mirrors this rational structure." This "God's Eye View . . . constitutes a universally valid reflective stance."[31] Rationality may draw upon sense data in some preliminary stage, but its essence is transtemporal, transcendent, abstract, formal, disembodied. Meaning and rationality are to be clearly distinguished from perception and imagination. That is, figurative, nonpropositional structures are too bodily and subjective, too private and idiosyncratic to function as shared general structures. Knowledge and meaning proceed with assurance only by route of a shared, transpersonal, conceptual framework – a giant rational mind that is available to plug into.

What this amounts to is academic fundamentalism, which, even several spheres removed, still shows its sympathy with traditional theological approaches. In Johnson's words, this position represents the idea that "meaning is, at base, literal. To grasp the meaning of an utterance is to know its truth conditions literally interpreted" (72). It is to deny that language has truth structures beyond its literal, propositional content. The objectivist stance works in mutual reinforcement with the "deeply rooted set of dichotomies that have dominated Western philosophy (e.g. mind/body, reason/imagination, science/art, cognition, emotion, fact/value"(140). To expand upon Johnson's list, we might add the binary oppositions of structuralism, all of which culminate in the classic dualistic partnership, male/female. Indeed, viewed from this angle, the fury of postmodern debates over representation and the disappearance of author/ity can be seen as arguments about the declining hegemony of Western ideas about rationality. At stake is nothing less than any assurance of old order and cultural authority: the transparency of language, the possibility of an objectively obtained truth, and the meaningful presence of self, author, and God as they have been defined through the authoritative male voice.[32]

31 Mark Johnson, *The Body in the Mind: The Bodily Basis of Meaning, Imagination and Reason* (Chicago: University of Chicago Press, 1987), x. Subsequent page citations in the text appear in parentheses.
32 McFague addresses the postmodern crisis in Western rationalism in *Models of God: Theology for an Ecological, Nuclear Age* (Philadelphia: Fortress, 1987). For a sense of the

In a profound challenge to the rationalized superiority of this objectivism, Johnson argues that understanding, reason, and meaning have their essence in preconceptual, nonpropositional language that arises directly from the physical body – the walking, standing, eating, farting, ejaculating, bleeding, birthing body – and that the image schemata and metaphors that emerge from our embodiment are the basis for language, meaning, understanding, and rationality.

The experience of balance, for example, is something we do before we think it. "It is an activity we learn with our bodies and not by grasping a set of rules or concepts. . . . The baby stands, wobbles, and drops to the floor. It does this again and again until a new world opens up, the world of balanced, erect posture" (74). By extension, we also know balance through the related experience of bodily equilibrium or loss of equilibrium. Our acts of balancing and our experience of systemic processes within our bodies generate the basic image schemata that are present in all such experiences, "a symmetrical arrangement of force vectors relative to an axis."[33]

Metaphor extends this physical experience of stability, weight, gravity, and distribution through a variety of conceptual domains such as our ideas of alignment, symmetry, equilibrium, equality. We value logical and mathematical symmetry (although we are not above conducting the kind of argument that might tip the balance in our favor; we might see more sides to an argument if we had more hands – "on the one hand . . . but on the other hand"). We value psychological balance (a buildup of excessive emotion may lead to an unbalanced mind), we are uncomfortable without systemic balance (it is not good to have too much gas in the bowel; we hope the president will honor the system of checks and balances), and we link mathematical and moral systems by weight and balance (an uneven distribution of material goods may challenge our ideas of social justice; a system of ethics may be devised by weighing costs and benefits, and the gravity of good and bad consequences).

Such reasoning depends upon metaphoric language – figurative, nonpropositional language without which we would have no way to articulate an orderliness of reason and understanding. Image schemata, the abstract structures of images, and metaphors (the way in which we project those abstract structures from one domain of experience to another),

postmodern discussion from feminist literary critics, see Carolyn Allen, "Feminist Criticism and Postmodernism," in *Tracing Literary Theory*, ed. Joseph Natoli (Urbana: University of Illinois Press, 1987), 287–305; Jane Flax, "Postmodernism and Gender Relations in Feminist Theory," *Signs* 12 (Summer 1987): 621–43, and Linda Hutcheon, *A Poetics of Postmodernism: History, Theory and Fiction* (New York: Routledge, 1988).

33 The discussion of balance that follows is based on Johnson, "Metaphorical Projections of Image Schemata," in *The Body in the Mind*, 65–100. Johnson provides diagrams of the prototypical balance schema and its schematic variations on pp. 86–7.

are "the pervasive, indispensable structures of human understanding . . . propositional in a special sense that makes them central to rationality" (xx). Metaphoric language is crucial, not disposable language, and intensely personal in the most enriching kind of way.

   Johnson's work helps us see how women, symbols of the disorder of body, would naturally be excluded from the logical and dignified process of creating and maintaining cultural authority, while the exclusionary function of that authority is based upon simply another kind of body – the male body – eloquent testimony to the power of the body even when the claim to a disembodied rationality is most powerful. The universal is not maleness, it is bodiliness, and it is inescapable. By insisting upon the felt, bodily basis for language and understanding, Johnson reembodies the mind, and frees it *from* the pretense of a disinterested notion of universal rationality and *for* a mature view of what it means to be objective or rational. "Objectivity does not require taking up God's perspective, which is impossible, rather it requires taking up appropriately shared human perspectives that are tied to reality through our embodied imaginative understanding" (212). Consequent upon this perspective is Johnson's understanding that "whatever human rationality consists in, it is certainly tied up with narrative structure and the quest for narrative unity" (172).

Through fictional narrative and the bioluminescence of metaphoric language I focus upon the fusion of religious and sexual experience. Usually I refer to my topic as "religion and sexuality," although I am aware that one outgrowth of feminist work is the currently popular discussion of "spirituality and sexuality," a designation used by both Christian and post-Christian commentators. I find the term "spirituality" troublesome, however, for the history of its usage privatizes, deinstitutionalizes, and disembodies the experience to which it refers, making it difficult to relate to actual practice and experience. Furthermore, our privatization of sexuality – acting as if sexual behavior had no particular or significant relationship to public institutional life – is one reason why women have found it so difficult to challenge the sexual politics of cultural life. Dominant usages of "sexuality" and "spirituality" make it very difficult to address the politics of the institution, and difficult to address the translation of institutional politics into personal relationships on the one hand, and the larger patterns of cultural meaning, on the other hand.[34]

34 My feminist contemporaries may well disagree with my characterization of "spirituality" here, for it is the purpose of many feminist writers to rehabilitate the word so as to experience spirituality, and especially women's spirituality, as a forceful presence in public life and policy. I am largely sympathetic to this project, but also skeptical at present. For the meanings that may be attached to a discussion of spirituality, see the

Hence, religion and sexuality. "Religion" forces us to contemplate institutional dynamics and specific public policies in a way that "spirituality" does not. Eros, sensuality, passion, desire are all good terms for encompassing the generosities of sexuality, but I usually opt for the starker word – sex or sexuality – as a way of keeping before us the physical reality of the body. Penises and pulpits, vaginas and vessels, spires and erections, coitus and communion, breasts and the milk of God's word – these are the physical realities that empower the remarkable edifices of religious doctrine, theology, and institution that are so important to the shape of Western culture.

The polarization of body and spirit in Western language is not simply the product of a conspiracy or an exclusively male-guided fantasy about experience, however. Vivid, anguishing experiences have led men *and* women to conceptualize a two-part self. The validity of this dilemma, dramatized by religion and sexuality, I refer to as "embodiment." Neurologist and writer Oliver Sacks vivifies the inherent ambiguities of embodiment in the story of "The Disembodied Lady," which is about a young woman who suffers a terrible body/mind estrangement when she loses her proprioceptive ability. (Proprioception refers to a hidden but indispensable body sense that enables us to feel our physical self.) "It is only by courtesy of proprioception, so to speak, that we feel our bodies as proper to us, as our 'property,' as our own."[35] Sacks's client, Christina, sustains a permanent, physiological injury that leaves her living as a mind encased in a body she cannot feel. "I feel disembodied," she says, and then, with mounting horror, she describes herself as a "pithed frog." Her body is like a "horrible, dead veil."

Depriving her of virtually all sensation or normal movement, her medical trauma illustrates how closely a healthy sense of self is moored to "corporeal identity, or the body-ego which Freud sees as the basis of self" (52). This extreme disruption of body/mind relations certainly con-

following: Paula M. Cooey, Sharon A. Farmer, and M. E. Ross, eds., *Embodied Love: Sensuality and Relationship as Feminist Values* (San Francisco: Harper & Row, 1987); B. Z. Goldberg, *The Sacred Fire: The Story of Sex in Religion* (New York: Horace Liveright, 1930); Hallie Iglehart, *Womanspirit: A Guide to Women's Wisdom* (San Francisco: Harper & Row, 1983); William James, *The Varieties of Religious Experience. A Study in Human Nature* (New York: Modern Library, 1902); John Moore, *Sexuality and Spirituality: The Interplay of Masculine and Feminine in Human Development* (San Francisco: Harper & Row, 1980); James Nelson, "Reuniting Sexuality and Spirituality," *The Christian Century* 104 (February 25, 1987): 187–90; Carol Ochs, *Women and Spirituality* (Totowa, N.J.: Rowman & Allanheld, 1983); Amanda Porterfield, *Feminine Spirituality in America: From Sarah Edwards to Martha Graham* (Philadelphia: Temple University, 1980); and Charlene Spretnak, *The Politics of Women's Spirituality: Essays on the Rise of Spiritual Power within the Feminist Movement* (New York: Anchor/Doubleday, 1982).

35 Oliver Sacks, *The Man Who Mistook His Wife for a Hat and Other Clinical Tales* (New York: Harper & Row, 1985), 43. Subsequent page citations in the text appear in parentheses.

firms the tenacity of human spirit apart from the body, for Christina does learn how to reassert some measure of physical capacity that enables her to return home to a seminormal, if physically inert, existence. All of us can think of other such instances when the spirit flares against the darkening of physical life, and from such knowledge we can appreciate a thought system that separates body from spirit in anticipation of the mortality of bodily life, in hope of the immortality of spiritual life. The body dies, and we have no choice in the matter. By urging that we take the body seriously, that we not subordinate or devalue the body, I am not suggesting that one must be happy about the inevitable prospect of physical dissolution.

At the same time, however, this story of proprioception reminds us that seeking to live as if the body were an incidental, disreputable or disposable covering is to take for granted the very medium that allows us such breathtaking carelessness in the first place. Christina's "loss of proprioception, her de-afferentation, has deprived her of her existential, her epistemic basis, and nothing she can do or think will alter this fact. . . . She has succeeded in operating, but not in being" (52). She cannot think or spiritualize her way back into sensual flesh, and her loss is irrevocable. The feeling-full presence of the body is essential to selfhood and the life of the spirit.

It is my intention to explore the language of embodiment without denying or dismissing the inherent ambiguities of our enfleshment and the anxieties expressed about this felt condition. To accept our physicality without fearing it is hard, for we know of no transport beyond this carriage of flesh. Yet, obviously, I also seek a way around the oppressive antagonisms of dualism and denial that have pocked much of Western theological language about bodies, especially the sexual body. To affirm the body in the spirit, to say that religious impulse and sexual ecstasy are a shared energy should not be regarded as reductionistic nor antagonistic to religious experience. To claim that it is reductionistic is to reveal one's disposition to subordinate the body to "spiritual" values.

Unfortunately, death has ruled the living in much traditional Christianity as though a lifelong strangulation of physical pleasure could somehow defer, thwart, or outwit that final exit of breath. Perhaps this is the meaning of losing one's life in order to gain it. If so, it is a terrible saying, for despite Christian wishful thinking, there is no script without body and no words or Word can efface or destroy the tenacious, risky eloquence of physical being. Certainly, here is an untapped capacity of Christian wisdom for understanding and accepting the contingencies of body life, for "incarnation is not simply past event. The Word still becomes flesh. We as body-selves – as sexual body-selves – are affirmed because of that. Our human sexuality is a language, and we are both

called and given permission to become body-words of love. . . . Body
language is inescapably the material of Christian theology and bodies are
always sexual bodies, and our sexuality is basic to our capacity to know
and experience God."[36]

On the other hand, Christianity's long relationship to Western misogyny seems to some insurmountable. For theorist Julia Kristeva, "Christianity is the distilled essence of patriarchy; it is the nervous system of
that organism called patriarchy displayed in its most involved form."[37]
A discussion of religion and sexuality that cannot endure the possibility
of disrupting and dislocating Christian systems may very well be not
much more than an exercise in dressing up old fears and prejudices in
more palatable public clothing. At some point, Christianity and deity
must be suspended in order to explore alternative dimensions of embodiment, especially if we wish to take women seriously. The ongoing
struggle of women writers from within our androcentric language system
is a disheartening, and in some instances, horrifying record of damage
and despair. Evading the body, spiritualizing the body, or blaming the
body on women has been in practice – whatever the periodic nobility of
intentions along the way – not much more than a shabby, selfish rescue
of androcentric interests.

In a dialogue with Herb Richardson, Tom Driver offers a glimpse of
how much Christian structure could be upset in a genuine encounter
with the body in the mind. Driver argues against spiritualizing sex.
"There must always be something higher and better than sex, mustn't
there," he observes, paraphrasing Richardson's comments. Then, continuing with his own remarks, he repudiates the idea that there is some
"higher" realm to which sexuality must apply for meaning. The value
question begins and ends with a question about how to live graciously
through the "inherent rhythms of my own creatureliness. . . . Sex is what
it is and you keep trying to make it something else."[38] If, as Driver is
arguing here, there is no "higher" realm to which one applies for meaning, are we bereft of meaning altogether, or might we have new incentive
for learning the lettered spirit of physical self in order to speak and be
what love we have to offer? Could we not learn "to feel the great richness
of the ardent," and know this to be enough?[39]

36 James B. Nelson, *Embodiment: An Approach to Sexuality and Christian Theology* (Minneapolis: Augsburg, 1978), 8, 36.
37 I am quoting from Martha Reineke's discussion of Kristeva in "Life Sentences: Kristeva
and the Limits of Modernity," *Soundings: An Interdisciplinary Journal* 71 (Winter 1988):
449.
38 Tom Driver and Herb Richardson, "The Meaning of Orgasm: A Dialogue," in *God,
Sex and the Social Project: The Glassboro Papers on Religion and Human Sexuality,* ed.
James H. Grace (New York: Edwin Mellen, 1978), 199.
39 Mary Gordon, *The Company of Women* (New York: Random House, 1981), 284.

The interactive intimacy of body and language is no evanescent novelty but an urgent reality for women and men alike, for from the midst of a gender-skewed vision, the androcentric writer also records his or her pain and terror at the prospects of mortal life. Perhaps the terror of mortality is something we share no matter what our alignment with gender issues. In the chapters that follow I honor potential common ground between women and men by gathering traditional fictional descriptions of religion and sexuality together with nontraditional accounts. The fierce, capricious, ecstatic, melting, and utterly engrossing demands of the body are no distance at all from the demanding, consolatory, arbitrary, and rapturous promises of institutional religion and its secular dispensations across the cultural landscape. To say so is not to reduce one thing to the other, or to imply a hierarchy of values, but to insist upon a truthful apprehension of how our ideas of male and female have shaped the intricacy of spirit *and* body, religious *and* sexual experience.

2

The Stubborn Density of Desire:
Religion and Sexuality in
Nineteenth-Century Fiction

For some critics, explicitly rendered sexuality is one unhappy, harrowing novelty of modern literary life. Francis Kunkel, for example, argues that too many contemporary writers "turn religious activity into sex," a "profane" transformation indicative of the "neurotic confusion" of the writer. Kunkel's protest assumes a comparison with some unspecified period of purity. He also assumes that any sympathetic treatment of religious and sexual energy is indulged in only by the "adolescent," "life-defeating," and "anti-intellectual" writer. His interpretation will bear little scrutiny when we read nineteenth- and twentieth-century texts with a less prejudiced literary eye, however.[1]

It is true that we usually do not think of nineteenth-century literature in terms of sexual content, and certainly not in terms of explicitly rendered sexual encounter in which religion is implicated. That does not mean the religiosexual content is not there, however. The sexual frankness of modern fiction did not suddenly create a "confusion" between religion and sexuality. The convergence has always been with us. Furthermore, an experiment in metaphoric process – putting unlike passages side by side as a mutually interpretive dialectical unit – reveals a shared density about religiosexual relations that decodes no more easily in its sexually explicit twentieth-century form than in the reticences of nineteenth-century literary form.

The first passage under consideration comes from *The Damnation of Theron Ware* (1896) by Harold Frederic. In this novel, a naive but ambitious young Methodist minister, Theron Ware, becomes increasingly disenchanted with the bludgeon-like simplicity of his Protestant circle. His disenchantment is hastened toward rebellion by his infatuation with the fiery-haired organist at the Catholic church, Celia Madden. The text

---

1 Francis Kunkel, *Passion and the Passion: Sex and Religion in Modern Literature* (Philadelphia: Westminster, 1975), 157, 164.

in question occurs about two-thirds of the way through the novel. Theron has been loitering about outside the rectory, hoping for an encounter with Celia, who is a frequent guest in the priest's household. His wish is shortly thereafter granted and together they stroll through the balmy spring evening. During the course of their conversation, Theron reminds Celia that she promised to play music for him on the church organ. She replies: "Oh, there's no one to blow the organ . . . and I haven't the key – and besides, the organ is too heavy and severe for an invalid. It would overwhelm you tonight."[2] Two pages later, it appears that Theron is being seduced by Celia in her sybaritic blue and yellow chambers, although she does so with the aid of a piano, and not an organ.

The text I want to put beside this comes from John Updike's *Rabbit, Run* (1960). Rabbit is displeased with the way his mistress, Ruth, has behaved during a dinner with friends. He asks her to fellate him as reparation for offending him, saying that he needs to see her on her knees. "After being a wife her old skin feels tight," the narrator tells us, but she accepts her punishment:

> He takes off his clothes quickly and neatly and stands by the dull wall in his brilliant body. He leans awkwardly and brings one hand up and hangs it on his shoulder not knowing what to do with it. His whole shy pose has these wings of tension, like he's an angel, waiting for a word. Sliding her last clothes off, her arms feel cold touching her sides. . . . She closes her eyes and tells herself, They're not ugly. Not.[3]

In both these passages organ blowing is a key activity, which is exactly what made me think of them in tandem. Updike is talking about fellatio. Could Harold Frederic, a nineteenth-century novelist, also be referring to fellatio? Bald and crude as this may seem, there is some shock value in this juxtaposition. Peter Gay's fine work on Victorian sexuality notwithstanding, the vaunted reticence, if not downright prudery, of much nineteenth-century fiction can be an intimidating barrier to thinking through possible connections. Moreover, as Michael Steig demonstrates, one of the biggest problems we will deal with in trying to assess sexual presence in nineteenth-century texts will be our own a priori assumptions about what was possible for the author to intend and the audience to understand.[4] We are not excused from dealing with religion and sexuality in American fiction just because nineteenth-century prose manages to be evasive while it is being suggestive.

2 Harold Frederic, *The Damnation of Theron Ware*, ed. Everett Carter (Cambridge, Mass.: Belknap, 1960), 193. Subsequent page citations in the text appear in parentheses.
3 John Updike, *Rabbit, Run* (Greenwich, Conn.: Fawcett Crest, 1960), 174.
4 Michael Steig, "The Intentional Phallus: Determining Verbal Meaning in Literature," *Journal of Aesthetics and Art Criticism* 36 (Fall 1977): 51–61.

In the case of *The Damnation of Theron Ware,* there are plenty of reasons to be suspicious of Frederic. The novel has been laid with various sexual charges, leading more than one critic to note the congruence of religion and sex in the novel. Frederic, a *New York Times* correspondent based in London, led a fast life. That is a nice way of saying that he was something of a polygamist, who also recommended "limited polyandry" or "affectionate and lasting concubinage" as antidotes for prostitution and prudish patriarchalism.[5] *The Damnation of Theron Ware* is clearly a skillful exploration of the uncertain faith-prints of Protestant America, but it is also a wry and astute account of the sexual pageantry of the pious life – which brings me to the text in question.

The vintage of church organ appropriate to the setting of *The Damnation* might well have needed blowing. The procedure was indeed called "blowing the organ," or "blowing the bellows," and the phrase describes the process by which air was fed into the instrument by hand, and later by mechanical contrivances. If human laborers were involved, they were referred to as "blowers," "blow-boys," or "bellows blowers."[6] However, "blow" was also used in various scatological capacities in the Victorian sexual underground, most notably: "blowing the groundsels," which meant to have relations with a woman on the ground; "blow" or "Blower" referred to a harlot or a finely built woman; "to get a blow" was a male reference to copulation; a "blow-book" contained indecent or smutty pictures; and finally, "to blow the bellows" meant to stir up passion.[7] It seems likely, then, that one might innocently or not so innocently "blow the organ" or "blow the bellows."

As with *The Damnation,* the Updike novel is energized by a variety of religious charges. Hero Rabbit is a modern tin angel who is especially eager to "make it" while the church across the street is full of Sunday morning worshipers (88). The long love-making sequence between Rabbit and his new-chosen mistress establishes her body as a symbolic counterweight to the church, whose night-lit stained glass windows seem a "hole punched in reality to show the abstract brilliance burning underneath." Ruth's eyes also seem to be "gaps in a surface" (78). Even when Ruth leaves the bed to go to the bathroom, Rabbit's momentary lone-

---

5 A Saunterer in the Labyrinth [Harold Frederic], "Musings on the Questions of the Hour," *Pall Mall Budget* 33 (August 13, 1885):12.
6 George Ashdown Audsley, *The Art of Organ Building* (1905; reprint, New York: Dover, 1965), 675–7; Oliver C. Faust, *A Treatise on the Construction, Repairing and Tuning of the Organ* (Boston: Tuners Supply, 1949), 18–19; and E. J. Hopkins and E. F. Rimbault, *The Organ: Its History and Construction* (1877; reprint, Hilversum, The Netherlands: Frits Knuf, 1965), 34–5.
7 John S. Farmer and W. E. Henley, *Dictionary of Slang and Its Analogues, Past and Present,* introd. Lee Revens and G. Legman (1890; New York: University Books, 1966); and Eric Partridge, *A Dictionary of Slang and Unconventional Colloquialisms,* ed. Paul Beale, 8th ed. (New York: Macmillan, 1984).

liness is assuaged by the comforting view of the church windows (84). Given this sort of symbolic juxtaposition, it is not terribly surprising to arrive at the text under consideration and again find religion and sex occurring as intertwined themes. Rabbit, whose phallus has earlier been likened to an angel's sword (139), now stands like an angel anticipating revelation – in this case, penitential fellatio from Ruth. "His whole shy pose has these wings of tension, like he's an angel, waiting for a word" (174). Notice the *lack* of sexually explicit language right when it might reasonably be expected. As the event draws near, Rabbit refuses to name the sexual act he seeks, although he originally initiated his demand with a discussion of Ruth's sexual history and a very clear question – "Did you blow guys?" (172). However, once they are alone, "he is too fastidious to mouth the words" and she has to say it to confirm they are indeed talking about the same thing, although even her reply is implied and not rendered in direct quotation.

Ruth, like Theron Ware, is in some relationship to an organ that needs blowing, but the religious tonality of the Updike text undercuts the event into such an ambiguous shape that perhaps it is strictly a religious event that can be said to define the entire scene. The opacity of the prose at the critical religiosexual intersection leaves us wondering – are we to think religion is sexual, or sex a religious act of submission? Are we reading about an act of prayer or fellatio, "blowing the bellows" or playing the church organ?

Set in relation, the two passages perform a metaphoric exchange in which each borrows the convention of the other, dramatizing the stubborn density of desire. The Updike passage is as veiled as any nineteenth-century text; Frederic's outlandish play with nineteenth-century scatology is something more likely to be associated with a twentieth-century production. Generally, although not absolutely, sex operates on the underside of religion in nineteenth-century fiction, undercutting religious action, but never fully revealed because of the conventions of reticence guarding public expression of private matters. And generally, although this is less of a sure generalization than the first, religion undercuts sexuality in twentieth-century fiction. In both nineteenth- and twentieth-century fiction, however, the dialectical ambiguity between religion and sexuality remains intact. Thus, by looking more closely at nineteenth-century treatments of religion and sexuality in this chapter, we prepare to look forward to our own time, and we see that even when there is license to say everything, we cannot. There is a stubborn density to desire that resists the dispersion and control of grammatical arrangements.[8]

8 I use the word "desire" with some sense of risk, given the popularity of the term in

The opaqueness of nineteenth-century writing can be clarified by attentiveness to two things. We must be aware of the drama of sound and
silence that informs the nineteenth-century text, for that metaphoric
dynamic between sound and silence expresses and preserves a nineteenth-
century boundary between public and private experience that we have
been wont to miscall "prudish" or "repressed." As Peter Gay has demonstrated, however, we may too often have mistaken reticence for repression, and modesty for prudery. Specifically, we assume that what was
said was what was heard and acted upon, as though nineteenth-century
people were too unsophisticated to have devised an intricate network of
communication between public and private spheres. Those sharing the
prejudice that "for the vast majority of Victorians . . . public character
was the same as it was in private"[9] are thoroughly discredited by Gay's
work:

> This much should now be plain: the bourgeois experience was far richer
> than its expression, rich as that was; and it included a substantial measure
> of sensuality for both sexes, and of candor – in sheltered surroundings.
> It would be a gross misreading of this experience to think that nineteenth
> century bourgeois did not know, or did not practice, or did not enjoy,
> what they did not discuss.[10]

Nineteenth-century writers understood the synchronicity of religion
and sexuality, and there is no mistaking this in the writing. They knew
that a shared sensuality provided much of the basis for articulating this
connection between religious and sexual experience, and they sought to
express and understand this commonality. Images of heat, color, food,
and animals, as well as carefully monitored body images such as hair,
arms, the throat, or eyes are all pressed into service both for their intrinsic
beauty and the ability to convey the intimacy of matters of body and
spirit.[11] The Victorians knew something about passion that goes far
beyond modesty about nakedness or the incongruity of sexual intercourse. Those physical items are part of a charged symbolic universe that
is at once menacing and ecstatic, an experience both desired and feared.

current literary criticism. The word seems attenuated in twentieth-century usage, perhaps too much an abstracted sign of transcendence, nor is it as powerful a word as
"passion," given the standard dictionary definitions. By using "desire" in a chapter
about passion, I wish to utilize the yearning it conveys in the postmodern twentieth
century but clarify that yearning with the fire and terror that is carried by the term
"passion" in the nineteenth-century novel.

9 Russell M. Goldfarb, *Sexual Repression and Victorian Literature* (Lewisburg, Pa.: Bucknell
   University Press, 1970), 46.
10 Gay, *The Education of the Senses* in *The Bourgeois Experience: Victoria to Freud,* vol. 1
   (New York: Oxford University Press, 1984), 458.
11 See Elizabeth Stevens Prioleau, *Circle of Eros: Sexuality in the Work of William Dean
   Howells* (Durham, N.C.: Duke University Press, 1983), especially her introductory
   remarks on reading nineteenth-century fiction.

As Gay says, "their defensiveness was a tribute to passion, displaying a wry respect for its powers. It invites the paradoxical speculation that the century of Victoria was at heart more profoundly erotic than ages more casual about their carnal desires and consummations."[12]

Religion and Sexuality in Harold Frederic and William Dean Howells

In an editorial commonly attributed to Harold Frederic, he says of sex that "no good will be done by railing against the 'base appetite.' Men do not really regard the appetite as base at all. Its existence is evidence of man's power to deal his only counterblow against his enemy, death. It is the mainspring of human activity."[13] In both *The Damnation of Theron Ware* and in his own life, Frederic explored the dimensions of this conviction about the centrality of the "base appetite" for meaningful human existence.[14] Although his literary output was devoted and rapid (thirteen novels and short story collections in eleven years), Frederic did not achieve the recognition he sought until the publication of *The Damnation of Theron Ware* (1896), which now stands as a literary landmark between two better-known novels dealing with religion and sexuality, Nathaniel Hawthorne's *The Scarlet Letter* (1850) and Sinclair Lewis's *Elmer Gantry* (1927). Frederic barely had time to savor his success with the *Damnation,* for he died in 1898, never knowing whether his hero, William Dean Howells, approved of the work.

The Damnation of Theron Ware, published in England under the title *Illumination,* is the story of a young minister, who, laboring in the vineyards of small-town Methodism, is captivated and then corrupted by modern knowledge. This knowledge is fourfold: the scientific skepticism of naturalism and evolutionary thought represented by Dr. Ledsmar; the sophistication of modern biblical criticism represented by Father Forbes; the sensual delights of pre-Raphaelite aestheticism represented by Celia Madden; and the honest fraudulence of the Yankee way represented by the debt-raiser Sister Soulsby. The fascination of the novel derives not so much from Frederic's skillful handling of the classic theme of the American Adam as from his undisguised interest in the sexual pageantry of the pious life. "What I took for experiencing religion was really a girl," says one of the characters, deftly summarizing the novel while alluding to his own interest in Theron Ware's wife (127–8).

Characteristially, Frederic treats sex as a deliberate current that gnaws at the most intimate regions of religious life, and Theron's interest in

12 Gay, *The Tender Passion,* in *The Bourgeois Experience: Victoria to Freud,* vol. 2, (New York: Oxford University Press, 1986), 422.
13 A Saunterer, "Musings," 12.
14 According to Edmund Wilson, "the appetite of Harold Frederic for attractive women was indomitable and persistent." See "Two Neglected American Novelists: II Harold Frederic, the Expanding Upstater," *New Yorker,* 6 June 1970, 114.

organ music with which I opened this chapter is by no means an isolated demonstration of Frederic's calculated repertoire of religiosexual thematics. Early in the novel, Theron, being much impressed with the erudition of Father Forbes and Dr. Ledsmar, decides that he will gain entrance to their esteem and admiration by writing a book. With astonishing speed, he determines that the book will be about Abraham. As Theron explains the genesis of his inspiration to Father Forbes, the reader catches Frederic perpetrating a literary wink. Theron is attracted to the topic by the "complexities and contradictions in his [Abraham's] character," especially the "strange and picturesque episode of Hagar," and the "craft and commercial guile of [Abraham's] dealings in Egypt and with Abimelech" (72). The portion of patriarchal history in question recounts Abraham's swapping of Sarah's favors for goods and safe passage, and his subsequent bedding of the servant girl, Hagar. Although the subject provides the priest with an opportunity to enlighten Theron about various insights of Biblical criticism, the sexual thematic underscores Theron's growing infatuation with Celia Madden.

In fact, none of Theron's various illuminations are free from the allure of the flesh. Even when it seems a religious discussion is taking place, religion is undercut by sexual interest. Theron is often described as being seduced by ideas – biblical criticism, evolutionary naturalism, aesthetic hedonism – but invariably his own inner ruminations revolve around sexual speculation. Much later in the novel, when Theron has begun his descent into a realm of knowledge he is clearly unequipped for, he sneaks away from his own camp meeting to spy on the Catholic picnic. Theron watches the gaiety on the Roman side of the forest, finding the contrast with the grim pieties of the Methodist campground to be quite unfavorable to his childhood religion. He wishes someone would bring him a glass of beer, "as if he were a pretty girl" (244). He is joined by Father Forbes and Celia, and for a moment they all watch the young women playing on the swings. It seems to Theron that far too much petticoat and stocking is revealed, and he averts his gaze. But a look from Celia mocks his reticence, so he recommences staring. He and Father Forbes strike up a conversation about the meaning of religious behavior, with Forbes concluding that sophisticated folks must take religious observances in proportion and "understanding what it all amounts to, make the best of it." Theron responds, "Yes, that is the idea, – to make the best of it, and he fasten[ed] his regard boldly this time upon the swings" (251). Theron's contribution to the religious discussion is minimal. Frederic makes it clear that what Theron makes the best of is this novel opportunity to peer at women's underclothing.[15]

15 Swings may have provided ideal opportunities for the nineteenth-century (clergy) voyeur. Ronald Pearsall, in *The Worm in the Bud: The World of Victorian Sexuality* (London: Macmillan, 1969), discusses a Rev. Francis Kilvert, who distinguishes his diary writing

Although *The Damnation* was well received, several reviewers criticized its frankness. Referring to a "first climax" in the novel, the reviewer in the *Dial* reproached the book for "touching upon the borders of the sensual, instead of remaining within the limits of the merely sensuous."[16] This kind of uneasy response – one reason for the editorial changes in the English edition that worked to diminish the sensual impact of the novel – was confirmed by the the ever-diligent Anthony Comstock, who arranged a ban against shipments of the novel from England.[17] Yet, there is nothing shocking about *The Damnation* except, perhaps, that the author of such varied religiosexual sensualisms was a nineteenth-century writer. Frederic, however, was writing in the shadow of the twentieth century, and both personally and literarily he had freed himself from many of the reticences that characterized earlier nineteenth-century prose. His willingness to push sensuality and symbolism to their limits, a trait that included the use of sexual slang and puns, and his cheerful disdain for the sanctimonious regard generally accorded the clergy might suggest an imagination working on the outer limits of literary respectability. Yet William Dean Howells, a man of considerable literary reputation then and now, and a personality far different from Frederic's restless and rather Bohemian proclivities, also registered a lifelong fascination with the intersection of religious and sexual ardor.

Howells's *A Foregone Conclusion* (1875) deals with an unhappy love triangle between a young woman, her would-be suitor, and a Catholic priest. The unfolding of the priest's sexuality occupies center stage in the novel, which is charged with a variety of sensual and obviously phallic imagery. Throughout his career, Howells investigated the enigma of human passion in secular circumstances, returning at the end of his career to the menacing density created by the exchange between religion and sexuality. In *The Leatherwood God* (1916), a novel explicitly devoted to an exploration of the confusing mutuality of religion and sexuality, Howells "pried out the heart of passion."[18]

This little-known novel is based upon a peculiar episode of Ohio history recorded by Richard Taneyhill and much later published and then

with his interest in young girls. One such incident features a child on a swing whose "clothes became tangled up in the seat of the swing, and to the amusement of the spectators, it was seen that she was wearing no drawers." Kilvert goes on to comment that "her flesh was plump and smooth and in excellent whipping condition" (362).

16 William Morton Payne, "Recent Fiction," *Dial* 20 (June 1, 1896): 336.
17 Stanton Garner, "History of the Text," in *The Damnation of Theron Ware or Illumination* (Lincoln: University of Nebraska, 1985), 392.
18 Prioleau, *Circle*, 183.

reviewed by Howells in the *Atlantic Monthly* in 1871.[19] Taneyhill reported how a Joseph Dylks appeared in eastern Ohio in 1828 claiming to be God. He disrupted the community and then disappeared. Howells relied so heavily upon Taneyhill's account that he insisted the publisher allow him a note preceding the text to inform the reader of his indebtedness. Howells's long-term fascination with the Taneyhill account and his development of the history in terms of some shrewd psychodynamic insights about religion and sex suggest that Harold Frederic need not have worried about the reception of *The Damnation* at the hands of his hero.[20]

The *Leatherwood God* explores the bewildering ecstasy released in Leatherwood Creek by the "god" Joseph Dylks. The power of Howells's prose derives from an understated diction whose economy serves to underline the maelstrom of misdirected vitality that has seized the village. The advent of messiah Dylks occurs at a camp meeting. Dramatically giving new meaning to the word "revival," Dylks leaps into the prayer circle and prancing like a skittish horse, bellows about salvation until his own animal vitality has electrified the room. A character reports on these astonishing events with a phallic symbolism whose simplicity effectively heightens the orgasmic drama: "Plenty of 'em keeled over where they sot, and a lot bounced up and down like it was an earthquake and pretty near all the women screamed. But he stood there straight as a ramrod, and never moved an eyewinker."[21] The shrewd and laconic narrator, lawyer Matthew Braile, attributes the longevity of the Leatherwood hysteria to the power of sexualized piety, noting that Dylks is a "handsome devil," and "some fool of a girl, or some bigger fool of a married woman is going to fall in love with him" (57–8).

Like Frederic, Howells commands an impressive sensual vocabulary, and does not hesitate to draw upon sexual slang and symbolism. The credulous Sally Reverdy felt like she was "just goun' to die," while Nancy Billings uses an even older metaphor than the Elizabethan "die" when she speaks of her experience with Dylks as having a "a plow" go over her. Howells orchestrates images of animals, heat, color, and sound into an atmosphere of sullen, electrical density that is all the more powerful for the austerity of language used to convey it. Chapter 12 marks the height of this tension as a crowd of believers and unbelievers gathers in the "hot sunset glow" of an August twilight to witness Dylks perform

19 Richard Taneyhill, "The Leatherwood God," *Ohio Valley Historical Series, Miscellanies* 7 (Cincinnati, 1871): 7–53, and William Dean Howells, *Atlantic Monthly* 28 (1871): 255–6.

20 In fact, Howells praised *The Damnation* in a lengthy review essay of favorite books and authors, calling it "very well imagined" and a book of "great power." See "My Favorite Novelist and His Best Book," *Munsey's Magazine* 18 (1898): 24.

21 William Dean Howells, *The Leatherwood God* (1916; reprint, Bloomington: Indiana University Press, 1976), 14. Subsequent page citations in the text appear in parentheses.

a miracle. He has promised to turn a bolt of handwoven cloth into a "seamless raiment," and a community woman tenderly carries the bolt of cloth she has contributed, bearing it as if it were "her babe which she was going to lay upon an altar of sacrifice." A group of ruffians jeer and make merry at the expense of the believers, and shifting restlessly like young men at a dance or a rumble, they joke suggestively with the young women. The red hair of the messiah-struck Janie Gillespie is like a "flame"; her would-be suitor, Jim Redfield, is a "sinewy young man with a soft jolt in his gait like a rangy young horse" who circles nervously about her, giving an inner coil of tension to the scene.

In a sullenly lit, cloying room, the crowd waits for two hours for a messiah who does not appear. Although Jim Redfield pleads with the crowd, the bolt of untransformed cloth is torn to pieces in the ensuing riot as believers and unbelievers contend in the fetid air and flickering light of the mill until the "tumult of destruction" is "striken silent" (81 – 92). Howells closes the chapter with the powerful image of the woman who had offered the cloth on her hands and knees on the mill floor, sobbing her despair for her children who would have no winter clothing. The restless animal energy of men and women is dissipated in a religious frenzy, the cacophony of sound and misdirected desire resolved into the solitary sobbing of a betrayed woman and a heated twilight that has become dark.[22]

The *Damnation of Theron Ware* operates as a sly literary elbow to the ribs, presenting a largely comic view of the hazards of sexuality relative to the limited religious life of rural America. If there is also more than a note of wistful cynicism to be detected, perhaps it is because in his hapless hero Harold Frederic reencountered his own youthful self who, like Theron, had been "busy saying goodbye" to his innocence ever since (329). Howells, too, is concerned with rural America, but by concentrating on the genuine terror of finding religious ecstasy so indistinguishable from bodily desire, Howells underscores rather than undercuts the utter seriousness of bodily, religious life.

These two novels are late, however, and it could be objected that Harold Frederic and William Dean Howells both demonstrate their location in a literary century other than the one of their birth.[23] Yet the

---

22 The phallic context and the ripping of the cloth suggest *sparagmos*, the ritualistic tearing apart of a sacrificial body found in a number of Greek myths and ancient cultic celebrations. According to Northrup Frye, *sparagmos* is an aspect of myth signifying "the sense that heroism and effective action are absent, disorganized or foredoomed to defeat, and that confusion and anarchy reign over the world.... " *Anatomy of Criticism: Four Essays* (New York: Atheneum, 1966), 192.

23 The *Damnation* appears four years prior to the close of the nineteenth century. The events on which *The Leatherwood God* is based occur in 1828 and Howells first became

Damnation and *The Leatherwood God* are preceded some thirty to sixty years by the fiction of Oliver Wendell Holmes, Nathaniel Hawthorne, and Harriet Beecher Stowe, all of whom have a specific word for the equivocal energy dramatized by Frederic and Howells: "passion." Neither Frederic nor Howells makes much use of the word "passion," although clearly Howells is writing about passion, with passion, while Frederic is charting the pecadilloes of religiosexual passion gone awry. In comparison, the earlier set of writers use the word "passion" so frequently as to be overwhelming. To this word "passion, whose utility and meaning seem to fade as one century closes upon the next, we look for a further clue to the nineteenth-century management of religion and sexuality.

*Passion in Oliver Wendell Holmes, Nathaniel Hawthorne, and
Harriet Beecher Stowe*

In addition to being a poet and novelist, Oliver Wendell Holmes was a physician who practiced medicine until 1844 when he accepted a post at Harvard as a professor of anatomy and physiology. His interest in biological life was complemented by his participation in literary life, and he expressed his doubled interest by exploring in fiction the mutual interactions of mind and body. Holmes wrote three novels, referred to by one reader as "medicated" because he so frankly set about to exercise his theories of psychophysiological dynamics, making the novels but thinly disguised excuses for medical speculation. The combination of sentimental, scientific, and pedagogic volubility that characterizes Holmes's novels is of tremendous advantage to the cultural analyst, for in trying to specify what may be unspecifiable, Holmes makes an important effort to move beyond the limitations of both his age and the subject itself in his use of key terms such as "love," "instincts," and "passion." In these he provides a vocabulary of unexpected access to the presence of religion and sexuality.

Thus, the three novels have the rather eccentric distinction of being fairly conventional as far as popular fiction is concerned, but quite interesting as medical and psychological inquiries. According to psychiatrist Clarence Obendorf, Holmes describes symptoms and behaviors that had yet to be named by the psychiatric community.[24] *Elsie Venner* (1859) is the tragic story of a young woman who was infused with snake venom

acquainted with them in 1871. *The Leatherwood God,* however, was not completed until 1916, although Howells indicates he had been considering the theme for a good twenty or thirty years. See Eugene Pattison, "Introduction and Notes," *The Leatherwood God* (Bloomington: Indiana University Press, 1976), xi–xii.
24 Clarence Obendorf, *The Psychiatric Novels of Oliver Wendell Holmes* (New York: Columbia University Press, 1946).

in utero and – excusably, Holmes thinks – acts very strangely. Holmes uses this device to discredit harsh theological doctrines of original sin and free will, another of his favorite topics, while exploring psychological and physiological alternatives to the grim pronouncements of the Calvinism of his youth. In the process, he describes what are later designated by the psychiatric community as schiziophrenia and psychic suicide. *The Guardian Angel* (1867) covers an even broader range of psychophysical behavior, including hysteria, transference, the collective unconscious, and multiple personalities. Finally, *A Moral Antipathy* (1885) explores Holmes's various Jungian-style prejudices regarding the true femininity of women and a case of gynophobia in a traumatized young man.

Although all three novels did well with the public, some readers and critics were uneasy. "What modern psychiatrists applaud as Holmes's recognition of the functioning of sex in relation to mental tensions and their cure was noted with high disapproval in his own day."[25] Holmes's coyness when speaking of women and matters of love is perhaps misleading to the twentieth-century ear, but his nineteenth-century audience rightly detected in the novels an impressive sensual and sexual vocabulary. Like Frederic and Howells, Holmes knew that religion and sexuality might well be experienced with the same kind of physical and emotional intensity, and he did not hesitate to speak of such matters.

The Guardian Angel features several parallel medical case studies, one of which deals with the effects of misplaced love and piety. In this instance, the victims are an impressionable young woman, Myrtle Hazard, and her philandering minister, Joseph Bellamy Stoker. The sensible scholar of the novel who functions as the alter ego of Holmes notes that when there is a young minister in town, "there's plenty of religious raving that's nothing but hysterics."[26] The Reverend Stoker is not one to ignore such an advantage and Holmes takes great effort to investigate the reason for and nature of this advantage. Stoker, he says, inhabits a shadowy territory where he may partake of "the pleasurable excitement of emotional relations with his lambs and enjoy it under the name of religious communion. There is a border land where one can stand on the territory of legitimate instinct and affections, and yet be so near the pleasant garden of the Adversary, that his dangerous fruits and flowers are within easy reach" (149). Such a dangerous territory exists because

> the paths of love and religion are at the fork of a road which every
> maiden travels. If some young hand does not open the turnpike gate

25 Miriam Rossiter Small, *Oliver Wendell Holmes* (New York: Twayne, 1962), 32.
26 Oliver Wendell Holmes, *The Guardian Angel* (1867; reprint of 1888 ed., Upper Saddle River, N.J.: Gregg Press, 1970), 167. Subsequent page citations in the text appear in parentheses.

of the first, she is pretty sure to try the other, which has no toll-bar. It is also very commonly noticed that these two paths, after diverging awhile, run into each other. True love leads many wandering souls into the better way. (159–60)

Love, or "legitimate instincts and affections," may be both the path to religion and yet also the path to a garden of pleasurable but "dangerous fruits and flowers" (149). This description, repeated in many ways in *The Guardian Angel,* explains why the "flame of religious excitement" may be used to "light the torch of an earthly passion" (142).

As Holmes understands it, there is love – true love – and there is a misleading impulse of such exaggerated sensual and emotional power that it may be identified as a serious threat to the spiritual integrity and physical well-being of the victim. Men and women may suffer the ravages of this look-alike love. True love, the one that may lead the maiden to the paths of religion, is an uplifting and ennobling experience. Unfortunately, the difficulty remains that true and not-so-true love both may be confused with exalted religious sentiment, as the seduction of Myrtle Hazard illustrates, so that distinguishing varieties of love impose an artificial intelligence upon an area of monumental perplexity.

Furthermore, Holmes is not simply enforcing a predictable distinction between spiritual and fleshly love, although he does incline in that direction. True love will most certainly include physical expression of a most tangible species, if the sensuality and fertility of his happily-ever-after couples are any indication. The mutuality of religion and sexuality takes its inspiration not from a shameful confounding of physical and spiritual desire, but rather, from the fact that sexuality and spirituality may both claim the same origin. All of us are born with what Holmes is pleased to refer to as *vis a tergo,* a force from behind.[27] Holmes uses this idea to explain why we are not necessarily accountable for our actions in any traditional sense of a theology of free will. We are shaped by this force, which seems to represent a matrix of the raw impulses of human nature, our personal, ancestral history and our cultural history, all of which contribute to the making of our "self." Holmes sometimes refers to this matrix of energy as "instincts." Love is powered by instincts, and although the instincts may be in mortal conflict and thereby create great physical and emotional anguish, they may also reside in harmonious adjustment. This adjustment is not a matter of repression, but rather a mature achievement that shapes the energy of the instincts to noble purpose. However, "instinct" has a fairly restrictive physical connotation, and Holmes prefers to use this word with reference to subhuman

27 Oliver Wendell Holmes, *Elsie Venner: A Romance of Destiny* (1861; reprint, New York: Houghton, Mifflin, 1891), 321.

forms of life. Regarding human "forces from behind," he uses a far more potent word – passion – that seems to extend well beyond the impulses of material, animal life.

As usual, Jonathan Edwards anticipates the baseline definition from which a nineteenth-century author such as Holmes operates. In his treatise *Religious Affections,* Edwards distinguished "passions" from "affections," the difference being one of purpose and degree. To control the passion for God is to produce gracious affections, which are "more extensive than passion," and refer to the "vigorous lively actings of the will or inclination." In contrast, passion refers to those activities of will and inclination that are "more sudden, and whose effects on the animal spirit are more violent, and the mind more overpowered, and less in its own command."[28] Controlled passion is a true affection (which in Edwards's view is the source of true virtue); passion that controls is another, dangerous form of affection that may mimic religious dedication when, in fact, a "false boldness" is the outcome. As noted in Chapter 1, Edwards discusses the wrongful channel of false affection, or passion, in *Some Thoughts Concerning the Present Revival,* indicating his clear understanding of the sexual possibility for religious passion. Perhaps this Edwardsean distinction between passions and affections can also be seen in the nineteenth-century concern for controlling the passions. Nancy Cott argues that for the nineteenth-century woman the ideal was passionlessness, while Charles Rosenberg offers the same observation relative to nineteenth-century culture at large.[29]

Certainly, nineteenth-century writers warned their readers about the negative consequences of passion, yet I wonder if the twentieth-century critic or historian might not overread the word toward its present-day sexual meanings rather than hearing the word as it would have been used by the nineteenth-century writer. In common twentieth-century parlance, "passion" refers to any strong emotion, but especially amorous feeling or sexual desire. As the 1966 *Random House Dictionary* reports it, passion is lust.

Nineteenth-century writers had a less constricted word at their disposal when they spoke of passion, and not all possible usages are negative. The 1858 edition of *Webster's Dictionary* tells us that passion is a vulnerability, as in "susceptibility of impressions from external agents." Some lexicons specifically suggest "passive" as an appropriate synonym such

---

28 Jonathan Edwards, *A Treatise Concerning Religious Affections,* ed. John E. Smith, vol. 2, in *The Works of Jonathan Edwards,* Perry Miller, general ed. (New Haven, Conn.: Yale University Press, 1959): 350, 98.

29 See Nancy Cott, "Passionlessness: An Interpretation of Victorian Sexual Ideology, 1790–1850," *Signs* 4 (1978): 219–36; and Charles Rosenberg, "Sexuality, Class and Role in Nineteenth Century America," *American Quarterly* 25 (1973): 131–53.

that passion is contrasted with action, although "receptivity" or "susceptibility" is the more common definition. But although people afflicted with a passion may be acted upon – susceptible to external influence – they are rarely passive in their response.[30] Rather, a good deal of mental and physical activity is produced by passion, and powerful and intense manifestations of passion constitute the most common definitions. Passion is "violent agitation of the mind," a "vehement desire," or an "intense or inordinate continuous affection or impulse." Passion is variously described as fear, hope, joy, love, zeal, pride, jealousy, avarice, inordinate appetites, fervid devotion. Finally, all nineteenth-century lexicons report the Latin root of the word – to endure, to suffer – as a working definition. To have passion is to suffer. Gradually the verb was reduced and used only with reference to the suffering of Christ and now is capitalized as a proper noun, but nineteenth-century dictionaries use passion in the sense of "to suffer" as both a proper noun and verb.[31]

Oliver Wendell Holmes uses the word in its variety of meanings. Passionate people are susceptible both to the force of outside agents, as is Myrtle Hazard to the ministrations of her lecherous clergyman, and to the force within themselves. A young man worries about his "growing" passion for Myrtle Hazard, clearly his own impulses and affectional instincts set in motion by an external agent, in this case a delectable young girl. Myrtle, roused to anger against another girl, nearly strikes her a savage blow and is horrified at "this passion such as her nature had never known" and hopes it is not definitive of her "true self" (274). In fact, Holmes will try to demonstrate that our true self, or "good" self, is but the product of transforming the raw energy of passion into positive channels such as love and religion. Passion itself is not necessarily good or evil. Thus Holmes can speak of the "tender passion" or the "great passion" that is love, but also refer to the "inner spirals of the passion which whirls men and women to their doom in ever narrowing coils, that will not unwind at the command of God or man" (140–1). In the Holmes oeuvre, passion is variously described as aching, sullen, violent,

30 Sandra Sizer's study of gospel hymns offers further discussion of the relationship between "passive" and "passion" in nineteenth-century religious discourse. See *Gospel Hymns and Social Religion: The Rhetoric of Nineteenth Century Revivalism* (Philadelphia: Temple University Press, 1978).
31 The following dictionaries were consulted for the discussion of passion: Noah Webster, *An American Dictionary of the English Language* (Springfield, Mass.: George and Charles Merriam, 1858); *A Dictionary of the English Language* (London: Spottiswoode, 1876); *Standard Dictionary of the English Language* (1890; reprint, New York: Funk & Wagnalls, 1895); *Universal Dictionary of the English Language* (New York: Peter Fenelon Collier & Son, 1897); *The Century Dictionary* (1889; reprint, New York: Century, 1903); *Webster's New International Dictionary of the English Language* (1929); *The Oxford English Dictionary* (1933); *The Random House Dictionary of the English Language* (1966); and *Webster's Third New International Dictionary* (1971).

fierce, blinding, tender, great, earthly, and engrossing. Passion seems to be the intrinsic impulses of emotion and instinct that make us vulnerable, that fill us with great or frightening force of emotional and sensual feeling. One does not "have" a passion so much as one is or is not passionate, and to be passionate may bring great joy or great suffering.

Holmes's understanding and use of the word helps us to see why the more inquisitive and daring minds of the nineteenth century might regard the intersection of religious and amorous activity with as much curiosity and compassion as censure. Holmes approves of neither lecherous clergy nor confusing sensual and religious rapture, but he is intellectually honest enough to wish to explore why such behavior can occur. When Reverend Stoker woos Myrtle Hazard in *The Guardian Angel* with his "passion kindled rhetoric," she hardly knows "whether she were in the body or out of the body" (160) because the source of the sensual and spiritual event is the same. Stoker's persuasive religious charms are attributed to his passionate nature, in this case most especially his "animal nature." Myrtle's religious enthusiasm is attributed to her passionate nature, namely her vulnerability to the machinations of the "professional experimenter" and her susceptibility to violent or vehement agitations of mind and body. The character in the novel who is described as a "passionless egotist" is the only suitor for whom the passionate Myrtle shows little attraction, and by the end of the novel he is as suitably punished for his lack of passion as Stoker is punished for his excesses.

Destructive anger, great love, religious enthusiasm, appropriate or inappropriate sexual desire all are manifestations of passion. Thus, sexuality can be seen to be but one manifestation of a basic ontological intensity, of which sexuality and religion are components, sensuality a shared potential, and passion the word most properly characteristic of the whole. Within this matrix of intrinsic vitality, religion and sexuality share a common urgency, and they often look the same. Holmes's interest in the mutuality of mind and body makes passion an especially appropriate word for what he wishes to convey, nor is his usage idiosyncratic. *The Guardian Angel* shares this understanding of passion with so unlikely a literary counterpart as the elegant *Scarlet Letter*.

The Scarlet Letter has been too well plowed to need introduction, and the more shrewd of our literary critics have noted Hawthorne's interest in religion and sexuality, not only in *The Scarlet Letter,* but also in several of his short stories. Critic Carl Berryman asks, for example, just what kind of conventional religious labels could possibly be meaningful when applied to a man who knew "how piety may be generated by sexual energy"?[32] Reverend Dimmesdale, who may be noted as the progenitor

32 Carl Berryman, *From Wilderness to Wasteland: The Trial of the Puritan God in the American Imagination* (Port Washington, N.Y.: Kennikat, 1979), 22.

of a long literary history of passionate divines, exercises a devastating appeal over his more nubile congregants: "The virgins of his church grew pale around him, victims of a passion so imbued with religious sentiment that they imagined it all to be religion, and brought it openly, in their white bosoms, as their most acceptable sacrifice before the altar."[33] Certainly, then, *The Scarlet Letter* may be said to be about religion and sexuality, although the sexual event that precipitates the story takes place prior to the opening of the novel. The novel is usually read as a tale of the terrifying religious aftershocks of sexual transgression, but too often the radical power of the woman created in Hester Prynne is overshadowed by the spectacular spiritual writhings of the hapless Dimmesdale. However, if we read the novel through the word "passion," Hester takes on electrifying proportions, and the novel seems to vibrate with a menacing vitality.

"Passionate" is one of Hawthorne's favorite words for Hester. Her needlework, expressive of a "rich, voluptuous nature," is a way of working out "the passion of her life" (59). She is of an "impulsive and passionate" nature (42); her "lawless passion" (113) has cast her beyond the pale of ordinary moral discourse. When Hester steps from the gloomy prison, she is surrounded by and empowered with a defiant sensual energy that works like a threatening, protective forcefield around and within her. Hawthorne lavishes her with words of vibrance and passion: fantastic, splendid, burning, richness, fertility, gorgeous, luxuriance, abundant, beautiful, reckless, illuminate, impulsive, passionate, glowing (36–43). Several times Hawthorne draws the reader's eyes to her bosom, as indeed are drawn the eyes of the onlookers. Hawthorne calls attention to the anatomy of sexuality, but also the passion that gives sexuality and religion their existence, for Hawthorne tells us that the crowd is also gaping at that scarlet letter that burns with such urgency. Thus do the letter and the energy it symbolizes "have the effect of a spell, taking her out of the ordinary," and enclosing "her in a sphere by herself" (40). Hester is so powerfully drawn in those opening pages that when she is returned to prison at the beginning of Chapter 4, Hawthorne simply reports that she is dangerously overwrought and must be watched lest she do violence to herself or her baby. There is no need for him to describe the tempestuous scene, for he has given the reader ample material with which to fill in the report.

After the novelty of Hester's humiliation is dissipated and she is left to her own privacy, we are told she appears to be cold and majestic, as one whom Passion would never dream to embrace (112). This may be what the rigid New England villagers see, but what we see is a woman

33 *The Scarlet Letter,* Norton Critical edition, ed. Seymour Gross et al., 3d ed. (1850; reprint, New York: W. W. Norton, 1988), 98. Subsequent page citations in the text appear in parentheses.

of volatile and rebellious vitality whose thoughts track lawless paths around conventional morality ("The scarlet letter had not done its office," 114) so that she can manage only an appearance of submission. She is a woman who only need shake down her hair in a forest glade in order for the radiant sensuality of her nature to be seen; who with only the feeblest encouragement from her lover can leap to imagine a future for them and so vivify the inspiration that she supplies enough passionate energy to propel them both out of the forest in a desperate, joyous (and in Dimmesdale's case, short-lived) quest for a second chance.

Hester's passion is of essentially tragic substance, for the time for reclaiming the vivid and sensual elements of her personality passes with the death of the minister she loved so fiercely. Her passion partakes of the full resonances of the nineteenth-century term. It is a receptivity, a sensuality, a power of feeling and mind, a suffering. Pearl is the beneficiary of Hester's passion. Perhaps we are to think she is endangered by such a legacy, but in Hawthorne, as in Holmes, passion is only potentially rather than necessarily dangerous. "Crimson and gold, the fiery lustre, the black shadow, and the untempered light" of the mother's "impassioned state" are transmitted to the otherwise "white and clear" moral life of the unborn child (63). Pearl inherits this "trait of passion, a certain depth of hue" whose presence endangers yet protects the strange child until we see the raw and impulsive energy transmitted into the tender passion of the scaffold scene. Pearl will grow whole, although she will not do so on American soil.

Whether they approved or not, reviewers contemporaneous with Hawthorne recognized the novel as an exploration of passion. Orestes Brownson, distinctly not a fan of *The Scarlet Letter,* announced in his review that he was "not among those who join the worship of passion, or even intellect," for that matter. George Bailey Loring, however, reviewing the novel in *The Massachusetts Quarterly Review,* understood precisely the vitality of which Hawthorne had written:

> For centuries the devoted and superstitious Catholic had made it part of his creed to cast disgrace upon the passions; and the cold and rigid Puritan, with less fervor, and consequently less beauty, had driven them out of his paradise, as the parents of all sin. There was no recognition of the intention or meaning of that sensuous element of human nature which, gilding life like a burnishing sunset, lays the foundation of all that beauty which seeks its expression in poetry, and music and art, and gives the highest apprehension of religious fervor.[34]

34 The reviews by Brownson and Loring are reproduced in *Hawthorne, The Critical Heritage,* ed. Donald J. Crowley (New York: Barnes & Noble, 1970), 75, 169.

Here the reviewer has approvingly identified the passions of Hawthorne's cautionary tale as the foundational element of human nature, the basis of beauty, and the "highest apprehension of religious fervor."

Passion in *The Scarlet Letter* is bewildering, tempestuous, lawless, sensual, tender; a stunning abundance of feeling whose presence in each character compels one to ponder the "strange sympathy between soul and body" (95), and Hawthorne, like many of his contemporaries, takes for granted a kind of portraiture writing wherein the face and physiology are lingeringly examined as the gateway to the soul. Although in writers like Holmes this expectation takes on a phrenological silliness that Holmes himself professed to decry even while practicing it, the technique also serves to remind us of complex physiospiritual interactions that the language of transcendence and dualism tends to obscure or deny. Dimmesdale's intellectual and spiritual inventory is visible in his "white, lofty and impending brow," as well as in his "tremulous" mouth and "melancholy eyes." The "furrowed visage" and slight physical deformity of Chillingworth speak of a harrowing already begun. As Chillingworth advances toward his infamy, we can see the stooped body become the unhappy container for the raging spirit that glows "out of his eyes as if the old man's soul were on fire" (116). With the preternatural insight ever available to the damned, he greets Hester, saying, "What see you in my face?" (116). The question is entirely appropriate; the passions will be written upon the flesh just as flesh may transform the expression of passion.

Dimmesdale, of course, suffers a most spectacular revenge of the alienated body and spirit, as the "tooth of remorse" gnaws through the heart, consuming him from within, marking him without. The essential health of Hester and her offspring also is visible. She needs only the encouragement to remove the external, physical disguises clamped upon her physical self in order for the sensual spirit to animate the waiting body. The denial of the ecstatic mutuality of spirit and flesh is what makes Hester seem so rigid and unnatural, and that same denial is part of what will slay the weak-willed Dimmesdale, who cannot survive being so moved beyond the mechanisms of control leveled against this force. To be passionate is to be possessed, and possessing, and there is no sure outcome promised in the encounter. Chillingworth, himself hostage of "dark passions" (133), says of Dimmesdale, "But see, now, how passion takes hold upon this man, and hurrieth him out of himself! As with one passion, so with another! He hath done a wild thing ere now, this pious Master Dimmesdale, in the hot passion of his heart" (94). Dimmesdale and Chillingworth are literally consumed from within by their passion, and Hawthorne tells us that they are consumed by the same power, for, "philosophically considered, therefore, the two passions [of love and hate] seem essentially the same except that one happens to be seen in a celestial radiance and the other in a dusky and lurid glow" (175).

In *The Scarlet Letter,* as in every other novel discussed here, passion is the life water – and sometimes torrent – upon which each author has launched a fictional negotiation. Hawthorne and Holmes use the word and its forms so often that once retrieved for the hearing, it is impossible to ignore. Similarly, Howells began his career with a calculated portrait of passion and its religiosexual dynamics in *A Foregone Conclusion,* and concluded with his novel of "tremendous things," a territory so forbidding he confessed that the "dreadfulness and the mystery of the story distressed him terribly." Still, in *The Leatherwood God,* "in the most explicit language he ever dared, Howells confronted his "darkest observations about passion."[35] A reviewer in *Bookbuyer* approved of Harold Frederic's "frank recognition of an undercurrent of some form of passion – hate avarice, jealousy, or what-not – as a controlling motive of the lives of men and women,"[36] and in a good essay on Frederic and Hawthorne, Samuel Coale says Frederic was trying "to reach the primal forces of the human psyche, that dark realm which has always been the primal core of the best American literature."[37]

In all of these writers discussed thus far, sexuality and religion are not antagonists in this life forcefield named passion, they are its (dialectical) expressions, providing an unavoidable language of relationship that points us to this terrifying density of vital origin. This passion may also cast a different gleam upon the writing we heretofore have regarded as repressed or prudish. The utility and veracity of leaning upon this word "passion" as an interpretive lever can be put to the test in the toughest possible case – that which is read as nothing but sublimated sexual fever masquerading as religious fervor or, following Foucault, that in which the seeming absence or denial is but excrescence – the wistful and troubled Harriet Beecher Stowe.

Despite recent reevaluations, Stowe seems certain to remain a favorite example of stereotypic femininity – hardly the author one would turn to for enlightenment regarding nineteenth-century sexuality.[38] Yet Stowe

---

35 Prioleau, *Circle,* 168, 184.
36 "Harold Frederic," *The Bookbuyer* 8 (May 1891): 151–2.
37 Samuel Coale, "Frederic and Hawthorne: The Romantic Roots of Naturalism," *American Literature* 48 (March 1976): 44.
38 See, for example, Elizabeth Ammons, ed., *Critical Essays on Harriet Beecher Stowe* (Boston: G. K. Hall, 1980); Nina Baym, *Woman's Fiction: A Guide to Novels by and about Women in America, 1820–1870* (Ithaca, N.Y.: Cornell University Press, 1978), and *Novels, Readers and Reviewers: Responses to Fiction in Antebellum America* (Ithaca N.Y.: Cornell University Press, 1984); Fritz Fleischmann, ed., *American Novelists Revisited: Essays in Feminist Criticism* (Boston: G. K. Hall, 1982); Mary Kelley, *Private Woman, Public Stage: Literary Domesticity in Nineteenth Century America* (New York: Oxford University Press,

uses the word "passion" in much the same manner as our other authors. In *The Minister's Wooing* (1859), a young girl may be "unwarned of the world of power and passion" slumbering in her heart, although a woman may be fortunate to be vitalized by a "grand passion." The heart of a scheming man is a "vase filled with boiling passions," while a noble man may also be tormented by a "boiling sea of passion."[39] Characters in the novel grieve, connive, exult, and declaim passionately. They do so, however, while glazed with a quantity of idealized writing arguably designated as sentimental or domestic, and (also arguably) evasive in its handling of certain realities such as sex and death. *The Minister's Wooing*, saturated with such writing, is a critical test of "passion" as an interpretive tool.[40]

The novel actually has less to do with the middle-aged minister of the title, Dr. Hopkins, than with the efficacy of suffering as a sure detour around Calvinism. The story, then, belongs to Mary Scudder and her rascally but adorable suitor, James. Mary is Stowe's version of a Protestant Madonna, a correspondence urged upon the reader throughout the text. Adorned with the same promise texts given to Myrtle Cummings Ballew (see Chapter 1), "The King's daughter is all glorious within," and "Thou art all fair my love, there's no spot within thee," Mary acts as the evangel for the wayward James. "The dear boy" goes to sea with a questing but unregenerate heart and when news is brought to the little village port of his death at sea, Mary must mourn not only the loss of her temporal happiness but also the loss of his soul forever.

But, unlike the minister Hopkins, Mary has never had doubt of her "evidences" and so through the example of teenage purity, Stowe tries to work past the torments of New England Calvinism. The angriest arguments against the fearsome decrees of Calvinism are launched by the boy's grieving mother, but the most effective testimony comes from Mary, who undercuts New England Calvinism through no speech, but rather through the ministry of her exalted suffering. Such spiritual heroism does not go unrewarded, for James returns home, not drowned after all. As a newly dedicated Christian, he is now a fit companion for the little saint, Mary Scudder. Such a happy ending is especially poignant

---

1984); and Ellen Moers, *Harriet Beecher Stowe and American Literature* (Hartford, Conn.: Stowe-Day, 1978).

39 Harriet Beecher Stowe, *The Minister's Wooing* (1859; reprint, Hartford, Conn.: Stowe-Day Foundation, 1978), 231, 304, 418, 552. Subsequent page citations in the text appear in parentheses.

40 Fred See has discussed Stowe and *The Minister's Wooing* from a Lacanian use of "desire," arguing that "her text shows how desire may be transformed into maternity as the heart is prepared for grace, and how this movement may transform the larger text of culture." *Desire and the Sign: Nineteenth Century American Fiction* (Baton Rouge: Louisiana State University Press, 1987), 48 and the surrounding discussion.

despite its sugar coating, because Stowe herself lost her unregenerate nineteen-year-old son at sea; her sister Catherine similarly lost a lover. In real life there are no trapdoors and miraculous exits, or if there are, they are self-created, such as we see in *The Minister's Wooing,* which seems to have been Stowe's effort at building an honorable exit from her own grief.

The title of the novel derives from the tragedy-tinged period during which the characters seek to absorb and understand the "death" of James. The gentle, absent-minded minister feels himself drawn to the spiritually precocious Mary, who in the passing months after James's "death" becomes the "sanctified priestess of the great worship of sorrow" (380). Eventually, the minister Hopkins asks her to be his wife and she accepts, thinking her true love gone. Then James returns. The minister is too fuddle-brained to comprehend the dilemma Mary's betrothal promise now presents, and it remains to a gossipy seamstress to straighten him out. In the meantime, Mary prays over the matter, and then she goes to church where a climax – or as Stowe titles it – a transfiguration occurs. The account of this event puts all this passion discussion to the test. I've reproduced nearly the entire chapter because the sheer quantity itself may be an interpretive clue:

> Everybody noticed, as she came into church that morning, how beautiful Mary Scudder looked. It was no longer the beauty of the carved statue, the pale alabaster shrine, the sainted virgin, but a warm, bright, living light, that spoke of some summer breath breathing within her soul.
>
> When she took her place in the singer's seat she knew without turning her head that *he* was in his old place, not far from her side; and those whose eyes followed her to the gallery marveled at her face there, . . . for a thousand delicate nerves were becoming vital once more – the holy mystery of womanhood had wrought within her.
>
> When they arose to sing, the tune must needs be one which they had often sung together, out of the same book, at the singing-school, – one of those wild, pleading tunes, dear to the heart of New England, – born, if we may credit the report, in the rocky hollows of its mountains, and whose notes have a kind of grand and mournful triumph in their warbling wail, in which different parts of the harmony, set contrary to all the canons of musical Pharisaism, had still a singular and romantic effect, which a true musical genius would not have failed to recognize. The four parts, tenor, treble, bass and counter, as they were then called, rose and swelled and wildly mingled with the fitful strangeness of an Aeolian harp, or of winds in mountain-hollows, or the vague moanings of the sea on lone, forsaken shores. And Mary, while her voice rose over the waves of the treble, and trembled with a pathetic richness,

felt, to her inmost heart, the deep accord of that as if the soul in that manly breast had come to meet her soul in the disembodied, shadowy verity of eternity. The grand old tune, called by our fathers "China," never, with its dirge-like melody, drew two souls more out of themselves and entwined them more nearly with each other.

And as Mary sang, she felt sublimely upborne with the idea that life is but a moment and love is immortal, and seemed in a shadowy trance, to feel herself and him past this mortal fane, far over on the shores of that other life, ascending with Christ, all-glorified, all tears wiped away, and with full permission to love and to be loved forever. And as she sang, the Doctor looked upward, and marveled at the light in her eyes and the rich bloom on her cheek; for where she stood, a sunbeam, streaming aslant through the dusty panes of the window, touched her head with a kind of glory, and the thought he then received outbreathed itself in the yet more fervent adoration of his prayer. (538–41)

The immediately outstanding feature of this passage is how the prose suddenly drops into a density from which it never entirely recovers. This occurs in the third paragraph, right after Stowe has said tantalizing things about Mary's physiology. Something about being in church with HIM has considerably enlivened her body. Before we can savor this delectable moment, however, Stowe hastens into an extended discussion of hymn singing, which turns her toward a consideration of spiritual communion between the two souls that transpires during the singing. This maneuver by which the sexually suggestive opening is diverted by the language thrown up in its path begs us to consider the evasion that is transpiring. Furthermore, as we emerge from the weighty dirge of the third paragraph and head into a resolution, a further fascination presents itself. By the time we reach the final paragraph, there are three lovers on the scene: James, Christ, and Dr. Hopkins. Which one is the object of the tingling of Mary's vital nerves is not entirely clear (although for charity's sake we might assume it is James), nor is it clear with whom the glorious ascension scene is taking place. At the least, James and Christ have become conflated as the divine lover, while the good doctor is left to watch, an interesting idea all together. To compound the confusion, we may also read Mary as the Christ figure through the passage, as the chapter title, "The Transfigured," encourages us to do. Indeed, the purpose of the novel is to encourage upon us this association between suffering womanhood, the suffering savior, and the sanctification earned by both.

The body of Stowe's works indicates her uneasiness with or at least disinterest in the physical aspects of love, and so there would be no reason suddenly to find her working some subtly liberated portrait of religion and sexuality. She tells us quite clearly, in fact, that all human love is but a shadow of the divine ideality. That which Mary loves "so passionately, that which came between God and her in every prayer" is her ideal image of James. Love rarely bears any relation to the reality of its subject because "the kindling of the whole power of the soul's love . . . is, in fact, the love of something divine and unearthly. . . . Properly speaking, there is but one true, eternal Object of all that the mind conceives, in this trance of its exaltation" (128–9). Earthly love is participation in divine love; flesh seems to have nothing to do with this mystic contemplation.

Thus, Stowe's treatment of passion is different from that of the authors discussed previously. We get no sense that she is trying to unmask the conjunction of religion and sexuality or that she is even aware of the sexual implications of her writing. On the other hand, her language in this passage is sensuous. Music is the attendant and catalyst for a rapture of some sort, and the writing itself rises and falls in similar waves. When Mary is transfigured, Stowe rapidly reverts to out-of-body language, but not before noting the simultaneous interaction of the spirit and flesh, saying of Mary, "you might almost say her body thought" (539). Clearly, Stowe does not need to be convinced of the interaction between body and divine language. Indeed, her understanding of embodied speech is acute throughout the novel. But in Stowe that is not the same thing as pointing to the mutuality of religion and sexuality.

It is not that Stowe is unaware of the sexual possibilities in religious realms. In *Pink and White Tyranny* (1871), published one year before the Beecher–Tilton scandal became front page news, Stowe remarks, "In fact, the clergy, when off duty, are no safer guides of attractive young women than other mortal men; and [the heroine] had so often seen their spiritual attentions degenerate into downright, temporal lovemaking, that she held them in as small reverence as the rest of their sex."[41] At the most, her writing is peculiarly suggestive, such as when she says of the love-stricken James that a "little weak hand was laid upon his manhood, and it shook and trembled" (118), or, as in the passage quoted at length, when she refers to the "delicate nerves" of holy womanhood, a phrase nestled within an effulgence of rapturous prose.

Stowe does not seem to be Peter Gay's discreetly liberated Victorian, nor does she dwell with a loving condemnation upon sexuality such as we might expect if we were disciples of Foucault. But, if passion may be considered the determinative category out of which springs both religious and sexual experience, then it would be as possible for a writer to dwell upon the religious and spiritual nature of love, even to the exclusion of sexuality, as for a writer to focus upon the sexual aspects

41 Harriet Beecher Stowe, *Pink and White Tyranny: A Society Novel* (Boston: Roberts Brothers, 1871), 50.

of religious experience. Stowe has much interest in religion, seemingly little in sexuality. She is depicting the richness of religious passion, and given an understanding that religion and sexuality are together grounded in this vitality, it is reasonable that whether she intended or not, her language of love and religious dedication bears considerable resemblance to depictions of the intense and overwhelming intimacy of sexual encounter. The passion that deepens and vitalizes human experience, that can be both suffering and exaltation – this is what is of importance to Stowe. The abundance and near incoherence of her prose at such passages is a paradoxical eloquence that reminds us of the difficulty of speaking of this passion, much less determining what territory of human experience is exclusively religious, exclusively sexual, or intricately entwined.

Sound and Silence: The Dialectics of Passion

The reticences as well as the effusions of nineteenth-century prose indicate something about the difficulty of talking publicly about passion. The enigma of passion may not be entirely attributed to the reticence of nineteenth-century literary etiquette, however. Perhaps because we do not cherish the same boundaries of public and private life, we are unwilling to countenance the way in which nineteenth-century language preserves those boundaries while still taking their measure. Silence, as well as sound, must be attended to.

As indicated earlier, scholarship has recognized the silences of Victorian literature, taking the lack of specific discussion to indicate absence or repression. But silence is not literally silent. As John Cage says, "There is no such thing as silence. Something is always happening that makes a sound," even if it is the blood pounding in your ears, the movement of careful breathing, or simply sound remembered.[42] Similarly, language is not simply present sound. It is also composed of silences, understood in the sense just described. Spoken language conveys both verbal and nonverbal messages and some of these nonverbal messages may be silences, the speaking of what has not been spoken. In the words of Susan Sontag, "Silence remains, inescapably, a form of speech (in many instances of complaint or indictment) and an element in a dialogue."[43] To speak of language as sound and silence is to acknowledge both its non-verbal spaces and the communication that can occur when we refrain from speech, and points us toward a well-worn paradox – that of the valences possible beneath deliberately uttered vocables whose literal signification plays with a hidden world of inarticulate communication beneath words. This feature of language is an organic function of human

---

42 Cage is quoted by Susan Sontag, *Styles of Radical Will* (New York: Farrar, Straus & Giroux, 1966), 10.
43 Ibid., 11, 28.

culture. Studies of aphasiacs, persons who have lost their ability to understand the signified meaning of words, demonstrate the powerful crosscurrents that electrify speech. "For though the words, the verbal constructions, per se, might convey nothing, spoken language is normally suffused with 'tone,' embedded in an expressiveness which transcends the verbal – and it is precisely this expressiveness, so deep, so various, so complex, so subtle, which is perfectly preserved in aphasia, though understanding of words be destroyed."[44] Similarly, the inverse deficit, agnosia, also underlines how much our words – the vehicle – depend upon the tenor for their meaning, for speech without that affective charge freezes the depth of feeling into a caricature of human emotion and significance.

But when we read we are not literally speaking, we are dealing with print – visual space – so that the valenced interplay between tone meaning and word meaning is compromised. Written language has a much harder time conveying the dimensionality of language and the silences that reflect eloquence rather than emptiness. What is lost in audio-immediacy is reproduced in metaphor, which in form and content enables us to distinguish between verbal and nonverbal communication, and so demonstrate this crucial distinction between what is said and what is heard. By this necessary indirection, we are pointed toward the dialectics of public and private life. Metaphor, speaking of one thing while sending another is, after all, the ultimate exercise in dialectic, and the method by which the dialectics of public and private territories are negotiated.

In print, the lost audio connection becomes a metaphor of sound/silence. That experienced below literal signification is rendered as primal, wordless communication. The surface is the spoken word, the publicly acceptable communication. But this communication is charged by what is not said but nonetheless present, the private given disguised utterance. Silence and sound belong to the same metaphoric transaction, for as Foucault says, "silence . . . is less the absolute limit of discourse, the other side from which it is separated by a strict boundary, than an element that functions alongside the things said, with them and in relation to them within overall strategies."[45] The sensuality of sound electrifies wordless silences, thereby underlining a vanishing wisdom, namely that restraint – in this case the nineteenth-century prohibition upon literal discussion of intimate matters – produces its own potent erotic charge.

Music and voices are primary agents of the metaphor of sound/silence. Music, "with its pulsating beat and baths of sound, its tantalizing delays,

44 Oliver Sacks, *The Man Who Mistook His Wife for a Hat and Other Clinical Tales* (New York: Harper & Row, 1985), 81.
45 Michel Foucault, *The History of Sexuality: An Introduction,* vol. 1 (New York: Pantheon, 1978).

thrilling climaxes, and exhausted decrescendos" has long been recognized
as a refuge and expression for sensuality. Tchaikovsky, vigorously contending with his patroness, declares that in matters of love, words may
often be ineffectual, and then "the more eloquent language, ie, music,
appears in all its power."[46] It is important also to understand that music
is felt as well as heard. That the sound of felt music – and I do wish to
underscore the simultaneous engagement of other senses – could have
been so powerful would have been of no surprise to any nineteenth-
century writer.

   In the long passage from *The Minister's Wooing* just discussed, music
provides the occasion and possibility for religious ecstasy, the crescendo
of emotion made voluptuous by the "romantic," "rising," "swelling,"
"wild," "moaning," waves of music. Harold Frederic makes lavish use
of music as a sensual device, and instruments and the sounds they make
provide him an opportunity for teasing the reader about religiosexual
experience. The most famous instance of this is the "Chopin" sequence
that begins with the discussion of organs that opened this chapter. After
this scintillating exchange, Theron is invited to Celia's private chambers
where she invites him to a feast of sensual experience. He struggles to
maintain the decorum proper to one seeking religious communion, but
the subtle confluence of color, clothing, sumptuous furnishings, liqueur,
and the murmur of Celia's voice brings him to a fever pitch of excitement.
He mistakes Celia's piano for an altar, and in bewilderment lurches
between his impulse to deify her as a traditional madonna figure or ravish
her as a pagan goddess. But it is Celia's passionate execution of Chopin
that sends the tingly young man into a sexual swoon as the "echoes of
the broken melody seemed panting in the air . . . for completion." "It
can't be the end," he says, protesting the interruptus style finish of the
sixteenth Mazurka. And, with all the religiosexual significance intended
by Frederic, he murmurs ecstatically, "What a revelation your playing
has been to me" (206–7).

   Oliver Wendell Holmes was also alert to the seductive potential of a
well-modulated voice or the murmur of mellifluous religious music. He
knew that some hymns could be "as much like a love song as [they]
dared to be in godly company" (179) and was fond of using musical
metaphors to explain the experience of passion. The minister in *The
Guardian Angel,* Joseph Bellamy Stoker, uses his voice like an organ, for
he "loved to produce a sensation, [and] would avail himself of the ex-
citable state of hi: audience to sweep the keyboard of their emotions,
while, as we may say, all the stops were drawn out" (120). He quickly
gets a reputation for "being too fond of prosecuting religious inquiries
with young and handsome women" (173). One object of his interest is

46 Gay, *The Tender Passion,* 259, 261.

quite vulnerable to the sensuality of sound with which he surrounds her: "She loved to sing the languishing hymns which he selected for her. She loved to listen to his devotional rhapsodies, hardly knowing whether she were in the body or out of the body, while he lifted her upon the wings of his passion-kindled rhetoric" (160). Sensuous sound sweeps the participant into a destabilized and liminal state where, just as her sense of embodied being is suspended, the usual barriers between religion and sexuality dissolve before the convergence of religious and sexual energy. Myrtle Hazard's hysterical condition – and her passionate nature – renders her susceptible to any unscrupulous experimenter "who would use the flame of religious excitement to light the torch of an earthly passion. So many fingers that begin on the black keys stray to the white ones before the tune is played out" (142).

Similarly, William Dean Howells, though much less impressed with the effect produced by the average Protestant hymn singer, nevertheless was aware of the persuasive powers of the well-trained voice. Joseph Dylks mesmerizes the entire village of Leatherwood Creek with the raw sensual power of his sermons, the texts of which are incoherent when contemplated rationally. His delivery of the scriptural message is so skillful, however, that "women who knew their Bibles by heart sighed their satisfaction in his perfectness; they did not care for the relevance or irrelevance of the passages; all was scripture, all was the one inseparable Word of God, dreadful, blissful, divine, promising heaven, threatening hell" (21).

These examples help establish the sensuality of sound as produced by music or voices, but they also disclose the second important function of this metaphor. Literal utterance is far less important than the affect conveyed. Whatever is said or sung in words is the vehicle for a second message, that which is communicated but never stated deliberately. As Frederic reports the dynamic influence of the revivalist Sister Soulsby, "those who watched her words most intently got the least sense of meaning from them. . . . What Sister Soulsby said did not matter. . . . The way she said it was wonderful" (159). Harriet Beecher Stowe tells us that the "greatest moral effects are like those of music," achieved not by the "sharpsided grammar of intellect," but through these words being given "a mysterious fullness of meaning, made living by sweet voices, which seem to be the out-throbbings of angelic hearts." Words are "melted in by a divine fusion" and the result is this wordless but powerfully affective communication of sound (396). Women are as accomplished at using silence as a language as they are at using music to circumvent the literal and limited designations of spoken language. "Do not listen to hear whom a woman praises, to know where her heart is!" Stowe admonishes us. Rather, listen for what she does not say, for one "whose name she never speaks" (312). Silence is a paradoxical sound, encompassing a world of message without dropping a word.[47]

The triumph of sound and affect over literal intent is thorough in all the writers discussed here. Although two messages are sent and received – the literal meaning of the words and the affect used to propel them into significance – only one message has the power of effective (affective) communication and that is what is *not* said. Nineteenth-century writers used this metaphor of passion to negotiate the transaction between public and private domains. This function is skillfully executed in *The Scarlet Letter,* a feature that did not escape the watchful ear of Hawthorne's contemporaries. Arthur Cleveland Coxe correctly, if prejudicially, identified this deceptive dynamic as the signature of the novel. Using words such as "licentiousness," "petrefaction," and "debauched," Coxe protests that *The Scarlet Letter* is characterized by a "running undertide of filth," which is all the more horrifying for its subliminality. The language of the author, like "patent blacking . . . would not soil the finest linen, yet the composition itself, would suffice, if well laid on, to Ethiopize the snowiest conscience that ever sat like a swan upon that mirror of heaven, a Christian maiden's imagination."[48] Here the reviewer protests the doubleness of the language that allows Hawthorne to confirm the transaction between public and private while preserving the modesty of both. Obviously, the reviewer did not think Hawthorne was successful in this most intricate of dialectical enterprises – a reminder of the high-risk negotiations carried on by nineteenth-century language and the ever-present danger of disruption.

As has often been commented, *The Scarlet Letter* operates upon a series of dialectics: head/heart, male/female, order/anarchy, wilderness/civilization, inner self/outer self, and perhaps the basepoint for all, a dialectic of public and private domain. The novel balances upon this dialectical tension between what we say we are and what we keep hidden. When Arthur Dimmesdale publicly entreats Hester to name the father of her child, his "voice was tremulously sweet, rich, deep, and broken. The feeling that it so evidently manifested, rather than the direct purport of the words, caused it to vibrate within all hearts, and brought the listeners into one accord of sympathy" (49). Dimmesdale sends two messages, and Hester answers the heart-sound that simultaneously electrifies and undercuts the words of his command. She refuses to name the father of her child. "She will not speak," he sighs with relief, although in fact

---

47 This paradoxical silence also "speaks" with great poignancy of the position of nineteenth-century women within patriarchal culture. Women knew what it meant to be seen but not heard. Tillie Olsen uses the paradoxes of female silence to great effect in her contemporary classic *Silences* (1965; reprint, New York: Laurel, Dell, 1978).

48 This review is reproduced in part in Seymour Gross et al., *The Scarlet Letter,* 190.

much has been spoken between them, and their private torment has been made public. This double function of speech, sound, and affect is duplicated in the symmetrically corresponding scene at the end of the novel. Hester is standing near the scaffold, straining to hear Dimmesdale's Election Day sermon. Hawthorne takes a long paragraph to describe the effect and affect of Dimmesdale's voice, the first few sentences of which are sufficient to underline my point:

> This vocal organ was in itself a rich endowment.... Like all of the music, it breathed passion and pathos, and emotions high or tender, in a tongue native to the human heart, wherever educated. Muffled as the sound was by its passage through the church walls, Hester Prynne listened with such intentness, ... that the sermon had throughout a meaning for her entirely apart from its indistinguishable words. (164)

Hester cannot hear the words at all, but she can hear the grieving heart, "telling its secret." To those who have ears to hear, the private is quite public. While cognizant of the intellectual and theological message, the audience, too, detects the "deep, sad undertone of pathos" which has so stirringly transported the sermon.[49]

Notice that the affect-borne words are not merely disguises or empty containers, although it is true that the literal words might be considered a "grosser medium clogging the spiritual sense" (164). When Dimmesdale urges Hester to publicly name the father of her child, his literal words do truly plead a part of his case. He knows that to be exposed would be a moral kindness, although the words are overwhelmed by the far more powerful desire for protection and secrecy, which is what Hester responds to. Similarly, when Dimmesdale prophesies great hope for the new land, those words plead part of his case. If there is sadness there, too, then his audience has been wisely forewarned of the inevitable ambiguity of all human hope. This is known by the Reverend Mr. Dimmesdale too well. In all of this, the literal signification of the words is not irrelevant to the message, although, as in all metaphor, the vehicle takes second place to the tenor. Just so are public and private realms involved in such a dialectical transaction. One does not show without the other, although there are boundaries to be patrolled and observed. What happens in private, contained by the tongue of the heart (yet sent forth) has everything in the world to do with our public lives. Even in his private love letters to Sophia, there was much that Hawthorne would not say, so that, as Leland Person has so astutely observed, "Hawthorne's

---

49 An article by Nina Baym, "Passion and Authority in *The Scarlet Letter*," *The New England Quarterly* 43 (June 1970): 209–230, also notes Dimmesdale's voice as an instrument expressive not of spirituality, but passion.

very wordlessness thereby becomes a secret language. Sophia, in effect, must read between the lines, understanding her fiancee's silences by reading in what she feels in her own heart. Repression becomes expression."[50] In this perhaps we have a glimpse of just how much Hawthorne wrote *The Scarlet Letter* from the heart of passion.

In Puritan theology, sin is deformity, and Hawthorne's account of human passion in *The Scarlet Letter* warns us that for all the splendor of passion, the splendor may as easily be turned to deformity as to beauty. All of the writers discussed here have a clear eye for the danger of passion misused. Theron Ware nearly kills himself in a drunken rage over his betrayal and foolishness. Joseph Dylks in *The Leatherwood God* drowns in the Ohio River, babbling religious inanities. In Stowe, the tormented heart may throb and pulse with such violence as to displace clothing, not to mention mortal life. Stowe reveals the terror of this force as the language of sexuality is overwhelmed by the language of religious ardor, which in turn is nearly always trailed by a meditation on death. Holmes executes a spectacular revenge upon the errant clergyman in *The Guardian Angel*. Reverend Stoker is preaching on the text, "the wolf shall also dwell with the lamb" when the old sounding board above the pulpit crashes upon him. "He received such a violent blow upon the spine of the back that palsy of the lower extremities is like to ensue. He is at present lying entirely helpless" (410). Hester Prynne, avatar of passion, is consumed and twisted by her own lucency, and Dimmesdale cannot survive it at all. Perhaps, then, another reading of *The Scarlet Letter* also tells us that the real deformity and danger occurs when trust is betrayed. We betray ourselves; we are betrayed by our social arrangements. The sin, or deformity, lies in passion wrongly used, whether by those who would repress it or those who would exploit it. Thus does Hawthorne warn with such poignant simplicity, "Be true, be true, to thine own self be true."

Sound/silence is not the only metaphor of passion available within nineteenth-century fiction, but it is a key metaphor, expressing how nineteenth-century writers explored religion, sexuality and their dialectical relationship as passions. It is an extraordinary example of language seeking to replicate life experience – how to express the inexpressible – by taking deeply private and personal experience and speaking of it in daylight so we may understand without violating the intimacy of the experience or without misusing the power vested in us. This language says exactly what it must about the experience of passion: its powerful and empowering vitality, the equivocal blessings it brings, its translation

50 Person, "Hawthorne's Love Letters: Writing and Relationship," *American Literature* 59 (May 1987): 217.

into external physical forms, and the intricate relationship between physical and spiritual expression, just as the body in nineteenth-century fiction
is not merely a container for the spirit, but the visible expression of what
is spirit. Our nineteenth-century writers tell us that this passion, restless
and radiant, is a transformative power of dying and rebirth with no
assurance that the rebirth is what one wanted, expected, or can survive;
that the connection between religious and sexual passion is troubling and
difficult to talk about; that the transition from private to public and back
again is not effortless or without pain.

Finally, our writers tell us that the privacy of the human heart is to
be cherished no matter how we choose to negotiate the dialectics of
public and private territory. Harriet Beecher Stowe, for all her lack of
interest in sexual passion, is, in her single-minded focus on religious
passion, as concerned for the privileged movement of the heart as Hawthorne, who knows very clearly how entangled are the religious and
sexual passions. In the end, religious beatitude and sexual intimacy look
the same because they participate in the same powerful force for human
life and love. Nineteenth-century writers knew, intimately, the stubborn
density of desire. Their word for it – passion – and their metaphor –
sound/silence – are as intense, skillful, and brave as any contemporary
foray into the enigma of religion and sexuality, if only we have the ears
to hear.

3

A Tradition of Divine Lechery:
Men Write about the Ministry

In 1885 Annie Burnham Cooper was twenty years old, and she recorded in her diary the events of an unexpectedly amorous spring. Her forty-four-year-old minister, a Mr. Camp, seemed to be flirting with her. The diary entries published in *Private Pages: Diaries of American Women, 1830's–1970's* introduce us to a sensitive, energetic, and healthy young woman who is alternately intrigued and repulsed by the attentions of her spiritual guide. She does not seem unduly alarmed at the attentions of men or even an older man, although like many a passionate and perceptive young woman, she fields the events of courtship with a sense of high drama. What separates this courtship from others is his profession. As she says, he "comes here and take tea & flatter me just lays it on thick, and then flirt, & do all sorts of things that would be charming in any other man, but for a minister,———! Well, I don't know!"[1] Between entries about her new romance, she meditates with great severity upon her own Christian shortcomings.

In late May she professes herself overwhelmed by the attentions of her forty-four-year-old minister. She continues: "I dare not put on paper the soft sweet words he tells me, if I were his 'sweetheart' he could not say or act much more, but he knows I understand and match him in that." The occasion for this sentiment has been a woodland ride and wishes made over a secluded spring. "We converse about *love* freely, & we understand each other," she says, and then records that two days after these irreproachable affections have been exchanged, he preaches a sermon on the text, "And their souls shall be like a well watered garden of the Lord" (158). This memory sends her forthwith into a contemplation of the joys of God's love, which immediately becomes a series of questions about Mr. Camp that are only partly rhetorical:

1 Penelope Franklin, ed., *Private Pages* (New York: Ballantine, 1986), 157. The italicized words in the quotations indicate Cooper's emphasis. Subsequent page citations in the text appear in parentheses.

> I love God & his love fills me with a love to all his creatures and all nature. What did Mr. Camp mean when he said in *soft, sweet tones* while he found my hand & *pressed* it gently, "I warn you against love, beware of love?".... When picking violets he takes his seat at my feet & hold my hand (when I allow it) & repeats poetry about love? When he takes my arm & looks into my face, *aye my eyes,* & says the sweetest *things imaginable,* sometimes in French & sometimes in English? Of course he *knows I know* it is purely *Platonic,* but then it *savors* of flirtation, too. He is a real good man, anyway, pure & high & noble in his impulses. (159)

Despite the protestation of that last sentence, however, the peculiarity of the situation asserts itself, and she vehemently repels the idea of this flirtation. Mr. Camp has "completely disgusted" her. She reconsecrates herself to Christ and bids Camp farewell, saying "I feel hurt & pained to say so, but I *must!* So *here goes* goodbye – – *Adonis! goodbye!*" (159). It seems to take another year before his importance to her resumes manageable proportions, apparently both because of her confusion and his persistent attentions. Camp disappears from her meditations until September of 1888. Then she records with compassionate detachment that Mr. Camp, under a cloud of illness and scandal has "cut his throat and jumped into a cistern where he was found dead" (173).

Annie Cooper went on to enjoy a long and loving marriage and a happy life as an artist and mother. Her encounter with divine lechery apparently left no lasting scars, although it seems clear that her periods of spiritual turmoil were exacerbated by this subtle seduction. Unfortunately, Annie Cooper's Mr. Camp joins a long line of ministers who are irreparably damaged, not only by the torque of their own passion, but – as this chapter demonstrates – by the demands and prejudices and arrogances of the profession itself.

Ministerial sexuality is as troublesome as female sexuality, and for the same reason – it is not supposed to exist. In *The Feminization of American Culture,* Ann Douglas opens her discussion of the relationship between women, ministers, and cultural values by pointing to the nineteenth-century lament for the "vanished virility" of Protestantism.[2] Douglas's work seems to have secured the historical judgment that the "masculinity" of Calvinism was replaced by a feminized Protestantism, the religion of sentimental affections, and with this shift and the disestablishment of religion, ministers lost cultural status and manhood both. Relegated to a cultural backshelf, ministers found women, also isolated from public relevance, to be their primary audience. The enforced mutuality was at once sustaining and damaging as women sought to exert the little "in-

2 Ann Douglas, *The Feminization of American Culture* (New York: Knopf, 1977).

fluence" available to them through the offices of religion, and ministers sought to protect their feeble institutional power from the female parishioners upon whom they depended for cultural visibility. Of the ministers in Douglas's sample, the common profile reveals a group of men who fear they are not masculine. They suffer from the same kind of poor health so stereotypic of the nineteenth-century lady and are often described in similar terms both by themselves and others: poetic, angelic, sweet, delicate, humble. As a group, they are sexless; many were unusually attached to their mothers.

Nineteenth- and twentieth-century fiction will verify this profile of the emasculated minister, as is evident throughout this chapter. However, Douglas's sample could not possibly be telling us the whole story. American fiction contains many examples of the kind of ministerial anxiety documented in *The Feminization,* but it is also replete with examples of lusty clergy who have little in common with Douglas's collection of shrinking liberals. From Arthur Dimmesdale to Elmer Gantry to Thomas Marshfield, and in marked contrast with the clergy in Douglas's sample, fiction has provided us with a remarkable and consistent record of clergy sexuality.[3] Furthermore, the tradition of divine lechery in American fiction tells us that the kind of enfeebled clergy found in Douglas's sample were as capable of sexual misconduct as their aggressively masculine counterparts.

Arthur Dimmesdale of *The Scarlet Letter* (1850) is the first of these miscreants and is clearly recognizable as one of Douglas's enfeebled elite. His "white, lofty and impending brow, large, brown melancholy eyes, and a mouth which . . . was apt to be tremulous, expressing both nervous

---

3 I am indebted to Douglas's work even where I disagree, for where prior books and articles tend to be surveys of "images of the minister," Douglas is one of the first to achieve clarity about the peculiar, gender-driven situation of the clergy. Some other sources on fiction about ministers include Horton Davies, *A Mirror of the Ministry in Modern Novels* (New York: Oxford University Press, 1959); Grier Nicholl, "The Image of the Protestant Minister in the Christian Social Novel," *Church History* 37 (September 1968): 319–34; Peter Raible, "Images of Protestant Clergy in American Novels," in *The Right Time: The Best of Kairos,* ed. David B. Parke (Boston: Skinner House, 1982): 17–31; Irving Sussman, *As Others See Us: A Look at the Rabbi, Priest and Minister through the Eyes of Literature* (New York: Sheed & Ward, 1971); and Gilbert P. Voight, "The Protestant Minister in American Fiction," *Lutheran Quarterly* 11 (February 1959): 3–13.

In addition, a number of dissertations provide an extensive survey of novels written about ministers: Ernest Eugene Bennett, "The Image of the Christian Clergyman in Modern Fiction and Drama" (Vanderbilt, 1970); David Glenn Davis, "The Image of the Minister in American Fiction" (University of Tulsa, 1978); Richard H. Gamble, "The Figure of the Protestant Clergyman in American Fiction" (University of Pittsburgh, 1972); Walter Mueller, "Protestant Ministers in Modern American Novels, 1927–1958: The Search for a Role" (University of Nebraska, 1960); Emerson Shuck, "Clergymen in Representative American Fiction, 1830–1930: A Study in Attitudes toward Religion" (University of Wisconsin, 1943); and F. Lannom Smith, "Man and Minister in Recent Fiction" (University of Pennsylvania, 1968).

sensibility and a vast power of self restraint,"[4] reappear periodically in American fiction as the fleshly signs of a delicate and highly organized spirit. Unfortunately, the exquisite refinement represented by the faint-hearted Mr. Dimmesdale is not equal to the demands of embodiment, for Dimmesdale cannot survive his experience in the material world. His successors, however, are better equipped. The majority of these peccant pastors are portrayed as hearty, masculine types, or they frankly aspire to such a title.

Many of the fictional ministers used as examples in this chapter have already been discussed as the avatars of passion in the nineteenth-century use of the term (Chapter 2). There is Rev. Joseph Bellamy Stoker *(The Guardian Angel),* a "hen hawk among the chickens – first he picks up one and then he picks up another."[5] Harold Frederic's Theron Ware is introduced to us with Hawthorne's Dimmesdale in mind, but the closer to apostasy – and illicit sexual fulfillment – Theron strays, the more masculine his appearance becomes. Joseph Dylks in *The Leatherwood God* (1916) is the first portrait we get of a coarsely masculine minister, a "stallion of a man," with black eyes like coals and a mane of black hair.[6] Henry Adams *(Esther,* 1884) offers a Calvinist minister courting an irreligious young woman because she is a challenge. Stephen Hazard is a descendant of Dimmesdale; he is "very tall, slender and dark, his thin, long face" so spiritual that the "great eyes seemed to penetrate like his clear voice to every soul within their range."[7] The title character and subject of his passion, Esther Dudley, cannot bring herself to profess his creed of faith, and Adams uses her scruples of conscience as a means of exploring the sexual politics of submission and conversion.

The popular and notorious account of ministerial concupiscence, *Elmer Gantry* (1927), decisively turns the fictional portrait of clergy toward its defensively masculine capabilities. Gantry dreams of himself as a "white-browed and star-eyed young evangel," but he is much less Dimmesdale than Dylks. He is a large man whose "black hair and venturesome black

4 Nathaniel Hawthorne, *The Scarlet Letter,* Norton Critical edition, 3d ed., ed. Seymour Gross et al. (1850; reprint, New York and London: W. W. Norton, 1988), 48. Subsequent page citations in the text appear in parentheses.
5 Oliver Wendell Holmes, *The Guardian Angel* (1867; reprint of 1888 edition, Upper Saddle River, N.J.: Gregg Press, 1970), 48 and 169.
6 William Dean Howells, *The Leatherwood God* (1916; Bloomington: Indiana University Press, 1976), 8. Subsequent page citations in the text appear in parentheses.
7 *Esther,* in *Democracy and Esther: Two Novels by Henry Adams* (1884; reprint, New York: Doubleday, Anchor, 1961), 211. According to biographer Otto Friedrich, Adams engineered a veiled attack upon his wife in the character of Esther, while Eugenia Kaledin reads *Esther* as prophetic, but not hostile. See, respectively, *Clover* (New York: Simon & Schuster, 1979), esp. 297–306; and *The Education of Mrs. Henry Adams* (Philadelphia: Temple University Press, 1981). *Esther* might profitably be compared with Margaret Deland's *John Ward, Preacher* (1888).

eyes," "manly laughter" and "heavy good looks" cause "the girls to breathe more quickly."[8] *Elmer Gantry* appeared during a period of exaggerated Christian masculinity, and the outcry against Lewis's polemic portrait of the sensual hypocrite was itself both hypocritical and historically uninformed, for Gantry was part of a well-established pattern.[9] Billy Sunday had been selling rugged Christianity for at least two decades, and other, lesser novels of this period had boldly taken up the theme. One outstanding example – perhaps outstanding because it has been so thoroughly forgotten – is Winston Churchill's *The Inside of the Cup* (1913), which was superseded in sales only by Charles Sheldon's *In His Steps* (1897), and ten years after its first publication was made into a silent movie by Paramount.[10] The novel is an apology for the Social Gospel, made through the person of a dedicated and sexy minister, John Hodder. Hodder's congregation finds some "anomaly in virility proclaiming tradition," but Hodder, with his "protesting locks of hair," "strong and sinewy" hands, and "wide, tolerant mouth" knows that "women are his great temptation."[11] Somehow he manages to proclaim the gospel of love, maintain his virtue, and claim the love interest in the novel without any diminution of his impressive sexual appeal.

The Savior himself was subjected to sensual renovation during this period. In *The Man Nobody Knows* (1924), Bruce Barton provides us with Jesus as the consummate businessman and man's man. He assures us that Jesus has been misrepresented as a "frail man, under-muscled, with a soft face – a woman's face covered by a beard." The real Jesus was a man recognizable by "the calm assurance of those blue eyes, the supple strength of those muscles, the ruddy skin that testified to the rich red blood beneath." The proof for these assertions is provided by "the health that flowed out of him to create health in others; the appeal of his personality to woman – weakness does not appeal to them; his lifetime of outdoor living; and the steel-like hardness of his nerves."[12] This kind of Christian concern for ministerial virility is of long standing, and, if anything, becomes more vehement as the century progresses. For example, an anonymous 1901 article entitled "Ministerial Virility" is concerned with the recruitment of believers, worrying that young men do not go to church because the minister is not virile enough. The author goes on to define "virile" in terms of vigorous intellectual life. William Horn, writing in 1961, thinks that one problem with the ministry is that it is

8 Sinclair Lewis, *Elmer Gantry* (1927; reprint New York: Signet, NAL, 1970), 8. Subsequent page citations in the text appear in parentheses.
9 See Mark Schorer's discussion in *Sinclair Lewis: An American Life* (New York: McGraw-Hill, 1961), 473–83.
10 Warren I. Titus, *Winston Churchill* (New York: Twayne, 1963), 102–3.
11 Churchill, *The Inside of the Cup* (New York: Macmillan, 1913), 31, 134.
12 Bruce Barton, *The Man Nobody Knows* (Indianapolis: Bobbs-Merrill, 1924), 42–45.

associated with women, leading the media to portray the minister as "effeminate." The solution is to seek ministerial candidates who are "regarded as models of young manhood" rather than encouraging those of timid, effeminate natures. In this modern usage, "virile" is more obviously associated with maleness.[13]

With the cultural permission for sexual frankness, later twentieth-century writers fully exploit the defensive masculinity of the Christian clergy, but they do so at a terrible expense to women. Fiction of the late nineteenth and early twentieth century does not blame women for the tensions of embodiment, but examines ministerial and female roles with equal severity, often finding Protestantism itself culpable for the failures of passion seen in Protestant clergy. Generally, women are spiritualized in the stereotypes of nineteenth-century rhetoric, whether the writer is condescending to the weaker sex or presenting her as a model of superior religious leadership. But women are recarnalized, if not simply brutalized, in contemporary fictional discourse. As a representative of twentieth-century fiction of embodiment, John Updike revives the ancient misogynism of Western Christianity, a revival that flourishes in writers with less overt religious interest, such as Norman Mailer or Ken Kesey. In his several novels of contemporary religious angst, most notably *A Month of Sundays* (1974), Updike returns women to the unenviable theological status devised for them by the church fathers, and *A Month of Sundays* functions as an apology for wayward clergy from a perspective that would have been abhorrent to earlier writers. The subject of religious authority coupled with the ability and willingness to write sexually explicit prose coalesces and magnifies an ominous hostility toward women, revealing our proximity to the source of cultural gender dysfunctions.

The Scarlet Letter establishes the complexities of divine lechery, and subsequent fictions pay tribute to the genius of the drama through imitation and dilation of the original narrative. This is no small matter of historical curiosity. Hawthorne told a story worth worrying many times over for its mysteries, not the least of which is the scandalous particularity exercised by the main character. His occupation is not incidental to the story; his fall is somehow more portentous. Stephen Crane, himself a minister's son, put it this way: "The bartender's boy falls from the Waldorf roof. The minister's son falls from a park bench. They both hit the earth with the same velocity, mutilated beyond recognition."[14] He might have spoken similarly for ministers as well as their children, for

13 *Biblical World* 17 (January 1901): 3–5; and "The Image of the Protestant Minister," *Lutheran Quarterly* 13:193–210.
14 Larzer Ziff, *The American 1890's* (New York: Viking, 1966), 189.

there seems to be an unnatural progress attached to the office. The hazards of the ministry explored in the following pages are these: (1) the aesthetic and intellectual sterility of Protestantism; (2) the adolescence of the clergy; (3) women, who are the necessary accomplices to and victims of his perpetual boyhood; and (4) the seductive power of performance that is enacted through preaching and the androcentric fascination with words that cannot, finally, be separated from women themselves. Although a number of writings will be illustrative of these points, Hawthorne's baseline narrative (*The Scarlet Letter,* 1850) sets the stage for the discussion of a tradition represented by *The Damnation of Theron Ware* (1896), *Elmer Gantry* (1927), and *A Month of Sundays* (1974).[15]

There is an intrusive anomaly, however, and it is this: what we know about the concupiscence of ministers, we know from the account of male authors, who, for the most part, focus on the male figure in the novel. Some of these fictional lecherous divines possess an exaggerated masculinity whereas others replicate the dubious physical attractions of the Dimmesdale prototype. Women, too, wrote about the ministry, but the portrait of the pastoral wimp seems to be the *only* image of the minister available in nineteenth-century fiction written *by women*. Twentieth-century novels by women about ministers boost his virility greatly, but still fail to note any lecherous clergy. In short, male authors seem quite conversant with the lustful clergy; women novelists, verifying Douglas with a vengeance, write as if such a thing never existed. The concerns in female-authored novels about ministers are so different, it is like reading fiction from two cultures who have had some minimal, and not especially amiable encounter. I honor this distinction by discussing novels

---

15 Some representative portraits of ministers (peccant and pure) in twentieth-century fiction appear in the following, chronologically listed: George Washington Cable, *Bylow Hill* (1902), presents us with an insanely jealous clergy husband who nearly murders his wife and then commits suicide; Robert Keable's *Simon Called Peter* (1921) is about an army minister who falls in love with a high-spirited sinner but gives her up for the Lord; in Robert Nathan's *The Bishop's Wife* (1928), the title character longs for a truly passionate relationship and is visited by a supernatural lover to replace her sexless clergy husband; Dan Brummitt, *Shoddy* (1928); T. S. Stribling, *Unfinished Cathedral* (1934); James Gould Cozzens, in *Men and Brethren* (1936), presents us with a worldly minister who condescends to a stream of pathetic parishioners; James Street, in *The Gauntlet* (1945), kills off the good wife in order to deepen the faith of her muscular, blue-eyed husband; Paul Wellman, *The Chain* (1949); Peter DeVries, *The Mackerel Plaza* (1958), creates an Updikian sort of clergy with a sense of humor and an attraction for women, while Gregory Wilson [pseud.] offers an interesting study in moral and psychological development in *The Stained Glass Jungle* (1962); the protagonist in Conrad Richter's *A Simple Honorable Man* (1962) decides in middle age to become a minister; Frederick Buechner, *The Final Beast* (1965); Martin Gardner, *The Flight of Peter Fromm* (1973); Dotson Rader, *Miracle* (1977), a preacher's son himself, exposes the sexual politics of big-time evangelism. Finally, John Updike's *Roger's Version* (1986) is narrated by a minister who has abandoned his pulpit and assumed the sacred podium of that most dangerous creature, the academic male.

by women in subsequent chapters, for I have no good way of effecting integration with the account from male authors.

Aesthetic Liabilities

One of the subtlest hazards of the Protestant ministry is the deliberate absence of the communion with the senses that has characterized Protestant worship and culture. In all the fiction examined in this chapter, a poverty of beauty – variously represented by music, art, literature, intellectual discussion, and even food – is a serious liability for the Protestant clergy.

Nathaniel Hawthorne, sometimes seen as the soul of Puritanism born out of time, calls attention to the Protestant deficit in grace and beauty, and in so doing, shows himself distinctly equivocal in his relation to his spiritual ancestors. At several points in *The Scarlet Letter,* Hawthorne contrasts the dreary rigidity of Puritanism to the aesthetic vitalities of earlier religious periods. Hester is so picturesque and beautiful upon that scaffold that "had there been a Papist among the crowd of Puritans, he might have seen . . . an object to remind him of the image of Divine Maternity" (41). Hawthorne says, "we have yet to learn again the forgotten art of gayety," and provides as the reproachful contrast Hester herself, who has "in her nature a rich, voluptuous Oriental characteristic – a taste for the gorgeously beautiful, which, save in the exquisite productions of her needle, found nothing else in all the possibilities of her life to exercise itself upon" (59). The arid comforts of his own faith drive Dimmesdale to penitential practices "more in accordance with the old, corrupted faith of Rome than with the better light of the church in which he had been born and bred." He lives on his anguish and little else, but, "had he once found power to smile, and wear a face of gayety, there would have been no such man!" (99, 101).

Hawthorne's suggestions that the aesthetic and sacramental qualities of other systems, most notably Catholicism, might offer greater comfort and expression for the questing soul are greatly expanded in Harold Frederic, whose debt to Hawthorne is considerable.[16] Theron Ware is immediately drawn to the priest, Father Forbes, and his organist, Celia Madden, through the beauty of the Catholic liturgy. Additionally, and not insubstantially, he takes note of the beauty of Celia herself, and the captivating image of Celia as a luminious Madonna intrudes upon Theron many times within the novel. Compounding the maternal, physical at-

16 See, for example, Stanton Garner, *Harold Frederic* (Minneapolis: University of Minnesota, 1969); George W. Johnson, "Harold Frederic's Young Goodman Ware," *Modern Fiction Studies* 8 (Winter 1962–3): 361–74, and Joan Zlotnick, "*The Damnation of Theron Ware* with a Backward Glance at Hawthorne," *Markham Review* 2 (February 1971): 90–2.

traction of Celia is the charm of the music she produces as church organist. Theron suffers from an almost "magical fascination" for music, so much so that "more than once he had specifically prayed against it as a temptation." He immediately confesses to Celia that his church has no organ – a deliberate attribute of the Protestantism he serves – and she replies that she couldn't play two anyway. The insinuations in this exchange prepare us for the climactic sexuality of the "blowing the organ" scene that determines the action of Section 3 of the novel (see Chapter 2). At this point – and it is very early in the novel – Theron lacks an organ, the instrument functioning as an effective symbol of the mutuality of the aesthetic and the sexual. His subsequent activities are efforts to supply a remedy. He will either have music or he will write a book, and in the encounters that follow, Frederic brings together what have become twentieth-century obsessions: fertility, writing, organs, pens, and penises.

Theron is suddenly enthralled with the prospect of buying a piano for his wife, an ambition given vitality by his encounter with Celia. Furthermore, in honor of his awakening intellectual self, he decides he will act upon his desire to write a book, and in a suggestive passage we see him "thrilled with a novel ecstasy" as he selects pens, paper, and a "virgin blotter" with which to begin his project. He notes in his diary that he pursues the piano and the book upon the same day.[17] Then, dramatizing the danger of organs and pens, or the lack thereof, Frederic sends Theron to an initiatory meal. Seeking assistance with his book project on Abraham, he calls upon Father Forbes and is invited to stay for supper. This supper introduces Theron to all of the temptations that will so confuse and bedazzle him. He is even enchanted by the food, but it is the intellectual and sensual atmosphere of the rectory that seems to prove so debilitating to his rudimentary Protestant sensibilities. He is treated to a variety of unsettling discourses by Father Forbes and Dr. Ledsmar, who make shocking announcements about genealogical theory in the Bible, paganism, the "Christ-myth," and the turpitude of women.

The ballast for this intellectual drenching is Celia, who is practicing the organ in the adjacent church building. With the "noble music throbbing through his brain," Theron stares out the rectory window at a stained glass likeness of a woman's head. "There was a halo about it, engirdling rich, flowing waves of reddish hair," which for a moment he takes to be a likeness of Celia herself. The sonorous tones of the bass pedals shake the rectory, and Theron takes pleasure imagining "the large, capable figure of Miss Madden seated in the half-light at the organ-board,

17 Frederic, *The Damnation of Theron Ware* (Cambridge, Mass.: Belknap, 1960), 55–9. Subsequent page citations in the text appear in parentheses.

swaying to and fro in a splendid ecstasy of power as she evoked at will this superb and ordered uproar" (80–3). As he leaves the rectory and begins walking home, the music comes to him with a "curious, intimate, personal relation," and it seems to him to be "something adapted to marriage ceremonies, – rich, vivid, passionate" (86). At the bidding of this seductive music, the untutored Methodist minister who has never been in a Catholic church before, enters the building and is nearly swallowed alive. He finds himself in a vast tomb or womblike darkness, a blackness spiced by the faint odor of cigarettes and electrified by the "burnished row of monster metal pipes," whose "deafening, angry" bellows make "everything about him vibrate." What follows next is a prophetic tableau of the helpless Protestant in presence of the unrestrained power of the aesthetic and the sensual. Theron cannot see Celia at all. Instead,

> there were only these jostling brazen tubes, as big and round as trees and as tall, trembling with their own furious thunder. It was for all the world as if he had wandered into some vast, tragical, enchanted cave, and was being drawn against his will – like fascinated bird and python – toward fate at the savage hands of these swollen and enraged genii. (97–8)

In the inflated phallicism of the tableau, the minister stands in the dark like an insignificant finger of flesh before these swollen and enraged giants, symbols of the psychosexual deformations produced by his own religious tradition, for we see the organ and its pipes through his eyes. It is invested by no other character with such dark and attractive power. The menace of the instrument and its manipulator, as well as the intellectual sophistications of Forbes and Ledsmar, are summarized in this remarkable image of threat and fascination, and all become devices in his downfall, representing the fatal richness of the aesthetic, intellectual, and sensual life available outside fundamentalist Protestantism.

Sinclair Lewis's portrayal of small-town Protestantism in *Elmer Gantry* is knowledgeable of both *The Damnation* and *The Scarlet Letter*, although the sheer polemic of Lewis's text is all his own. Lewis is rarely anything but cynical as he spotlights the barren cultural life of the average fundamentalist as a vital factor in the creation of the errant clergy. The church is the center of Elmer's cultural life, and all music, art, and literature have been reduced to the thin and soporific sentimentalities acceptable to rural Baptist America. When Elmer thinks of church, he thinks of missionary dinners, numbing sermons, and "flexible little girls in thin muslin" (31). Like *The Damnation,* the sexual interest undercuts the religious at most points, and if anything, Lewis deepens his indictment of Protestantism far beyond calling attention to its cultural deficits or sexual hypocrisies. The church is capable of invoking in Elmer tender thoughts about his mother, probably the few instances of genuine emotion expressed by the character throughout the novel, but when all is accounted for, he has gotten everything from the church "except, perhaps, any longing whatever for decency and kindness and reason" (34).

John Updike's quarrel with his Protestant contemporaries runs in parallel tracks to those laid down by *The Scarlet Letter, The Damnation,* and *Elmer Gantry.* Aesthetic/sexual anxiety seems to be the epicenter of ministerial discontent. In *A Month of Sundays* Updike provides a convenient distillation of American Protestant tradition in the three ministers: Ned Bork the effeminate liberal, Thomas Marshfield the enraged Barthian, and Marshfield's senile father, the "undressed mind" of the vocation. All are equally lecherous. Updike's hero, however, is Marshfield, who sees himself in mortal combat against the feminized intellectual and aesthetic life of liberal Protestantism. He cannot plead ignorance or innocence for his willing entrance into professional debauchery, for he is educated and cultivated, but he will plead a distinctly Roman sacramental theology: "The Catholic church in this at least was right; a priest is more than a man, and though the man disintegrate within his vestments, and become degraded beyond the laxest of his flock, the priest can continue to perform his functions, as a scarecrow performs his." Thus he arrives at the end of the novel just where he began, arguing a theology of forgivable specificity. With Ned he insists, "Love thy *neighbor.* Love what is near, not what is far."[18] We cannot change the world, for God is unchangeable, and so our only response to this remote transcendence is to fill the absence with our own immanence. Fornication is the logical conclusion of the gospel. Marshfield intends to live his theology of particularity, and he, unlike his literary predecessors, is handsomely equipped to do so.

Marshfield has an organ *and* his own personal organist, Alicia, who plays him as she would the other instrument. Just as she bends over the keyboards of her "gorgan," so she curves over him, "and brings me up to pitch, and the throbbing church would swim in one sea of love" (102, 134). Marshfield is interested only in sexual music, however, and thinking about music makes him think about masturbation, "the saving grace note upon the baffled chord of self." He makes his own music this way at several points during his narrative, the metaphor now reduced to a literalism of erect flesh. The entrance of the sensual and the aesthetic in the form of the energetic Alicia and her willing instrument apparently has not improved the Protestant cultural complexion, however. Now

---

18 John Updike, *A Month of Sundays* (New York: Fawcett Crest, 1975), 249, 86. Subsequent page citations in the text appear in parentheses.

there is too much and the wrong kind of aesthetic, so Marshfield bans the music but continues to pass the pipe, so to speak. He acts upon his theological and aesthetic complaints by firing Alicia, "a plumping for the Word as against pretty liturgy" (241). But the hypocrisy of this is no less profound for its ubiquity. His third lover, Frankie, complains that Alicia is imposing too much music upon the service, and Marshfield immediately redirects the accusation by admiring Frankie's bottom as she flounces away from him (88). It is not real music overwhelming the liturgy, it is sexual music, it is not Alicia or even Frankie who are inappropriately "musical," it is Marshfield himself.

In all of these novels, the various cultural and theological deficiencies of Protestantism contribute to the floundering of the clergyman, but the logic of narrative and metaphor drives beyond this institutional criticism to the individual himself. The lush and ominously Freudian entrance to Theron Ware's spiritual stumbling that occurs in the first hundred pages of *The Damnation* is yet further elaborated by Frederic's unrelenting scrutiny of Theron's sexual fantasy life, apparently the only sexual life available to him. A good deal of Theron's history in *The Damnation* illustrates the proposition that the role of minister is incompatible with that of maleness, and it is Theron's conviction that his "miserable ecclesiastical bandages have dwarfed [his] manly side" (299). At several points in the novel, Theron sees himself as female, usually a girlish figure, and as his intellectual, aesthetic, and sexual discontent increases, so he is correspondingly worried about his own masculinity. He complains that people think of ministers as some sort of "hybrid female," and as he willingly enters the twilight of moral ambiguity and doctrinal apostasy, he devotes more attention to his clothing, which give a "masculine bulk and shape to his figure." He boldly announces to Celia that she should not regard him as a minister, but as a man (257).

The paradox in this line of thought, however, is that while Theron pursues his own manhood with increasing conviction, he persists in viewing Father Forbes not only as a rival for Celia's affections, but as an object of his own fascination. When Theron meets Celia, he is unaware that her relationship with Forbes is a "delicately sore spot" for the Catholics of Octavius (97). Later Theron prompts Dr. Ledsmar to gossip about Celia and Forbes, for not only has he begun to suspect something "puzzling" about their relationship, but their relationship becomes an increasing threat to his own satisfaction. As Edmund Wilson points out, Frederic's first readers must have shuddered at these intimations that Celia is having an affair with the priest, but this is not the worst that could be thought.[19] Theron's simultaneous jealousy of *and* attraction to

19 Edmund Wilson, "Two Neglected American Novelists: II Harold Frederic, the Expanding Upstater," *New Yorker*, 6 June 1970: 112–34.

the priest is unmistakable, a plot feature that has escaped any notable mention in critical evaluations of the novel.

Father Forbes is presented in androgynous terms, although he is seen by Theron as a powerful sexual presence. As Father Forbes appears at the dinner in Section 1, he is wearing "a long house gown of black silk, skillfully moulded to his erect, shapely, and round form. Though he carried this with the natural grace of a proud and beautiful belle, there was no hint of the feminine in his bearing, or in the contour of his pale, firm-set face" (70). This same description is later rendered in less flattering terms. The priest appears to Theron as a "soft-voiced, portly creature in a gown," with "white, fat hands" and a "feline" manner. Nonetheless, Theron is impressed with the "commanding and unique effect of virility" produced by the priest, and Theron responds to the ambiguity of his presence by speculating about what Forbes really thinks about celibacy.

Theron's internal ruminations are part of the ongoing fantasy-text of the novel through which Theron invests the celibate life with tremendous sexual power. He envisions women prostrating themselves at the priest's feet as they perform the "lascivious mysticism" peculiar to their sex. Then, with imaginative alacrity, he replaces the priest with himself, "looking down on those worshipping female forms." Theron initiates this swift dream sequence, however, by thinking of *himself* as one of the adoring female throng in relation to Forbes. Using the same words his wife, Alice, had once spoken to him in their courtship days, he says to Forbes, "I love to hear you talk," as if he were courting the priest. He feels as "a romantic woman must feel in the presence of an especially impressive masculine personality" (288–9). It is not necessary, although it is certainly possible, to understand such passages in terms of latent homosexuality, but of larger importance is the decisive presentation of Theron's indecisive gender identity. In such images, Frederic repeatedly offers us the idea that the institution of married clergy is so deficient in its affirmation of normal manhood that even those who officially partake of no sexual congress whatsoever, enjoy a sensual advantage over those who live under a matrimonial mandate.

Theron Ware's anxiety about his sexual identity is at the heart of this novel, as it is in nearly every other novel treating the subject in either century, and examples of the fragile masculinity of the Protestant clergy abound in twentieth-century fiction. Gantry is converted to Christianity by a Billy Sunday–style evangelist, whose "manly handshake" and "virile laugh" proclaim "the team captained by Christ! No timid Jesus did he preach" (51). For all his bluff masculinity, however, Gantry is aware that other men think of him "as though he were an old woman in trousers," and a gentle, liberal colleague feels the insult that "as a parson, he was considered not quite virile ... that he was barred from knowing the real thoughts and sharing the real desires of normal humanity" (311, 320). Jesse Bentley in Sherwood Anderson's *Winesburg, Ohio* (1919) is a God-tormented minister who "did not look like a man at all. He was small and very slender and womanish of body."[20] Reverend Pick in John Gardner's short story, "Pastoral Care," who is "not as tall as [he] would have been if anyone had given [him] a vote in the matter," is further distressed that his gestures have come from his mother. He preaches while balanced upon a footstool behind the pulpit, and waves his hands with their "long white fingers like the lady choir director."[21] Thomas Marshfield protests his feminized status as a minister, and is annoyed that Frankie Harlow's husband doesn't seem to consider him a threat – "I had put on skirts in his eyes" – and longs to tell him everything (209).

The resentment accruing to these sentiments is a rather standard cultural conceit – a man is naturally insulted to be thought of as a woman since "female" is our shorthand for a variety of cultural and biological deficits. "Female" is a negative "other," clearly a horrifying social and existential condition for a man. Vociferous lamentation about his marginal masculinity, however, should not divert us from the fact that institutional or social prejudices are not the only things that rob him of masculine stature. Male clergy are accomplices to their own impotence. At the conclusion of *The Damnation*, for example, Alice Ware ponders her husband's near vocational fatality, and she doesn't think it was the ministry at fault. She wonders if the town itself was to blame, but Sister Soulsby says, "If there hadn't been a screw loose somewhere . . . Octavius wouldn't have hurt him" (351). Aside from the vocational liabilities already discussed, whatever is wrong with Theron seems to be wrong with a good many of his literary companions. It is not just the institutional church, but the kind of man who selects the vocation that figures in ministerial dysfunction. It is not simply that male ministers are regarded as "hybrid females," it is also that they perceive themselves as children, boys who are perpetually experiencing the promptings of adolescent sexuality.

Peeping Parsons

Arthur Dimmesdale with his "simple and childlike" air (48) is the progenitor of these unhappy good/bad boys, and by the end of *The Scarlet Letter* he has been reduced from childhood to infancy (169, 174). Harold Frederic has underlined and enlarged upon what is begun in Hawthorne's novel. As Theron walks home after the fateful first supper with Father Forbes, he is so excited by the evening, he steps over the

20 Sherwood Anderson, *Winesburg, Ohio* (1919; reprint, New York: Viking Compass, 1975), 66.
21 John Gardner, "Pastoral Care," in *The King's Indian* (New York: Ballantine, 1972), 4.

cracks in the pavement as he had done as a boy. He approvingly notes "something exceptionally juvenile and buoyant about his mood" (85–6). Specifically, his sexual identity is boyish, childlike, immature. He sniggers over George Sand and Chopin, and is thrilled when Celia winks at him and says, as if he were a small boy with a dirty secret, "Naughty, naughty!" (219). Much later, when he proudly presents himself to her as a rival to the priest, Celia tells him he has acted like a "nasty little boy." From this blow, he finally staggers to Sister Soulsby's house in a state of metaphysical drunkenness. There he weeps, his face surrendered to the "distortions of a crying child's countenance, wide-mouthed and tragically grotesque in its abandonment of control" (347).

One of the consequences of this arrested development is that Theron is a voyeur to adult life, reduced to peeking at the girls on the swings for his sexual excitement. The dramatic summary of this profile occurs in the forest scene that concludes Section 3 of *The Damnation*. Theron has been preaching at the annual camp meeting of the local Methodists, but after impressing his rustic cohorts with his eloquence, he sneaks off in search of the Catholic picnic that is proceeding on the other side of the woods. There he encounters Celia and Forbes, and he is greatly impressed by the carefree and rowdy Romans who are doing nothing more worshipful than drinking large amounts of beer. He wishes someone would bring him a glass, "as if he were a pretty girl" (244). Celia's drunken brother makes an insinuating remark about the "Protestant parson coming meddling" with Catholic girls, and Theron takes advantage of the insult to make good the gossip. He draws the infuriated Celia off for a soothing walk in the woods. There, in a scene ironically resonant of the reconciliation of Hester and Dimmesdale near the brook in the forest, Theron renounces the ministry in favor of his manhood, and then variously prods Celia to discuss her sex life. He speculates about her chastity, but when she asks him what made him think she had never known love, he buries his head in her skirts and imagines he is "a little boy again, nestling in an innocent, unthinking transport of affection against his mother's skirts," and he weeps with the beauty of his own "infantile purity and sweetness" (264).

Theron's response to Celia's denial of her chastity is part of a pattern of juvenile behavior. Theron is always caught in the act of peeping, either literally or figuratively, and he is never quite able to bear what he sees. He dwells with pleasure upon the attractive Sister Soulsby, but when he contemplates her rather lurid past and wonders whether she is really married to Brother Soulsby, he "drives the impertinent query down again under the surface of his mind" (190). When it first occurs to him that Levi Gorringe seems to like Alice very much, Theron's mind, like a camera, snaps "a shutter down on this odd, unbidden idea" (152).

Later, he faints when he sees Gorringe, who has announced that the church owes him a girl, join Alice at the confessional altar. When under the influence of liberated religious and intellectual thought, Theron muses upon the necessity of "wifeless calm" the life of genius demands, but he promptly stocks his wifeless dream space with other women, usually in the form of Celia or Soulsby. It is during such reveries that his thoughts turn to the priest, whom he has invested with magical sexual presence. But then Theron speculates about life in the rectory with the haglike doorkeeper who attends its portals, and just as quickly he drops the thought.

Frederic's portrait of Theron as a spying adolescent is consistent with later novels. Elmer Gantry's only endearing moments occur when he yearns for maternal consolation, and the hollow and lonely soul appears as a "little beaten boy, . . . a bothered, unhappy child" (181). In *Winesburg, Ohio,* Rev. Curtis Hartmann becomes obsessed with spying upon the school teacher Kate Swift. From his bell tower office, he peeps at her through a leaded glass pane depicting Christ blessing a child. In order to improve his view, Hartmann breaks a hole in the window, just nipping off the heel of the boy staring at the Christ. Hartmann is that boy, his sexual peeping the Achilles heel symbolized by the hole in the window.

John Updike offers the most complex portrait of this pastoral peeping. Bare-bottomed, Thomas Marshfield sneaks out at night to spy on his organist, Alica, and his assistant pastor, Ned. Later, having been relieved of his duties because of his own indiscretions, he hopes that Ms. Prynne, proprietress of the home for wayward clergy, is spying on him, and he eagerly seeks signs of this coveted intrusion. Marshfield operates out of a willed innocence, and with a calculated image he justifies the focus of his perpetual boyhood. His mother once had a beautiful singing voice, now roughened by time, and she protests the loss by refusing to sing in church. "Her silence pealing in [his] heart," becomes a paradoxical sound of fear. He is terrified of silence, and he understands his spying upon Ned and Alicia as an attempt to fill that silence with vision. But hearing, not seeing, is believing, and Marshfield immediately moves to establish music as the voice of sexuality in the novel. Having confessed this, Marshfield explains that his

> mother's singing voice was, for me, her sex; that her hoarseness I transferred in my childish innocence to her lower mouth, which was, as I stood small beside her in the pew, at the level of my mouth; that I equate noise with vitality; that silence, chastity, and death fascinate me with one face; that Alicia's power over the organ keyboards was part of her power over me (26–7).

Notice how the nineteenth-century metaphor of sound has been remodeled. Silence is no longer of the partnership, no longer a necessary function of what can be expressed but not said, but rather, the enemy; not part of a realm of nonverbal meanings, but the end of meaning altogether. Alicia provides his first line of defense against silence with the infidelity of sound, but she will be replaced, because she "was like those brimming golden afternoons of boyhood, that yet we do not wish to live again, because we do not wish to be again the pint-size, allergy-ridden, powerless person who enjoyed them" (241). He dismisses Alicia as part of adolescence, as though we are now to see how he has grown, but his narcissism is merely refocused. He replaces music with words, and the omniscient Ms. Prynne becomes the next vortex of desire. In the image of the little boy mourning his mother's lost voice Marshfield appeals to our tenderness and respect for the innocent wisdom of children here, but this is not a child's reflection, but that of a grown man looking back, a grown man who has never grown taller than his mother's hymn-book (27). He did not think these symbolically portentous things when he was a boy, he thinks them now that he is a boy trapped in a man's body.

This image of the clergy, trapped within the innocence, loneliness, and turbulence of sexually awakening boyhood, is both moving and tragic, for perpetual boyhood demands an indulgent but protective parent somewhere in the wings. The cry of the bewildered child cannot but tug at the reader, while at the same time the movement of metaphor and image makes clear that the troubled adolescent is a boychild, the listening and accused parent is a woman. In this is both shame and tragedy, for one consequence of this perpetual male adolescence is the blaming of women for the adulthood of the world. In *A Month of Sundays,* women are "porters for the great train of guilt" with which Marshfield is afflicted. "Babies and guilt. Women are built for lugging" (201). They are not just beasts of burden, however. They are also indicted as the cause of his debacle. As Marshfield says, it was a "common fall, mine, into the abysmal perplexity of the American female" (238).

Of Falls, Balls, and the Music of the Spheres: Women

Religion exists because of women. On this, nineteenth- and twentieth-century fiction agree. Women are the inspiration for religious ardor, vulnerable to religious persuasion, victims of passionate confusion. The gentlest such explanation of this phenomenon comes from Squire Braile in *The Leatherwood God,* who says that the faith in Joseph Dylks would die out if it were confined to men, but "some poor fool of a girl . . . is going to fall in love with him. . . . And nothing can be done to prevent it." He first attributes the aberration of Messiah Dylks to "what women are," but his wife remonstrates that women "are what men make 'em." The Squire concedes that it's "six of one and half a dozen of another," and concludes that "the real God put it into human nature and

all Hell couldn't stop it" (58). Harold Frederic offers an even more deliberate explanation in *The Damnation*. Dr. Ledsmar announces to Theron
that the entire ministerial profession "would have perished from the
memory of mankind, if it hadn't been for women" (224). Women, who
are superstitious and not of a metaphysical nature, "want their dogmas
embodied in a man," and the clergy offer an exciting aura of "pagan
sensuality and lascivious mysticism" (225–6).[22] Nathaniel Hawthorne
argues in *The Scarlet Letter* that Hester Prynne ponders the dark questions
of passion and religious meaning with such fierce and anguished ab-
sorption because of the unalterable channels of her female nature (112–
14). Oliver Wendell Holmes thinks that women are victims of seduction
and passionate disarray because they are more instinctual and vulnerable
in their emotional composition, and he uses a variety of organic metaphors relative to women (water, vegetation, horses, among others) to
underscore this idea. No nineteenth-century author suggests, however,
that women are responsible for lecherous clergy, and it remains to twentieth-century fiction and commentary to blame women for the dilemmas
of the ministry. For example, in 1982 *Christianity Today* published an
article on clergy divorce, then one of the few public acknowledgments
that male clergy sexuality is a problem within Protestantism. Ten reasons
for the alarming escalation of the divorce rate among clergy are offered;
five of those reasons are assigned to women.[23] Nowhere does the author
consider that the theology of Protestantism turns upon a gender sickness
that cannot help but produce a damaged and damaging vocation. The
blaming of women in twentieth-century fiction is testimony to a serious
theological and vocational dysfunction.[24] Thus, we are returned to the

22 But Frederic also has Celia challenge the entire history of misogyny in Christian theology when she says, as part of a long and impassioned speech about female dignity,
"Jesus himself appreciated women and delighted to have them about him, but those
brutes they call the Fathers . . . hated women" and so Christianity was deformed by
"cranks and savages like Paul, Jerome and Tertullian" (265).
23 Robert J. Stout, *Christianity Today* 26 (Feb. 5, 1982): 20–23, lists the following: the wife
doesn't understand his work, she doesn't support his vocation, or she is looking for a
Daddy figure; the working wife may make too large a paycheck; and some women
think of the pastor as a conquest. Stout does not mention the possibility that some
pastors may think of female congregants as conquests.
24 A fascinating historical document on the problem of miscreant clergy is W. F. Jamieson's
The Clergy: A Source of Danger to the American Republic (Boston: Colby & Rich, 1874).
For a sense of the contemporary discussion in religious periodicals and other accessible
kinds of public writing prior to about 1986 (when feminists began writing specifically
about clergy sexual abuse), see the following: Andre Bustanoby, "The Pastor and the
Other Woman," *Christianity Today* 18 (August 30, 1974): 7–10; Ann Davis, "A Single
Woman Speaks Up about Ministers," *Pastoral Psychology* 18 (December 1967): 39–44;
Joan Clayton, "My Minister Kept Making Passes at Me," *Ladies Home Journal* 102 (July
1985): 16, 20; Janet F. Fishburn, "Male Clergy Adultery as Vocational Confusion,"
Christian Century 99 (September 15–22, 1982): 922–5; and Dean Merrill, "The Sexual
Hazards of Pastoral Care," *Christianity Today* 29 (November 8, 1985): 105.

ironies uncovered by Ann Douglas in her study of nineteenth-century clergy and women. The minister's identity depends upon the presence of a captive and captivated audience, but that same audience will be his undoing.

"Ours is a religion of women and slaves," says Thomas Marshfield (*A Month of Sundays*), whose entire apology will manage to suggest that "slaves" refers more to ministers than the actual victims of political oppression. Like Theron Ware, who travels from his wife to Celia to Sister Soulsby in his religiosexual quest, Marshfield moves through a succession of women. His journey from Jane to Alicia to Frankie is a performance of Søren Kierkegaard's three spheres (the ethical, the aesthetic, and the religious), until he arrives on the doorstep of the ultimate proprietress of passion, Ms. Prynne. All three spheres will prove to be unsatisfactory options, as indeed they were for Kierkegaard, who tested a variety of ontological postures. The aesthetic, the ethical, and the religious are integrated by passion, the "how" of subjectivity, denoting the duality and intensity of inwardness that enables the famous leap of faith.[25] Marshfield, however, is not preparing to leap, he has already fallen, and his "how" is literally all screwed up.

Marshfield's wife, Jane Chillingworth, is the daughter of an ethics professor. In Kierkegaardian terms, she represents the domain of universal principle, the telos of human existence. Jane is unexceptional, but also alien to warmth and passion. In a grating and ugly image, Marshfield says that viewing Jane naked was like "bending over a long porcelain sink where a single Brillo pad has been left lying, unmoistened, expectant, abrasive, symbolic of weary worlds of work to come" (71). The ethical Jane with her cool porcelain body and pubis as inviting as steel wool is hardly competition for the sun-caped Alicia. Her vagina is like a mischievous child, and she and Marshfield play in each other like children in puddles (45). But although Alicia calls him forth from the ethical and into life, he (like Theron Ware) is finally overwhelmed by her music.

More recently, feminist commentators have named the problem of lecherous clergy as "sexual abuse" (which in turn has been developed into the larger rubric of "authority abuse"). Here are some sources for this discussion: Marie Fortune, *Is Nothing Sacred? When Sex Invades the Pastoral Relationship* (San Francisco: Harper & Row, 1989); Christine Hamilton-Pennell, "Pastoral Sexual Abuse: One Congregation's Order," *Daughters of Sarah* 13 (July-August 1987): 20–4; Ann-Janine Morey, "Blaming Women for the Abusive Male Pastor," *Christian Century* 105 (October 5, 1988): 866–9; and Mary Pellauer, "Sex, Power and the Family of God: Clergy and Sexual Abuse in Counseling," *Christianity and Crisis* 47 (February 16, 1987): 47–50.

25 A number of critics have explored the Kierkegaardian dimensions of Updike's fiction. For such a discussion, see Sue Mitchell Crowley, "John Updike and Kierkegaard's Negative Way: Irony and Indirect Communication in *A Month of Sundays,*" *Soundings: An Interdisciplinary Journal* 68 (Summer 1985): 212–28.

So he turns to Frankie Harlow, the only one of his women who believes in God. Unfortunately, in the gossamer net of her devotion, he is impotent because if she believes in God he cannot believe in himself, and so he cannot perform.

We are given to understand that Marshfield goes haywire because his wife is too good, and she does not adore him enough, although Frankie adores him too much. Alicia tells the truth about him, and so all have failed him. Marshfield conveys this in a tone designed to assure us that he really knows better, but his assumption of responsibility is only seeming. Marshfield is a dishonest narrator, for although he seems to be confessing his transgressions, he does so with an eye to committing the next. He is engaged in apology, not confession. The fact of *A Month of Sundays* is that women bear the burden of his collapsed career, if not for all the traumas of manhood in America. The novel is self-consciously dated by the women's movement, and the integrity of the women is undercut by his snide attributions to feminism, "lib-lubbers," he jibes in a footnote that reduces his wife to an "indentured cunt" (67). This kind of hectoring creeps in at several points, surfacing the political energy of the novel and underlining the misogyny that is basic to the text.[26] The point of his sniping is that "women's rights may not be established as symmetrical to men's." This is an especially nasty piece of work, for this discourse, directed toward unhappy women, counsels them from the midst of his own infidelity that "marriage is a sacrament and not a contract of convenience . . . , that our task is to love not what might be but what is given" (161).

Marshfield pities his young, liberal associate who represents an entire generation of fellows who have been made impotent by girls deprived of shame by the pill. Now, like locusts, these voracious women besiege Marshfield with complaints about men. They have reduced their male partners to "toothless, spineless, monosyllabically vocal, sticky in texture and tiny in size, deaf and blind" creatures, a "race of infant monkeys" (159). And so he "goes down"; like a hunted animal going down, he has a smell about him (158), and he is flooded with the sexual demands of these devious, insatiable women. Everyone, in fact, is interested in "going down." "Head and heart, tongue and cunt, mouth and cock – what an astonishing variety of tunes were played on this scale of so few notes" says the reluctant piper (160). Although he is clearly repulsed by their whining, he sleeps with a few as a private concession to his public occupation. "They begged me for a touch, begged though the strength went out of me" (162), he says in mock-scriptural, mock self-pity, for

26 Other important places where Marshfield attacks the women's movement appear on pp. 100, 119, and 174.

his tone – quite to be distinguished from his words – mocks them and pities himself. As a Barthian, Marshfield should be lofting the awful power of the Word against these hordes, but instead, he gives head. It's what they want, he says, and so oral sex becomes an alter (altar?) preaching, a transformation remarkable in its candor, inevitable in its context.

According to Marshfield, Barth provides the tough, masculine voice that was so lacking in his own father, so lacking in modern Protestantism altogether. Yet Barth is more of a presence for Marshfield than God, for God in most Updike novels is suspected by his absence. In *A Month of Sundays,* the absent father has become the deranged father. Some of the most moving passages in the book occur between Thomas and his own father, who is the portent of his present decay. Marshfield still approaches him as a child, calling him "Daddy" because Father belongs to God. For Marshfield there doesn't seem to be any Father, just this lunatic Daddy, and his assumed childhood is stripped from him by the sandpaper of his father's senility – the final childhood.

Thomas's "Daddy" has already slipped into an abyss of appetites now fulfilled in a stream of obscene language. "The baseness of his undressed mind shocked me" (150) says Marshfield, who finds himself accused of sleeping with his mother by the virile wreck who is absent before him. Yet the senior Marshfield tells the terrible truth about God's absence and man's terror both. Punning in French, he advises his son that an engagement is "a *compromis.* Hear it? *Com-promis!* A promised cunt!" Or, more chillingly, a compromise, a dangerous promise, for "*le con est le centre du monde*" (151). "The cunt is the center of the world," and the old man has said out loud what Marshfield has been enacting all along. Thus, speaking of golf and God, a not-so-subtle metaphor of balls and holes, Marshfield offers the controlling image of the novel: the "poor cunt men" slipping around on the edge of the hole "like fearful fetuses," saved only by the clatter-ladder rope of words that will lasso the reader into submission to his emission.

Ecclesiastical Theater: Preaching as Performance

For Søren Kierkegaard's Knight of Infinite Resignation, "silence is the snare of the demon,"[27] and so, too, for Thomas Marshfield. Silence, death, and chastity are symbolized by the vagina, and Marshfield's "troublesome and mortal bone" (212) is the instrument raised in defiance of these terrifying silences. Preaching occupies the same space as this penile rebellion. Marshfield tells us he listened to his father type out his sermons, "ejaculations of clatter after long foreplay of silent agony. These sounds

27 Søren Kierkegaard, *Fear and Trembling* (Princeton, N.J.: Princeton University Press, 1973), 97.

of ministerial activity engraved themselves upon a deadly silence" (25). Then, as noted above, he offers us the tender image of the little boy, standing ear level with his mother's lower mouth, "her silence pealing in his heart." The sequence of imagery here and elsewhere makes clear how much this "deadly silence" is carried and conquered by women, at least the ones who know their fingerings and chord charts. Yet while they can make music, they may not speak. Women do not ejaculate, and following metaphoric logic, women are discouraged or prohibited from entering the pulpit, making the ministry the special territory of the death-defying male.

The nineteenth-century metaphor of sound and silence has suffered considerable transformation, and the dialectic of public and private life expressing the mutuality and mystery of religion and sexuality, spirit and body, has been polarized. This movement also can be tracked in the shifting function of preaching from nineteenth- to twentieth-century fiction. With the polarization of public and private life – another way to speak of this would be the increasing dualism of body and spirit – we find a corresponding polarization between performance and honesty in preaching. Theater becomes the paradigm for the dissemination of the Word.

In *The Scarlet Letter*, preaching is disciplined, solemn, and eloquent, but as we have seen (Chapter 2), Dimmesdale uses the sermon as a means of double communication. Successive fictions unveil the theatricalization of the pulpit, coming uncomfortably close to suggesting that this is all it ever was. Theron Ware becomes a very good preacher when he begins to "puzzle out and master all the principles which underlie this art and all the tricks that adorn its superstructure. . . . He practiced effects now by piecemeal, with an alert ear and calculation in every tone" (23). Elmer Gantry loves the pastorate in the way an actor enjoys greasepaint and call boards (252). For his poor family, Sundays were a "hell of keeping out of his way," for they "had the strain of a theatrical first night" (310). His first sermon in Banjo Crossing is like many other such performances. "Voice, sureness, presence, training, power, he had them all. Never had he so well liked his role; never had he acted so well; never had he known such sincerity of histrionic instinct" (264).

Although a performance is not necessarily a counterfeit of genuine conviction, meaning, or dedication, the use of theatrical language in the context of the ministry casts a shadow upon the integrity of the profession and its practitioners. This is not just a matter of being realistic or un-realistic about what it takes to put across a good sermon. The self-conscious application of dramaturgy to the composition of preaching cheapens the project, for as fiction persists in reminding us, "act" means "feign" or "pretend" as much as it does "represent" or "perform."

There is also congregational complicity in this. The vocational demand for a sustained witness to eternal assurances that most ordinary mortals cannot achieve for themselves encourages the minister to learn to counterfeit that sacred emotional and intellectual pitch. It is a tragic movement that seeks to preserve his sanity and stability by gaining detachment from the perils of self-reflection and from any genuine encounter with others.

The bitterness of this mechanism of preservation and betrayal is fully exploited in *A Month of Sundays,* for the entire novel has about it the air of a performance. From the beginning, Marshfield is aware of his audience and of his power in directing their perceptions. As he begins his third-person narrative of his first-person story, he discovers that "This is fun! First you whittle the puppets, then you move them around" (17). Later he recreates an encounter between Alicia and Jane as a stage play, a demonstration that gives him distance and trivializes them by reducing them to characters in his controlling fantasy (111). Even at the end of the novel, he is pleasurably aware of his immensity as the author of his own drama, a giant observing and manipulating dolls. Again, he reduces others around him to stick figures, suggesting that all the remembered emotions and experiences were artificial and contrived, the people of little consequence on the stage of his ego.

In this context, his treatment of women is no worse than his treatment of anyone else in the novel, but his power over women in particular is essential to his own survival, which is why preaching – the performance and act of the gospel – must be his and his alone. Before they've even slept together, Alicia reproves Marshfield for the kind of preaching he's putting out. "I mean, this isn't meant to be your show, it's theirs" (40) she says, referring to the congregation. But that's not how Marshfield sees it. Alicia protests that by filling the service with so much music she is trying to protect him from making a display of himself (108), but he is not impressed with her altruism, and fires her because "she toots her horn too loud" (174). In his own sense of performance, he is huge, exalted, rapt: "There is a grandeur, an onslaught of *vouvs* and of dizzying altitude, in the act of placing a communion wafer between the parted lips of a mouth that, earlier in the very week of which this was the Sabbath day, had received one's throbbingly ejaculated seed" (163). Marshfield, who is as ready to ejaculate as profess, achieves this grandeur upon the receptivity of the worshiping female body, which, symbolically, is what every congregation is reduced to in the presence of the Lord. In this, Updike is merely following the not-so-subtle metaphoric logic of centuries of patristic theology. The domination of women (the silence of women) is essential to the proclamation and male well-being both. Intercourse and preaching amount to the same thing.

Transparency is one of Updike's favorite ways of talking about God.

By this he means that the world is transparent at certain moments so that the presence of God is revealed in the ordinary details of human existence. Marshfield offers a unique angle on transparency, however, telling us that "the women who came to me as dark bundles and resistant tangles became transparent in being fucked" (226). How are men made transparent? Well, men are already transparent to each other – "spirits naked to one another" (226) – and so our wayward clergy are transported to the desert to be bleached clean by the sun of God. There they minister to one another, restored, shaken, but "hearty, boyish, mortal, minister" (235). This recuperation is presided over by a giant, but ultimately manipulable, female who provides Marshfield with a further chance at transparency. Having her is a necessary part of his own sense of revelation and the fitness of things, for if women become transparent "in being fucked," men must become transparent by performing the act upon her, the primeval occupation of mortal life in pursuit of the immortal.

Marshfield's summary of his journey dismisses all actual women as persons. Rather, his fall and restoration are megamythic, the courageous, suffering phallus pushing through a "translucent hellish chute of intricate folds and bannister like turns" (241), his description of his position between faith and ethics, Frankie and Jane. His story is as old as the Bible itself: because they were there, because they were unhappy or discontent, because they offered, the fall is womanborne, and the story of mankind a persistence of phallus against the labyrinthian body of original sin. In *A Month of Sundays,* Updike has only offered us an unblushing view of distilled Christian theology, and in that he gives us nothing new under the sun. It is remarkable that with so phallic a theology ministers could have such trouble claiming their manhood, an indication, perhaps, of how much the performance of Christianity is at odds with its text and how far theology has traveled from its source. Jesus is no sexual sharpshooter. But this is not all. The entire novel – and this is truly a tour de force – is a performance, not only upon the female but upon the reader of the novel. The redoubtable Ms. Prynne is the agency of this accomplishment.

From the beginning of his "rehabilitation," Marshfield is aware of her presence, an awareness that is pleasurable for him even though at this early stage she is physically unattractive to him, a "self-congratulating turtle," to be precise. His therapy consists of writing "about what interests him most," and he is at once interested in her interest. He hopes she is spying on him, and he is increasingly concerned with arranging what she will read and scatters invitations to her throughout his journal ("you prying Prynne," "I know you are praying for me, Ms. Prynne"). She is not just his keeper, she is the watcher, for to be watched is to be loved; also, to be cherished by something you fear and desire at the same time. "God is watching over you" is both a promise and a threat; Marshfield seeks proof of the promise. Usually the watcher has tremendous power over the unsuspecting subject, and in the looking translates the vulnerability of the subject into the helplessness of the appropriated object. But Marshfield is not vulnerable to Ms. Prynne as Ned and Alicia are to his earlier spying, because he courts her observation and arranges what she will see. Her omniscience is only seeming, because being male, Marshfield has an inside track on this God-thing.

As he grows in confidence his references to her become more flippant and patronizing. Finally he is assured enough of himself to carry on an outright mimicry of *The Scarlet Letter:* "You with your figure of perfect elegance on a large scale. . . . You have been inflexible and chaste. Wondrous strength of a woman's heart!" (253–5). He alternately cajoles and bullies her in tones of both an appealing adolescent and an embittered lecher: "Ms. Prynne, am I trying to seduce you? Help me. . . . I will treat you real swell, Ms. Prynne. Screwing optional. . . . I want my merit badge. You, Ms., pynne it on me. . . . Then don't come, you bitch, you sashaying cunt" (228, 264, 266). On the final page, she yields.

But in between his appeals to her by name, he also summons a "gentle reader," "Ideal Reader," "You, my reader, my only love," addresses that certainly refer to Ms. Prynne, but given the feminized status of any congregation or audience, refers to you, the reader of the novel, as well. "Spent an hour now rereading, between winces of embarrassment, the pages we (you and I, reader; . . .) have accumulated" (239). So he calls to us both, "my ms.sterious Ms." (231), "ms." being the abbreviation for manuscript as well as female person of unknown marital status. We/she have become the manuscript, the female body, the silence upon which the word is scattered. We/she never speak. We are silent, and in reading the novel we, too, have submitted to a rapture of the word. You have been fucked, not to put too fine a point on the matter, and "nothing left for me to do, dear Ideal Reader, but slip and topple off, gratefully" (271), says the unrehabilitated and unrepentant Marshfield. Good preaching is like good writing, the triumph of the authorial phallus, a necessarily sexual act, for how else could the abstraction of the W/word be given the life necessary to sustain it? The reader, like every congregation, is subject to the W/word, which in this context is dependent upon female submission in order to live.[28]

---

28 Updike's exploitation of the reader in *A Month of Sundays* is a perfect illustration of John Barth's erotic theory of reading in "Dunyazadiad." As it is described by Brian McHale, "the author plays the masculine role, the reader the feminine role and the text

Many fictional explorations of divine lechery are rooted in living testimony, often self-consciously so, as though the author were fearful that the credulity of the reader would be strained without some obvious justification for the account. Oliver Wendell Holmes tells us in his preface to *The Guardian Angel* that the portrayal of Rev. Joseph Bellamy Stoker is "only a softened copy of too many originals."[29] William Dean Howells similarly documents his account of *The Leatherwood God* in a publisher's prefatory note to the text. Sinclair Lewis spent months in Kansas City, observing and interviewing ministers, and according to his account, "getting them drunk enough to tell the truth about themselves" (afterword, 422) until in May of 1926 he was ready to begin *Elmer Gantry* (1927). John Gardner translates the rumored sexual escapades of a former Carbondale, Illinois, minister into the harmless indiscretion of wishful thinking in "Pastoral Care," the lead story in the collection, *The King's Indian* (1972).

All of these examples, including the fact that I have felt it necessary to point them out, indicates the extreme tenderness of the territory involved. Like the idea of religion and sexuality, there is something disquieting about the idea of adulterous clergy, and it tends to be an item from which we would prefer to avert our gaze altogether. At the same time, like the scene of an accident, it is utterly fascinating.[30] It is only in theory that the Protestant tradition has been able to demand an absence of carnality in its representatives, and yet efforts to deal with the unusual demands of the profession are often as ignoble as they are ignorant.

Michel Foucault argues that "today it is sex that serves as a support for the ancient form so – familiar and important in the West – of preaching."[31] This is correct. Thomas Marshfield jeers at liberal Protestantism for its loss of sexual vitality. Ned and Jane would rather talk than make love, much to Marshfield's dismay. But it is not the intellectual softening of Calvinism that is responsible for the loss of ministerial manhood. It is the freedom of women. It is not really intellect that has been the

functions as their intercourse." See *Postmodernist Fiction* (New York: Methuen, 1987), 226; and John Barth, *Chimera* (New York: Random House, 1972), 3–56.
29 Holmes, *Guardian Angel*, x.
30 For example, public excitement over the sexual and financial scandals involving Jim and Tammy Bakker and the PTL ministries ("God and Money," *Newsweek* 6 April 1987, 16–22; "Heaven Can Wait," *Newsweek* 8 June 1987, 58–65) and the fall of evangelist Jimmy Swaggart ("A Sex Scandal Breaks over Jimmy Swaggart," *Newsweek* 29 February 1988, 30ff.; "Now It's Jimmy's Turn," *Time* 7 March 1988, 46–8). See also: "Weeding Out Clergymen Who Go Astray," *U.S. News and World Report* 2 October 1978, 63–5; "Their Pastor an Adulterer," *People* 7 February 1986, 99–100; "A Pastor Claims Dancing," *Christianity Today* 30 (August 8, 1986): 32–33, which includes a follow-up notice about three congregants filing sexual harassment charges; and "It Isn't the First Time," *Newsweek* 6 April 1987, 23.
31 Foucault, *The History of Sexuality: An Introduction* (New York: Pantheon, 1978), 7.

hallmark of masculinity all these centuries; it is the obsession for power masquerading as intellectual superiority, a posture that inevitably carries the source of its own disease. So much depends upon the silence of women in this universe, and when women speak, the cosmos crumbles. If a man must fear the adult sexuality of women, then he must fear his own as well. The blaming of women perpetuates the childhood of the male clergy. This is an outcome already offered theologically, but reinforced by the fury of the male clergy for their own fragile position, which seems so dependent upon the scapegoating and subordination of the female. This obsession represents the major pressure point of Christian theology, because so much of social, ecclesiastical, and metaphysical order rides upon controlling women. At stake is access to some ultimate sense of power and self-worth that sets up a sick exchange between ministers and women. He needs them to be sick in order for him to be well.

In addition, the Protestant flight from beauty, sensuality, and the body not only ill prepares the minister for life in the material world, it also works against the magnetism of human yearning that produces such an investment in physical symbols. The longing to be cherished unconditionally, the hunger for touch, warmth, and protection depends upon the presence of sensual, physical comforts as well as an innocence of belief, often a willed simplicity. The intellectualizing of theology offers nothing here. How could the minister be otherwise than boyish (like the idealized youthful savior of popular iconography) lest the threat of knowledge (adult sexuality) sink the whole enterprise? Both the kind of man who chooses the profession and the demands of the congregation, operating within the parched aesthetics of Protestant sensibility, create the deformities of passion documented from fiction to real life. A sympathetic account of this complicity appears in *The Leatherwood God* as Joseph Dylks explains his performance:

> You're tempted by what's the best thing in you, by the hunger and thirst to know what's going to be after you die; to get near to the God that you've always heard about and read about.... It's something, a kind of longing, that's always been in the world.... You think I had to lie to them, to deceive them, to bewitch them. I didn't have to do anything of the kind. They did the lying and deceiving and bewitching themselves, and when they done it..., they had me fast, faster than I had them. (117–18)

Finally, denying his adulthood produces the paradox of the sexless, effeminate public figure that often disguises a predatory private sexuality. The danger of ministerial histrionics is not simply the calculated but unevenly managed power that is unleashed by effective performance, although this danger is considerable. In twentieth-century discourse, the performance takes over the witness, giving us an oratorical splendor whose basis is a clever counterfeit of genuine conviction. In twentieth-century discourse, and particularly since the advent of televangelism, preaching has become, metaphorically speaking, a sound without silence. This widening gap between performance and conviction invites and sustains a parallel dualism between public profession and private behavior, hence the scandal of particular clergy. This dualism takes an enormous toll. As Hawthorne says, "No one can wear one face to a multitude and another to himself without getting bewildered as to which may be true" (146).

The dialectic of sound and silence, for all its irritating reticences, shows in its twentieth-century sundering the effectiveness of its device. The presence of silence, a sort of revealed concealment, to use Kierkegaard's terms, is what is heard but not said, the nonverbal articulations carrying the double action of words. It gives people a way to acknowledge and confront the unspeakable while protecting what must be the dignity of public life and the honesty of private life. But now the course of our language tells us that silence, symbolized by women, is to be feared. Borrowing Updike's mixed metaphor, language becomes the light against the darkness, revelation in the outpoured word, just as the Bible says. But this fear of silence also removes some crucial balance between honesty and privacy, and often we are left with just a public persona and an empty performance, divorced from the genuine movements of uncertainty, grief, joy, and dreaming that give a being depth and dignity. Is this not a symptom of the age, that we fear our silences, that we are so desperate for life that any sound will do? No silence, no private life, only the terror of being alone is left, and so we learn to be satisfied with performance devoid of content, sex instead of passion, religion instead of passion, and the word instead of the thing itself. Thus, religion becomes a performance enacted as compulsive speech about women, on women's bodies, in order to fill the silence and prevent that silence from being heard, closing off all ambiguous depths.

Did the dialectic of sound and silence always work for nineteenth-century discourse? Were the people who wrote and talked this way more confident of essential existence and God? Well, it was always fragile at best, and no, it could not always save them from madness. Witness the ways in which the adulterous clergyman was disfigured in his falling in nearly every novel available on the subject. But there was some certainty we lack. The nineteenth-century writer knew how powerful passion could be, and the metaphoric dialectics of sound and silence attest to their respect. In the twentieth century, we are like children playing with matches, recklessly plunging into speech as though that could banish our fear. And so, mistaking silence for the enemy, the androcentric voice hastens to say everything lest the "other" should speak, a performance that has left us utterly naked, whistling in the dark.

4

A War of Words:
Women Write about the Ministry.
The Homiletic Writers

Errant ministers suffer a variety of mutilations and humiliations for the transient pleasure of sexual intrigue: lynching, drunkenness, paralysis (and other forms of symbolic and literal castration), ostracism by public scorn and ridicule, death (by drowning: in rivers, wells, guilt), and madness. The hazards of the ministry relative to sexuality are well documented in fiction, but the consequences portrayed may be more a product of the suggestive rather than mimetic function of literature. That is, poetic justice is not the same as actual justice, and literature may not be used uncritically as sociological evidence. Only the polemic of Lewis's *Elmer Gantry* comes close to reporting another aspect of the tradition of divine lechery. Elmer Gantry is nearly exposed several times in his career, and yet he flourishes wherever next planted, both because of his own psychic agility *and* the unwillingness of his congregations to see more than pleases them. More than most, Lewis underlines the congregational complicity in Elmer's successful recoveries. In fact, congregations are as apt to forgive an errant clergyman as they are to run him out of town. This is not simply a matter of Christian charity, for the same generosity may not be extended to the female participant. The history of Henry Ward Beecher and Elizabeth Tilton provides an instructive and documented dramatization of this outcome.[1]

Henry Ward Beecher, known for his preaching of a comforting love religion, was the pastor of the powerful and wealthy Plymouth Church in Brooklyn Heights. Elizabeth Tilton was a parishioner and the wife of a friend, Theodore. Beecher became intimate with Elizabeth sometime in 1868, opportunity having been afforded by pastoral visits to console her for the loss of her infant child. Henry advised Elizabeth that the world would not understand their love, and so they must practice "nest-

---

1 My primary source for the following account is Altina Waller, *Reverend Beecher and Mrs. Tilton: Sex and Class in Victorian America* (Amherst: University of Massachusetts, 1982).

hiding." But despite such ecclesiastical counsel, the emotionally vulnerable Elizabeth found herself unable to sustain the deception. Confessing to her husband that Henry had justified their union by an appeal to "pure affection and a high religious love," Elizabeth told Theodore that she had found Beecher's arguments "overmastering." A series of clandestine maneuvers involved the pathetic young woman in writing and then retracting and then rewriting her confession upon the contradictory demands of her husband and her minister, who was understandably anxious to conclude what was at this point a largely private controversy. Rumors of the affair, however, had exceeded the Tilton household, and in 1872, Victoria Woodhull apprised the entire nation of it. Woodhull urged Beecher to have the courage of his convictions and openly proclaim the doctrine of free love he was practicing in private. The pressure of the scandal was varied, but ultimately unrelenting, and in 1875, gossip having regained national attention, Tilton brought suit against Beecher.

Aside from the spectacle itself, what is so fascinating about the history of these sorry events is that despite overwhelming evidence against Beecher, Plymouth Church steadfastly refused to believe the charges. Their confidence in Beecher's integrity was incompatible with the evidence, so the evidence must be false. One early response to the accusations was to dismiss Theodore Tilton from church membership in 1873. Then, under pressure from the public outcry, a church investigating committee gathered testimony, and in spite of "almost irrefutable evidence . . . issued a report completely exonerating Beecher." In fact, Beecher's sufferings brought them to pronounce themselves possessed of "sympathy more tender and a trust more unbounded" than ever before.[2] The legal trial that followed this demonstration of ecclesiastical jurisprudence produced an undecided jury and an acquittal. Later, during a second church council investigation, Beecher was once again affirmed, and those bringing testimony against him were excommunicated. In 1878 – ten years past the precipitating event – Elizabeth Tilton reversed her prior defense of Beecher and confessed her adultery anew. She too was excommunicated. "Ostracized by Plymouth Church, Elizabeth Tilton died in 1897, lonely and blind, at the home of her daughter in Brooklyn."[3]

The case illustrates the powerful social protections afforded the clergy. The respect naturally invested in the office, coupled with the unwillingness of the congregation to believe their judgment to have been wrong, are two such protections. According to one biographer, "an overwhelming majority of people agreed with Mark Twain, who expressed his regret that 'so insignificant a matter as the chastity or unchastity of an

2 Ibid., 10–11.
3 Ibid., 11.

Elizabeth Tilton could clip the locks of this Samson (ie, Henry Ward) and make him as other men.' "[4] A third protection involves cultural attitudes toward women. In this case, there is the suspicion that she is more accountable than he for their affair, and a history of past indiscretion or mental weakness may be discovered of the female participant. Along with the relentless public shredding of her reputation, she will suffer the loss of a personal and community relationship, what may amount to a devastating social and spiritual exile, for who does she turn to when her minister is her violator? While the impressive resources of the institution are rallied on his behalf, what happens to the woman involved?

With the ironic exception of her outraged husband, there was apparently no one to speak for Elizabeth Tilton, and his fame was as degraded as hers by the course of events. Not surprisingly, Beecher was sheltered by both the relationship – his intimacy with Elizabeth Tilton – and his office. Not only did she defend him in court and once retract her accusations, but Beecher violated the trust of power invested in his office when he approached Elizabeth and then employed that office to defend the illicit activity. Elizabeth had no such office to protect her, and even less cultural or religious power. The fond stereotypes of Victorian America about the purity of women proved little protection from public willingness to believe in her perfidy rather than his sexuality. So while the two men jousted over their various honors for nearly a decade, Elizabeth Tilton virtually disappeared, both in the records of the time and in contemporary analysis.[5]

When we turn to fiction, we note *The Scarlet Letter* as the rare novel that treats the woman with sympathy. Otherwise there is little in male-authored fiction that encourages us to look for her story, although much of the fictional record is acute, complex, and sympathetic in its dialogue about this issue of embodiment and clergy sexuality. Given the intensity of involvement between women and clergy documented by Ann Douglas and others, it is not surprising to find numerous novels written *by* women

---

4 Noel Gerson, *Harriet B. Stowe. A Biography* (New York: Praeger, 1976), 198.
5 For example, Leon Oliver, *The Great Sensation: A Full, Complete and Reliable History of the Beecher-Tilton-Woodhull Scandal with Biographical Sketches of the Principal Characters* (Chicago: Beverly, 1873), says in his concluding summary that "the four great 'Stars' [of the scandal] . . . are Henry Ward Beecher, Theodore Tilton, Victoria Woodhull and Henry C. Bowen" (341). Elizabeth is mentioned in passing, and is given no biographical attention. Abbott, Lyman, and Halliday also fail to mention Elizabeth or any particle of the scandal in *Henry W. Beecher: A Sketch of His Career* (Hartford, Conn.: American Publishing, 1887). More recently, William G. McLoughlin assesses *The Meaning of Henry Ward Beecher* (New York: Knopf, 1970) as a symbol of middle-class sensibilities. The fate of Elizabeth relative to that meaning is unimportant – she is mentioned four times, and only in passing. Other contemporary biographers and historians mention Elizabeth Tilton, but only Altina Waller, *Reverend Beecher and Mrs. Tilton* (1982), takes sympathetic note of her fate.

about the clergy that speak clearly about embodiment and women's role relative to the institutional church and her male representatives. In this chapter, I take up such a group of writings that begin in the nineteenth century and follow their thematic progress into the twentieth century.

Homiletic Fiction

My resources for this chapter include several of the writers referred to by Douglas as "sentimental," but I do not find this category sufficiently respectful of their purposes or product to continue using it. As noted before, Douglas's work spotlights the intense and mutually destructive relationship between women and clergy in the nineteenth century. But she gives short shrift to the religious concerns of these women by labeling them as purveyors of the "sentimental." Her discussion is not without some sympathy for their cultural dilemma, but she moderates much of the sympathy ostensibly extended by so clearly lamenting (and often mocking) their literary and aesthetic shortcomings. Along with Helen Waite Papashvily, Douglas focuses on the bitterness and anger toward men in general and male clergy in particular expressed by these writing women, but her concern for them is abbreviated relative to her eulogizing of the intellectual (read: masculine) rigor of a defeated Calvinism.[6]

Following (and also expanding upon) readings by Nina Baym and Jane Tompkins that helped me understand the "sentimental" writer differently, I distinguish two phases of woman-authored fiction about the ministry.[7] These phases, what I will designate "homiletic" and "romance" writing, can be roughly, although not absolutely, plotted in a chronological relationship. Unlike the consistent thread of concerns de-

6 Helen Waite Papashvily, *All the Happy Endings: A Study of the Domestic Novel in America, the Women Who Wrote It, the Women Who Read It, in the Nineteenth Century* (New York: Harper & Brothers, 1956).
7 In *Woman's Fiction: A Guide to Novels by and about Women in America, 1820–1870* (Ithaca, N.Y.: Cornell University Press, 1978), Nina Baym argues that Harriet Beecher Stowe did not intend to write about real women, nor was a figure like Little Eva intended to be a model for earthly life. "Stowe was not talking about womanhood, but sainthood" (234). Jane Tompkins, *Sensational Designs: The Cultural Work of American Fiction, 1790–1860* (New York: Oxford University Press, 1985), argues that the distinguishing literary features of *Uncle Tom's Cabin* are of typological narrative and identifies this writing with the American literary preaching tradition of jeremiad (135–40). These discussions were helpful in formulating the idea of homiletic fiction. My classification is not sufficient to the diversity of women's writing, nor is it intended to replace the broader patterns suggested by Baym in *Women's Fiction;* Mary Kelley's discussion of "literary domesticity" in *Private Woman, Public Stage: Literary Domesticity in Nineteenth Century America* (New York: Oxford University Press, 1984); or Susan Harris's discussion of "exploratory" fiction in *19th-Century American Women's Novels: Interpretive Strategies* (New York: Cambridge University Press, 1990). It does take into account the unique literary, religious, and cultural ambitions of a particular grouping of fiction, the impact and integrity of which may be lost in other kinds of literary nomenclature.

lineated in male-authored fiction, homiletic and romance writers display successive rather than recurrent themes, those of romance writing being mirrored – that is, reversed – images of the homiletic novel.

The first phase is the homiletic, the war of words that gives this chapter its title and focus.[8] These writings, many of which were produced between 1850 and 1900, are a gynocentric fiction that sustains a powerful attack upon the clergy while pleading the cause of enlightened and superior womanhood. Barred from access to the pulpit, often discouraged from speaking in public under any circumstance, women with religious concerns seized the novel as their podium, fused writing and preaching, reading and hearing, and thereby created an unprecedented and effective entrance into the public arena they had earlier been denied. In doing so, they upset patriarchal privilege in both secular (writing) and sacred (preaching) realms, which may go far to explain the vehemence of the androcentric response – then and now – to their efforts. They launched a holy war, and they certainly intended to join men in religious authority or perhaps replace them altogether. They were ardently and unabashedly pro-woman, often writing with a warmth for women that is reduplicated only in the resurgence of feminism in the latter twentieth century.[9] At the same time, their writing reveals tremendous ambivalences toward women and men. The anger of their uncertainties combined with the passion of the spiritual vision often gives the homiletic novel a jagged and interesting, if not powerful, literary edge. My primary, although by no means exclusive, examples of homiletic fiction come from Harriet Beecher Stowe, Elizabeth Oakes Smith, Elizabeth Stuart Phelps (Ward), Margaret Deland, and Ellen Glasgow. These last two writers carry homiletic fiction well into the twentieth century, and rhetorically and thematically, they provide important transitional material, for they are some of the last women writers to address sympathetically the position of women relative to the male ministry.[10]

There are also two variations of homiletic fiction that provide back-

8 This chapter was named in manuscript draft prior to the publication of Sandra Gilbert and Susan Gubar's fine new study, *No Man's Land: The Place of the Woman Writer in the Twentieth Century* (New Haven, Conn.: Yale University Press, 1988), the first volume of which is entitled *The War of the Words*. I retain my similar title because it is still an accurate metaphoric model for my material, but I am happy to acknowledge the assistance that Gilbert and Gubar's work has provided my own.
9 I do not claim that they were feminists in any extensive contemporary sense of the word, but rather in the simplest use of the word: they made public their concern for and support of women's right to a dignified autonomy of identity.
10 Barbara Welter discusses several of these writers in "Defenders of the Faith: Women Novelists of Religious Controversy in the Nineteenth Century," noting that "No course in American thought, no text on American religion mentions Augusta Wilson, Elizabeth Ward, or Margaret Deland. Yet they were read by many more Americans than were Emerson, Rauschenbusch and William James." See *Dimity Convictions: The American Woman in the Nineteenth Century* (Athens: Ohio University Press, 1976), 129.

ground resources for the homiletic writers I have selected for discussion. One of these variations I call "lamentation" literature, referring to a small but poignant group of works that record the travails of the impoverished minister's family. These writings have as much an air of documentary as fiction about them, and they often speak with special urgency of the plight of the minister's wife, in an account that does not reflect favorably upon the minister or the congregation.[11] Martha Stone Hubbell's *The Shady Side* (1853), which sold 50,000 copies on first appearance, is one of the most poignant of this group.[12] Hubbell is sympathetic to the minister, but the larger narrative purpose is her mourning for the wife who follows him into premature death. There is little biographical data available on Hubbell save her dates and the fact that she was married to a minister, but the grim realities of infant mortality, the grinding penuriousness of congregations, and the utter lack of privacy all read true and clear as a firsthand account. Hubbell was dead three years after the account was published, at age 37. The wife in her narrative dies at age 33, which is probably how old Hubbell was when she wrote the book.

The second variation on this homiletic theme is represented by those writers who devote the novelistic homily exclusively to the idea of the saintly and spiritually superior woman. The saintly woman is a mainstay in Stowe, Smith, and Phelps, but in writers such as Elizabeth Payson Prentiss, Susan Warner, Marion Harland (Mary Virginia Hawes Terhune), Augusta Jane Evans, Caroline Chesbro', and Mrs. G. P. T. Parker, the woman has already replaced the minister, so much so that if he appears at all, he is a shadowy and inconsequential figure on the stage of her self-

11 Examples of these works include: *Prairie Missionary* (Philadelphia: American Sunday School Union, 1853); Eunice White Bullard Beecher (1812–97), *From Dawn to Daylight, or The Simple Story of a Western Home by a Minister's Wife* (New York: Derby & Jackson, 1859); Almedia Brown (no dates available), *Diary of a Minister's Wife* (New York: J. S. Ogilvie, 1881); E. M. Bruce (no dates available), *Thousand a Year* (Boston: Lee and Shepherd, 1866); Corra May White Harris (1869–1935), *A Circuit Rider's Wife* (Philadelphia: Henry Altemus, 1910); Martha Stone Hubbell (1814–56), *The Shady Side, or Life in a Country Parsonage* (Boston: John P. Jewett, 1853); and Elizabeth Stuart Phelps (1815–52), *The Sunny Side, or The Country Minister's Wife* (Philadelphia: American Sunday School Union, 1851) and Phelps's pseudonymous [H. Trusta] *A Peep at Number Five, or a Chapter in the Life of a City Pastor* (Boston: Phillips, Sampson, 1855). See also, "Shady Side Literature," *New Englander* 12 (February 1854): 54–70.

Phelps, Hubbell, Beecher, Harris, and the anonymous *Prairie Missionary* were minister's wives; the marital identity of Bruce and Brown is undetermined. In *The Minister's Wife: Her Role in Nineteenth Century American Evangelicalism* (Philadelphia: Temple University, 1983), Leonard Sweet optimistically suggests that the role of the minister's wife was a stepping-stone to her own preaching vocation. For a different description of her fate, see my "Lamentations for the Minister's Wife, by Herself," *Women's Studies* 19 (1991): 327–40.

12 *The Shady Side* was a response to Elizabeth Stuart Phelps's *The Sunny Side*. The publication figure for Hubbell's book is given by Emerson Shuck, "Clergymen in Representative American Fiction, 1830–1930: A Study in Attitudes Toward Religion" (Ph.D. diss., University of Wisconsin, 1943), 511.

determined spiritual triumph.[13] For example, the imperious and remarkable Edna Earle in Evans's immensely popular *St. Elmo* (1867) is
born wonderful and takes her only instruction in religious development
from her struggle against her debauched but fascinating would-be lover,
St. Elmo. St. Elmo's charm is his distinctly unministerial virility, and
so the sign of his acquiescence to her spiritual superiority is that he
becomes a minister, an event that, given the sexual energy of the novel,
cannot help but read as a castration. Enter minister, exit man, end novel.
Edna, in contrast, is revealed to be simply more of what she always was
– the mature, self-created embodiment of spiritual womanhood. Marion
Harland's heroine in *Alone* (1854) is more interesting, for Ida Ross is not
born with her spiritual achievement, but must work and grow in order
to gain power as a religious leader in her small community. She "loved
her pastor, but her acquaintance with him was slight," and although she
maintains contact with the institutional church, she finds it lacking in
basic Christian spirituality, and so wields her quiet influence outside
organized religion.[14] Although this chapter focuses on homiletic fiction
that offers more clues to the male–female dynamic and women writers'
portrayal of the male ministry, these depictions of the saintly woman
are also part of the homiletic canon, and will be useful resources for
further illustration.[15]

The second phase of woman-authored fiction about the ministry, successor to the homiletic voice, begins in the late nineteenth century, peaks
in the 1920s and 1930s, and fades by the 1950s. This is romance fiction,
much of it produced in the heyday of Social Gospel idealism. These
writers confirm the erotic difficulties inhering in the ecclesiastical office
and its keeper, but they do so with a distinctly androcentric outlook,
making the minister the desirable but innocent subject of romance in the
parish. Characteristically, this fiction blames women for whatever dilemmas may occur regarding the sexual behavior of ministers, making
their handling of the material a nearly complete inversion of the concerns
of the homiletic writers. This body of literature is so extensive and
contradictory to the first that it is necessarily placed in a separate chapter
(Chapter 5). Writers such as Grace Smith Richmond, Caroline Atwater
Mason, Helen Reimensnyder Martin, Agnes Sligh Turnbull, Nelia Gardner White, and Elsie Oakes Barber contribute to this phase, which is the

13 One exception to this displacement of the minister in the fiction of the spiritually
   superior woman is Susan Warner's *The Wide, Wide World*. Ellen Montgomery is involved
   with a powerfully directive minister whom she eventually marries. But, as Nina Baym
   pointed out to me in correspondence, Ellen Montgomery is not nearly as subservient
   as she appears; her tears and humility are often quite effective tools for exerting her
   will.
14 Mary Virginia Hawes Terhune [Marion Harland], *Alone*, 5th ed. (Richmond, Va.: A.
   Morris, 1854), 282.
15 For a listing of the novels used to define the homiletic voice of women's fiction, see
   Appendix A.

last time we see any sustained interest in the clergy on the part of women writers. Overall, contemporary women novelists are not particularly interested in the clergy, for the context of the political, social, and religious battles being waged by the homiletic writers has changed. The church is no longer the solitary outlet for female expression and influence, and relative to other kinds of offices, the members of the clergy are not seen as powerful in society at large.[16]

The inevitable exceptions to the diminishing interest in the ministry on the part of woman novelists, however, are anomalous and powerful enough to be worth noting. Of the few women who have written specifically about ministers since the 1960s, Joyce Carol Oates and Flannery O'Connor provide a countercommentary that is neither andro- nor gynocentric in its profile. They write of the deformity and cruelty of religion, of a manic and primitive hunger of the tormented self for resolution. The ministers involved in these novels are seized by the absurdities of flesh in relation to spirit, mutilated and destroyed by the confounding appetites represented in the dualisms of embodiment and the pitiless demands of Christian grace.[17] The record of woman-authored fiction is of psychic dislocation and verbal warfare, and the naturalistic brutality of Oates's and O'Connor's prose offers a suggestive symbolic conclusion to the story of female interest in the clergy. Oates and O'Connor are far away from their female predecessors, but the romance and homiletic writers are not much closer to each other. If there is anything shared across time, it is an intense anger and scorn, sometimes directed at women (the romance writers) and sometimes directed at men (the homiletic writers) that, metaphorically speaking, has taken recent shape in the writing of Oates and O'Connor. The unbearable suffering of embodiment, focused and then exaggerated within the ministry, becomes a strange and beautiful battery of words. These are tales of sound and fury, told about maniacs imprisoned in bodies they can't trust, abandoned by a deity they can't escape. It is the pain, the terrible eloquence of dislocation, that survives in the writing of contemporary women as a de-evolved text, the war of words rendered in the raw, red light of yearning become primeval hunger.

Yet despite the numerous and various female-authored novels dealing with ministers and their female parishioners, there are virtually no voices for the Elizabeth Tiltons of this world, nor is there any discussion of the

16 The noteworthy exception to this generalization is organized fundamentalist religion, which continues to make its power appreciated. Margaret Atwood's treatment of the savagery of fundamentalism given absolute social power in *The Handmaid's Tale* (Boston: Houghton Mifflin, 1986) reminds us that the war of words is far from concluded.
17 See Joyce Carol Oates, *Son of the Morning* (New York: Vanguard, 1978); and Flannery O'Connor, *Wise Blood* (1962) and *The Violent Bear it Away* (1960) in *Three by Flannery O'Connor* (New York: NAL, n.d.).

equally vulnerable position of the minister's wife amidst the events of clergy transgression. Noteworthy exceptions appear in a short story by Harriet Prescott Spofford; in Catherine Read Arnold Williams's *Fall River: An Authentic Narrative* (1834); and in Catherine Beecher's *Truth Stranger than Fiction* (1850).[18] The last consists of Beecher's trial notes accounting for the proceedings brought by Delia Bacon against clergyman Alexander McWhorter for calumny, falsehood, and disgraceful conduct. Similarly, Catherine Williams gives an account of the trial of a Methodist minister for the murder of a young woman with whom he was involved. Williams indignantly protests the postmortem character assassination that was applied against the victim in order to exonerate the minister. (I discuss the Williams narrative in Chapter 5.)

As if presciently aware of the immense silence she was entering, Spofford titled her piece, an exploration of the psychological dynamics of grieving, "Her Story." The narrator, speaking from the mental asylum to which she has been committed, tells us of her descent into madness as she realizes – or suspects, we are never sure – her minister husband has betrayed her with another woman. Other than this lonely fictional lamentation on behalf of the wife, however, and Williams's and Beecher's early, vigorous defenses of women, I have found no fiction by women in either century that speaks on behalf of the female victim of divine lechery. In fact, I have found no woman novelist, whether working in a homiletic or romance mode, in the nineteenth or the twentieth century, writing about adulterous clergy as we find male authors doing. Although I certainly may have overlooked some evidence amidst the untapped reservoir of women's writing, this is a significant finding. According to the record of women writers, there is no such tradition of divine lechery. Whereas male authors have been consistently fascinated with the spectacle of illicit clergy sexuality, this is not what engaged the woman writer, and before examining the homiletic writers more closely, I want to consider some of the larger cultural reasons for this resounding silence.

The homiletic writers did not hesitate to seek equal footing with male ministers, and their combined writings sustain a steady attack upon the ministry, and sometimes upon the manhood of the officeholder. They wrote about seductions and romance, and they wrote with great hostility in an area of high tension. Despite the kind of risks they took, they never wrote about sexual intrigue between a minister and a female parishioner. Given the peculiar dynamics between religious women and the clergy,

---

18 "Her Story," in *Old Madame and Other Tragedies* (1872; reprint, Boston: Richard G. Badger, 1900), 205–49; *Fall River: An Authentic Narrative* (Boston, Marshall, Brown, 1834); and *Truth Stranger than Fiction: A Narrative of Recent Transactions Involving Inquiries in Regard to the Principles of Honor, Truth and Justice* (Boston: Phillips, Sampson, 1850). I am grateful to Anna Shannon Elfenbein for bringing the Spofford story to my attention.

it is impossible not to give credence to Douglas's observation that these imaginative writings reveal a "testament of sexual tension," and we know from the historical record that (to use a metaphor of appropriate delicacy for the era) where there was smoke, there was fire.[19] It is impossible for these women not to have known of instances of sexual involvement between clergy and female parishioners, for the press was filled with news of "ministerial sex scandals . . . in the 1860's and 1870's."[20] Harriet Beecher Stowe, who had distressingly immediate knowledge of the possibilities, engaged in a spirited defense of her brother.[21] Although neither Stowe nor any other of the homiletic writers could have been ignorant of clergy seductions, they did not write about them.

There is, of course, no point in chastising the authors for not writing the book you think they should have. Silence, however, is an eloquence in nineteenth-century discourse, and this silence may very well be articulate with the fear, ambiguity, and rage experienced by the intelligent, religious nineteenth-century woman. The meeting of religion and sexuality, especially as embodied by the male minister, was controversial even when handled by male writers, and such a subject would have been even more dangerous for a woman writer who was not supposed to know about such matters in the first place. In addition, and this is extremely important, a number of these homiletic writers were the daughters or wives of ministers (and in some instances, daughter to one minister and wife to another), and the plaints of uneasy male writers and ministers notwithstanding, they were living in a culture redolent of patriarchal prerogative.[22] This put the religiously ambitious writing woman in the fearsomely uncomfortable position of attacking or displacing her own husband, brother, or father, and the nineteenth-century woman was acutely aware of her powerlessness relative to any material or culturally

19 Ann Douglas, *The Feminization of American Culture* (New York: Knopf, 1977), 228.
20 Ibid., 100.
21 Harriet Beecher Stowe, *Pink and White Tyranny* (Boston: Roberts Brothers), wherein Stowe remarks on how a minister's "spiritual attentions could degenerate into downright temporal lovemaking" (50), appeared in 1871, but it is impossible to ascertain whether the passage about unreliable clergy was penned before or after Stowe's knowledge of Henry's difficulties. Alice Crozier, in *The Novels of Harriet Beecher Stowe* (New York: Oxford University Press, 1969), holds that Stowe "was aware of her brother's distress almost from the first," which would place her involvement about 1870, but believed him innocent "until her dying day" (201). In *Runaway to Heaven: The Story of Harriet Beecher Stowe* (New York: Doubleday, 1963), Johanna Johnston points out that although Stowe was willing to think the worst of Lord Byron, she immediately repulsed the similar account of her own brother's transgressions. She sprang to his defense, maintaining that he was the victim of male jealousy and female foolishness.
22 Phelps, Stowe, and Elizabeth Prentiss were minister's daughters; Stowe and Prentiss were married to ministers, as was Marion Harland. Phelps's mother, Elizabeth Stuart Phelps (1815–52), was one of the writers contributing to the lamentational literature on behalf of the minister's wife. Gilbert and Gubar's discussion of the powerful father-daughter paradigm that shaped the writing of twentieth-century women also has relevance here. See *The War of the Words*, esp. 170–6.

effective sense of the word. The unhappy exchange of dependencies between clergy and woman, coupled with her very real economic servitude may, also have contributed to the silence of homiletic writers about lecherous clergy. It is also possible that they were not interested in clergy sexuality for positive and for the culturally coercive reasons mentioned above. This is not flattering to the male involved, and especially not to a profession already nervous about its masculinity, but the writers of homiletic fiction do little to reassure the male reader on this score. They are writing for a female audience, and therein may lie the last of several keys to this silence about divine lechery.

Nina Baym argues that between 1820 and 1870 women writers produced a distinctive kind of narrative, a "woman's fiction" that featured heroines who, despite various domestic and cultural confinements, learn to be independent and resourceful. These spirited female creations will give way to the passive heroine of the gothic romance, a female who is unable to choose effectively for her own destiny in the way that the heroines of women's fiction are empowered. Baym suggests that one strategy for independence was to defy the cultural notion that "anatomy is destiny" by ignoring sexuality. Unwilling to show women as the inevitable sexual victims of predatory men, women wrote about a different kind of heterosexual encounter, one that emphasized the mutuality and spirituality of worthy heroes and exemplary heroines.[23] Augmenting this account is my discussion of the meaning and usage of the word "passion" relative to Harriet Beecher Stowe's treatment of religious ecstasy (Chapter 2). In nineteenth-century discourse this term carried an extended tribute to the reality of embodiment, and given the cultural circumstances of the woman writer such as elucidated by Baym and others, it is quite plausible to have a writer like Stowe describe religious ecstasy, have it sound suspiciously sexual to twentieth-century ears, but, in fact, simply be a genuine expression of how the religious experience might feel without having to suspect Stowe of repression or a surreptitious titillation.

One of the distinctive meanings of passion in nineteenth-century discourse is suffering, with its close correlation to the suffering and passion of Christ. Jane Tompkins points out that "the pain of learning to conquer her own passions is the central fact of the sentimental heroine's existence" and the strength of these novels "lay precisely in their dramatization of the heroine's suffering as she struggles to control each new resurgence of passion."[24] Tompkins is correct in all but her distinction between passion and suffering. Suffering is also a passion, is, in fact, *the* passion

23 Baym, *Woman's Fiction*, 18, 26, 162–3, 254, 313.
24 Tompkins, *Sensational Designs*, 172–3.

in a religious sense, and this sense of passion is common and distinctive
to the woman writer. Through one kind of passion (suffering and redemptive love), the woman may conquer the darker passions that might
threaten her spiritual and physical well-being (jealousy, avarice, fear,
lust, pride). It is regrettable that physical desire may have been seen as
a darker passion, but the realities of medical knowledge and cultural
attitudes meant that for nineteenth-century women sexuality was a language of powerlessness and damage. Women did not have to be literally
raped or seduced in order to feel the prison of their gender this way. In
contrast, the language of spirituality is the language of power, both
present and promised. Unlike the body, the mind and heart cannot be
so readily invaded. With good reason, then, the focus of this writing is
on religious passion, not sexual passion, for it is only religious passion
that may redeem and preserve her. That not all women felt this way is
a matter of record, but this cannot erase the ambiguity that many felt
regarding the treachery of physical life and the corresponding imprisonment of cultural life.

From the manipulative humility of Susan Warner's Ellen Montgomery
to the more overtly independent and spiritually proud heroines of Stowe,
Phelps, Smith, and other homiletic writers, all share this use of the word
"passion" and the sense of cultural confinement that gives their presentation of the passion of redemptive suffering such intensity. Jane Tompkins points to the "claustrophobic atmosphere" of The Wide, Wide World
that works effectively to convey the sense "of someone utterly at the
mercy of implacable authorities," and it is this sense of imprisonment
or confinement that, in varying degrees, characterizes all the homiletic
writers.[25] It is an extended grammar expressive of the suffering of religious passion as a product of both cultural and physical imprisonment.
The homiletic writers, then, are writing about religious passion, by-
passing the sexual possibilities involved in order to focus on the redemptive, spiritual possibilities of passion.

Ann Douglas has pointed to the institutional isolation and spiritual
narcissism of "sentimental" fiction (what I have reappropriated as several
kinds of homily), noting that these women never joined a group or
reform society, that their incredible spiritual gifts are employed strictly
within the private realm, and usually to no good social effect.[26] But many
women may have felt they had no choice relative to an institution where
they were to be seen and not heard, and the various portraits of ministerial
women in homiletic fiction can be read as an effort to imagine a plausible
alternative to their cultural stalemate. It should not be surprising that

25 Ibid., 177.
26 Douglas, Feminization of American Culture, 103, 157.

their fictional solutions might work in uncertain and perhaps self-defeating cross-purposes to their ambitions, for the psychological and cultural combat in which they were engaged was an event of excruciating and perilous intensity.

A War of Words

The pretense for Henry Beecher's repeated visits to the Tilton household beyond the consolatory was that he was reading to Elizabeth portions of his forthcoming novel, *Norwood* (1869). The affair progressed by way of words, discourse giving way to intercourse with the infusing of Beecher's literary emissions into the ear and heart of Elizabeth Tilton. Words were also a means for concealing the event as the boundaries between words, sexual power, preaching, and fiction became clearer. As Ann Douglas points out, Beecher

> claimed he had not seduced Libby. Tilton accused him of "sexual in-timacy"; he admitted to "improper advances." What kind of defense was that? What, after all, was seduction anyway? But in a sense Beecher's confusion was genuine, no matter how manipulated. Had he seduced Libby, or was it just "nesting"? If you close your eyes, does anything really happen? Did he read her a novel, or act out a novel?[27]

The interlocking power between preaching and reading that seems to have operated between Beecher and Tilton was not an anomalous, private event, and their understanding of that same power led women to write and publish in the first place. Elizabeth Oakes Prince Smith had an active sense of the imprisonment of women, and she was an energetic writer and participant on behalf of women's rights. The mother of five children, four of whom survived childhood, her writing made a necessary financial contribution to her household. Smith's concern for the religious and cultural integrity of women took personal shape in 1877 when she became the minister of an independent congregation in Canastota, New York. Her portrait of a female saint in *Bertha and Lily: Or the Parsonage of Beech Glen* (1854) must have been an early effort at thinking through her own developing sense of religious virtuosity and commitment.[28] The novel acts as a documentary of the passions, for Smith uses the word almost

---

27 Ibid., 243.
28 Her diary entries offer interesting insights into her ideas about the spiritually pure woman. See Joy Wiltenburg, "Excerpts from the Diary of Elizabeth Oakes Smith," *Signs: Journal of Women in Culture and Society* 9 (Spring 1984): 536–48.

as frequently as does Stowe. "The majesty of human passion" dwarfs
Niagara, love is an omnipotent passion, the body is a chalice of passions.
There are the "grosser" passions and there is divine passion, inspired
passion, and poetic passion.[29] The imprisonment of Bertha takes place
prior to the opening of the novel, however, for Smith concentrates on
the triumph of suffering as the torment of a violated heart is purified
and freed from the constraints of the past and the conventions of the
present. As the novel opens, Bertha is a woman well on her way to
independence and spiritual beatitude.

The source of Bertha's secret and tragic suffering is a series of multiple
violations: her seduction, impregnation, and abandonment by one Nathan Underhill and the loss of her infant child. She has retreated to the
quiet village of Beech Glen to allow the sanctification of suffering to do
its work, for "there is a finer essence in women, which if encouraged,
will save the race." On these and other grounds, Bertha "seriously ad-
vocates the admission of woman into the pulpit" (55), and toward that
end, she slowly takes over the position of the town minister, Ernest
Helfenstein.[30] This is only natural, because women "live in nearer relations with the Divine than is the nature of the more material masculine
element to do" (83–4). Like the Christ, she seems harsh to those who
oppose her, but her seemingly peremptory activities are easily justified
once her redemptive purity, purchased by her suffering, is fully revealed.
Bertha, never one to be modest, says this of herself:

> I am accustomed to sorrow, and my body is but a medium by which
> the soul makes itself manifest to those about me.... The passions of
> people about me are so poor, petty, miserable in their kind, that I am
> filled with a sort of disgust at their exhibition. Good God, how would
> they be confounded could they penetrate the lava depths of my soul.
> (48)

This language of the volcanic soul is common to descriptions of holy
passion as well as of the grosser passions, for Helfenstein uses the same
kind of language to depict his infatuation for a shallow society woman.
In Bertha's case, she is purified by her suffering, her molten soul poured
into the purity of religious passion. We see this process throughout the
novel until she is ready for the conclusive interview with her former
lover, after which he is immediately struck dead, and she is transfigured,
fully revealed as a female savior. Even her body looks different after this

---

29 Elizabeth Oakes Prince Smith, *Bertha and Lily: Or, the Parsonage of Beech Glen, A Romance*
   (1854; New York: Derby & Jackson, 1858), 16, 225, 256, and *passim*. Subsequent page
   citations in the text appear in parentheses.
30 The name is something of a joke, because Helfenstein was Oakes Smith's *nomme de
   plume*. Wiltenburg, "Excerpts," 538.

rechanneling of passion into its divine form. Faint rays emanate from her fingertips, her face takes on a new luminosity, and she becomes a vegetarian.

Helfenstein, on the other hand, is unable to conquer his baser passions, and only when the society girl renounces his attentions does he finally turn to the incomparable Bertha as a life partner. For his retarded spiritual progress, he is relegated to the role of the admiring beloved disciple, while she is the Comforter and Savior both. Like Jesus in the Gospel of John, it is "hard to believe that thought had ever grown in her mind; hard to believe she had ever been a babe" (275). "The thorn hath pierced her brow, the gall hath touched her lips; she hath bent beneath the Cross, but lo! She is transfigured before us" (332). This Bertha, who is similar to the later Edna Earle of *St. Elmo,* is a difficult heroine to appreciate. To the modern mind, unattuned to the context and purpose of all this passion and suffering, she is merely arrogant, incredible, and often cruel in her implacable assurance of righteousness. But she is also powerful, intelligent, and independent, scorning the conventions of human relations and institutional religion, qualities that have never been endearing to an androcentric culture. Her narrative is instructive and cautionary, a homily on the journey of the soul, exaggerated in its message-bearing function, but vital with an ardent confidence in the power of the spiritually ambitious woman.

Harriet Beecher Stowe, who specialized in female saints, preferred a more modest hagiography. Stowe's writing is typically associated with the limitations of the domestic and the aesthetics of the sentimental. But as Karen Halttunen argues, the preoccupation of sentimental culture with the details of decor and fashion served the purpose of cultivating sincerity and simplicity through "moral" manners and fashion. The body (and its surroundings) was to be a transparency to the soul.[31] Stowe's writing urges us to consider how a woman's body reveals her spiritual nature, and to that purpose, her writing is built upon domestic interiors, from the hearthside to the precious interior within that interior, a woman's heart.[32] Stowe's theological facility in a book like *The Minister's Wooing,*

31 Karen Halttunen, *Confidence Men and Painted Women: A Study of Middle-Class Culture of America, 1830–1870* (New Haven: Yale University Press, 1982), 75–81. Linda Kauffman's work in *Discourses of Desire: Gender, Genre and Epistolary Fictions* (Ithaca, N.Y.: Cornell University Press, 1986) also is helpful in rethinking "sentimental." She says, "I have tried to expose the devaluation of the sentimental as another form of repression, with ramifications as serious at the end of the twentieth century as sexual repression was at the end of the nineteenth" (316).
32 See my "American Myth and Biblical Interpretation in the Fiction of Harriet Beecher Stowe and Mary E. Wilkins Freeman," *Journal of the American Academy of Religion* 55 (Winter 1988):741–63. In a similar vein, Elaine Showalter has written a good study of Stowe by relating the practice of quilting to the art of novel writing. In "Piecing and Writing," she argues that *Uncle Tom's Cabin* is built upon the famous quilting design

which uses the Edwardsean spirit of religious affections against its darker Calvinistic underpinnings, should not be hidden by literary labels. In fact, she is very difficult to place, and her writing illustrates the utility of this category of homiletic fiction.

The Minister's Wooing (1859) is one of those novels in which the spiritually precocious woman again displaces the minister who by the title would seem to be the center of the narrative.[33] As Baym notes, Stowe does envision the earthly sanctification of the soul as a possibility for men as well as for women, but in this novel, as in most of her others, it is the female character who shows us how to do it.[34] Simply put, women are better at it than men are. "All her outward senses are finer and more acute than his, and finer and more delicate all the attributes of her mind."[35] Furthermore, Christ, "as to his human nature, was made of a woman, it leads us to see that in matters of grace God sets a special value on woman's nature and designs to put special honor upon it."[36] Elsewhere Stowe specifies that it is the "life of Christ *and* his mother" that turns us heavenward, and although Stowe was not a Catholic, she obviously appreciated the theological possibilities for women afforded by the presence of Mary, for she wastes no opportunity to praise the maternity of God.

The uniqueness of Christ and the gospel message was his bodily assumption of the suffering of humankind. In The Pearl of Orr's Island (1862), Stowe tells us that the ministry of Christ began with the declaration "Blessed are they that mourn." While "prosperity was the blessing of the Old Testament," it is adversity that defines the New Testament.[37] This perspective is even more exhaustively explored in The Minister's Wooing. Sorrow is simply part of the human condition, born when the soul awakens and in terror realizes the metaphysical darkness of her confinement: "Oh how narrow the walls! Oh how close and dark the grated window!" (358). But if we are to follow in the Savior's footsteps,

---

known as "log cabin." See Nancy Miller, ed., *The Poetics of Gender* (New York: Columbia University, 1986): 222–47.

33 Lawrence Buell discusses Stowe's use of Hopkins in an interesting essay, "Calvinism Romanticized: Harriet Beecher Stowe, Samuel Hopkins, and *The Minister's Wooing*," in *Critical Essays on Harriet Beecher Stowe*, ed. Elizabeth Ammons, (Boston: G.K. Hall, 1980), 259–75.

34 As Baym says, "Stowe is not talking about womanhood, but sainthood, and since the condition cannot be achieved by imitation, these characters are not models of what every woman should try to achieve or become. They exist on another plane . . . and their Christlike function is not limited by or directed to gender" (234).

35 Harriet Beecher Stowe, *The Pearl of Orr's Island: A Story of the Coast of Maine* (1862; reprint, Boston: Houghton Mifflin, 1896), 122.

36 Harriet Beecher Stowe, *The Minister's Wooing* (1859; reprint, Hartford, Conn.: Stowe-Day Foundation, 1978), 364. Subsequent page citations in the text appear in parentheses.

37 Stowe, *Pearl*, 365.

we must recognize that "sorrow is the great birth agony of immortal powers. . . . Sorrow is divine" (358–60). The personality of Stowe's sense of the suffering and cultural confinement of women is inescapable, and her writing examines the cultural and existential location of this situation and then translates it into its spiritual significance. She presents us with a biblically based model of spiritual virtuosity centered upon the experience of the grief and self-sacrifice of women.

Here, then, is the equation: just as the shed blood of the lamb was necessary in God's salvation plan, so, too, is the purifying confinement of women within the prison of life's sorrows. The equation simultaneously explains the achieved divinity of Christ and the potential, if not actual, divinity of women. In *The Minister's Wooing,* Mary Scudder reincarnates the Christ, for her heart will be "wrung, pierced, [and] bleeding with the sins and sorrows of earth" (74). The loss of her lover at sea destines Mary to her course "as a sanctified priestess of the great worship of sorrow," and she turns her grieving heart to minister to others, for otherwise the river of love in her heart so cruelly thwarted would have "drowned her in the suffocating agonies of repression" (378). Her achievement is so obvious that minister Samuel Hopkins, who always had a "reverential spirit towards women which accompanies a healthy and great nature," regards her as a "miraculous messenger from Heaven," and brings all the delicate questions of internal, spiritual experience to her to be resolved (379). As sexless as this writing seems, it depends upon an experience of a particular body, a woman's body. In *Oldtown Folks* (1869), Stowe identifies this precisely. "If we suppose two souls, exactly alike, sent into bodies, the one of man, the other of woman, that mere fact alone alters the whole mental and moral history of the two." She identifies a religious type of woman so spiritually intense that "one might almost say her body thought."[38] She quotes the same line with regard to Mary Scudder at the moment of her transfiguration in church (see Chapter 2), and it seems clear that although the body may be an unreliable container, the movement of spirit may also act in harmony with its fleshly container. The container most likely to respond to the divine vocation is a woman, for it is the female body and mind – the two inseparable – that render her open to such virtuosity.

Thus, the emanating fingertips of Bertha in *Bertha and Lily* and the radiance of Mary Scudder, whose face glows "as when one places a light behind some alabaster screen sculptured with mysterious and holy emblems" (362) indicate not a denial of the body, but a re-creation of the body. The characters move from the realm of sorrow, the physical, sexual

<hr/>

38 Harriet Beecher Stowe, *Oldtown Folks* (1869; reprint, Cambridge, Mass.: Belknap, 1966), 408, 465.

world, to a realm of spiritual beatitude. In doing so, they are no longer
the sexual, physical body that gave them first entrance to such mysteries,
but they become a religious body, possessed of holy language. Bertha
first takes over Helfenstein's teaching and then builds a little chapel to
accommodate her audiences. By the end of the novel, "her lectures were
better attended than mine," says the awestruck minister (245). Mary's
sanctification is most spectacularly displayed during prayer group, her
petitions so powerful that "they who heard her had the sensation of rising
in the air, of feeling a celestial light and warmth descending into their
souls" (366). Obviously, the average minister would have difficulty com-
peting with this perfect union of body and soul, given tangibility in
prayerful peroration.

The refinement of woman's nature in its remarkable agreement with
the female body is one explanation for her readier translucence to spiritual
verity, but the other factor is her cultural confinement. Men, vigorous
and active in the outside world, have not the slightest conception "of
that veiled and secluded life which exists in the heart of a sensitive woman,
whose sphere is narrow, whose external diversions are few, and whose
mind, therefore, acts by continual introspection upon itself. . . . Man's
utter ignorance of woman's nature is a cause of a great deal of unsuspected
cruelty which he practices toward her."[39] Being female in American
culture gives a woman special entrance to divine mysteries, for the same
ear that is trained to listen to the needs and wants of male companions
listens that much more acutely for God, who is, after all, the ultimate
male and father in this universe. Women bear the burden of grieving for
the loss of children and loved ones (and women's fiction testifies to the
frequency of such loss), but this sorrowing prepares women for the most
universal of sympathies, mourning on behalf of unredeemed humanity.
"If we suffer with him, we shall also reign with him" (361).

Stowe may have been presenting us with an ideal (women should
suffer), but she was also engaged in truth-telling. Women did suffer. In
The Women's Bible, Elizabeth Cady Stanton remarks tartly that men seem
to find self-sacrifice extremely attractive – in women – and the ultimate
heroism is demonstrated by Stowe's heroines when they suffer in sacrificial silence. But Stowe violates an unspoken cultural fastidiousness by
refusing to do so herself, and it would be a mistake to underestimate the
anger registered in much of her writing. In The Pearl of Orr's Island, she
predicts that the thoughtless arrogance of men will encounter a reckoning
day, for woman owns a moral authority that fits her to be an "angel in
the Apocalypse, to whom was given the golden rod to measure New
Jerusalem. . . . There may perhaps come a time when the saucy boy, who

39 Stowe, Pearl, 216.

now steps so superbly . . . will learn to tremble at the golden measuring rod, held in the hand of a woman." Perhaps even more chilling for any male beneficiary of the current androcentric order is the heroine's death-bed satisfaction that her demise is providential for the relationship. As a wife, her charms would have faded for him, but now, she says, "I may have more power over you, when I seem to be gone, than I should have had in living."[40]

The Minister's Wooing was written after Stowe's son died by drowning in 1857 and her sister Catherine had lost her fiancé in an earlier drowning death. Although Mary Scudder may represent Stowe's ideal coping strategy, the figure of the embittered mother in the novel may more closely argue Stowe's own anguished feelings in the matter. "We women have secret places where our life runs out. . . . Nobody ever knows what we women die of" (383, 528), says Stowe dramatically, although she has certainly made a good effort to tell us. From bleeding hearts to bleeding feet, this language of the spiritual suffering of women creates poignant symbolic connections with the actual bleeding of women (the ability and disability of the reproductive body) and the ultimate bleeding of the passion (the wounds of the cross). Again, the intimacy of religious and sexual matters as passions becomes apparent. Women know the hazards of passion on the most personal and ordinary level possible – that of the vulnerability of the body, but this damaging and dangerous experience is also the reason that women know the divine portion of passion as well. In that knowledge there is satisfaction, and the point of the homiletic writers is to announce, document, cultivate, and confirm these unique conditions. The language of suffering, however, betrays the enormity and terror of their position, for despair and anger compete with their labor toward vindication.

Their suffering, in other words, was as debilitating for their goals as it was efficacious, and nowhere is this clearer than in the writing of Elizabeth Stuart Phelps (Ward). Phelps married relatively late in life, and apparently so unsatisfactorily that many commentators drop her married name in ordinary reference. She wrote throughout her lifetime despite continual illness, and she devoted her uneven energies to a number of social issues, women's rights key among them. *The Silent Partner* (1871) was the first American novel to treat problems of urban, industrial blight.[41] *Doctor Zay* (1882) is a remarkable study of a successful professional woman dealing with the gender-generated pressures inhibitory to her career as a physician.

Perhaps like Smith's realized vocation as minister later in her life,

---

40 Ibid., 162, 391.
41 Carol Farley Kessler, *Elizabeth Stuart Phelps* (Boston: Twayne: 1982), 50.

Phelps, too, had experienced a call. An interesting short story in the collection *Sealed Orders* (1879) imagines "A Woman's Pulpit." Phelps's account shows a woman overriding the prejudices of her denomination against female ministry and successfully filling her position in a small mountain town. She worries about what to wear in order to properly command her post, but the bulk of her attention goes to preparing her sermons and lessons and calling upon her parishioners. In evaluating her first months on the job, she leans toward continuing the ministry, for she is clearly very good at it. But inexplicably, Phelps has her called home for some emergency involving the measles and a minor character whose relationship to the narrator is never clear. The hasty ending looks as though Phelps did not know what to do once her heroine was clearly in command of the situation, nor, apparently, could she imagine simply leaving her there in a lifetime ministry, so she whisks her offstage and ends the story. This abrupt conclusion is characteristic of Phelps when she extends her characters into a future sociology too far beyond her own imaginative reach, and her writing about women and religion is particularly distinctive of this stop-start feeling. In Phelps's novels and short stories about religious life, we find the most intense and painful renditions of nineteenth-century women's position, relative to her own work and relative to the other homiletic writers.

Phelps's sense of life imprisonment is acute.[42] In "A Woman's Pulpit," a paralyzed man looks at the sunset over the mountains and sees "lines and bars . . . red hot and criss-cross like prison gates." This image is resolved by the narrator into a vivid compression of the hopelessness of village life: "When I turned my head for a farewell look at my parish, the awful hills were crossed with [the] red hot bars, and Mary Ann, with her mouth open, stood in her mother's crumbling door." This image of the idiot daughter barred by the hot, imprisoning light does far more work than Phelps's announced moral that "it is in repression, not extension, that the danger of disease lies to an immortal life."[43] Announced or not, however, the point should not be lost – repression is the enemy of the soul. But Phelps's sense of repression was most urgent in relation to women, and this is the unspoken theme of all the *Gates* novels. In the first of this immensely popular series, *The Gates Ajar* (1868), Mary Cabot is so "walled in" and "shut up" with grief for her recently slain brother she despairs of any religious comfort. The novel retails her instruction through this sorrow at the hands of Aunt Winifred, who assures her that heaven is like coming home on a cold evening to warmth and light, and

42 In addition to the *Gates* series, two other novel titles are indicative: *Hedged In* (Boston: Fields, Osgood, 1870) and *Walled In* (London: Harper & Brothers, 1907).
43 Elizabeth Stuart Phelps, "A Woman's Pulpit," in *Sealed Orders* (1879; reprint, New York: Garrett, 1969), 195–200.

that her love for her brother will be gratified in tangible reconciliation. In *Beyond the Gates* (1883), the middle-aged heroine visits heaven while in a death-like coma, and, indeed, finds that heaven "moves on in the dear ordered channel" of family love, which for Phelps means harmony, growth, happiness, and fulfillment. Of particular concern to Mary is the restoration of a long lost lover, and she finds that, in heaven, each person can look forward to enjoying a loving family life and a lover's intimacy. Just as she is about to be reunited with her lover, however, she wakes up from the expansiveness of heaven to the narrowness of her sickbed. The morning is frosty, and her world looks shrunken. There are no celestial gates ajar, only her bedroom shutters, from which she can see the poor girls going to work in the factory, and on this realistic disappointment the novel ends.

In Phelps, heaven is expansive of the best of human passions and physical possibility, whereas present life is a confinement and repression. Home is reimagined, not as the domestic and marital prison it was for Victorian woman, but as she thought it should be – the fulfillment and perfection of the highest human passions as they are instructed and purified by the divine model. Women are more alert to the possibilities of passion, and more likely to seek and achieve its realization. All the *Gates* novels feature exemplary female heroes who instruct the duller males around them. In *The Gates Between* (1887), a deceased physician who was arrogant of his powers and thoughtless of his wife while he was alive is reduced to a "female" status in heaven, for his spiritual skills are quite rudimentary, and his earthly authority of no use. As a dead man, he can't heal a child, but the dead mother, watching over her living child from her heavenly vantage point, is able to strengthen and save her child through the power of her spiritual presence.

The role reversal in *The Gates Between* conveys much the same satisfaction as Stowe's various revenges upon patriarchal presumption, and, with Stowe, Phelps reads the transparency of women to the divine passion as scriptural and ordained. Her portrait of Jesus is especially revealing, for she concentrates on the sympathetic healing function of the savior. He does not "insult the nervous patient by expressing doubts as to the reality of his disorder. He did not prejudge hysterical symptoms, or underestimate the nature of a suffering only too evident to his refined perception" (157). But Jesus really shines in his understanding of women,

> always treating women with respect, always recognizing their fettered individualism, their force of character if they had it, their undeveloped powers, their terrible capacity for suffering, their superiority in spiritual vigor. . . . For the heartbreak that only women know, for the woe that women of their times endured, as a matter of course, without complaint,

he had been divinely sorry. He had been the only man who ever understood.[44]

Jesus is crucially shaped by his spiritual heritage from his mother, and his nurturing and healing skills make him more stereotypically female than male. Phelps uses the word "delicate" with reference to him so often that it is hard to take seriously her other descriptions of him as "manly."[45] The reason for his "delicate perceptions" of women stems from his origin as the son of Mary. "The suffering element in the life of the son began early in the soul of the mother," for "the awful law of sacrifice that was to become the ruling passion in the life of the son, began in the courageous and noble maternity foreshadowing his character" (12, 14). Jesus, then, is the perfect woman, comforter and healer who means "a power in the world of men gentle as that of motherhood, strong as that of worship."[46]

Phelps's emphasis here on the importance of bodily and spiritual health is not just autobiographically important. It is of a piece with her vision of heaven. Ann Douglas's assessment to the contrary, Heaven is not just the ultimate refuge for a materialistic, consumer-oriented society. For Phelps, much like Stowe and Smith, heaven is the perfection of embodiment. She offers a vision of a body both corporeal and celestial, a heaven in which touch would still be a pleasure, and a celestial body would refer to a spiritualized corporeal form without sickness, sin, or misery.[47] She is writing about a religious body, a transformed sexual body, and she is eager to incorporate those simple and essential experiences – the pleasure of physical contact as it expresses love, the exuberance of healthy flesh, the satisfaction of hearty passions. Her vision of heaven is poignant with longing for the life-giving warmth of human intimacy, and as brave a reconciliation of body and spirit as those arising from the church that apparently gave her so little succor.

The utopian visions of perfected embodiment that characterize Phelps's writing are disturbingly offset by the unmistakable anger that is often

44 Elizabeth Stuart Phelps, *The Story of Jesus Christ: An Interpretation* (Boston: Houghton Mifflin, 1897), 157, 200, 387.
45 Some examples of the delicacy of Jesus: "flushed delicately" (95), "quick delicacy" (101), "delicate instincts" (103), "a delicate task" (112), his "delicate perception" of what it meant to be touched by humanity (162). His voice (167), hands (169), complexion (236), face (257), and lips (146, 212) and throat (384) are "delicate"; he demonstrates delicacy in his handling of the woman caught in adultery, or maybe a "delicate sturdiness" (201, 207); and he is received into heaven upon a "delicate" cloud (412).
46 Phelps, *The Story of Jesus Christ*, 12, 14, 347.
47 Elizabeth Stuart Phelps, *The Gates Ajar* (1868; reprint, Boston: Fields, Osgood, 1869), 117–19.

directed at ministers, for they and their office are unhappily related to the suffering of women. Phelps shares this antagonism with her homiletic sisters who, rightfully so, identified the minister as a key opponent to the spiritual and social equality of women. Gilbert and Gubar review several stories by women about "the tragic destruction of women's manuscripts and female literary aspirations by censorious male ministers" who were hostile to writing and speaking women, within the pulpit and without.[48] Writing women, often overtly defiant of the condescension used to keep them in their place, turned it back upon their tormentors. Ministers in these novels are unattractive, inhibitory to mature spiritual life, destroyers, persecutors, bumbling fools. They are *not* sexy, they are not even effective subjects of romance.

Ernest Helfenstein, the luckless clergyman of *Bertha and Lily*, spends a fair amount of time sitting around daydreaming and whining about his lack of professional energy. He is snobbish and critical of those around him, and he has to record irksome events at the parsonage as an incentive to duty. Yet he never manages to get anything done. He opposes Bertha's every move toward an enlightened gospel of social transformation, but fails to enact any program of his own. In short, "Ernest Helfenstein is but a milksop."[49] The minister in Caroline Chesebro's *The Children of Light: A Theme for the Time* (1853) is similarly weak and unadmirable. He has trouble maintaining his faith and accepts the assistance of the compassionate Vesta. But he accepts her love without returning it, preferring the arrested and childlike piety of another parishioner. Thus, the two women friends in this novel, Asia and Vesta, affirm their love for each other, and then proceed in their conjoined life ministry apart from the traditional patriarchal structures. In *St. Elmo,* the hero's fascinating Byronic apostasy is caused by the cruelty of the clergy. Reverend Hammond has raised St. Elmo with his own son, Murray. When St. Elmo goes to school, he entrusts the care of his fiancée, Agnes Hunt (a minister's daughter), to his beloved stepbrother. But he returns only to find that Agnes and Murray are secretly in love, and he overhears them ridiculing his love for her. St. Elmo duels with Murray and kills him, and so bitterness and evil enter his soul, all because of – and Evans makes sure we don't miss this— "a minister's daughter, a minister's son, a minister himself."[50]

Harriet Beecher Stowe is kinder to the ministry, but although her Samuel Hopkins of *The Minister's Wooing* is gentle and well-intentioned, he is also foolish and helpless. Margaret Deland writes with tolerance,

---

48 Gilbert and Gubar, *War of the Words,* 176.
49 Smith, *Bertha,* 166.
50 Augusta Jane Evans Wilson, *St. Elmo* (1867; reprint, New York: Grosset & Dunlap, 1896), 271.

but her later career also reflects a confidence that was culturally unavailable to those women writing closer to the middle of the nineteenth century. Her Dr. Lavendar of the Chester tales is a kind and tolerant spiritual leader who has little in common with the collection of weak and spiteful clergy that inhabit the fiction of the mid-nineteenth century.[51] The title character of *John Ward, Preacher* (1882), Deland's first novel, however, clearly belongs to the period of warfare under consideration here. John Ward is a hard-line Calvinist minister. Helen Jeffreys is religious, but not an ideologue, and finds the old doctrines of depravity and predestination abhorrent. They are an unlikely pair, but once smitten with the independent Helen, Ward decides it is his sacred duty to marry her and convert her. The relationship of the newlyweds reads like a translated seduction story, with the sorrowful Helen struggling against this attempted violation of her spiritual integrity. She thinks they can agree to disagree, but she is wrong, for Ward is a fanatic, "the perfect Presbyterian . . . , logical to the bitter end."[52] Ward insists that she must adopt his view or they cannot live together as husband and wife. He fails to carry his point with her, so he banishes her from the house, and she, seeking to respect his principles while not violating her own, agrees with this solution. The impasse is concluded with yet another ironic vindication. Ward sinks into a fatal illness, and Helen returns to his empty arms as a healing mother. There is no indication that she has relinquished her beliefs, but the dying man cherishes the hope that his death is "the climax of God's plan for her" (454). God's plan seems to have diverged from Ward's plan, however, for Helen is now free to enunciate the victorious conclusion of the war: that faith is not a matter of "holding certain dogmas; it is simply openness and readiness of heart to believe any truth which God may show" (459).

With rare exception, then, the collation of images of ministers remains distinctly unflattering. Fools, fanatics, oppressors of women – all the varying resonances of anger, determination, resignation, and despair that are covered by these portraits are distilled with terrible vehemence by Phelps, whose writing is pressed into deformity by the internal fury of its inspiration. A wayward daughter in "One of the Elect" (1869) is repulsed by a congregation and the timid minister, but the suffering

51 A very unusual minister appears in the story "Where the Laborers Are Few." Deland explores the longing and loneliness of three elderly women who befriend an injured acrobat who preaches in barrooms after getting the attention of the patrons by performing gymnastic exercises. One of the women, Jane, is ardent with an unnameable longing that is translated as her desire for him to be a proper minister. But Dr. Lavender encourages him in his unique ministry, and he takes to the road again. See *Old Chester Tales* (New York: Grosset & Dunlap, 1898), 225–64.
52 Margaret Deland, *John Ward, Preacher* (1882; reprint, Ridgewood, N.J.: Gregg, 1967), 188. Subsequent page citations in the text appear in parentheses.

Christ beckons her home and her last vision is of the Savior calling to his Magdalene, "most precious to him, whom he had bought with a great price." A story conveying a remarkable anticipation of the "nothing happened" atmosphere of minimalism is "His Relict" (1891). Obedience Binney marries ordinary, boring Eliakim Twig, who leads a dull career as a minister no one wants to hire. Obedience has but one source of dignity, which is her identity as Mrs. Eliakim Twig, and when he dies, she nourishes his memory, although even their only son is uninterested in his father, and visits her only on her deathbed. The flatness of the story acts as a pointed commentary upon the mediocrity of the ministry and the tragedy of ordinary women involved with the office who have no way or will to live as autonomous persons.[53]

In *The Gates Ajar,* the portrait is intensified. Reverend Bland's name says about all that is needed about his efficacy as a minister. He is in unsuccessful theological combat with Aunt Winifred, although he hasn't the wit to see the triumph of her viewpoint until tragedy visits his own household. His wife burns to death while rescuing their child from a household fire, and Bland's fearful and abstract God is no comfort to his grief. He burns his sermon on heaven and seeks the consolation of Aunt Winifred. Note here the necessary damage done to women before the arrogant male can be persuaded of the light. Although these novels can seem laughably melodramatic with their numerous and protracted death and weeping scenes, in fact, it is tragic and sobering that so many women writers saw the death of the heroine as either the persuasive instrument of last recourse, or (perhaps) as the only way out of an unwinnable war. Aunt Winifred, after all, dies shortly after converting Bland, her life's energies apparently too diminished for her to survive the effort of her witness.

The most excruciating and revelatory portrait of the clergy in Phelps appears in her study of ministerial martyrdom, *A Singular Life* (1894). This novel begins as a social gospel story about Emmanuel Bayard, son of Mary and Joseph Bayard, who is assigned a parish in a slum section of Boston because he preaches a simple gospel of repentance and love, and is not concerned with the finer points of the Trinity or predestination. Phelps launches him as a relatively sympathetic character – the poor, idealistic, struggling young minister who is in love with Helen, the daughter of his major professor. But the tone of Phelps's portrayal becomes more uneven as the novel progresses, until there is a noticeable difference between what she tells us to think about him and what she actually shows us about him. She tells us he is pure, idealistic, lovable,

53 "One of the Elect," in *Men, Women and Ghosts* (Boston: Fields, Osgood, 1869), 199; and "His Relict," in *Fourteen to One* (Boston: Houghton, Mifflin, 1891), 346–69.

cordial, compassionate, dedicated to his parish, a man longing for the companionship of Helen. But what she shows us is an arrogant, self-involved, self-righteous, snobbish man who carelessly and even cruelly uses the women around him to support his ministry.

Phelps's language is especially bizarre regarding his behavior toward his fiancée, Helen. Helen herself is ambiguously portrayed as idle, beautiful, intelligent, warm, hopeful, foolish, and shallow, as though Phelps could not decide whether she would be the supportive woman or the shallow society woman, so she gets to be both. One day Bayard and Helen go rowing, and she announces her admiration for him while professing her own unworthiness to say so. He seizes her hand, "warm, soft, quivering." "He could have devoured it – her – soul and body; he could have killed her with kisses, he could have murdered her with love."[54] He then returns to his rooms for a sexual Gethsemane, which proceeds as an internal military struggle between himself and the "forces of evil whose master he had been so long. . . . 'This is an insurrection of slaves,' he thought. . . . 'Down!' he said, as if he had been speaking to dogs" (275). He picks up his Bible, but is distracted by the dried flowers that fall from it, which he "seizes," "devours," kisses "passionately," as he "hungrily" searches for other evidences of Helen. Then he turns to the picture of Christ on his wall, crying, "Anything but this – everything but this – Thou knowest. . . . Only this – the love of man for woman – how canst Thou understand?" (276–7).

Again, here is a fine example of the indissoluble confluence of religious and sexual passion, for although it is unlikely that Phelps wished to suggest his problem was physical in any crude or literal sense referential to male anatomy, it is certainly possible to translate the sexual charge of the speech in precisely such a manner. Furthermore, he is left speechless and inarticulate by his passion, for one does not need words when the alternate energy is physical potency. The conjoint power given him by religious speech and physical desire overrules his initial reticence about his worthiness to claim her love, and he assumes her mastery. He "commands" Helen to tell him when she first loved him, and she "turned her head from side to side rebelliously, as if she had flown into a cage whose door was now unexpectedly shut. . . . His imperious voice fell to a depth of tenderness in which her soul and body seemed to drown" (339). In these few sentences, Phelps surfaces the latent violence of all her writing about ministers, and displays the damage – spiritual cannibalism, imprisonment, death, murder by love – the spiritual and physical destruction of women at the hands of their jailers.

---

54 Elizabeth Stuart Phelps, *A Singular Life* (1895; reprint, Boston: Houghton, Mifflin, 1896), 271. Subsequent page citations in the text appear in parentheses.

Not surprisingly, *A Singular Life* moves toward a resolution congruent with its intense and cross-purposed presentation. Bayard can marry Helen after all, and in anticipation of the nuptials, she resumes the role of the supportive woman. But Bayard has made enemies because of his anti-alcohol stance, and on the day of dedication of the new chapel he is felled by a stone on the church steps. Like some eerie prophetic vision of modern assassinations, Helen sees him transfigured, sees him struck down, and she accompanies him to a nearby town for medical care. As they embark, there is a flash of red light that illuminates his face turned toward her and stains her white bridal dress crimson so that they are both drenched in this symbolic sacrificial blood (415–16). Helen watches ceaselessly at his bedside, and he becomes progressively stronger. But when she succumbs to fatigue and sleeps, he dies. Was he too good to live, or too cruel to live? Is he alive only when a female audience is watching? Did he die because Helen was faithless to her watch or because it was the only way for Helen to be free?

The punishing rage for and against women, that same rage for and against the male minister evident in Phelps, is visible in all the homiletic writers.[55] Bertha's female antagonist in *Bertha and Lily* is a nagging unimaginative housewife named Defiance. Stowe inveighs against useless vain women in *Pink and White Tyranny* and *The Minister's Wooing*. The sick universe Phelps creates in *Walled In* (1907) features a vain, independent wife (Tessa), a paralyzed man (Myrton, who is like a "mummy," a punning sign of his impotence?), and a rescuing angel, Honoria. Tessa bears the invective of the novel, but conveniently dies, leaving Honoria to spurn an able-bodied lover in order marry Myrton, because she'd rather have someone helpless to wait on as a life's vocation. The conclusion of the novel presents us with a view of heaven as a place where damaged men are waited upon by smug and smothering women – quite a contrast with the peaceful and independent afterlife Phelps imagines for women in the *Gates* series.

The seemingly tranquil waters of Stowe's orderly domestic universe, the serene vision of Bertha for a new social order, the warmth and peace of Aunt Winifred's heaven – all spring from the riptides of dramatic and violent fantasies about death and suffering. These damaging psychic currents come to the surface in the language of imprisonment, drowning, death, wounds, bleeding, sacrifice, suffering – the language of religious passion. This is a language so extravagant, however, as to have become a cultural silence because the outward events of a nineteenth-century woman's life do not seem commensurate with the suffering she says she

---

55 Gilbert and Gubar in *The War of the Words*, have named this ambivalence of women writers toward women the "female affiliation complex." See pp. 168–207.

endured. Phelps, Stowe, Smith, and many others like them tell us that women suffered. They show us the damage done in the helter-skelter energy of the violent and contradictory solutions they create for their confinement. Writing fiction may serve as a way of verbalizing and therefore controlling the disruptive life of the mind, and violent fantasies are often an expression, not of longing for the event, but of the despair and anger of helplessness turned inward.

The parallels between this report and the experiences of a rape victim are not incidental, for this fiction created from the pain of their experience turns as much punishment upon themselves (and other women) as upon their persecutors. Not surprisingly, then, homiletic fiction functions as a displaced seduction narrative, for religious and sexual passion do not disengage so easily as the homiletic writers would have willed. In most of these novels, there is a seduction story in the plot, perhaps in the heroine's past, perhaps regarding a dear friend, but as noted at the beginning of the chapter, the minister is never the seducer in this fiction. Yet the anger and self-loathing of these writers is directly connected to the minister as if he, in fact, were the literal seducer. Because, of course, sometimes he was. Furthermore, his was a seduction more egregious than any other possible, for he presumed not only upon her body, but upon her very soul.[56]

The Thinking Heart

The theological disputes between women and the clergy in these novels are the climax and final evidence of this war of words. The battle is both sexual and religious, but the merits of the women's confinement are also engaged on intellectual and theological grounds. Writing women took the war to high ground, the enemy's territory of words, discourse, and preaching. In all of these fictions, the spiritually autonomous woman defines her right to interpret or ignore the Bible relative to her own inner integrity and she claims her right to speak and write authoritatively, in public and in church, upon all such matters. In particular, she speaks out against the oppression of male-created theological systems, and she identifies these systems as the source of her suffering. The cold, rational language of patriarchal systems is damaging, invasive, killing. Male theological language, like sexuality, is the language of powerlessness for women. So they created their own, first by demonstrating their ability to engage on traditional territory and then by offering an alternative to the unacceptable tongue.

Smith's Bertha attributes the dullness of clergy preaching to the fact

---

56 In a sense, all of these novels involve a spiritual seduction. Deland's *John Ward, Preacher* makes this connection explicit, as does the singular *Esther* (1884) by Henry Adams.

that "the mind is bent to solely establish and elucidate old dogmas" (32). Furthermore, if the Bible sanctions such evils as slavery, orphanages, or prohibitions against female preaching, then "it has ceased to be a truth to us. We are beyond it in human justice and mercy, and must cast it aside as an obsolete letter" (42). She has examined all the old doctrines, studied the scripture, consulted her heart, and begins her ministry confident in her repudiation of all the prejudice and smallness that characterize the systems of men. In particular, what characterizes the integrity of Bertha's theology is its source in her purified woman's heart, the thinking heart that is not the antithesis of intellect, but the crown.

That is – and this is a crucial clarification – these women do not scorn the process of reason and intellect; they scorn a *disembodied* process of reason and intellect. Their agreement on this union is universal. As Marion Harland's heroine asserts, only men may enjoy the exercise that is purely of intellect, but in doing so, the heart is dwarfed, whereas "in woman, intellect and the affections are united from their birth."[57] To think from the heart means to think with the whole body, intellect and affect united in the highest form of apprehension. Unfortunately, this harmonious quality of being has been degraded and scorned by men, who claim the higher function by virtue of their operation of disembodied intellect, a process untempered by the warmth of human emotion, and therein springs the enslavement of the gentler female creature.

Harriet Beecher Stowe takes up this theme of the cruelty of man-made theological systems so consistently in her writing that if there is anything to be identified as her province beyond her testimony against slavery, it is this. *Uncle Tom's Cabin,* a triumph of homiletic fiction, is given its distinctive character by this critique of rational, intellectual man-made systems. In this novel Stowe repeatedly quotes scripture against the legal and religious systems that perpetuate slavery, and women and Negroes, inhabiting a similar natural and (therefore) spiritual space, are the most successful missionaries to the sinful slave system. In *Oldtown Folks,* Stowe says that children were like shuttlecocks being whacked about between Arminian and Calvinistic theologies until they were, religiously speaking, quite dizzy. Worse yet, these systems were constructed without consultation with woman's nature. "Theological systems, as to the expression of the great body of ideas, have, as yet, been the work of man alone. They have had their origin, as in St. Augustine, with men who were utterly ignorant of moral and intellectual companionship with woman, looking on her only in her animal nature as a temptation and a snare. Consequently, when, as in this period of New England, the theology of Augustine began to be freely discussed by every individual in

57 Harland, *Alone,* 222.

society, it was the women who found it hardest to tolerate or to assimilate it." Many women, she proceeds, "half refined to angel in their nature," found themselves torn between their stern intellectual training and ancestry and the "exquisite moral perceptions" of female nature, and so "many a delicate and sensitive nature was utterly wrecked in the struggle."[58]

The Minister's Wooing prosecutes this same argument with vigor. Women may feel free to interpret the Bible unencumbered with patriarchal expectations and doctrines because a woman's heart and the Bible are the same kind of text. Both must live under the reign of man's theological system building, and both are damaged by that weight. These systems have the "effect of a slow poison, producing life habits of morbid action very different from any which ever followed the simple reading of the Bible." Under the "anatomical demonstrator" of theological systems, the living embrace of the friendly New Testament becomes a lifeless body, invaded by "the chill of death in the analysis" (339). Tragically, men never see the damage done, for they are too busy tinkering with minute abstractions to consider the life laboring beneath those abstractions. "But where theorists and philosophers tread with sublime assurance, woman often follows with bleeding footsteps; – women are always turning from the abstract to the individual, and feeling where the philosopher only thinks" (25).

Men, on the one hand, pursue the intellectual and rational aspects of religion, which are wrongly – and arrogantly – taken by them to be the sum of significant religious experience. Women, on the other hand, resist "the chill of analysis as a healthful human heart resists cold" (289). Heart here is not operative apart from mind; rather, it is the source of all thought, for "intellections all begin in the heart, which send them colored with its warm life into the brain" (342). The good news, then, is that although the Bible may be helpless before the ruthless dissections that have passed for theology in the androcentric world, it may be restored when translated through the warmth of a woman's heart. Under that condition, the Bible is always more effective than "sharp-sided intellectual propositions. . . . So one verse in the Bible read by a mother in some hour of tender prayer has a significance deeper and higher than the most elaborate of sermons, the most acute of arguments" (396). Stowe is willing to give men credit for the possibility of this complete humanity already possessed by women. The abstracted Dr. Hopkins, after all, is so moved by the simple, heartfelt testimony of Mary's lover, James, he is unable to see his examining notes for his tears, and James is confirmed for church membership without ever having to display his reverence for

58 Stowe, *Oldtown*, 456.

the awful doctrines of Calvinism. So much for the coolness of logic in religion.

Phelps, with much more ambivalence and much less conviction, tries to create male characters with female hearts. Emmanual Bayard is one such effort; so is Reverend Malachi Matthew in the story named for him in *Fourteen to One* (1891), and so is, for that matter, her loving portrait of Jesus Christ. None of these male characters survive their own alleged tenderness, and it is more common for Phelps to examine the consequences of androcentric theology upon women. All the *Gates* books are dedicated to the illustration of the difference between intellect and the thinking heart of woman. Mary Cabot finds church, with its useless abstractions about heaven and universal love, a real impediment to worship and spiritual comfort. Aunt Winifred's competition with Reverend Bland proceeds as a contest between intellect and the thinking heart, or in translation, between the letter of the law and the logos of the heart. As with all other such homiletic heroines, Winifred doesn't hesitate to trust her own reading of scripture even when she is reading its silences, for "the mystery of the Bible lies not so much in what it says as in what it does not say."[59] Therefore, she lives in unshaken assurance of her meditations on heaven, for her knowledge is verified by her own longing, her own experience of the gospel promise.

The most elegant treatment of this essential theme of women's homiletic fiction appears in Margaret Deland's first novel, *John Ward, Preacher.* Deland is not a familiar name in American literary history, but she should be. She maintained a lifelong interest in social issues, especially as they affected women, but she refused to sacrifice her sense of complexity for the expedience of ideological purity. Deland routinely offered her home to unwed mothers in order to give them another chance, and her writing reflects the many facets of experience this charity afforded her. Her concern for the integrity of the human soul and the quality of human life and her lively interest in the process of moral growth and decision making, especially as such matters affected women and children, would make her novels interesting even aside from her literary gifts.

As noted earlier, Deland's writing career is later, both chronologically and culturally in relationship to Stowe, Phelps, and Smith, and her portrayal of the warring of the law and the spirit, the female heart and male mind, benefits from the distance. Her investment in the issues is undisguised, but her rendering is surer, kinder, more sorrowful than angry. Again, the terms of the war appear as a battle between the letter of the law (John Ward and the logical bitterness of Calvinism) and the spirit of the law (Helen Ward and the warmth of the human heart). She argues

59 *Gates Ajar*, 93.

the priority of love, while Ward, who could have been a model for Carol Gilligan's principle-driven male, argues the priority of doctrine.[60] The difference between them is demonstrated by their treatment of the widow of an alcoholic. Helen is concerned for the woman's grief for her husband, and how she will feed her family now that he is gone. John is concerned for the man's soul, and refuses the widow the consolation of thinking her husband might have been saved. Helen is appalled that John would tell the stricken woman that her unsanctified husband is likely suffering the torments of hell, and regarding John's doctrine of predestination and damnation, says, "I should be ashamed to be saved if there were so many lost" (252).

Perhaps surprisingly, Deland does not make John out to be a monster, for she also takes care to show his genuine compassion for human suffering as well as his own heroic efforts at self-honesty. He suspects that he loves Helen better than he loves God, suspects that he wants her salvation for himself, and not the higher purpose he claims, and in order to thwart his own selfishness, he devises the plan of sending her away, thinking that their mutual suffering may conclude their dispute. He is also compared with Helen's uncle, the rector of Ashurst, Dr. Howe, in both favorable and unfavorable ways, demonstrative of Deland's sense of the complexity of the stakes. The rector is a pleasant man who has never been terribly troubled by theological perplexity and so fails to grasp the issues at hand. At the same time, his easygoing acceptance of life also yields him an honest doubt, lending itself to genuine compassion. Dr. Howe must visit his old friend Mr. Denner and prepare him for his death, and he doesn't know what to say. With dignity and courage, Denner helps him out, requesting that he be allowed to meet his death with a simple conversation about the afterlife without religious jargon. Reduced to personal witness, the rector speaks honestly and haltingly, admitting what he doesn't know, refusing to say what he doesn't believe. Denner responds by talking about his own beliefs, and then they sit together, hands clasped in wordless tranquility (339). This sort of religious encounter would be impossible for John Ward, whose principles will always drive him to place priority on the theological condition of a soul (the abstract) rather than the need of the dying man for the reassuring intimacy of human companionship and love (the personal).

Helen is told that it is "unfeminine for a woman to think" (193, 405), and her father thinks she should stop bothering her little head over

---

60 I refer here to sociologist Carol Gilligan's much-debated thesis that the process of ethical decision making is a gender-determined characteristic in which men tend to apply fixed principles to every situation, no matter what the variables involved. See *In a Different Voice: Psychological Theory and Women's Development* (Cambridge, Mass.: Harvard University Press, 1982).

theological questions (85, 191), but Deland is clearly not sympathetic to this view. The book takes for granted the necessary concern of women for such issues. Helen is an admirable woman who will not be bullied into professing a belief she does not respect. At the same time, both she and John will suffer, not because she is meddling in matters too deep for her, but because they are both so principled in their inflexibility. Nonetheless, the victory is hers, tempered though it may be with sorrow, for the law-tormented intellect of John Ward cannot live without her.

Deland's account of the war of words rehearses the simultaneity of discourse and sexuality, power and preaching, body and spirit that so troubles the homiletic writers. John is determined to possess Helen's spiritual capitulation and so proceeds with yet another enactment of the tyranny of love the nineteenth-century writing woman knew so well. By situating the debate concerning head/heart/law/spirit within the context of a marriage rather than a courtship, Deland softens the literal sexual implications of the struggle without diminishing the emotional impact of the power struggle that defines so much of heterosexual encounter.

The novel bears much of the impress of its nineteenth-century context – there is the requisite romantic subplot involving two other characters, for example – but for the first time we also see an affirmation of love, not charity, condescension, worship, or pity, between women and men. Although the terms of the relationship between John and Helen are odd, Deland convinces us that, given who he is, John Ward really does love his wife, that he has correctly identified his own sin relative to a Calvinistic universe (loving her and his own happiness more than God), and that Helen returns and understands his love. Helen does not undergo a conversion after John's death and she makes no false promises to his memory. But she does promise to love him always, for "the only thing which makes life possible is love, because that is the only thing that does not change" (460). As a mature writer, Deland will modify her assertion about the unchangingness of human love, but she will also affirm its physical consequences. The sexual and sensual as components of heterosexual love are only hinted at in *John Ward,* but Deland's later novels demonstrate a profound appreciation for the sensual beauty of the body with all the mixed blessings of pain and happiness that may involve.[61]

For Deland, theological and social issues between women and men remain, but they are not represented by the polarity of minister and his female congregant. That time is passing, and with Ellen Glasgow, Deland's writing marks an important, if evanescent, literary moment – a

---

61 Two fine Deland novels that ought to be better known are the sequential histories of moral development in *The Awakening of Helena Richey* (New York: Harper & Row, 1905) and *The Iron Woman* (New York: Harper & Brothers, 1910).

time when the brightness of spirit is forged from hope and suffering rather than despair and suffering.

Seeking the Radiance in Vein of Iron

Ellen Glasgow's *Vein of Iron* (1935) takes up the same tension between male reason and the mystic female heart, and like the novels of the homiletic writers, features a minister as the champion of the rational, systematic life and a woman as the embodied, thinking heart. John Fincastle is a minister whose pursuit of systematic thought has unchurched him. This, says Glasgow's writing, is the conclusion of the systematics protested nearly a century before by Harriet Beecher Stowe – the lonely champion of a disembodied truth that is admirable in its principle but pathetic in its consequences.

Fincastle ekes out a living as a schoolteacher and works on his philosophy book into the early morning hours. Like Stowe's Samuel Hopkins of nearly a century earlier, his private work proceeds because of the women of his household (wife, daughter, mother, sister) who provide the structure and continuity that permit him to disappear into his search for truth. The counterpoint for his abstracted rationality is his daughter Ada, the practical, passionate mystic with the "vein of iron." When her fiancé, Ralph, is implicated in the pregnancy of another girl, Ada's father insists Ralph marry the girl. Protesting his innocence, Ralph nevertheless submits to "the law of the tribe" and the "wrath of God," which demands atonement.[62] Her fiancé is "sacrificed to a tradition in which he did not even believe," and her father is "a martyr to truth but it was his own truth, not hers" (143–4). Ada has a different truth because of her mother, who taught her that "it is only in the heart . . . that anything really happens" (170).

Ada's heart/word is defiant of theistic religion, and despite her own pain of betrayal, she repudiates any religion that suggests her suffering is necessary to a divine plan. "Ralph's will had been broken and his life ruined because his mother had . . . found a thrill of cruelty in the Christian symbols of crucifixion and atonement . . . had discovered that salvation was better than happiness" (210, 211). Although she rejects a theology of female suffering, Ada follows the faint path carved by her homiletic foresisters, for she finds no consolation in traditional Christian doctrines. In fact, her insistence upon the authority of her own heart encourages her to abandon any necessity of God whatsoever. "Resignation to the will of the Lord was the one thing more that would drive her wild" (131). Ada's assurance of her own integrity of experience derives from

62 Ellen Glasgow, *Vein of Iron* (1935; reprint New York: Harbrace Paperback, 1963). Subsequent page citations in the text appear in parentheses.

the thinking heart, and it is the prompting of this inner mind that urges her to seek for the radiance she once knew as a girl.

Radiance is a recurrent word in *Vein of Iron*, the immortality of the heart that lights the body from within, a reembodiment, not a disembodiment. Ada knows such radiance briefly with Ralph, when they are reunited after his marriage dissolves and before he goes to war. Again, the physical impact of language is underlined. Ralph, who has been betrayed by false words into an unhappy first marriage, has "hated words as long as words had been weapons of conflict and treachery. But with her, while they strove to reach each other through the veils of the flesh, while they sought with passionate tenderness the reality within realities, words had become as natural and as unguarded as impulses" (186). In this, words are reembodied, speech and sexuality both a natural token of the marriage of spirits in an embodied context.

The "reality within realities" is the radiance of the spirit, different from, but not apart from, the joy of flesh. The world, sometimes so obdurate and forbidding in its solidity, can also become transparent with this inner light. "All his life" John Fincastle "had obeyed reason" but as the certainty of his death nears he is "controlled by some faculty deeper, stronger, wiser, than the power he had called reason" (389). He marshals his waning energy to leave the city where wartime necessity has driven the family in order to return home to God's Mountain. "The power of speech, as he had once known speech, had deserted him" and he knows that with his dying the reality of logic and reason is being resolved into "the only element that endures . . . , the natural speech of the heart" (372). "Pure philosophy," he discovers, "is a wordless thing."

Hearing the speech of the heart, the eloquent silences of an inner logos, gives him the passion necessary to journey home. Even before he leaves the city, the world has worn so thin he can "see through it" (388). When he reaches God's Mountain he finds the earth shimmering with the energy that answers his own guttering spirit. "Spring was running in a thin green flame over the Valley . . . luminous patches of green and blue sprinkled the earth" (396), and God's Mountain, huge, yet no more than a hummock, floats upon the radiance, fully transparent with the unity of "world and life. . . . Every dandelion, every clover-leaf, every pointed blade of grass, stood out in a spear of light that would melt at a breath, at a touch, at a whisper. Was this vision the reality? Not brick and mortar, stone and iron, but this vision?" (400).

John Fincastle, minister, systematic philosopher, encounters at his death natural speech in the heartbeat of the material world. This is the language Ada has heard, nurtured, and been nurtured by all her life, by the generations of Fincastle women. "Her smoky blue eyes, so like her mother's in expression as she grew older, held the darkened radiance that

proceeds from within outward" (264). That is why she, always passionately embodied, fluent in the logos of the thinking heart, is the one with
the vein of iron. Neither her father nor her husband is capable of living
as part of the world as she can, and *Vein of Iron* is the story of how they
borrow the radiance from her even as she is learning to cherish it. The
blue bowl once belonging to her mother is the simple, solid symbol of
the embodied light of spirit, and it is Ada's one valuable possession
linking her to the strength of family women. Even when they have sold
all valuables for rent and food money, "the blue bowl, which had ac-
quired an ethereal value, as if it were the symbol of some precious bowl
of the spirit, stood in its old place and shone with the radiance of firelight"
(324).

Simple, circular symbol of heart, logos and light together, the blue
bowl reminds us of the commitment of the homiletic women to the
speech of the heart that calls us home. It represents the "invisible network
of affection and security" that was so important to the homiletic writers
as they strove to tell us why the thinking heart of women represented
the better vision of spiritual happiness within the embodied life. The
tentative reembodiment of mind and spirit that is begun by Stowe, Smith,
and Phelps is claimed and strengthened in later writers like Margaret
Deland and Ellen Glasgow. From the transfiguration of Mary Scudder
or the glowing fingertips of Bertha to the darkened radiance of a bowl
and the bodies of women, the homiletic writers demonstrate the common
sympathy of their efforts to claim their own language and then their own
bodies. The two – bodies and speech – are inextricably linked, just as
they are for male characters and authors in novels about the ministry,
and as they will be for the contemporary male writer, striving within
the longed-for imprisonment of natural circles (Chapter 6).

Deland and Glasgow clarify and deepen the sermonic polemic inherited
from the earlier writers, but their writing is not ravaged by the same
kind of internal fury, nor do they report the same sense of confinement
and suffering. They take for granted the spiritual and physical authority
of women in a way that was not possible for the homiletic writers, who,
desperate to be heard, wrote as through a literary megaphone. Having
learned to mistrust received words, even the Word, they tried to create
their own, arguing the superior logos of the thinking heart. They understood the double charge of holy speech, the use of words created and
conveyed by passion. They knew the physical impact of language as part
of their own confinement, and so they knew how important it was to
own it. Thus, when the dead, dismayed Dr. Esmeralde Thorne (*The
Gates Between*) finally realizes he squandered his life in self-importance,
he yearns to return to earth as a witnessing spirit, to show families that
angry words in the home are "as degrading as a blow." He would replace

the irritations and strife of daily communication with "the sacred graces of human speech. I wished to emphasize the opportunity of those who love each other. I groaned within me till I might teach the preciousness and poignancy of *words*" (author's emphasis).[63]

There are words here for the Elizabeth Tiltons of this world, although not the direct communication we might have hoped for. Their understanding of the invasiveness and alienation of male systematics and their knowledge of the reciprocity and power of words and body led the homiletic writers to create models of female religious authority. By urging women to be their own spiritual mentors they suggested a lonely but courageous protection for one such as Elizabeth Tilton. The ambivalence, anger, and fear of the homiletic writers is clear, as well as the literary hazards of writing from such pain. Their confinement and suffering were inevitably damaging. But they were preaching, not just writing, speaking, not just hearing, creating, and acting against the culture of passivity and victimization that was their religious inheritance.

They told the truth about their embodied experience by engaging their tormentors in the only public territory available – religious speech in the novel. They may have sacrificed literary felicity to theological necessity, but they also created a unique literary legacy, a theological literature that should have had a respectable place in the halls of American literary-religious history. Like Dr. Thorne of *The Gates Between*, they labored to teach the preciousness and poignancy of words. That they have been so readily dismissed – usually on grounds incidental to their purpose and achievement, usually by those approaching these texts with a prepared hostility – confirms their own report of suffering under cultural silence, confirms the necessity of daring to create their own literary language in their efforts to be heard.

63 Elizabeth Stuart Phelps, *The Gates Between* (Boston: Houghton, Mifflin, 1887), 214.

5

Comfort to the Enemy:
Women Write about the Ministry.
The Parsonage Romance

On December 21, 1832, the frozen body of Sarah Maria Cornell was found hanging at Durfee's farm, near Fall River, Rhode Island. Her cloak was "hooked down before and her hands under it, her knees within four inches of the ground, and her clothes smoothed under them." There was a cord imbedded in her neck and her tongue protruded from her swollen lips. Those who prepared her body for burial found "marks of violence" about her person – bruises on her hips, back, knees and face, and a broken arm. Still, the death was ruled a suicide, and she was buried. But after letters to her that incriminated a local minister were discovered with her belongings, her body was disinterred and reexamined. Physicians concluded that she had been strangled prior to being hung, and that she had been pregnant. Shortly thereafter, Rev. Ephraim K. Avery was charged with her murder.[1]

---

1 Catherine Read Arnold Williams, *Fall River: An Authentic Narrative* (Boston: Marshall, Brown, 1834), 27–35. Subsequent citations in the text appear in parentheses.
   Mary Orne Tucker, in *Itinerant Preaching in the Early Days of Methodism, by a Pioneer Preacher's Wife* (Boston: B.B. Russell, 1872), says of the Avery trial: "The whole country was painfully agitated by the arrest and trial of E. K. Avery, a well known Methodist preacher, for the murder of Sarah M. Cornell. We were well acquainted with Mr. Avery and his previous good character; we also knew the wretched girl for whose supposed murder he was tried for his life. She had been a member of Mr. Tucker's congregation, and was well known to our brethren and sisters in Rhode Island. She was a bold, bad woman, and capable of committing any crime; yet Mr. Avery's relations to her, and the unexplained mystery of her fearful death, environed his character in a sombre cloud which was never fully dispelled. The affair was a sad blow to our church at the time, and was keenly felt, particularly by his ministerial brethren" (89–90).
   Fall River Outrage: Life, Murder and Justice in Early Industrial New England (Philadelphia: University of Pennsylvania Press, 1986) by David Kasserman provides an exhaustive account of trial particulars, but no clear verdict about Avery. David Reynolds mentions Williams's *Fall River* in *Faith in Fiction: The Emergence of Religious Literature in America, 1785–1850* (Cambridge, Mass.: Harvard University Press, 1981) as "sensational satire," but his brief plot summary is grossly inaccurate. Otherwise, I find no mention of Williams or the Avery murder trial in any standard account of American revivalism or American religious history.

141

These and subsequent events are recorded in *Fall River: An Authentic Narrative* (1834). The author, Catherine Read Arnold Williams (1787–1872) is one of the very few writing women to address the problem of clergy seductions, and her candid entry is all the more remarkable for its early nineteenth-century date. Williams was a poet and historian, and in *Fall River* she applied herself to recording a particularly sordid portion of New England history, the alleged murder of Sarah Maria Cornell (1802–32) by the Reverend Ephraim K. Avery (d. 1869). She writes for the explicit purpose of warning young women "against that idolatrous regard for ministers . . . , which at the present day is a scandal to the cause of Christianity" (vi).

Sarah Maria Cornell was an itinerant textile worker in the mills that were common in industrial New England. She was, in Williams's words, "a moving planet" (46), and an avid follower of camp meetings. Based upon her reading of Cornell's letters and her restless and nomadic existence, Williams shrewdly assesses Cornell's religious devotion as a

> religion of feelings and frames. Though there is no doubt it was sincere, yet it was of the unstable kind that is most apt to fail when most needed. She had engaged in it in a time of high excitement, and its existence was preserved – while it was preserved – by constant application of the means which created it, viz: by frequent attendance on those exciting meetings where highly wrought feeling and sometimes hysterial affection is often mistaken for devotion. (85–6)

In early October of 1832 the thirty-year-old Cornell sought the assistance of a physician, who was horrified to find his client unmarried, and pregnant by a married, Methodist minister. The doctor insisted that if she would not ask Avery to acknowledge her, she must at least demand some financial assistance from him. One brief meeting between Cornell and Avery concluded with Avery's offer of a potion "to prevent future trouble and expense, and at once obliterate the effects of their connexion." The potion was oil of tansy, which, according to the physician, "was one of such deadly effect that she would probably have expired on the spot had she taken it" (24), and the doctor advised her against any other private meetings with Avery. Cornell saved the letters exchanged between herself and Avery (whom she addressed as "Betsy Hill"), together with a message: "If I am missing enquire of the Rev. E. K. Avery" (31).

Although there is much that is not clear about the events of Cornell's death, Williams's account of the trial indicates that Avery's congregation

---

Two recent novels are based on the events of Fall River. *Avery's Knot* (New York: G.P. Putnam Sons, 1981) by Mary Cable stays close to historical particulars, and is largely sympathetic to Sarah Cornell, whereas Raymond Paul's *The Tragedy at Tiverton* (New York: Viking, 1984) takes more liberty with the story while portraying Cornell as a nineteenth-century Pandora who seduced helpless men.

performed as well for him as Beecher's would do on his account decades later. Their perjured evidence turned "public indignation from the murderer, whoever he might be, to the person murdered," and the deceased was convicted of being "utterly bad, capable of any sort of wickedness" (68). After a four-week trial, Avery was found "not guilty" and his congregation "pronounced him perfectly innocent, and freed from all suspicion, and continued him in the service of his office" (71).

Williams's account is fascinating simply as a record of what life must have been like for the newly emerging class of mill workers in industrializing America. But aside from this, her narrative, despite its omissions, is also a keen analysis of the dysfunctions of religion and sexuality. Although Williams tends to emphasize Cornell's virtues, she does not portray Cornell as a total innocent, but sees her as luckless and foolish, the victim of her own religious immaturity, her rudderless existence, *and* the overweening power of the ministry. Williams indignantly protests the postmortem character assassination that was performed upon Cornell, and she writes to challenge the efficacy of orchestrated revival hysteria, and to expose the abuse of power in which ministers and congregations may conspire together.

The story of Cornell and Avery stands as a brutal reminder of the underbelly of the parsonage romance that succeeds the homiletic novel. The jury of Fall River found it easier to believe ill of Cornell than of the minister, and the same is true of all the romance writers. Without exception, what characterizes the parsonage romance is the proclamation of clergy innocence and female culpability, no matter what the circumstance. Indeed, the contrast between the mid-nineteenth-century writings on behalf of women's religious authority and dignity and the novels that succeed them is astonishing. For example, writing in the lamentational voice, Corra May White Harris tells the story of *The Circuit Rider's Wife* (1910), a series of episodic narratives in which the fictitious Mary Thompson reflects upon the cultural and material poverty endemic to the life of rural (Methodist) ministry. We see her husband, William, through her eyes.

Like the earlier lamentational writers, Harris is in sympathy with the minister's wife, and not always greatly admiring of the male minister's accommodations to professional pressures. Many of the problems – poverty still chief among them – remain the same. Unlike her nineteenth-century foresisters, however, Harris directly addresses the vocational dynamics between a male minister and certain types of female congregants:

> When we hear of a minister who has disgraced himself with some female member of his flock, my sympathies are all with the preacher. I know

exactly what has happened. Some sad lady who has been "awakened" by his sermons goes to see him in his church study. First she tells him she is "unhappy at home,"... finally [she] confesses she is troubled with "temptations...." He sees her reduced to tears over her would-be transgressions, and before he considers what he is about he has kissed the "dear child." That is the way it happens nine times out of ten, a good man damned and lost by some frail angel of his church. A minister is always justified in suspecting the worst of a pretty woman who wants to consult him privately about her soul, whether she has sense enough to suspect herself or not.[2]

This passage is important first simply because Harris is able to address the problem of ministers and sex without subterfuge. She does not assume the reading public will be shocked by this discussion. On the contrary, she assumes common knowledge of such events in that first sentence: "When we hear of a minister who has disgraced himself with some female member of his flock," and her comments are a clear and forceful judgment of the situation. Herein lies the second important point. Her judgment reverses the labor of the homiletic writers.

Harris disperses blame for this possible vocational dysfunction toward two parties – idle parish women, or, indirectly, the minister's wife herself. In the case of the latter, the "preacher's wife who does not cultivate the wisdom of a serpent and [the]...harmlessness of the dove...in protecting him from such women...may have a damaged priest on her hands before she knows it." The wife is responsible for protecting him from the sexual politics of his vocation, and an incompetent wife may be the cause of his downfall. In the case of the former, Harris is unequivocal. The minister is a sitting duck for unscrupulous women, and the depth of her anger can be measured by her remedy. Harris says that there ought to be a new set of civil laws that would apply to the "worst class of criminals in society...the real rotters of honor and destroyers of salvation." Such laws would give us a new kind of population in penitentiaries, by which she means "the women who make a religion of sneaking up on the blind male side of good men, without a thought for the consequences."[3]

Harris's comments clarify the reemergence of the patriarchal norm, away from the homiletic apology for women, toward the romance apology for ministers. In the romance writer, the lamentations for the minister's wife and the exalted narrative sermonizing of the homiletics are inverted by a mirror image narrative in which the minister is the ever innocent subject of parsonage romance. The singularity of the homiletic

2 Corra May White Harris, *A Circuit Rider's Wife* (Philadelphia: Henry Altemus, 1910), 163–70.
3 Ibid., 169–70.

achievement stands out clearly when we realize that Harris is writing about the same "problem" as was Williams when she took up her pen on behalf of Cornell more than 80 years before. The sexual politics of the ministry is a recognized, long-standing dilemma, but Williams, allied with the homiletic writers, gives the problem to the institution, the officeholder, and the woman; Harris, like her romance-writing contemporaries, gives the problem exclusively to women.

Defining Romance and the Parsonage Novel

The shift in fictional perspective from homiletic advocacy to the parsonage romance begins in the late nineteenth century and lasts well into the late 1940s. The parsonage romances are part of the growing wedge of female-authored narratives written with women in mind, having far more in common with the romance novels associated with contemporary popular culture today than they do with the "women's fiction" described by Nina Baym. The contemporary use of the term "romance" provides an important interpretive paradigm in relation to these novels.

The tradition of romance in popular literature may be traced back to such classics as Margaret Mitchell's *Gone With the Wind* (1936) and Daphne du Maurier's *Rebecca* (1938), but the designation as a term of aesthetic opprobrium is more properly located with the first wave of mass-marketed romances introduced in 1957 by Harlequin, now almost a generic term for this kind of writing.[4] The Harlequin romances are courtship narratives featuring adventuresome but virginal women in a relationship with a mysterious, cruel, but ultimately accessible and protecting male who always proposes at the end. Sexual tension is exploited but not explicitly enacted until the singular kiss that inevitably seals the story. Romance in this sense has little to do with classical forms of yearning and tragedy. Rather, the tradition of romance – more often than not female-authored – involves the development of a highly idealized love relationship between a man and a woman, in which love is "triumphant and permanent, overcoming all obstacles and difficulties."[5] There is a fairly rigid formula for romance fiction involving stages of encounter and unrecognized love, misunderstanding (by the heroine about the hero), cruelty (by the hero toward the heroine), and peril, rescue, and

---

4 My summary discussion of the roots of the romance novel is drawn from Tania Modleski, *Loving with a Vengeance: Mass Produced Fantasies for Women* (Hamden, Conn.: Archon, 1982); Janice Radway, *Reading the Romance: Women, Patriarchy and Popular Literature* (Chapel Hill: University of North Carolina Press, 1984); and Carol Thurston, *The Romance Revolution: Erotic Novels for Women and the Quest for a New Sexual Identity* (Urbana: University of Illinois Press, 1987).

5 John Cawelti, *Adventure, Mystery and Romance: Formula Stories as Art and Popular Culture* (Chicago: University of Chicago Press, 1976), 41–2.

resolution (marriage). In the 1970s the basic formula was revitalized by the exploitation and expansion of the covert eroticism of the romance, so much so that Ann Douglas has referred to the second wave as "soft core porn."[6] Yet the lingering and detailed exposition of sexual encounter in the "bodice-rippers" of the past two decades does not change the essential structure and function of romance.

Janice Radway argues that in important ways the romance is an "exploration of the meaning of patriarchy for women" who are unconscious of this structure as a normative condition of their lives or who do not care to challenge its parameters.[7] A happy ending is a requirement for a "good" romance, and the formula assures the reader that "when properly interpreted, masculinity implies only good things for women" (168). Romances with ambiguous or less than happy endings are "bad" because they "fail to convince the reader that traditional sexual arrangements are benign" (133). Romance is a compensatory narrative form in that it seems to offer readers assurance of something they do not find readily in their own lives, while at the same time the heavy hand of formula encourages the reader not to look too hard at the reasons she feels a need for compensation in the first place.

Radway's study helps us see romance as compensatory *and* compulsory, an exploration of the given and accepted condition of woman in patriarchy. Her analysis is also helpful in discerning the interlocking of romantic and religious structures that appear in the thematically selected novels under consideration here. Both religion and romance offer certainty in the face of contingency, and the formulaic romance nicely buttresses the internal religious promise of these fictions – that faith (in God) in male leadership promises the certainty of (eternal life) marriage. Both invariably bypass the real works of the physical body by idealizing the longings and impulses of the flesh as a purity of (spiritual rapture) true love. In so doing, both religious and romance formulas also mask the covert violation of female integrity by presenting his sexual command as an irresistible (grace) necessity. In the religious romances studied here, sexuality is felt, not seen, although some of the later novels do feature a fair amount of pulsing, throbbing, and heated and wavelike encounters between the hero and heroine that anticipate the aggressively realized sexuality of post-1960s romance writing. The religious/romance systems assume sexuality within a male-dominant system as natural and inevitable – so much so that the system itself is never under discussion – and yet a suspicious amount of the energy of the religious/romance formula is

6 Ann Douglas, "Soft Porn Culture," *New Republic*, 30 August 1980, 25–9.
7 Radway, *Reading the Romance*, 75. Subsequent page citations in the text appear in parentheses.

spent in proving that this natural destiny is freely chosen and accepted
by the heroine.

At the same time, it is the purpose of romance to deny the actual
cruelty of male sexuality in patriarchal society by showing it to be the
opposite. In the romance, the threatened violence of male sexuality is
portrayed as misinterpreted and once the heroine learns to "read" the
male hero, she sees that his seemingly brutal or exploitative actions are
really the loving consequences of his passion for her. In the religious
romance his endless innocence is a product of this mythos of the misread
male. He only *appears* to be guilty of a sexual abuse of power. What
seems to be an egregious violation of female trust and integrity is, in
fact, either her misunderstanding of his conduct, or her malicious or
misguided attempt to manage him, and not the other way around. Once
the heroine learns to "read" this embodied Word correctly, she will see
that what appears to be evidence of reprehensible sexual activity on his
part is quite the opposite, and she learns that he represents only good
and right things for her future.[8]

These novels, then, are concerned not with women aspiring to ministry, but women aspiring to marry a minister. Compared to their foresisters – both those who lent their word power to the cause of female
ministry and those who sought to recognize the heroism of the minister's
wife, the romance writers have no such sympathy. They do have a
preaching mission, however, and in this sense they are the heirs to the
homiletic tradition, but their purpose is antithetical to the goals of the
homiletic writers. This fiction undoes the religious ambitions of their
sisters and engages in a wholesale relionizing of the male ministry by
romanticizing and idealizing him while putting wives and dangerous
single women back in their place.

The women writing these novels are largely unknown to literary history today, and in many cases, even basic biographical information is
not available (see Appendix B). Some of the thirty women I've identified
with the parsonage romance were prolific and popular writers who may
have written one or two novels about ministers during their long careers,
although others found a favorite theme in the figure of the fascinating
clergyman. A few wrote only one or two novels and then disappeared
from publication altogether. Early twentieth-century novels tend to feature a story line in which the central couple is engaged by a loosely

---

8 In a good essay discussing the sexual titillation of romance in relation to pornography,
Anne Barr Snitow also points to the motivating discrepancy between what the hero
seems to be (cruel, remote) versus what the heroine is supposed to learn about him by
the last page. See "Mass Market Romance: Pornography for Women Is Different," in
Anne Barr Snitow, Christine Stansell, and Sharon Thompson, eds., *Powers of Desire:
The Politics of Sexuality* (New York: Monthly Review, 1983), 245–63.

constructed Social Gospel drama. A typical plot would be composed of two thematic strands: (1) the private romance of the minister (2) as it hinders or helps his idealistic public battle against the wealthy industrialist or landowner. In addition to the Social Gospel interest of many of these novels, the trauma of wartime romance with its challenge to ministerial manhood, and the social issue of divorce, with its implications for sexual and theological purity, provide various thematic excitements that are peculiar to the novels written in the late 1930s and early 1940s. Some of the novels under consideration here are about a marriage rather than a courtship and so do not strictly qualify as a romance. Others involve political or religious discussion that adds an element of seriousness that is missing in a conventional romance. The writing may proceed from an idealism and fervor that is not entirely vitiated by the formula used to convey it. There are also a significant few that offer only an ambiguous conclusion to marital stress and religious issues. But in one way or another, nearly all these novels are romances: they present a happy-ending love relationship between an idealized male minister and his stylized female parishioner. He is masterful, omniscient, and tender; she is spirited but dependent, perky but feminine, nominally rebellious but actually waiting to be awakened to true womanhood and faith by the same event – falling in love with (or confirming her wifely submission to) her minister.

Falling in Love with the Compleat Clergyman

Although the parsonage romance denies that there is any tradition of divine lechery, it agrees with the male-authored account of ministers about one thing. No matter what his age, the minister is likely to be depicted as youthful or boyish, a designation that at once denotes his innocence but also his potential if not actual virility. Robert McPherson Black in Grace Smith Richmond's *Red and Black* (1919) is thirty-five years old, but his best friend is positive he has "not been strictly truthful about his age," and thinks of Black as a "mere boy." Black is admired by the ladies for his irrepressible curly black hair and by the men for his muscular grip and athletic frame, and they all revere Black for the vigor of his pro-war (World War I) preaching. Similarly, minister Robert Van Brunt, in Louise Platt Hauck's *If with All Your Hearts* (1935) is boyish, charming, and athletic. Twice we are treated to scenes in which fisticuffs are required of Van Brunt, who thrills his future wife and impresses his congregation with these displays of masculine authority. In *Canon Brett* (1942) by Mary Badger Wilson, the Episcopalian priest is in his forties, but still has a "golden quality of youthfulness," and the young minister in Ruth Lininger Dobson's novel *Today Is Enough* (1939) dies with his "little boy smile, half-pleading for forgiveness for the thing he must do."[9]

The charm and vigor of his boyish physical presence may also be paralleled by his intellectual prowess. In Lucretia Gray Noble's *The Reverend Idol* (1882), Reverend Kenyon Leigh, who is thirty-four, is so "adored of women" he flees to a Cape Cod boardinghouse to get some privacy for the summer. He is tall and powerfully built, but his "intellectuality" is the source of his charismatic presence. Reluctantly, he gets involved with a young woman staying at the same boardinghouse and soon takes her in hand. Monny Rivers has embarked upon a reading program about the lives of the saints, but Leigh confiscates her books on the grounds that they are unsuitable reading material for a young woman. She is astonished at his "cool assumption of authority over her," but, of course, the point of the novel is her true education in submission to his intellectual, spiritual, and social authority.[10]

While claiming this intellectual prowess, however, the parsonage romance is also likely to attribute the power of his ministry (and his special appeal to female congregants) to an intuitive spirituality coupled with an engaging idealism to change the world. Specific doctrinal debates are rare, especially when compared with the homiletic writers, and his denomination is not always identified unless the plot turns upon a distinctive denominational policy. The proximity of the Episcopal priesthood to the ideal of the Catholic priesthood, and a specific denominational prohibition on divorce, for example, is the device determining the personal drama in *Canon Brett*. In general, however, specific Protestant doctrine is less important than an overall cultural debate between Christianity and secularism, paganism, or the nondenominational goals of the Social Gospel.

In fact, in some of these novels the rebellious female character is portrayed as the cold, intellectual soul in desperate need of the warmth of intuitive religion that only a man can provide – another mirror image of the homiletic writers, who believed that the heartfelt religion of women offered a much needed panacea to the doctrinal and intellectual chill characterizing male religious leadership. Often, the romance novel is to be read as an explicit strike against homiletic fiction. Jane G. Austin's *The Desmond Hundred* (1891) features an educated minister whose appeal

9 Grace Smith Richmond, *Red and Black* (New York: Doubleday, Page, 1919), 7; Mary Badger Wilson, *Canon Brett* (New York: Greystone, 1942), 1; and Ruth Lininger Dobson, *Today Is Enough* (New York: Dodd, Mead, 1939), 220–1.
10 Lucretia Gray Noble, *The Reverend Idol* (Boston: Osgood, 1882), 2, 6, 72. In this connection, Sandra Gilbert and Susan Gubar mention other writings in which "censorious male ministers" seek to destroy "female literary aspirations," obviously a related activity to that of censoring her reading material. See *The War of the Words,* vol. 1 of *No Man's Land* (New Haven, Conn.: Yale University Press, 1988), 176.

stems from his message of the warmth, simplicity, and particularity of love. His foil in the novel is the cold and intellectual Nazareth Sampson who argues a religion based upon the abstracted purity of an intellectual, universal love. Naturally, she is a very unhappy character.

Even more explicit in its coercive agenda is *If with All Your Hearts* by Louise Platt Hauck. Boyish Robert Van Brunt marries the intellectual skeptic, Faith Llewellyn, who learns that intelligence and reason are not always the best way to reach people. "There was no one in the world for her save this big simple man whose education was inferior to her own, whose intellect she suspected was not markedly developed but who possessed an intangible something, a strength which looked out of his eyes, rang in his voice, controlled or dictated his every action."[11] In fact, Robert helps Faith see that she directly contributed to the suicide of her first husband, who could not survive her strength and intelligence. She realizes that her "sophomoric learning" prevented her from understanding the true gospel message, but as she grows in this intuitive wisdom and relinquishes her pride in intellectual understanding, she becomes more beautiful and womanly. The sign of her true womanhood is her pregnancy.

The bulk of these novels claim for the male ministry a comprehensive power, often managing to close the dualism between head and heart by giving both to him. He emerges as an omniscient, spiritual superior to all women, and in some of these novels, the future or present wife adopts a positively worshipful attitude toward her minister husband. Elsie Oakes Barber offers a representative sample of this attitude in *The Wall Between* (1946). Society girl Christy Gardner experiences tremendous awe when she sees her minister husband at prayer, and "she is terribly frightened because she had seen a man of God greet the morning and that man was her husband." She knows that if her husband Mark is forced to choose between her and God, he will let her go, but she recognizes that his dedication is to something "far bigger than she was and finer," so she determines she will submit to and support his ministry. For his part, Mark knows "she loved him. There was no doubt about that. He was her beginning and her end, her alpha and omega. . . . She was just completely his."[12]

Women gain no religious authority in the parsonage romance, and it is rare for them to provide any sort of religious insight to the minister at all. Occasionally, turn-of-the-century novels feature her religious leadership. Usually she's a champion of Social Gospel principles so that as the minister falls in love with her his own latent idealism is enlarged and

11 Louise Platt Hauck, *If with All Your Hearts* (New York: Grosset & Dunlap, 1935), 114.
12 Elsie Oakes Barber, *The Wall Between* (New York: Macmillan, 1946), 33, 230.

activated by his doubled passion for her and Christian activism. In Caroline Atwater Mason's *A Minister of the World* (1895) and *The Minister of Carthage* (1899), the minister, in consultation with an idealistic fiancée, abjures the glamour of big-city ministry in favor of a life with the poor or humbler rural congregations. Slightly later are Elizabeth Neff's *Altars to Mammon* (1908) and Lillian and George Randolph Chester's *Ball of Fire* (1914). In these novels the heroines are unusually assertive in their independent religious opinions when compared with other romance novels, although their pertness in the face of established authority never seriously threatens anything more than the peace of mind of the minister who is falling in love with her. Although she may be the goad to his conscience, the ironic sign of his acceptance of her example is that he proposes marriage, which in these novels is the same thing as underlining her submission to his lifetime leadership. Furthermore, Neff and the Chesters created heroines whose independence seems to depend largely upon her wealth. As romance writing proceeds, even wealth cannot secure the heroine's religious independence.

Not only does she rarely offer any behind-the-scenes religious leadership, virtually no woman in a parsonage romance is ordained or even seriously considers such an option. The exceptions to this generalization are few and serve to highlight the veracity of the observation. In what reads as a throwback to the homiletic platform, Helen Reimensnyder Martin creates the only truly critical portrait of a minister in *The Church on the Avenue* (1923). Robert Watts is pastor of a wealthy congregation in Leitersville, Pennsylvania, and when the underpaid teachers of the town strike against the captains of industry who control the school board, Watts decides there are too many wealthy industrialists in his congregation for him to support the working class. His wife, Jane, however, speaks out for the strikers against his explicit wishes, and she tells him what she thinks he ought to say: "I've been preaching it in my mind to your congregation every since I became its co-pastor," referring to both her fantasies about her own authority and the actual unpaid position she occupies as a minister's wife.

Unlike the other parsonage romances, there is no happy ending for *The Church on the Avenue* – clearly a "bad" romance. The Episcopal minister in town takes the courageous stand Jane is urging upon Robert and is forced to leave town. Jane realizes that the popularity of her husband's ministry depends upon his "uncompromising commonplaceness; he had a positive genius for safe mediocrity," and she concludes that a "preacher's got to be intellectually childish to be popular."[13] Fur-

13 Helen Reimensnyder Martin, *The Church on the Avenue* (New York: Dodd, Mead, 1923), 59, 215–16.

thermore, she is too loyal to her marriage to leave him, but too intelligent not to see the shape of her future. Her resignation to her marriage and clarity about the state of Christianity are the tones that close the novel, with no easy resolution offered. At no point, however, does the author follow up on that one passage in which Jane asserts her interest in preaching, and although Jane refuses to compromise her conscience, she is faced with few options for effectively exercising her own principles. In *Yours for the Asking* (1943), author Jane Ludlow Drake Abbott marries a stuffy Methodist minister to a high-spirited and kind young woman whose generosity in their small Kentucky parish nearly capsizes the marriage because he feels she is undercutting his ministry. Abbott's sympathies seem to be with her heroine, who has a brief flirtation with a virile young man, but she is unable to sanction divorce for her unhappily married couple, and the marital crisis is unconvincingly resolved in favor of the ministry. Again, the religious contribution of the wife is unofficial and highly threatening to the male involved.

The only other novelist to suggest any institutional responsibility for a woman is Elsie Oakes Barber. In *The Wall Between,* Mark Gardner goes to war and his wife is asked to assume some of his duties in order to hold his position for him. Significantly, this does not include preaching, and there is no suggestion that this is anything other than a very unusual accommodation to wartime circumstances. In a later novel, Barber produces a cautionary tale about the barrenness of female ministry. *Jenny Angel* (1954) is an ambitious, faithless woman who rises from the Italian slums of Boston to become a sexually corrupt, wildly popular evangelist, the "Scarlet Angel." She exploits and seduces the men around her, and she is a negligent mother who prefers the public adulation of her career to the private sacrifices of motherhood. Barber punishes her properly, though. After an older, male minister convinces her of her loathsomeness, she drives her car off a cliff in suicidal penance for the emptiness and idolatry of her life. Thus, although some of these novelists wish to show how a supportive woman can be an asset to the ministry, there is no serious suggestion that she could ever be a minister herself except with the most disastrous of consequences.

The parsonage romance writers, then, insist that the male clergy can have it all. They depict his youthfulness as an engaging vulnerability that will protect him from the hazards of the office, especially sexual temptation. At the same time, we are left no doubt that the magnetism of his ministry can be attributed to the promise of virility that is associated with his youthful energy, curly hair, and broad shoulders. He is, in short, an immensely sexual creature, although his sexual power is permissible partly because it is an unconscious power, and partly because it is applied toward the proper ideals: defeating the robber barons, proclaiming the gospel, converting a cynical young woman. The tradition of divine lechery (Chapter 3) retailed by many male novelists also agrees on the boyishness of the ministry, but these writers are not so sanguine about the consequences of this condition, reading his boyishness as a dangerous vulnerability or a psychological immaturity that does not wear well under the extraordinary demands of the profession. In particular, the clergyman is completely unprepared for the sensual temptations of the world, especially those of sexuality. In the male-authored fictions, he often uses his innocence and inexperience as an excuse for his sexual adventures, and the male clergy in male-authored novels express tremendous conflict about their sexual identity. They claim that they are treated as though they were a "hybrid female"; manhood seems to be completely incompatible with the ministry, and their sexual malfeasance is devoted to disproving this terrible fear about ministerial virility.

The parsonage romance draws upon these fears but with a different inflection. These novels are frank in admitting the sexual hazards of pastoral care, but in the "now you see it, now you don't" formula for romance, no matter how bad it looks for him, he only appears to have been guilty of sexual indiscretion. His purity will be proved uncompromised in the end. This is an inversion of both the male-authored account of the ministry and a reversal of some nineteenth-century wisdoms. One formula for a nineteenth-century seduction story usually involves an attractive, innocent, and trusting young woman who is seduced and abandoned by a predatory male. The androcentric fiction by women about ministers reverses this formula of seduction and betrayal so that he occupies the pedestal position of the nineteenth-century woman, a strategy that at some unconscious level does seem to verify the oft-expressed fears of the male clergy about their masculinity. In two of the parsonage romances, the minister is presented as physically frail (Dobson, *Today Is Enough*) and even rather neurotic (Helen Abbot Beals, *The River Rises*, 1941). Like the nineteenth-century heroine who is too spiritual to live, both ministers die, leaving their widows to learn from their example and, not incidentally, marry a more hearty specimen of male. But these frail ministers are unusual in the parsonage romance, whose standard story line is about the attractive and pure minister who is led to the appearance of evil by unreliable women: lonely widows, unscrupulous divorcees, unworthy wives, and frivolous society girls. At no point can it be said that he deliberately exploits his sexual magnetism for public or private gain.[14]

14 The only remote exception to the absolute purity of the minister in the parsonage romance is *Terry* (1943) by Harriet Teresa Smith Comstock. The upright minister once committed an indiscretion in his youthful past with a common sort of woman. Unknown to him, the product of his one moral slip is an utterly charming daughter who

On the other hand, the fact that "nothing happened" cannot be taken as a sign that he has drawn a sexual blank or is foolishly innocent about the possibilities. The romance novelists insist that his vulnerability to the sexual dynamics of his vocation is not the same thing as ignorance on the matter. In a disappointingly conventional successor to *The Church on the Avenue,* Helen Reimensnyder Martin tells us in *Whip Hand* (1934) that the virility and personal charm of the clergyman is often like that of a movie star who is refreshingly innocent of the reason why women are chasing after him. Rev. Hilary Hammand may be innocent, but he is not ignorant, and later in the novel he confirms that the ministry is much like the theater. When his impeccable reputation is on the line, he observes that the source of his difficulty is the fact that women would love a scandal about him – "You know what women are!" Similarly, when there is gossip about Canon John Brett and a parish woman, the virtuous title character in Mary Badger Wilson's let's-build-a-cathedral novel, it is because his "very purity makes him such a shining mark."[15]

Even an early novel like Lucretia G. Noble's *The Reverend Idol* (1882) is quite clear about who to blame for the sexual hazards of the pastorate. Rev. Kenyon Leigh is so magnetic that "respite from adoring women had been denied him," although "clerical philandering was forever impossible to him." Not without insight, but largely without sympathy, the author's opinion about the terrible attractiveness of ministers is that women "are full of troubles," and they want some man to say "I'm sorry, and you'll be appreciated in heaven. . . . Women, you know, are not considered to have much influence in this world except a moral influence. . . . So the man whose business it is to proclaim the importance of virtue is the magnifier of their office."[16] The author, however, has no intention of suggesting that there is something wrong with a social or religious system that robs women of their adult dignity, and the novel becomes a sustained attack upon women's independence, as seen in the gladsome submission of the spirited Monny to the omniscient benevolence of Kenyon Leigh.

In *The Bishop's Mantle,* Agnes Sligh Turnbull (1888–1982) offers a latter-day reverend idol, noting through her idealistic and boyish Episcopal minister, Hilary Laurens, that "sex and religion" are "the two most powerful forces in life."[17] Even his secretary is in love with him, and Turnbull goes to some length to emphasize how unattractive she is and

decides to protect him from knowing she is his child because he has already paid enough for his guilt and sin.
15 Helen Reimensnyder Martin, *Whip Hand* (New York: Grosset & Dunlap, 1934), 222; and Wilson, *Canon Brett,* 322.
16 Noble, *Idol,* 21, 13, 25.
17 Agnes Sligh Turnbull, *The Bishop's Mantle* (New York: Macmillan, 1948), 83.

thus how foolish and pitiable her infatuation. Laurens has a passionate, if vaguely rendered, sexual relationship with his wife, so we are assured of his virility, while his boyishness assures us of his purity. He is largely unaware of his secretary's devotion, for example. Yet he is quite cognizant of the peril of his position, and the following passage aptly summarizes the viewpoint of the parsonage romance:

> In spite of himself, he thought of the ministers, from Beecher down, who had had trouble with women. Every city clergyman had to recognize this menace. A few to his own knowledge through the years, *in spite of their utter innocence,* had yet escaped scandal by a hair's breadth. A few here and there had not even escaped. There were always the neurotic women who flocked not only to the psychiatrists but also in almost equal numbers to ministers, pouring out their heart's confessions and their fancied ills. There were those pitiable ones in whose minds religion and sex had become confused and intermingled; there were those who quite starkly fell in love with a clergyman and wanted love from him in return. Yes, a man of God had to be constantly on his guard in connection with this problem of women.[18]

While acknowledging that religious and sexual energies are related disturbances – and this is the frankest discussion available in the parsonage romances – Turnbull's minister emphatically defends the complete purity of the ministry by defining the difficulty as "this problem with women." This is seen as a personal deficit on the part of women, and is never addressed in terms of institutional or theological dysfunction. Turnbull's description indicates a veritable flood of female complaints, giving evidence, along with other writers of her era, of the rise of the psychiatric profession as a resource for unhappy women. A number of the World War II vintage novels excoriate women for their manufacture of imaginary woes, their vacuousness and lack of life purpose, their refusal to have children, and their neurotic quest for attention. Sounding much like Turnbull's minister in the above quotation, Wilson's Canon Brett observes that there are two kinds of women, practical and neurotic. "Thank heaven the neurotics had turned to psychiatrists of late years, which was a break for the clergy."[19] Similar criticisms of women can be found in Nelia Gardner White, *No Trumpet before Him* (1947), Elsie Oakes Barber, *The Wall Between* (1946), Ruth Lininger Dobson, *Today Is Enough* (1939), and Mildred Lee, *The Invisible Sun* (1946). In fact, this later set of novels involves the same generation of women that is slowly suffocating under the benevolent despotism of the "feminine mystique" so brilliantly de-

18 Turnbull, 267. My italics.
19 Wilson, *Canon Brett,* 19.

fined and described by Betty Friedan in 1963.[20] That is, the parsonage romance writers have rightly identified that there is a problem, and it is exactly the problem that finally received a sympathetic ear from the renascent feminist movement. The romance offers the same cure that was applied by the psychiatric community to middle-class women who sought relief from this miasmic condition of the soul. The solution, according to the romance, is to redouble one's efforts to teach women to submit to the higher authority of cultural and biological necessity. In this thematically selected set of novels, of course, that necessity is even more impelling, for a woman's position is not merely social or biological but also cultural, as defined by religious authority, and her inability to accept and submit to this definition of herself is a personal, spiritual problem.

Mirror Image: The Dangerous Single Woman and the Unworthy Wife

From 1915 on, most of the parsonage romances will be preoccupied with the problems of city ministry, usually in the context of a well-heeled congregation coming to terms with urban social distress, and we find no instances in which a young woman provides religious leadership to a minister. Instead, the parsonage romances become increasingly coercive in their agenda for the future or present minister's wife, who causes him trouble in his ministry by her unwillingness, unworthiness, or ignorance relative to his goals and her proper role in a clergy marriage. Late nineteenth-century novels of this persuasion quote a good deal of scripture toward the goal of enforcing her identity. Early to mid-twentieth-century novels quote little scripture, relying instead on institutional precedent and shared cultural wisdom about such matters.

The perils of the male-embodied ministry are the fault of women, who appear in these novels in two varieties: the dangerous single woman or the unworthy wife. The dangerous single woman usually appears as an exciting side-bar to the main plot line. Some of these single women are idle or selfish society girls who, in *A Minister of the World* (Mason) and *Red and Black* (Richmond), try to turn the clergyman's head toward marriage, but they cannot compromise him as effectively as can the woman of experience. In *Reverend Idol* (Noble), *Whip Hand* (Martin), and *No Trumpet before Him* (White), she is an unscrupulous widow whose efforts to marry the minister or somehow control his personal life results in a seeming and temporary compromise of his reputation. In the lead story in *A Minister of Grace,* she is a lower-class girl with blackmail in

20 Betty Friedan, *The Feminine Mystique* (New York: Dell, 1963) was a study of female Smith College graduates of 1942.

mind;[21] in *The Wall Between* (Barber), she is a lower-class whore who resents the good work of the minister on behalf of her daughter; and in *The Bishop's Mantle* (Turnbull), she is a rich divorcee who spends a lot of time lounging around in filmy negligees. She, too, has blackmail on her mind. All of these women somehow contrive to entrap the minister in a sexually embarrassing scene. Although there is a brief period where it looks as though he is guilty, it always turns out that, despite her cunning and malice, nothing has happened except that he was framed.

Sometimes the dangerous single woman can be subdued by turning her into a wife, or at least thinking about it. This strategy is used in *Canon Brett* (Wilson) when Brett's vocational integrity is challenged by his love for divorcee Lisa Trimble. In this instance, as in *No Trumpet before Him* (White), the divorcee is a Christian skeptic who urges the minister to act on his passion with her so they can build a new life together. The resolution is the same in both cases. Divorce is wrong, and he cannot leave his vocation, and so he gives her up. In *Red and Black* and *If with All Your Hearts* (Hauck) the dangerous single woman is not a divorcee, but she is still a Christian skeptic and cannot be married until she converts or submits to the minister's interpretation of the gospel. In the extreme, however, just loving a woman – not even a wild woman like a divorcee or a skeptic – may be enough to jettison his entire career. In *Penelope Finds Out* (1927), the novelist explains that "religion and sex are very closely allied. And it has saved many a single woman from worse than a nervous collapse to have an orgy of services and church work to plunge herself into."[22] But this novel is not about a sex-crazed woman, it is about a fanatic minister who is incredibly attractive to women. His sexual appetites are in irredeemable conflict with his religious impulses – he cannot be a sexual creature and a minister at the same time. He is entirely honorable, however, until he releases his bestial sensuality by marrying the luckless Penelope. He is so unbalanced by his raging hormones that he drags her to India, assumes an ascetic life in the jungle in penance for his marriage, and then tries to murder her to rid himself of these terrible cravings. Clearly, women pose a real threat to a man's vocational integrity just by being available for a relationship. In addition to the novels just mentioned, *The Desmond Hundred* (Austin), *Terry* (Comstock), *The Wall Between* (Barber), and *The Bishop's Mantle* (Turn-

---

21 Margaret Widdemer, "Of the Clan of God," in *A Minister of Grace* (New York: Harcourt, Brace, 1922). According to an older, experienced minister in the tale, "none knew better . . . the tight-rope a clergyman's name, more fragile than a woman's, must walk. There had been times when it took all his own caution, combined with the resources of a clever and resolute wife, to keep the wives of leading parishioners in a safe frame of mind" (24).

22 Winifred Mary Scott (Pamela Wynne) (New York: Macaulay, 1927), 49. I fudge a bit here; the novelist is British, but the plot line is too irresistible to omit.

bull) all handle the conflict of interest created by the dangerous single woman. It is imperative, if she is turned into a wife, that she not misunderstand her place.

In *The Wall Between*, Christy Gardner has a hard time adjusting to her life as a pastor's wife, and the novel shows how her husband's tutelage makes "a fine woman of her." There are two kinds of scenes in this novel that are paradigmatic for all the parsonage romances. One is the anxious wife looking up at her preaching husband and feeling disoriented and alienated from him at those moments, as if she doesn't know him at all. The other is the wife hovering outside the study door. Both scenes reinforce the distance between the watching wife and the word-possessed husband, and the dislocation between them is repaired by her readiness to serve as an enlarging mirror for his spiritual/sexual leadership. In *Today Is Enough* (Dobson), Judy feels that John is far away from her when he is in the pulpit, and her alienation from him is eased only by her recollection of his voice – when he proposed to her. From preaching to propositions – this is perilously close to suggesting a similarity between loving God and loving a woman, and as mentioned earlier, many of these novels present the woman in her unsubdued condition as a threat to his vocational purity. In the case of Barber's Christy Gardner, she is intimidated by the majesty of her husband as a minister, and she tries not to listen to his sermons because "the man up there, beyond his dark eyes, his eloquent hand, his soul-stirring voice, was not her husband. The man in the pulpit was a priest of God and had nothing to do with her."[23] From the beginning, she is impressed with his otherness, and she is often in the position of being a spectator to his religious passion:

> Maybe, when she understood more, when she learned what had made him pray outloud that dawn on the cliff, what had brought the radiance to his face last night by the window, what had drawn him away so completely just now, like a man whose body and soul belonged to someone else, someone he called God – pronouncing the words quietly and gladly and with a faith that made the back of her neck prickly and heated her blood – maybe when she understood better, she would accept better.[24]

The language in the passage puts the watching wife in a peculiarly voyeuristic position – both because of the distancing function of voyeuristic activity and because this religious tableau arouses her in a way that clearly indicates the confluence of religious and sexual passion. It is peculiar, however, because she is robbed of the usual objectifying power

23 Barber, *Wall*, p. 55.
24 Ibid., 33.

of the voyeur by the fact that she is female, in a doomed sexual competition with God. Unlike the male ministerial voyeur, for example, who can appropriate God's watching for his own carnal purposes (Chapter 3), a woman cannot appropriate this divine function for herself, for she cannot be a God-symbol any more than she can be a minister. As we have seen, moreover, if he is pressed, the dedicated minister will always prefer God to the blandishments of female companionship. In this passage where she inadvertently sees him at prayer, the implications of her position are all sexually and religiously passive. Her looking becomes the reflecting glass for the theater of his religious display, emphasizing the distance between herself and her more spiritual husband. Furthermore, we find that Mark, like God, always seems to have been watching her, so that even when he goes to war, she feels his presence and guidance, for Christy is "you might say, his disciple."[25] And that, after all, is the point of the novel – to watch over the growth of the willful wife into the tractable wife.

It is a common affectation in these novels to describe the Protestant minister as a "priest," a titular costume that manages to borrow the more exaggerated institutional alienation of the Catholic priesthood from womankind and apply its power to the Protestant office. This more formidable title further defines his exclusive territory, especially when we see the same kind of distancing emphasized in the other archetypal scene: the awestruck wife hovering outside the closed study door as the Protestant priest studies or writes his sermon. In the case of Barber's novel, Christy is worried about something trivial, like whether or not to call him to lunch, and she quickly discovers that to interrupt his creative and meditative time is an immediate cause of household distress. She must learn to respect the sanctity of his word, which invades and dominates even her household, and his remoteness on the domestic front reinforces the larger lesson of his separateness from her in the spiritual realm. Whether the activity is preaching, praying or writing about God, then, these various dispensations of the Word are used to underline his otherness from the world of women, and she is isolated and diminished by the encounter. Even in the rather shallow prose of the romance, the sexual charge of such encounters is never far from the surface, and this, too, is something these writers confirm about the report of male authors regarding the male ministry. The ministry, and by implication, the gospel itself, depends upon the grand and enlarged isolation of male embodiment for its power and appeal; the shrinking of the female character is necessary to achieve this effect.

All of these novels end with the woman's acceptance of the man's

25 Ibid., 351.

religious leadership, the most visible signs of which are either a marriage or a pregnancy. The authors are kindly but firm about the necessity of her acquiescence to the feminine mystique, nor is it possible to find the same kind of cross-purposed language that characterizes the homiletic woman's encounter with the ministry. At the same time, there is a very fine line indeed between the kind of earnest social and religious coercion that is the agenda of these fictions and the appearance of a plainly punitive enactment against women. The subtle message of these novels is that no woman is ever good enough to be a minister's wife, and that is probably why there is so much need for instruction. In some of the novels, the minister's wife fails to observe or learn the established boundaries of her embodied condition, and her fate is most instructive.

In cases where the wife fails to occupy her God-given position, her unworthiness derives from her inability to recognize the sacred priority of his calling. In combination with other kinds of personal character flaws, this turns her into something of a moral monster. *Steadfast: The Story of a Saint and Sinner* (1889) by Rose Terry Cooke features two minister's wives. The first is the saintly Rachel Hall whose tragic paralysis works in her an ethereal purity. She is attended devotedly by her equally pure husband, Philemon, until her death early in the novel. After a suitable grieving period, Philemon courts Esther Dennis. Esther is in love with another man, and for his sake has destroyed valuable legal documents regarding her own inheritance. She is dishonest and unadmirably impressionable, in other words. Worse, when her lover proves fickle, she abandons any vestiges of religion she might have professed. The rest of the novel retails the purgations of Esther's various character flaws so that she can accept the position as a minister's wife that Philemon presses upon her. She is the sinner of the title; Philemon is the saint; Steadfast is their infant son, named in honor of the quality of his father's faith. Esther is treated kindly by her creatrix, so that we can see that she is as much foolish as she is bad, but it seems that even once purged, she will never be as good as the dead Rachel Hall. Rachel, however, is necessarily dead, for no woman could possibly emulate her wifely perfection, a not so subtle clue as to the kind of demand facing any aspiring minister's wife.

Even more cruel than this suggestion that the only good minister's wife is a dead minister's wife is the horror of *The Parsonage Secret* (1898) revealed by Annette Lucille Noble. Reverend Stoughton, patient and pure, is married to a vain and idle woman named Alice. Says one parish scold, "When she comes to church she is dressed fit to kill, but around the house she don't care how she looks."[26] Alice's remarkable lassitude

26 Annette Lucille Noble, *The Parsonage Secret* (New York: J.B. Dunn, for the National Temperance Society and Tract House, 1898), 25.

is caused by her morphine and alcohol addictions. She drugs her children to keep them quiet, forges prescription orders to keep herself in supply, and on the afternoon both children drown she is drunk on whiskey. Flushed with an enjoyable sympathy, a veritable army of parish women watch this parade of parsonage tragedy, and all are admiring of the divine patience and forgiving nature of her long-suffering husband. No one is too sorry when the unworthy wife dies of a drug overdose. Stoughton has been ennobled and strengthened by these adversities, and at the close of the novel he marries a modest, pious, and beautiful village girl.

The melodrama of this particular tale is undoubtedly inflated by the fact that it was a publication of the National Temperance Society and Tract House, but the vindictiveness in assigning the moral monstrosity to a minister's wife surely is another matter, and a far cry from the pleadings on her behalf that issued from minister's wives themselves. Other examples include a novelette by Margaret Deland, *The Promises of Alice: The Romance of a New England Parsonage* (1919), which features an unlikable (and soon dead) minister's wife whose religious fanaticism overpowers her husband and daughter even from the grave, and Nelia Gardner White's *No Trumpet before Him,* which depicts a gentle minister married to a vain and selfish woman who refuses until the end of the novel to be humbled into her appropriate position. Perhaps most remarkable of these vengeful tales is Alice Brown's *The Willoughbys* (1935). David Willoughby is a retired pastor whose energetic wife takes a trip abroad to tend to Uncle Henry. In her absence, Willoughby's adoring, unmarried daughter, Hannah, determines to free her father from his domineering wife. Her efforts occupy much of the narrative, until the absent wife has been enough diminished and father enough revitalized for a triumphant conclusion of patriarchal restoration. Wife Willoughby returns a broken woman. Uncle Henry has told her she is a domineering shrew, and she has discovered she has breast cancer. Now she looks smaller and less awesome to David Willoughby, who says to her, "you're so different – so small and young and lovely. When you went away, you were tall and splendid and not in need of anybody."[27] Hannah rejoices in the return of love as her diminished, dying mother submits to the care of her father.

This beatific vision of the sexually disfigured mother who is supplanted and conquered by a father–daughter partnership is not really a romance, however. The novel violates the fastidiousness of romance by exposing in raw psychological terms a skeletal structure in the closeted body of romance. The minister as boyish lover has become a castrated father, the female parishioner has become the ardent daughter, and the unsuitable minister's wife has become the devouring mother who is manageable

27 Alice Brown, *The Willoughbys* (New York: D. Appleton-Century, 1935), 308.

only when absent, disabled, and dying. Her fatal wounds are the key to his restoration and the daughter's triumph. Brown was not a minister's wife or daughter, but a fair number of the romance writers were, and as with the homiletic writers, we can speculate that writing wives and daughters carried a daunting psychological weight to their enterprise. The parsonage romances offer an undisguised dramatization of the compelling father–daughter paradigm that shaped the writing of twentieth-century women *and* the simultaneous ambivalence of women writers toward women – what Gilbert and Gubar refer to as "female affiliation complex."[28] Noting that romances do punish women who get out of line, Janice Radway suggests that this activity by women, upon women, is not so much a sign of female masochism or antifeminist sentiment as it is an "impulse toward individuation and autonomy, a step that must be taken, at least within patriarchy, against the mother, that is, against women" (124). Ann Douglas, however, observes that the "prodigious success" of the contemporary romance has "coincided exactly with the appearance and spread of the women's movement, and much of its increasingly anti-feminist content reflects this symbiotic relationship." She agrees with Radway's understanding that the tension in the romance formula is connected to female independence and adulthood, however, noting that the idea of adulthood is a taboo in romance that "constitutes one of its great attractions. . . . In the soft porn fantasies of the Harlequins, woman's independence is made horrifically unattractive and unrewarding, her dependence presented as synonymous with excitement."[29]

These explanations for vindictiveness toward women – antifeminist sentiment, and daughters seeking to escape the enormity of their mothers without appearing to do so – are not mutually exclusive and taken together offer a compelling insight into the enigma of the romance formula. The homiletic women sought to confirm their identity by challenging *his* power, although sometimes they, too, can be extremely punitive toward women. The writers of the parsonage romance seek to confirm their identity by confining and challenging *her* power in whatever form it may take: feminist power, mother's power, or wife's power. In order to do so, however, they have to be on his side, "borrow" his power. These are women writing, poised in tenuous approximation of male authority by sending a reflection of women they themselves violate, if only for a moment by writing in a patriarchal voice. They disembody

28 Gilbert and Gubar, *War of the Words,* 168–207. Of the thirty novelists considered here, Caroline Atwater Mason, Elsie Oakes Barber, and Nelia Gardner White were minister's wives. Sarah Jenkins, Grace Smith Richmond, Margaret Widdemer, Helen Reimensnyder Martin, Mildred Lee, Dorothy Walworth, Ruth Suckow, and Sarah Barnwell Elliott were minister's daughters. This list may well be incomplete, however, for it was not always possible to obtain basic biographical information on some of these writers.
29 Douglas, "Soft-Porn Culture," 26, 28.

themselves, claiming a representational distance that is, in fact, impossible from the context of the patriarchal eyeball. Women are never disembodied, not even writing women. It is only the heavy hand of formula that allows the romance writer a sense of controlling distance that is the natural asset of the writing, watching male. In the language of mirrors, they get to pretend that the reflection they create is not to be associated with the self who creates, for we cannot see and be seen at the same time. Indeed, written as if to confirm the language universe of Lacan, the female-authored romance underscores the view that the "phallomorphic standard prescribes that woman will never be able to represent her difference but will serve as a mirror for the masculine subject."[30] Realizing the paradox of herself as the mother in the mirror, Luce Irigaray, for example, expresses the sense of loss and frustration of knowing oneself as a reflection of androcentric desires. She writes as the silenced daughter in address of her own mother:

> Each of us lacks her own image; her own face, the animation of her own body is missing. And the one mourns the other. My paralysis signifying your abduction in the mirror.... I, too, a captive when a man holds me in his gaze; I, too, am abducted from myself. Immobilized in the reflection he expects of me. Reduced to the face he fashions for me in which to look at himself.[31]

We can guess that the act of binding and framing women may have been a similarly ambivalent experience for the writers of the parsonage romance, but there is little in the prose save the heavy hand of the formula wielded against recalcitrant wives and dangerous single women to confirm or deny this speculation. Romance writing is not intended to be psychologically dense or revealing, quite the opposite, in fact. A mirror implies a frame and a restriction of field, and the glassy surface of formula reflects back, an imitation of dimensionality, and not the thing itself. In opting for the flat surface of the romantic formula, the writer automatically agrees to exclude the eccentricity of possibility. In these novels, the possibility the formula keeps under wraps is the possibility of challenging the cosmic male eyeball. "Looking ... is not indifferent; it is always implicated in a system of control," and the formulas of romance restrict the gaze of a female audience to a flattened field of opportunity while reaffirming the enlarged privilege of the male vision.[32] Romance colludes with patriarchal mirrors to deny the independence of the looking self from the mirrored self, for in "a world ordered by sexual imbalance,

---

30 Kate Linker, "Representation and Sexuality," in *Art After Modernism: Rethinking Representation* (Boston: New Museum of Contemporary Art, 1984), 400.
31 Luce Irigaray, "One Doesn't Stir without the Other," *Signs* 7 (Autumn 1981): 66.
32 Linker, "Representation and Sexuality," 407.

pleasure in looking is split between an active male/passive female."[33]
That is, men watch women in order to act upon them; women watch
men in order to be acted upon. Even when it seems she is visually active,
she's not, such as with Barber's Christy Gardner watching her husband
at prayer. As Virginia Woolf says, "Women have served all these centuries as looking glasses possessing the magic and delicious power of
reflecting the figure of man at twice its natural size."[34] The image of the
little wife looking up at her remote and majestic husband as he issues
the word is an important distancing device that transforms the activity
of looking into the passivity of reflecting, so that her eyes become the
mirrors for his magnitude. Her watching and waiting is part of his
performance; her goal is not to see, but to be seen, for "you never can
tell when you may be seen and being seen is a precious opportunity" to
advance oneself toward the goal of submitting to male mastery.[35]

   The female self in romance fiction is the effacement of the living self
with the reflected self, an enforced regression and paralyzation enacted
by the formula upon the selfhood of adult women. In her study of mirror
scenes in literature, Jenijoy La Belle points out that there are "precious
few [scenes] in which men use the mirror for acts of self scrutiny. Men
look at their faces and their bodies, but what they *are* is another matter
entirely – ultimately, a transcendental concept of self." Women, on the
other hand, may be condemned as unfeminine if they are not narcissis-
tically involved with mirrors, for when a woman looks into a mirror,
it is an act of identity.[36] Nonetheless, while a woman should know herself
only as a reflection in the slick, framed surfaces of romance, she will still
be condemned for her vanity in looking into a mirror to find a body, a
self, and a soul. Thus, the metaphor of the mirror image is not just a
handy rhetorical device for describing the difference between the homiletic and romance writers. It is intimately connected with the distancing
between male and female that is accomplished in the formula-bound
certainties of the romance.

   This inversion from a real self to the reflected self in the parsonage
romance is accomplished as formulas for romance and religion similarly
negotiate the boundaries between fantasy and realism, myth and history.
As Radway points out, popular romance may acknowledge stylistically
that the tale of sublime masculinity and picturesque femininity is a fantasy, but it also exhibits "a marked attention to the material details of

33 Laura Mulvey, "Visual Pleasure and Narrative Cinema," in *Women in Cinema: A Critical Anthology* (New York: E.P. Dutton, 1977), 418.
34 Virginia Woolf, *A Room of One's Own* (New York: Harcourt, Brace & World, 1957; 1929), 35.
35 Snitow, "Mass Market Romance," 249.
36 Jenijoy La Belle, *Herself Beheld: The Literature of the Looking Glass* (Ithaca, N.Y.: Cornell University Press, 1988), 9, 17.

the world in which that fantasy is set. The effect is so overpowering that the technique may well persuade the reader that the tale need not be considered a fantasy at all" (193). The romance thereby sets up a sort of confusing hum between its fantastic and realistic meanings so that the reader, along with the heroine, is advised to understand any discontinuity between what she actually experiences and what is promised and mandated by the fantasy as the product of her own shortcomings. At the same time, she is encouraged to use the romance as escape and compensation for this deficit. Thus, the system that deprives her, rewards her.

Religious systems conflate the same boundaries with much the same results. Any perceived slippage between the historical reality of Christian systems and the mythological promise is a product of the faithlessness of the believer. Viewed in terms of its proximity to the coercive structure of romance, Christianity assumes a sobering aspect. The relationship of God and the sinner is much like that of the male hero and heroine. Christianity offers worshippers a chance to understand the confusion and anguish of existence by blaming themselves. Is there suffering and evil in the world? This is caused by human sinfulness, or perhaps this is a mystery of God's love we are not to question. God graciously inaugurates an opportunity for forgiveness by staging a distracting savagery – the execution of himself – although the benevolent effects of this event are eternally future-promised. Pain, suffering, and death still train the course of mortal life, while the worshipper is taught to love the author of her torment. This is a theological trick done with mirrors, since God, in effect, offers us himself as a protection from himself, thereby being in two places at one time, while managing to convince us that what we think we see going on is entirely the opposite.

The relationships between the romantic hero and heroine, the minister and his congregant, are built upon the same model – the looking-glass relationship of God to the sinner. God is not really cruel or unjust; rather, the sinner misunderstands the Word, or the sinner is simply unworthy. The hero is not really cruel and rapacious; rather, the heroine misinterprets his actions, or she is unworthy of his love. The minister is not really a lecher; rather, the heroine has failed to understand and support him, or the heroine is really a whore. Nothing really happened. A woman under patriarchal religion must learn that the distances and cruelties this condition entails are the product of her own unworthiness, a lesson whose efficacy depends upon dividing her not only from him, but from herself by convincing her that what she feels and experiences is not as real as the image provided in the androcentric mirror. What she thinks she knows about him and his religion proves to be entirely wrong, just as the persistent rumors of the maladjusted and misfired sexuality of the clergy prove to be entirely the opposite.

The pervasive, repetitious nature of romantic formula accrues the hypnotic power of cultural incantation, a triumph of the symbiosis of the religious and romance universe. In short form: the hero is not really cruel, the minister is not really a lecher, and God is not really unjust. Nothing happens, and the "nothing" that happens is not his or his or His responsibility. We have misunderstood everything. What happened, then, to Sarah Maria Cornell, who fell in love with her minister and died? According to the parsonage romance, nothing happened, and the "nothing" that happened was entirely her fault.

6

The Fox in the Well:
Metaphors of Embodiment in the
Androcentric Imagination

In his first sermon of the month, Thomas Marshfield (*A Month of Sundays*) quotes St. Paul: "So ought men to love their wives as their own bodies." That this is not so generous a charge as it might seem is immediately confirmed by Marshfield, who goes on to comment: "But most men dislike their own bodies, and correctly. For what is the body but a swamp in which the spirit drowns? And what is marriage, that supposedly seamless circle, but a deep well out of which the man and woman stare at the impossible sun, the distant bright disc, of freedom."[1] Marshfield's name announces his own boggy predicament, but the language of entrapment specified by the well and the swampiness of the body is not peculiar to this novel. Updike's Rabbit usually seeks a burrow but just as often finds himself in an uncomfortable well, pit, or endless tunnel. In *Rabbit, Run* he feels "reconciliations rising up like dank walls" as he shrinks from the prospect of returning to his marriage. In *Rabbit Redux* it is not surprising to find Harry living "in a tight well whose dank sides squeeze and paralyze him."[2]

In the brief passage from *A Month of Sundays* above, Updike presents several of the antimonies that characterize the androcentric experience of embodiment. Men are bade to cherish wives and bodies despite a distrust of both. Yet there is a mutuality of experience somewhere along the line, for in this brief image, men and women stand together in that deep well. The longing and sorrow that defines this passage is typical of much androcentric literature about embodiment, for Western literature faithfully dramatizes a good portion of the heritage of theological discomfort regarding religion and sexuality. In this chapter I explore the wheel of metaphors used by four male authors – William Faulkner, John

---

1 John Updike, *A Month of Sundays* (New York: Fawcett Crest, 1975), 57.
2 John Updike, *Rabbit, Run* (Greenwich, Conn.: Fawcett Crest, 1960), 97, and *Rabbit Redux* (New York: Fawcett Crest, 1971), 249.

Updike, William Gass, and Walker Percy – to express their experience of embodiment.

With the possible exception of William Gass, whose fictional corpus is small, these writers are recognized sources in the field of religion and literature. Faulkner, along with other first-generation religion and literature resources such as Hemingway and Fitzgerald, has achieved, according to Nathan Scott, "quasi-scriptural eminence."[3] Of Faulkner I have made the most use of the four novels that are generally recognized as his best: *The Sound and the Fury* (1929), *As I Lay Dying* (1930), *Light in August* (1932), and *Absalom, Absalom!* (1936).[4] John Updike, whose popular contemporaries include Saul Bellow and Norman Mailer, represents a renewal of resources in the field. Arguably, Updike has provided the most influential exploration of the modern Protestant imagination that we have. I rely primarily upon the first three Rabbit books (*Rabbit, Run*, 1960; *Rabbit Redux*, 1971; *Rabbit Is Rich*, 1981) and *Roger's Version* (1986).[5]

William Gass should be better known in the field of religion and literature than he is. The novel used extensively here, *Omensetter's Luck* (1966) is a philosophically dense and demanding narrative that is convincingly energized by Gass's treatment of embodied anxiety.[6] Gass, in terms that are important for this chapter, trusts the gravity of metaphor to do its work. This is not true of Walker Percy (*Love in the Ruins*, 1971; *Lancelot*, 1977; *The Second Coming*, 1980), who has been a much ballyhooed newcomer to the scholarship of religion and literature.[7] Compared to the other works mentioned here, his writing often comes off as a clumsy pop psychology or science dressed up as profundity. Percy is influential right now, however, and the things he shares with Faulkner, Gass, and Updike makes him a useful, even if lesser, resource.[8]

3 Nathan Scott, *The Broken Center* (New Haven, Conn.: Yale University Press, 1965), 217.
4 I use the following paperback editions of Faulkner's novels unless otherwise noted: *Light in August* (1932; reprint, New York: Vintage, 1987); *As I Lay Dying* (1930; reprint, New York: Vintage, 1987); *The Sound and the Fury* (1929; reprint, New York: Vintage, 1987); and *Absalom, Absalom!* (1936; reprint, New York: Vintage, 1987). Page citations in the text appear in parentheses.
5 I use the following paperback editions of Updike's novels: *Rabbit, Run* (Greenwich, Conn.: Fawcett Crest, 1960); *Rabbit Redux* (New York: Fawcett Crest, 1971); *Rabbit Is Rich* (New York; Fawcett Crest, 1981); and the hardcover edition of *Roger's Version* (New York: Knopf, 1986). Page citations appear in the text in parentheses.
6 *Omensetter's Luck* (1966; reprint, New York: NAL, 1972). Page citations in the text appear in parentheses.
7 I use the following paperback editions of Walker Percy's novels: *Love in the Ruins: The Adventures of a Bad Catholic at a Time Near the End of the World* (1971; reprint, New York: Avon, 1978); *Lancelot* (New York: Avon, 1978), and *The Second Coming* (New York: Pocket Books, 1981). Page citations in the text appear in parentheses.
8 Percy is popular for his apocalyptic existentialism. Sympathetic accounts of this dimension in his writing can be found in Raymond Boisvert, "Walker Percy's Postmodern

Faulkner, Updike, Percy, and Gass have two things in common that are of interest in this chapter. First, they all create fictions energized by an androcentric account of gender-polarization, an outlook rarely mediated or editorialized by an implied author's voice. This is an important critical and theoretical point. It is customary to respect the distance between the living author and his fiction, and usually I try to do so by implicitly observing Wayne Booth's distinction between the flesh and blood author and the implied author.[9] I often have trouble doing so with these authors, however. For example, in *Roger's Version,* Updike teases our scruples about never confusing the author with the textual voice by playing with point of view. Roger speaks in both the first and third person. Correspondingly, the voice of Walker Percy's ironic, world-weary heroes is largely indistinguishable from Percy in his interviews and nonfiction essays.[10] Certainly the New Critics taught us to respect the distance between the author and the text, but as Tobin Siebers points out, although the prohibition of the intentional fallacy may rightly protect writers from "unfair identification with their characters and works, . . . the separation that it creates between the poet and the poem acts to shield authors from aggressive criticism."[11] Theoretically, I wish to give these writers some room for their creations as separate voices, but in practice, I fall short of this generosity. I think this a defensible shortfall, for even if we impute everything to an implied author, the view of gender relations seen from one novel to the next within each writer's corpus is so consistent that we may reasonably assume some congruence between the mind of the living author and the fictions he has created.

Moreover, and perhaps compounding my intransigence on this point, the continuing popularity of these writers can be partly attributed to the consistent view of male–female dynamics found in their fiction. In a field already dominated by theological and literary androcentrism, prominent scholars, mostly male, have had precious little to say about the andro-

Existentialism," *Soundings; An Interdisciplinary Journal* 71 (Winter 1988): 639–55; and Gary M. Ciuba, "The Omega Factor: Apocalyptic Visions in Walker Percy's *Lancelot,*" *American Literature* 57 (March 1985): 98–112. A generous overview of Percy's work as it is of interest to religion and literature studies can be found in Ralph Woods, *The Comedy of Redemption: Christian Faith and Comic Vision in Four American Novelists* (Notre Dame, Ind.: University of Notre Dame, 1988).

9 Wayne Booth, *The Rhetoric of Fiction* (Chicago: University of Chicago Press, 1983), esp. 71–6.

10 Note, for instance, the tone and image structures in *Lost in the Cosmos* (New York: Farrar, Straus and Giroux, 1983), and then consult Lewis A. Lawson and Victor A. Kramer, eds., *Conversations with Walker Percy* (Jackson: University Press of Mississippi, 1985), in which, for example, he defends his portrayal of the female TA psychologist in *Lost in the Cosmos* on the grounds that "using a woman was a better way to bring out the demonic spirit of sexuality" (288).

11 Tobin Siebers, *The Ethics of Criticism* (Ithaca, N.Y.: Cornell University Press, 1988), 48.

centrism (and all too often, misogyny) in the fictional worlds of Faulkner, Percy, Updike, and Gass. This suggests, I suspect, that the view of women presented in these fictions is largely a comfortable one to these critics. My focus on the gender-polarized worlds of our most popular religion and literature authors not only encourages a reassessment of those fictions as they speak to issues of difference, but also spotlights the lamentable, complicitous critical silence that upholds the patriarchal hegemony of these favorite canonical texts. I am not necessarily suggesting these texts need be eliminated from our canon. I am saying that they can no longer be read as if their presentation of gender is an incidental or trivial feature of their literary and theological purpose.

Second, in addition to their androcentrism, all of these writers share a concern, if not self-consciousness, about language and authorship. There is a fear that telling the story is not enough, although it may be all we have; that words, like bodies, will betray us, although we are ineluctably fond of both. Faulkner uses stream of consciousness, a technique also employed by Gass and Updike, to evade the story altogether, as if in fiction we could somehow leap to experience directly. Sometimes the result is a snarl of language, the words a torrential and terrifying performance of the distress of embodiment. In fact, along with women, water is an important source of embodiment language, for its literal and metaphoric significations help our writers talk about words, and metaphor can be understood not as simply clothing for the idea, but the idea itself.

Concern for the terms of embodiment often produces a language of multiple containment. Percy likes to use a story within a story (the movie within the novel in *Lancelot,* for example), a structure that replicates the box within a box effect that is enacted by many of the metaphors of embodiment. In larger kind, Faulkner does the same thing within and between novels. There are two stories in *Absalom, Absalom!*: the story of Thomas Sutpen, and the conversation between Shreve and Quentin as they recreate Sutpen's story. The interior story to those in *Absalom* is Quentin's section of *The Sound and the Fury,* a narrative that is only a shadow in *Absalom.* The story within a story is another way of underlining our narrative helplessness by showing us that our cleverest creations produce these fictions of infinite regress. Nonetheless, words, like bodies, still seem to be our only life raft, and sometimes they are what we do because we cannot bear a touch. The concern with our slippery, distrustful relationship with words and the androcentrism of that relationship are the central ingredients in these fictions of embodiment.

The Fox in the Well

The master metaphor for this chapter comes from Gass's *Omensetter's Luck:* the fox in the well. Gass, too, is fascinated with wells, pits,

caves, and burrows.[12] *Omensetter's Luck* is not really about the title character, but rather, the responses to him from the minister, Jethro Furber,
and his landlord, Henry Pimber. Unlike the minister or Henry Pimber,
Omensetter is a man who is very comfortable with water, and his life
looks so natural and uncomplicated that the villagers in Gilean, Ohio,
begin to refer to "Omensetter's luck." A prelapsarian Adam, Omensetter
collects worms and twigs and stones, laughs at the threat of the flooding
river, plays with his daughters, and complacently waits for his wife to
deliver a third child, a son.

The fox in the well is Henry Pimber's story, recounted in the second
section of the novel. Henry thinks Omensetter a "foolish, dirty, careless
man" but is enchanted with him nonetheless. "He was a dream you
might enter" (37, 43). One morning Omensetter finds his oldest hen
dead by the shattered well cover. From the bottom of the dry well gleam
the green-gold eyes of the luckless fox who, at the moment of leaping
triumph, seized his prize only to fall through the rotted well cover into
the earth below. Omensetter tells his daughters that the fox is a giant in
the earth; his eyes are like emeralds that can put spells on dogs and melt
the coldest snow. The well, once "empty belly," is filled with the glowing spirit, and Omensetter says, "he'll have to stay where the hen has
put him"; after all, "you can see how bad the well wanted him" (38–9).

Henry, however, is appalled, and feels the enraged helplessness of the
fox:

> That would be like Omensetter's luck, certainly – for the fox to seize
> the bitterest hen, gag on her as he fled, and then fall stupidly through
> the ground. What an awful thing: to have the earth open to swallow
> you almost the moment you took the hen in your jaws. And to die in
> a tube. Henry found he couldn't make a fist. At best, the fox must be
> badly bruised, terribly cramped, his nose pressed into the damp well
> wall. By this time his coat would be matted and his tail fouled, and his
> darkness would extend to the arriving stars. A dog would bloody his
> paws and break his teeth against the sides and then wear out his body
> with repeated leaping. By morning – hunger, and the line of the sun
> dipping along the wall, the fetid smells – bitter exhaustion of spirit. No
> wonder he burned with malice. (39)

Henry is tormented by these thoughts: "suppose he'd fallen there himself?" and he returns at nightfall and shoots the fox. But the fox persists,
"leaping against the sides of his skull," and Henry is driven to a more
permanent resolution.

Henry meets Omensetter in the woods to collect the rent, and, as
usual, Henry watches him carefully for a clue to a mystery he can't quite

---

12 Gass is currently at work on a novel entitled *The Tunnel.* See "The Tunnel," *Salmagundi*
   55 (Winter 1982): 3–60; and Arthur M. Saltzman, *The Fiction of William Gass* (Carbondale: Southern Illinois University Press, 1986), chap. 5.

name. But this time Omensetter acts just like a man troubled by the usual cares of life – paying the rent, hanging out the clothes, the weather, the future of his unborn child. He tells Henry they have to move, for the cabin is too wet for a new baby, and the river has now become a danger to him. He takes leave of Henry, "no miracle, [but] a man, with a man's mask and a man's wall." Omensetter is going "to leave the fox where he has fallen" (61), and, weeping, Henry realizes that "Omensetter lived by *not* observing," his luck merely the innocence of ignorance and a perishable product of the hopes of those around him. "If Brackett Omensetter had ever had the secret of how to live, he hadn't known it. Now the difference was – he knew. Everyone at last had managed to tell him, and now like everybody else he was wondering what it was. Like everybody else" (63). In Omensetter, Henry fastened his teeth in some desperate and fatal lunge for "a chance of being new" and, falling, found himself with no secret beyond his own captivity: "Ah – god – the fox, Henry thought, knuckling his eyes. He'd had the hen in his mouth, life in his teeth, saliva running. Feathers foamed over his nose. And then the earth had groaned. Just a moment ago. He'd never nailed the well shut, though now when he closed his teeth it all latched" (57–8).

Once Henry felt he had been a stone with eyes, and then Omensetter showed him how to be a body and he thought there was some dizzying and glorious secret to it all. Now, climbing the mountain for the last time, Henry says, "I shall be my own stone . . . my own dumb memorial, just as all along I've been my death and burial, my own dry well – hole, wall and darkness. . . . Don't look for Henry here, my dear, he's gone. He's full of foolishness, and off to kill a fox" (60, 63). In a last attempt to thwart the ignominy of a well-death, Henry hangs himself from the highest tree he can find.

This extended metaphor for the clever, restless (male) spirit and its containment in an unexpected hollow employs a language common to much androcentric fiction: falling, containment, longing, sorrow, water, stones, and words. Moving away from these specific terms of the metaphoric enactment of the fox in the well and yet still occupying the same territory is Faulkner's tableau of embodied irony seen in the psychic captivity of Rev. Gail Hightower in *Light in August*. Hightower is one of several narrators of this story on the warfare of embodiment, the primary expression of which is the history of the racially tormented Joe Christmas. But Hightower, too, has lived a drama of embodied captivity, and the inclusion of his story serves to widen the implications of the struggle of Joe Christmas. Hightower, like many other fictional ministers, is a child trapped in a man's body, and he recalls living his childhood with his mother "like two small weak beasts in a den, a cavern" (524). As with many of Faulkner's people, he is time-tormented, his life "ceased before it began," frozen at the moment when his grandfather was shot from a galloping horse at the end of the Civil War. As a child, he is eternally hypnotized by this story, and his entire life becomes a circle around an event that occurred twenty years before he was born. He aggressively seeks a parish assignment in Jefferson, the town where his grandfather died.

Relative to Faulkner's work, Hightower's endless rehearsal of his grandfather's death enacts a typical Faulkner theme – that although we have some notion of progress or motion in life, in fact, it is the ghost-filled light of time that moves through our helpless bodies. The body itself becomes a stilled emblem of living, acted upon rather than acting. In Hightower's case, the arrest of his fleshly self has to do not only with the lasting trauma of the Civil War and the white Southern obsession with miscegenation but – and here is but one of many instances in which Faulkner's realization of the psychic tableau extends far beyond its regional origins – with the monstrous joke of life itself. The glory of war, the thunder of horses and the fearsome glint of sabers, and maybe even the magnitude of the cause itself, all these are part of Hightower's perpetual daydream, but his life stops not with these mementos of rationalized dedication, but with the thunder and rattle of these portentous things as a backdrop to the moment of his grandfather's death. How did Hightower's grandfather die?

The old fox "killed in somebody else's henhouse wid a han'ful of feather. Stealing chickens." Furthermore, it was "likely enough the wife of a Confederate soldier who fired the shot" (535). *This* is the ignominious fall of the crafty spirit. The death is laughable, a terrible joke upon which Hightower has built his entire existence in unwitting honor of its absurdity. As Hightower locates this performance in the context of his ministry, he sees himself as if he were "a fish in a bowl," "a figure antic as a showman," shouting homilies about horses and fire and guns and religion at a bewildered congregation. He has been a "charlatan preaching worse than heresy, . . . offering instead of the crucified shape of pity and love, a swaggering and unchastened bravo killed with a shotgun in a peaceful henhouse" (539). His reflections pick up the terms of performance so common to ministers (Chapter 3), but this time they stress the staginess and the craziness of our contained performance. It is a circusy thing, this life, as much like a high-wire act as a feat of prestidigitation, a play in the body that the spirit is fated to perform no matter how ludicrous the costume or senseless the script or cruel the director. Furthermore, Hightower's moment of truth in this vision of the absurdity of origins is his guilt in the drama, for "if I am my dead grandfather on the instant of his death" (542), then through that inheritance he is the author of his own destruction and of those around him. Past and future form a seamless net in which we are the dead we thought to escape.

Similarly, as Updike's Rabbit gets older, he is aware of the dead, apart

from but increasingly part of himself. With the aging of his hero, Updike's present-tense narrative begins shifting toward a Faulknerian awareness of the claim of the past – not simply the historical past, but the
eternal past and our responsibility even for that. The fox in the well or
the henhouse is not always a victim of falling and fate, but may choose
to jump or burrow into the earth, seeking the past and the dead in order
to understand or activate the future. Walker Percy's Lancelot Lamar of
Lancelot refers to himself as entombed in the past, but also indicates his
own volition in the matter: "A fox doesn't crawl into a hole for a year
unless he is wounded. But after a while he begins to feel good, pokes
his nose out, takes a look around" (112). In *The Second Coming,* the
suicidal Will Barrett carries on a subterranean conversation with his dead
father, whom he calls "old mole." His father killed himself, burrowed
into death, so to speak, and even tried to take his young son out with
him. So, rather like Hightower, Barrett has lived his entire life as an
aged child, knowing that when his life was spared by a misfired gun
blast, his life began and ended. So he incarcerates himself in a cave in
order to tempt God to let him live. Hightower, too, has looked for an
escape into quiescence, hoping that if "there was shelter, it would be the
church. . . . That was what seminary meant: quiet and safe walls within
which the hampered and garmentworried spirit could learn anew serenity
to contemplate without horror or alarm its own nakedness" (*Light:* 527–
28). The search for "quiet and safe walls" and a rest for the "garmentworried spirit" is as ubiquitous as is the quest for escape from those walls,
and sometimes escape and captivity are simultaneous.

This last statement is especially applicable to the symbolic function of
women in these fictions. The fleshiness of their spirit usually qualifies
women as a symbolic immensity rather than as a partner in the well.
Women are often the final resort for the clever, lovely spirit, and like
the walls of the well, they can be seen as shelter or the ultimate form of
entrapment, an imprisonment both chosen and railed against. Hightower
learns that women do what he thought the seminary would do: "Woman
(not the seminary, as he had once believed): the Passive and Anonymous
whom God had created to be not alone the recipient and receptacle of
the seed of his body but of his spirit too, which is truth or as near truth
as he dare approach" (514–15). Updike's Rabbit, who is often able to
think of woman as a welcoming funnel, can also look at her – reduced
to the enormity of her genital significance – as "a vertical red aperture
that seems to stare back . . . out of blood-flushed nether world, scarcely
pretty, an ultimate which yet acts as a barrier to some secret beyond"
(*Rich:* 429), and in *Rabbit Redux* he flees his wife's vagina as though it
were "a tiger's mouth" (33).

Hightower confuses seminaries with women, and Dr. Tom More is told that his problem is that he doesn't "love God, he loves pussy" (*Ruins:* 44). This is a seminal confusion, for these authors detect an unsettling idolatry in the relation of men and women. "Women are holes," says Rabbit's well-tutored son, and in fact, female holiness – all puns intended – is a key to the frustration and mystery in the androcentric language of embodiment. Women may very well be that gateway to the land of giants that Omensetter tells his children about, and here is the fox, stuck in perpetuity at the gateway, leaping to enter, frantic to leave, astonished and angry at the unexpected push and pull of existence. "No wonder he burns with malice" (*Luck:* 39).

Foxes, moles, and rabbits: the hub of embodiment language in male-authored fiction is containment (captivity, protection) from which various metaphoric spokes radiate. These radiating and often radiant tropes may seem far from their origin, yet each can be traced to the hub of the circle: *women* (vessels, houses, wells, infinity, and earth), *water* (fish, nets, hooks, tears, rain, rivers or streets, wells, falling, running, stream of consciousness), and *words* (water, women, stones, bodies, and circuses). Each metaphor leads to the other. Their closure and circularity is part of the essence of containment, a rooted figure that mimics and expresses something basic about the embodied human mind. As Lucy Omensetter says, it all began with the well, "that simple circle in the ground" (179).

Women

"Who made a woman's body? God, we have to keep reminding ourselves," says Roger in his version (321). Is the word "God" an answer or an oath? The double tonality displays the intense ambivalence toward women enacted in these novels. It also serves as a reminder that not only is the narrator male (which is not that easy to lose sight of), but that he is not just speaking for himself, but on behalf of and to a male audience (hence, "we"). Androcentric fiction typically carries on a sort of *National Geographic*-style commentary about women, wherein individual female characters are defined by their generic qualities as women and these qualities are periodically summarized as the narrator of this safari points out the fascinating and repulsive features of the natives to the traveler, as in the samples below:

> Women are monkeys (*Run:* 54).
> A blank check. A woman is a blank check until you fuck her (*Redux:* 270).
> She does know something. All cunts know something (*Rich:* 113).
> Women do have an affinity for evil (*Sound:* 120).
> Women are never virgins (*Sound:* 132).

They lead beautiful lives, women. Lives not only divorced from, but irrevocably excommunicated from, all reality (*Absalom:* 240).
In women, revenge takes the form of religion (*Luck:* 96).
Women are mythical creatures. They have no more connection with the ordinary run of things than do centaurs (*Ruins:* 85).
Women have only just now discovered the secret, or part of it . . . the monstrous truth lying at the very center of life: that their happiness and the meaning of life itself is to be assaulted by a man . . . to be rammed, jammed, stuck, stabbed, pinned, impaled, run through (*Lancelot:* 239).

The exclusivity and power of this ongoing conversation is heightened in *Roger's Version*. As noted earlier, Updike seems to have given Roger both first- and third-person narrative voice. Roger provides us with the narrative of events only the implied author could know, unless we choose to believe that Roger is only guessing at what has transpired and all that he reports is a product of his imagination. This possibility is engendered in the text, and certainly we should allow for the unreliability of the narrator. Yet because of the absence of any implied author apart from this unreliable narrator, and despite the rotation between first- and third-person narration, Roger's version of events is the only version we ever get. The result for the reader is that this central male character possesses a wicked omnipotence. It is under these tolerant narrative circumstances that Roger often "turns to the camera," so to speak, and addresses a male audience: "The chemistry between two women we have fucked fascinates us, perhaps with the hope that a collusion will be struck to achieve our total, perpetual care" (287). The sentiment expressed in this man to man aside is important, for although women are frequently defined by their voracious sexuality, women's fertility and its products are not that important. The productiveness of female sexuality is evaluated in terms of its significance for and relationship to full-grown men. Perhaps this is only to say that here the boundaries of male experience are visible. Men do not give birth nor (despite contemporary rhetoric) are men primary caregivers for children, and so these events are important only inasmuch as they locate or dislocate the male character. In these novels, mothering seems to be as restricted a word as fathering has been traditionally.

Children do not fare well in these novels, and the novels themselves have about them the cry of a lost child as women take on a symbolic immensity that contains and traps all life. Faulkner shows us Dewey Dell getting out of the wagon and measures her absolute significance by her body. Her leg "coming from beneath her tightening dress" is "that lever that moves the world, one of that caliper which measures the length and breadth of life" (*Dying:* 98). The sum of woman's immensity is at once reassuring and terrifying, the object of a near idolatrous veneration that leads the androcentric author to persist in juxtaposing the language of religion and sexuality, which, in the androcentric world is, at best, a language of uneasy dualism. William Faulkner, for example, will emphasize the sheer power and impact of flesh as if the body were the essence of being. Yet in other places, the body is a "barracks" or "tenement" for the soul, an "unsentient barrow of deluded clay" (*Absalom:* 177). The dualism is the traditional one of body and spirit, and in various metaphoric analogies to the impermanent, material world, women are the body, the container (or gigantic bulk) against which the male spirit struggles.

All of Walker Percy's novels are concerned with estrangement as experienced by a weary, cynical, and often suicidal male hero. Dr. Tom More of *Love in the Ruins* identifies the human condition as "More's syndrome, or chronic angelism-bestialism that rives soul from body" like some "poor ghost locked in its own machinery" (98). Angelism is an excessive abstraction of self; bestialism an excessive incarnation that caricatures the bodily appetites (223), the latter usually seen in exaggerated or perverse sexuality. The hope of Percy's heroes is to banish these polarities by somehow mending the broken soul back into flesh, although Percy is too uncomfortable writing about sexuality for this to be a believable goal. More returns in *The Thanatos Syndrome* (1987) to engage the same problem, but as with earlier efforts, the sci-fi, pop psychology Percy uses as his vehicle makes it hard to take him seriously, and his characters act more like a cartoon population than flesh and blood persons. *Lancelot,* however, for all its overdetermined literary resonances, emerges from his work as a more honest and symbolically complex fiction in its intensity than the fantasies in *Love in the Ruins* or *The Second Coming.*

Amidst numerous other literary allusions, the novel draws upon several versions of the Arthurian cycle and the legends of the Fisher King.[13] The title character, Lancelot Lamar, is telling a story of misbegotten sexual quest and purity to a silent listener, presumably a priest, who is also variously identified as Prince Hal, Percival (the original Grail hero in Chrétien de Troyes who sees the Grail), John the Evangelist, and even Christ. Walker Percy complicates the suggestiveness of this apparatus,

---

13 The following articles were helpful to me in understanding the mythic resources as a way of reading the novel: Deborah Barrett, "Discourse and Intercourse: The Conversion of the Priest in Percy's *Lancelot,*" *Critique: Studies in Modern Fiction* 23 (Winter 1981–82): 5–11; John Bugge, "Merlin and the Movies in Walker Percy's *Lancelot,*" *Studies in Medievalism* 2 (Fall 1983): 39–55; Corrine Dale, "*Lancelot* and the Medieval Quests of Sir Lancelot and Dante," *Southern Quarterly* 18 (Spring 1980): 99–106; John F. Desmond, "Love, Sex and Knowledge in Walker Percy's *Lancelot:* A Metaphysical View," *Mississippi Quarterly: The Journal of Southern Culture* 38 (Spring 1986): 103–9; and Stephen R. Yarborough, "Walker Percy's *Lancelot* and the Critic's Original Sin," *Texas Studies in Literature and Language* 30 (Summer 1988): 272–94.

however, by juxtaposing the ancient mythic structure with the seductive, structured illusions of contemporary moviemaking. The mythic past invoked by the novel works just like the movies. Whether myth or movie, we can't tell if we are dealing with something symbolically significant and serious or just playacting for shallow and sinister purposes. Identities shift, take on portentous meaning, dissolve; Lancelot may be merely a murderous madman, an adulterous knight betrayed by his own sexual obsessions, or perhaps there is indeed something gallant about his fury with the licentiousness of the world. The presence of the listener can be seen as the cautionary comment of the implied author on Lancelot's vision, although the point of view of the silent priest must be inferred entirely from Lancelot's first-person narration, so we can never be certain about the priest's relationship to Lancelot and his story. What also makes getting perspective on the novel so challenging is that despite the enigmatic mediation of Percival, nearly everything Lancelot Lamar says about women under the exaggerated license of madness and confession can be found in more civilized costume elsewhere, in the mouths of other Percy characters and in essays and conversations with the author.

Lancelot Andrewes Lamar is a dissolute southern lawyer whose life is given new purpose by his discovery that his daughter is not his biological child. His worshipful obsession with sexual love becomes an equally powerful holy obsession to expose his wife's betrayal and to exact retribution. He identifies himself as a crusader for sexual purity and gender propriety, but in so doing, becomes a prisoner of sex, showing us how the language of apocalypse can be detonated by religiosexual claustrophobia. *Lancelot* illustrates the traditional dualisms of Christian theology through a reel of images in which men are related to houses and women *are* houses. Women are like tradition-riddled houses, both sanctuary and prison, containers of ambiguous value. Lancelot happens to live in two kinds of structures that function as both kinds of things: the family mansion, Belle Isle, and his actress-wife, Margot. Lance suggests that Margot married him partly because she wanted to restore the old house, saying that "the house Belle Isle was she herself, a Louisiana Belle." Sadly, however, "she came to prefer restoration to love. Certain architectural triumphs became for her like orgasms" (126–7). A woman, he notes elsewhere, "is at home in a room. The room is an extension of her." She is like a house one would like to make home, and indeed that is how Lance first experiences Margot, for kissing her was like being welcomed "into a new home" (39, 83).

But not only is Margot the inn, she is also the innkeeper. Margot busies herself with restoring Belle Isle, a project that includes refurbishing the abandoned pigeon roost in the house for Lance's personal retreat. Inside Belle Isle, Lance lives inside a "pigeonnier." The metaphor of containment is doubled, giving the effect of a box within a box. It heightens the sense of claustrophobia and thus warns of entrapment as well as protection. The claustrophobic is imprisoned by a mind that fears being imprisoned by a small space. Lance – inside the pigeonnier, inside Belle Isle – is twice trapped in literal space (the house), which is the metaphor for his entrapment in sexual space (Margot), which he mistook for spiritual space. Margot, in fact, is a sacred enclosure of ambiguous value, for Lance has idolized her sexuality, saying, "She was like a feast. She was a feast. I wanted to eat her. I ate her. That was my communion Father . . . , that sweet dark sanctuary guarded by the heavy gold columns of her thighs, the ark of her covenant" (182). Elsewhere Lance builds on this blasphemy, exulting that the love of a woman is far better than the love of god. She is infinity. With such an overpitched sense of sacrament, it is no wonder that he is made mad by his discovery that the sexuality he loves so much is not his exclusive covenant. Having first sexualized spirituality in his woman worship, but finding the combination treacherous, Lancelot turns in fury to the task of spiritualizing sexuality, which really seems to mean destroying it altogether.

He begins at home by installing movie cameras in all the guest rooms, using the hidden spaces of the house to spy on his wife and her lovers. It is like using her own body to reveal her treachery, just as she and her body have deceived him. His confirmation of her continuing adultery also confirms the pervasive perversity of sexuality all around him – his daughter, his guests, his wife are all carrying on this unholy communion. Incensed by this corruption of his sanctuary, Lance launches his revenge during a hurricane that isolates the plantation. In order to begin, however, he has to hack his way out of the pigeonnier, whose door has been barricaded by a falling tree. Having freed himself from the interior prison, he dramatically frees himself from the outer walls. He blows up the house with Margot and her lover in it.

He tells this story to Percival from a single-celled room in a psychiatric hospital, the room and the sexually ravaged girl next door being all he can deal with at present. He decides that Anna, her sexuality punctured simply by her violation, will be a suitable New World partner for him, a mutilated Eve for his maddened Adam. They communicate by tapping on the shared wall between their rooms, timid, solitary spirits tapping for passageway through the fleshly walls that divide them, from self and from each other. Anna, however, is suitable as his New World partner as long as she is silenced by her humiliation and in her silence Lancelot can invest her with a paradoxical purity and simplicity. But when they finally talk, even words cannot construct her sexual self as he wills it. She is annoyed that he defines her by her rape, saying, "Are you suggesting . . . that I, myself, me, my person, can be violated by a *man?* You

goddamn men. Don't you know that there are more important things
in this world? Next you'll be telling me that despite myself I liked it."
In fact, this is exactly what Lancelot is telling her. Furthermore, in Lancelot's new world, Christ will be all male, and "there will be virtuous
women who are proud of their virtue and there will be women of the
street who are there to be fucked and everyone will know which is which.
You can't tell a whore from a lady now, but you will then. . . . Freedom?
The New woman will have perfect freedom. She will be free to be a
lady or a whore" (190–1). With these two words, "lady" and "whore,"
Lancelot cuts her back down to size.[14]

The symbolic immensity of woman moves androcentrist language far
beyond recognizable containers like houses, vessels, or controlling labels
like "lady" or "whore." She is so huge, she is the earth and life itself.
The gravid Lena Grove (*Light*) moves with the steadfastness and serenity
of the "implacable and immemorial earth" of which she is a symbol.
The maternal-sexual woman John Updike's Rabbit admires so much is
an enormous, comforting presence. His mistress, Ruth, is an "incredible
continent," her "pushed up slip a north of snow . . . , her belly a pond
of shadow" (*Run:* 79). Percy's Lancelot has the same perspective on
Margot, who was "life itself, as if all Louisiana . . . had been gathered
and fleshed out in one creature. . . . She was a big girl" (125–6). Woman's
hugeness seems to come from the awesome vibrancy of her sexual nature.
When Rabbit sits behind the minister's wife in church, he immediately
notes "something sexed in her stillness in the church." He is so fascinated
with the radiance, he is shocked when she turns around. "The luminous
view he had enjoyed for an hour did not seem capable of being so swiftly
narrowed into one small person." Later, while walking home with her,
he imagines her as a piece of land he is destined to dominate (*Run:* 220,
222). As Rabbit says in *Redux,* naked women have an "absolute bigness"
(38).[15]

Women, then, are huge enclosures of uncertain purpose – welcome
shelter, blasphemous sanctuary, comforting lands, jail and jail-keeper
both. Their bodies are metaphors of containment, a psychic and literal
space so inviting it rivals the established sanctuaries of civilized religious
life. Like those enigmatic and ancient statues of priestesses and goddesses,
the metaphor of containment built upon a woman's body offers the
inanimate serenity of an icon, displaying her receptivity, patience, and

14 Lancelot's vision for a future society is very much like the chilling prophecy explored
in Margaret Atwood's *The Handmaid's Tale* (Boston: Houghton Mifflin, 1986).
15 This language of incredible, natural immensity is repeated so many times in these novels
that there is no need for extensive documentation, and the connection between human
females and a female earth with all the usual metaphors of sowing and plowing and
harrowing has been thoroughly discussed in feminist scholarship.

endurance. They also suggest a link to a forcefield of great but impersonal power. There can be peacefulness in this iconic presentation, and her potential to give life (which, as noted earlier, is not the same as actually giving birth to babies and nurturing children) is a continuing source of wonder. In a particularly generous passage, Updike shows us Rabbit's unlikely wife exercising her iconic potential. Janice, a "gateway of love," literally holds her lover in his body as he suffers a heart attack. "He grits his teeth 'Christ!' and strains upward against her as if coming and she presses down with great calm. . . . She widens herself to hold his edges in, she softens herself to absorb the spike of his pain. She will not let him leave her" (*Redux:* 335). She wins. Here the literal function of her sexual body has been translated into an effective performance of affirmation and containment. It has little to do with the actual details of her reproductive function, but everything to do with her metaphoric function. But life is not the only thing present in this iconographic narrative. By successfully absorbing the death of her lover, Janice erases an old score – the drowning death of her infant daughter (*Run*), a reminder that she who challenges death may also bring it with her. The circle of sex-death-life played out between Janice and her lover is present in most of the metaphors of containment related to women's bodies, and the dark side of woman is unavoidable.

This iconic view of woman is an effort to control and borrow her power, representations that in various ways seek to contain the container. Yet as the dark side of the icon persists in juxtaposition to her passive serenity, we can see how closely containment is related to engulfment, for the interior of her body is as immense and lonely as outer darkness. When the searchers finally locate Henry Pimber's body, they find him at night, hanging from a high tree in the "cunt colored darkness" (*Luck:* 211). Despite his effort, he died in that well. Walker Percy's Lancelot says that woman is "not a category, not a sex, not one of two sexes, a human female creature, but an infinity" (137). Even the physical presence of her sexual organs is incomprehensible, and the "vector of desire" is a "sheer negativity and want and lack" (84), rather like the emptiness of outer space. In fact, the analogy that dominates *Rabbit Redux* is the calendar of space shots, "all about emptiness . . . a big round nothing" (28) set against the terrifying and demanding immensity of women. Janice, who was "opened up about the time of the moonshot" by her affair, frightens Rabbit. "Her appetite frightens him, knowing he cannot fill it anymore than Earth's appetite for death can be satisfied." Rabbit's son, Nelson, says, "Women. They are holes, you put one thing in after another and it's never enough, you stuff your entire life in there. . . . That's what cunts do to you when nature takes over: go out of control" (*Rich:* 45, 68, 336).

According to Roger, the iconic view of woman is a rear view as she is walking away ("she looks grand, a piece of the earth," *Roger's Version:* 220). This is a perspective Roger seems to have on God as well, and what is true of many of the Updike novels is also true of other novelists. God is experienced through his absence, and the way we know there is any reason for the idea of God is the "longing which is . . . our only evidence of His existence" (67). Women, functioning as embodied inspirations for longing, are experienced as both vast and absent holes to some unknown world. Dale tells Roger's wife Esther that without faith "there's this big hole, and . . . the hole is a certain shape, that it [faith] just exactly fills" (203). Retranslated: women's genitals represent absence and the lack, while the penis promises presence and abundance, just exactly the right shape for filling the emptiness. This is an unusually cheerful description, however, for filling the hole is typically seen as a hopeless task. All of these androcentric novelists are concerned with the risk of the enterprise, for one never knows when even just thinking about things will open "flimsy trapdoors . . . under the weight of our attention into the bottomless pit below" (*Roger's Version:* 74). The male spirit is perpetually in danger of leaping or falling into that hole or well.

The negativity of woman's holiness is one aspect of her galactic darkness, and her essential filthiness is the other. The incarcerating well is dark, but also dank and slimy, and inevitably, the fox is bloodied, smeared, and fouled by his captivity. The metaphor of the fox in the well that is the guiding image for this chapter is part of the language of all these authors, but it is Faulkner above all who articulates with such ferocity and repugnance the archaic androcentric terror of woman's blood filthiness.

Although *Light in August* may be inflected in terms of racial conflict, it is more accurately described as a text on embodiment. It dramatizes in the body of Joe Christmas the ancient wisdom that what produces life is what will kill it. Specifically, this comes down to the unmanageable sexuality of women. Joe Christmas is doomed and drowned by a conflict of blood, racial blood and sexual blood, and one cannot be distinguished from the other. His early life is marked by various religiosexual initiations, and learning of the filthiness and betrayal of women is simultaneous with encountering the uncleanness of his own racial lineage. He hears that women are "doomed to be . . . victims of periodical filth" and then rejects this horror by killing a sheep, a paschal cleansing of blood with blood, saying, "Not in my life, and love" (204). He is wrong, of course, as are all men wrong about the deathly origin of life. When the waitress, Bobbie, tells him she is having her period he translates what she has said into its iconographic significance:

In the notseeing and the hardknowing as though in a cave he seemed to see a diminishing row of suavely shaped urns in moonlight, blanched. And not one was perfect. Each one was cracked and from each crack there issued something liquid, deathcolored, and foul. He touched a tree, leaning his propped arms against it, seeing the ranked and moonlit urns. He vomited. (208–9)

Through this woman Joe Christmas is presented with the essential filthiness of life, women as broken vessels of some rotten flow, and so he discovers the putrefaction of his own particularity. She first betrays him simply by being female, and then she betrays him again, when she discovers he is not just foreign, but tainted. She and her cohorts beat and rob him, this last treachery the same as the first.

Faulkner's characters are such intense and fisted representations of passion we feel more awe and horror for them than pity or sympathy. There is rarely uncompromised laughter or any clarity of joy, and when children appear as characters they are simply the small, tormented twists of flesh that they will be as adults, for they already have seen too much. This is certainly true of Joe Christmas, and yet more so than for most of his characters, Faulkner takes care to underscore the lonely and even appealing innocence of Joe's childhood and young manhood (198, 215, 228, 244). He did not create his torment, and in the helplessness that defines the rest of his life we are not allowed to forget the child trapped in the flesh of adult complicity. The man who learns about women's bodies "with the curiosity of a child" (215) is struck down by the perfidy of a woman. After Bobbie and her cohorts have brutalized him, he lies on the floor, "licking his lips now and then as a child does" (244), and then gets up to enter "the street which was to run for 15 years." Like Updike's Rabbit, however, he is not really running, for he does not move but rather, the street, like time, moves around and through him. "It made a circle and he is still inside it," he realizes at the end of the novel, as the "black tide" creeps up his legs as death moves (373–4). But he is not just drowning in racial torment, he is also engulfed by the swampiness of sexuality in the form of the spinster Joanna Burden.

When he breaks into her house, he is "a shadow returning ... to the allmother of obscurity and darkness" (252–3), and making love with her was "as though he had fallen into a sewer" (281). Using the same kind of regressed containments we've seen in *Lancelot*, Faulkner shows us Joanna's house as the hub in the sewerlike universe of her land and being (282) and her body inside the house a "richness ready to flow into putrefaction at a touch, like something growing in a swamp" (287). Joanna's appetites are unnatural in both source and object, an overflow of sterility even when it is finally channeled into the false pregnancy of words:

talking, teaching, and praying. Therefore, Joe Christmas, "who feels himself being sucked down into a bottomless morass" or "the bottom of a pit" will (like Lance Lamar) destroy both containers, her and her house. He beheads her and sets fire to the house.

Joanna Burden's restless and voracious sexuality is the demonic side to Lena Grove's placid and overwhelming fecundity, but both icons – the demonic and the maternal – are treacherous. Joanna literally cannot give birth, and therefore her sexuality is purposeless and destructive. Lena simply dwarfs and absorbs the men around her, feeding upon them with a slow and gentle assurance. Reverend Hightower tries to warn one subject of her feeding away from her, saying, "No woman who ever has a child is ever betrayed; the husband of a mother whether he be the father or not, is already a cuckold" (347). Woman is filthy: it is her essence; it is essential to life and whether she is Lena Grove or Joanna Burden, slut, earth mother, virgin, or crone, woman has that "natural affinity for evil" – a favorite Faulkner phrase in every novel.

It is within this context that Caddy's lost virginity in *The Sound and the Fury* becomes comprehensible. Quentin has staked everything upon a galactic joke – the absurdity of her purity as the gateway back to an innocence he never actually had. Upon "the minute fragile membrane of her maidenhead" is balanced his entire world, as if "poised upon the nose of a trained seal."[16] But "women are never virgins" (132), and Quentin, like all men, is playing a rigged game balanced upon the hope of her purity and the fact of her betrayal. No wonder he is mad. Caddy is absent in the novel because she never could have been present except as an impossibility, for purity "is a negative state" (132). Therefore she has no voice, although the entire history of the Compson family swirls around the void of her absence – her holiness – and the confirmation of her essential impurity until all are sucked back into that immensity of expectation. Only men, in other words, fall into that well, are betrayed by the tricky earth, swallowed into darkness even in life.

Knowledge of and submission to that destiny of containment and engulfment gives definitive articulation to all these novels, although the act of writing each novel is also a protest against that eventuality. Anger and longing compete in these novels, one as fierce and despairing as the other. What tenderness there is in androcentric fiction is usually reserved for men, and nearly all these novels are structured by male friendships or the more ambivalent but no less essential relationship of father and son. As the biblical cry of the title suggests, *Absalom, Absalom!* is the

16 This quotation comes from the appendix to the 1929 Random House edition (New York: Vintage), 411.

story of doomed love between men. Most of the novel is an excavation of the past, and Rosa Coldfield's death is the only present event in the novel. Besides Rosa's own account, the rest is conversation between men as they reconstruct the story of Sutpen's Hundred: Quentin Compson and his father, and most important, Quentin Compson and his roommate Shreve as they rehearse and identify with the interior story of Charles Bon and Henry Sutpen, also a love story between men.

Lancelot is similarly constructed as a confessional conversation between Lancelot and his priest friend, Percival, and there are various indications of longing and intimacy between the two men that conceal an intriguing substructure to the story of Lance's treacherous wife. In addition to this sharing between male friends, Lance is also one of several fictional characters trying to come to terms with a father. Quentin Compson in at least two novels, Thomas Marshfield (Updike, *A Month of Sundays*), Will Barrett (Percy, *The Last Gentleman* and *The Second Coming*), Rabbit Angstrom, and then into the next generation, his son Nelson (Updike, *Run, Redux,* and *Rich*), are all involved in a long-term reckoning with father–son relationships. At rare times we do see children in these stories, especially in Updike, whose Rabbit tries to be a father in his feckless and bewildered way, but "child" is present more fully in these grown men as they turn to their fathers for closure or resolution and find only a deathly silence upon which to build meaning. In that sense, the abstracted cry that closes *The Sound and the Fury* and *Absalom, Absalom!* is the signature for all these novels. Benjy's voice in the first novel, duplicated by the idiot Negro in the second, "might have been all the time and injustice and sorrow become vocal for an instant... the grave hopeless sound of all voiceless misery under the sun" (*Sound:* 333, 366).

There is no reason why androcentric authors should not write about male relationships, but the subtle and elegiac understructure provided by the sorrowing comradeship of men is buoyed by the persistent seepage of anger that is a component of every grieving, and these things in combination emphasize the radical alienation between men and women. Most of the anger, unlike the elegy, is directed toward women. Some of this is visible in the ridicule that goes on: of women's bodies, sexual expression, and quest for personal identity. As I noted in Chapter 3, the virulence of male misogyny intensifies as the century grows older, so that in some ways the condescension and contempt for women found in Faulkner's prefeminist writing are cleaner than those of his postfeminist brothers.[17] Updike and Percy are both persistent in their denigration of women, – especially feminist women, – and rarely pass up a chance to

17 Faulkner's view of women is still a matter of debate. For a good survey of the question, consult Doreen Fowler and Ann J. Abadie, eds., *Faulkner and Women; Faulkner and Yoknapatawpha, 1985* (Jackson & London: University Press of Mississippi, 1986).

reduce them to their androcentric significance. There's "a ton of cunt in the world" (*Redux:* 292), says Rabbit, as if he had been in conversation with Lancelot, who blames much of the evil in the world upon the "100 million voracious cunts" out there terrorizing young men into homosexuality (189). William Gass follows Faulkner's footsteps. He gives two of his female characters the same first name, underscoring their identity as a single unit of meaning. Like the Lena Grove and Joanna Burden pairing of *Light in August,* Lucy Omensetter is the earth mother to Lucy Pimber's voracious sexual obsessions.[18] Sometimes this scorn erupts into violence (*Lancelot*), fantasies of violence (Updike's men entertain fantasies of brutalizing their wives or lovers), or the violence of ridicule, as noted above.[19]

The anger of this writing emphasizes the profound estrangement enacted through the metaphors of embodiment. Rabbit decides that women are a different race, like plants or stones (*Run:* 89); Tom More says that "women are mythical creatures. They have no more connection with the ordinary run of things than do centaurs" (*Ruins:* 85). But far more serious than the rather ingenuous cruelty of such observations is how effectively the androcentric mind has amputated women from the realm of human experience. According to this prose, women are untouched by life, which is probably the key to their endurance. They simply don't feel like men do. Rabbit says that he is now the sole heir of grief for their lost child because Janice "seemed to forget: like a cat who sniffs around in corners mewing for the drowned kittens a day or two and then back to lapping milk and napping in the wash basket. *Women and nature forget*" (*Redux:* 41, my emphasis). Tom More decides that "men are the only single-minded lovers, loving for love, that women love with the idea of winning" (*Ruins:* 323). Hightower, summarizing the heart of *Light in August,* says, "But what woman, good or bad, has ever suffered from any brute as men have suffered from good women?" (347). Finally, there is Mr. Compson, rehearsing the tragedy of Sutpen's Hundred in which the calculated exploitation of women is not incidental, saying:

18 Perhaps another clue to Gass's outlook is detectable in *Willie Master's Lonesome Wife* (New York: Alfred A. Knopf, 1971), a postmodern experiment in interrogating art and life through that old whore, the poetic muse.

19 For a fascinating and chilling historical study that confirms my metaphoric material here, the reader should consult Klaus Theweleit, *Women, Floods, Bodies, History* in *Male Fantasies,* vol. 1, foreword by Barbara Ehrenreich (Minneapolis: University of Minnesota Press, 1987). The dense and troubling material Theweleit has amassed here cannot be easily abbreviated, but it is important to note that this meticulous study of warrior psychology (in this case, the German Freikorp) reveals the deep-seated male fear and hatred of female bodies, and the deliberate violence that is an outcome of that loathing. As Ehrenreich puts it, the motivating force of male violence seems to be the "dread, ultimately, of dissolution – of being swallowed, engulfed, annihilated. Women's bodies are the holes, swamps, pits of muck that can engulf" (xiii).

They lead beautiful lives, women. Lives not only divorced from, but irrevocably excommunicated from, all reality. That's why their deaths . . . are of no importance to them since they have a courage and fortitude in the face of pain and annihilations which would make the most spartan man resemble a puling boy, yet to them their funerals and graves, the little puny affirmations of spurious immortality set above their slumber are of incalculable importance. (*Absalom:* 240)

Shortly thereafter, Quentin repeats this affirmation that women have no connection to reality, that the facts of "birth and bereavement of suffering and bewilderment and despair" move by them with "the substanceless decorum of lawn party charades, perfect in gesture and without significance or any ability to hurt" (*Absalom:* 264).

She is life, she contains and engulfs life, but she herself is unaffected by it. The arrogance and narcissism of this collective utterance is astonishing. Women, who take such physical and psychic life risks in pregnancy and childrearing, who have survived the centuries of rape, abuse, disfigurement, abandonment, and murder that occur simply because they are women, are emptied of humanity by this language, and the words are turned to justify the events. The accumulation of images, symbols, and metaphors seeking to contain women by making them containers is sometimes overwhelming, and it is hard to imagine any common ground between men and women, so decisively have androcentric writers barricaded the territory. As though centuries had not passed between Tertullian's pronouncement that woman is a temple built over a sewer and the American male writer of the late twentieth century, women are still implacable, iconic flesh, and men are the spirit of that temporary shelter. Or, to use another metaphor that will take us closer to words themselves, women are water creatures and men are not.

Water and Words

The well that the fox falls into is clammy, but no longer productive of water. The well's column is like "blackened body hollows" (*Luck:* 41) thinks Henry Pimber, who watches Omensetter to see how it is he has avoided this fate. To Henry, Omensetter's luck suggests that being part of a body does not have to be experienced as a dry tunnel, and for a brief time Henry feels he is "newborn in that waltzing body; he had joined it as you join a river swimming" (47). Henry's buoyancy is short-lived, but the abundance of water language in this novel is not. Updike and Faulkner share with Gass the use of water language, as well as a flow of language that demonstrates the metaphoric reciprocity of water and words. They call upon the sacramental meaning of water – baptism, living waters, the waters of life – while reminding us of the threat as well as the promise. In baptism, one must die to the old life in order to live anew, and so one is simultaneously cleansed and drowned in order to be reborn through the ritual. According to these novelists, however, this can be a dangerous procedure, and water is not a natural element for human beings, even if it is essential to life. In water, as in life, as in our very bodies, we drown, and there is no particular confidence that there is life after baptism.

Congruent with the metaphoric definition of women as the unmoved icon of fleshly being, Updike's Rabbit sees women as natural denizens of the waters of life that are menacing to the male spirit. "Himself, he was not a water animal" (70, 81, 134), for as we have seen, he and his male cohorts are burrowing, tunneling animals. Nevertheless, the land-locked Rabbit is making a water journey. Much of the world in *Rabbit, Run* is rendered in "green aquarium light," while Rabbit's car is like a "seaworthy boat" (180, 93). Rabbit's mistress, Ruth, is a great, green fish, or a mermaid swimming in the pool while Rabbit sits on the side flexing his muscles. In one of the few obvious references to the Christian content of such language, the parsonage is marked as a water world, with the Christian symbol of the fish hanging as a door knocker and the roof glistening like the scales of a big fish. Furthermore, when Rabbit visits the parsonage and bangs with the fish-knocker to gain entrance, the door is opened by a "crisp little number with speckled green eyes" (110). The minister's wife sounds like fried fish. This water world follows Rabbit into *Redux,* and much of what he does or sees occurs as if un-derwater (32, 43, 83, 92, 133), although the presence of a woman can change his experience of the element. His bed is a "resisting raft he is seeking to hold to a curving course" until Janice climbs aboard and turns it into a "nest, a laden hollow, itself curved" (32). Or, in bed with Jill, "he is floating rigid to keep himself from sinking in terror," and she "is a mermaid gesturing beneath skin of the water" (248).

Faulkner, American master of the stream, points toward the use of water language as the definitive structure for these fictions. Stream of consciousness, a literary term that manages here to designate both struc-ture and metaphoric content, works to subvert deliberation by immersing the reader directly into experience, as if the flow of words were enough that one could be literally swept from observation into participation in the interior life of the mind. It is a way of using language to avoid language, and it is in the flow as much as in the literal meanings that the words take on significance. The action of the words against each other is like gemstones in a tumbler – all glitter, polish, babble, an incessant sound whose coherence occurs in the torrent, and not individual signi-fications. This rush of sound that intends to replicate the most private processes of thought and experience is a denial of silence and, in the doing, a profound invasion of privacy – the end of silence and distinctions between public and private in any nineteenth-century sense of those realms (Chapter 2). The cataract of words that streams through the center of Updike, Gass, and Faulkner is an expression of the stress carried by language once religion and sexuality have been named together and the shapes of embodiment given public utterance. Sometimes there is the effect of a studied incoherence as a way of expressing the fact that even when everything can be said, some things cannot. At other times the explicit language about religion and sexuality is simply distorted and often out of control. Indeed, what Robert Detweiler notes of texts in which bodily space is literally violated by language is also true of fictions in which language threatens to violate the text itself. "The narratives describe charged texts that are too much for their context and a charged corporeality too forceful to be fully articulated in language."[20]

In *The Sound and the Fury*, Quentin says "I suppose that people, using themselves and each other so much by words, are at least consistent in attributing wisdom to a still tongue" (135). Unfortunately, he is unable to be silent himself and so talks himself into fatal water. Quentin destroys the hands on his watch and sets himself awash in several time zones during the space that designates his narrative. He purchases the iron weights he will use for his suicide and then walks outside of town where he befriends a little girl who seems to be lost. The urgency of his monologue is bounded by the presence of this silent little girl on the one side, and, in a dark burlesque, he will be charged with kidnapping her ("You steala my seester," 160), as if to be literally convicted of what he has secretly desired. Balancing this not-so-funny enactment is the presence of three little boys going fishing. Quentin, who is carrying on a constant interior conversation with and about Caddy, has hidden his irons under the end of the bridge. He stands with the three boys and looks down at the trout below, who is a "neighborhood character" (134). They speculate about the fish and how hard he is to catch, and how much he'd be worth, doing what Quentin has done with Caddy – "making of unreality a possibility, then a probability, then an incontrovertible fact, as people will when their desires become words" (134). That fish, however, is as unattainable as Caddy's purity, and giving much better advice than he is able to take, Quentin wishes them luck, saying, "Only dont catch that old fellow down there. He deserves to be let alone" (137).

Quentin, who feels the water before he even gets to the bridge (132), is no fish himself. Like Rabbit, he is a land animal, and he is drowning in his obsession with Caddy. Water, the odor of honeysuckle, and the flow of his own words carry him toward the headwaters of his memories

20 Robert Detweiler, *Breaking the Fall: Religious Readings of Contemporary Fiction* (San Francisco: Harper & Row, 1988), 123.

of Caddy, and his knowledge of her sexual activity. Like Ophelia, "she was lying in the water her head on the sand spit the water flowing about her hips," and as she holds him "against her damp hard breast I could hear her heart going firm and slow now not hammering and the water gurgling among the willows in the dark and the waves of honeysuckle coming up" (171, 175). He remembers her as a child who sat down in the water and got her drawers all muddy, and the memory of her innocence, that upon which he has balanced his entire world, is what will undo him – not innocence itself (which doesn't exist and which is why he cannot exist) but his memory of that which never could have been real. He pleads with her ("Caddy you hate him dont you," 173) and she pities him and herself and allows him the consolation of contemplating her murder and his suicide. Finally, the conclusion of his muddy memories is that sex and death are confirmed together, all senses and significances converging into "liquid putrefaction like drowned things floating like pale rubber flabbily filled getting the odor of honeysuckle all mixed up" (147). Caddy, like water, runs through his madness and disappears into the bellowing of Benjy whose voice is the authoritative all-sound of the novel, the conclusion of all streams (92). Quentin could die no other way than by drowning.

The flow of language in Quentin's section, following upon the inverted eloquence of Benjy's section, is what creates the remarkable force and impact of Quentin's madness, and it is impossible by discrete quotation to convey the intensity of the water as metaphor, language as water achievement of Faulkner's stream of consciousness in *The Sound and the Fury*. William Gass uses the same doubled enactment (water as metaphor, language as water), as does Updike, but both writers use this structural torrent as less a fury and more an elegy, more passion grieved than passion expressed. Perhaps this is because language itself moves to the forefront as the key to the embodied dilemma, and somewhere in that transition, the force of the physical is translated into the lurking absurdity of mortality rather than its anguish.

In *Omensetter's Luck* we are warned far in advance of the central stream of consciousness by the narrative of Irabestis Tott that opens the novel. Tott, now an old man reflecting somewhat erratically back on the story of Omensetter, warns us we are about to take a water journey. He himself often mind-travels, following the cracks and rills in the faded wallpaper in his room: "Gently closing his lids to allow an eyelash of light, he would push off from the bank and coast by the torn hills, poling the grease-spot march, and by the time he had baited his hook and dropped his line in the plaster chip he was in the history of his life, out of the wall, in the old slow world" (17–18). Irabestis makes his way from wall-water to world-water, in spite of the fact that "he knew no nautical terms and nothing of seamanly action" (17). Swimming, he says, takes away your weight, which explains why Omensetter is at home in the water, as in life. "It was Omensetter's luck. Likely. To lose the heaviness of life. That Furber fellow, for instance, was nothing but bones, and even those you could have wrapped in a hankie. Yet he weighed a ton" (15–16).

This imagery of a life water in which some sink and some swim continues throughout the novel, and, as Tott has made clear, Furber is the leaden counterweight to the buoyant Omensetter. We first meet the minister confined within the clammy walls of the parish garden. If he makes the effort, Furber can see beyond the walls to the Ohio River, along whose banks the lucky Omensetter and his brood of children are wont to frolic on pleasant Sundays. Sometimes most of Furber's parish is out there with Omensetter, bathing, skipping stones on the river, fishing, sunning. Their shouts of laughter and sport send Furber into homiletic seizures. Beginning slowly, and then going faster and faster, Furber paces the walls of his garden with words and footsteps until he collapses, incoherent and physically spent. The physical pacing of the caged animal is paralleled by the verbal pacing of the caged spirit – the spirit inside the animal inside the walls of the garden, and language of containment is doubled, giving a box within a box effect. Furthermore, the absurdity and terror of the confinement is seen in the distorted imagery that Furber sends flying about within the walls, his stream of consciousness a dense, textured leaping of thought about sex and religion, the meeting of which seems to produce a circus.

Furber declares that he has been misunderstood. He knows he did not choose Jesus, but "the Lord of Hosts, His Tent, Tights and Trapeze" (95). Sometimes the master of ceremonies is the devil, "dressed in pink tights and carrying a striped umbrella" as he reigns over the Big Top. At other times Furber himself is the magician and ventriloquist, the devilish host of the carnal show. Often he pauses in his declamation to chant scatological verses about himself or his congregants. The effect is of a breathless calliope cranking out urgent, jerky tunes in the midst of the acrobatic discourse. Furber returns to the circus imagery often, because he can't talk about sex without defiling religion and he can't talk about religion without arriving in the midst of raffish sexual imagery. The circus language suggests sideshow deformations and peepshow sniggering, and where Hightower in *Light in August* uses circus language to ridicule his own absurd performance, Furber uses the gaudy carnival imagery to expose the sexual underside of the proper pious life, which of course includes his own.[21]

21 The postmodern discussion of carnivalized language certainly has relevance here, although with Wayne C. Booth, we would do well to ask, just who is the object of laughter in the carnivalized language of *Omensetter's Luck*? See Booth, "Rabelais and

The truth that Furber wants to say, but cannot seem to get into proportion, is that every act, every life performance, is simultaneously religious and sexual. Furber remembers his pious Aunt Janet and the day she fell off her chair. Presumably she dies in the fall, in the middle of a tea party, and Furber recalls that "she'd had too much of life and she'd let go at last and left the high wire," the metaphor reminding us that living is at best a precarious business. But Furber also says that in his mind she seemed to fall infinitely through space, her skirts ballooning up to reveal beneath them a woman's private parts. Private parts have spoken to Furber before, although he was not sure what it meant. "Well, even Moses was slow-witted with the burning bush," he puns, before rushing on to recapture the memory of Aunt Janet's fall, continuing his play with the sexual theology contained in the word "fall." His Aunt Janet somersaults herself into one large private part, becoming a "single, broadly grinning, comic mask," a Medusa head (93–5). This is Furber's obsession – the sexual smile carved on the underside of the rock of pious life. The ghost of a ministerial predecessor advises him that "pounding on the pipe won't punish the plumber," and Furber agrees: "You can't feel the spirit through the body, it's far too thick and wooly" (98). But neither his wisdom nor ghostly wisdom tells him what the parts we keep hidden have to do with the parts we say we truly are. What does the public part have to do with the private part? Furber doesn't seem to have a double language for managing the tension, even though he knows language can act that way.

Furber's response to the press of physical life is to make language the container and boundary, content and mediator against the threat of physical experience. "Words are superior; they maintained a superior control; they touched without your touching; they were at once the bait, the hook, the line, the pole, and the water in between" and so Furber is all talk, a hungry fish in skywater, hooked in the root of the tongue (113, 76). Furber's nemesis, the word-ignorant Omensetter, however, is prelapsarian, which explains his effortless existence. Omensetter is a water creature, all body. Like women in any Updike or Faulkner novel, he is natural and at ease in physical life, representing the thoughtless innocence and the cruelty of the natural life – a "stony mindlessness" that always makes Jethro Furber think of Eden (126).

The modifier "stony" in this last quotation is hardly casual. Stones, like bodies and words, have a significant relationship to water. Furber's interior rush of words is set up in direct relationship to Omensetter's physical sport in the water, Furber sending his words tumbling around

the Challenge of Feminist Criticism," in *The Company We Keep: An Ethics of Fiction* (Berkeley: University of California Press, 1988), 383–418.

the garden walls, Omensetter skipping stones in the river. Furber's interest in stones goes back to his childhood, when he was entranced with biblical accounts of stoning. As an adult, he chooses his stones carefully (117). As he paces around the garden, he strides from stone to stone, one word chasing another as he hurls them upward, giving "the semblance of life to the stone." But like Omensetter's skipping stones, "whatever he gives them, it lasts only a moment. There's no help for it, they have to come down to a stone's end." Thus, following the trajectory of water, words, stones and bodies, Henry Pimber, cut loose from his hanging tree, will plummet to earth "like a stone" (208).

Omensetter is the one who finds Henry's body, and the villagers even suspect him of foul play, but Omensetter's only crime has been his preverbal life, and now he is falling into necessary knowledge. The mission to recover Pimber's body proceeds at the same time that Omensetter's baby is stricken with diphtheria. Doggedly following through with his fox-logic ("he'll have to stay where the hen has put him . . . ; you can see how bad the well wanted him," 38–9), Omensetter ignores the pleas of his wife, and refuses to send for a doctor. Instead, he goes outside his cabin and begins collecting stones as if to build an altar or perhaps to skip them in one last simulation of flight above the drowning waters, not knowing how to make them the words that he wants. Omensetter asks Furber to pray for the boy (207). But Furber, frantic with insight, scatters the pile of stones, shouts at the flesh-struck Omensetter. The baby is not dying from a theological test, but from diphtheria. Talking won't save the baby, and neither will trusting the body to itself; he needs a doctor, not prayers. Words alone cannot save us any more than can the body be sufficient expression of living – essential though it is.

Lucy says of the search for Pimber, "What's any body good for, emptied out. . . . How hard did you hunt for him when he was alive?" (178, 180). That's a fair question about how we have treated living beings, but Furber knows that even without its filling, the body is worth something to us. We can't help it. Strangely enough, he has learned this from Omensetter, who, all body and unreflected feeling, is helpless in the face of perishing spirit. With a redemptive sadness that supplants his earlier mockery, Furber responds to Henry Pimber's suicide by using the carnival language to express the absurdity and sorrow of corporeal life: "Why did he have to do it in such a circusy way?" and then wrapping a world in simple forms, answers himself: "Ha ha. Yeah. Why? Boy" (185). The question is rhetorical, because whether you fall into a well or hang from a tree, every life performance is subject to the precarious partnership of word and body; one will finally outweigh the other, and we cannot live fully except with both. Words, like bodies, like stones, have weight, gravity, and are as essential an element to life as water itself. Sometimes, like water, we drown in language, or as Furber does, we use language to make distance instead of human connections. We are like stones given temporary flight, something our words may do for us, but sinking is always the conclusion of every sky journey. Grave/stones – the matter of language is of the utmost seriousness, even though "the body of every symbol is absurd" (208), and eventually words and bodies both will fail us.

Although Henry on his way to his final leap says, "I shall be my own stone . . . just as all along I've been my own dry well – hole, wall and darkness" (60), Gass is more sanguine about words and bodies than is that despairing fox, Henry Pimber. If anything, words ("spiritual stones") can be a triumph over body because they can be so much more powerful in structure and effect. Updike and Percy are similarly disposed. Percy, for example, in much simpler metaphoric construction than Gass, regularly sends his characters in search of new language. Lancelot wants to devise a new code with Anna; Allie in *The Second Coming* designs a relationship with Will Barrett by insisting upon using her own tongue, and as they reclaim language, is able to think of speech as a form of lovemaking. The fondness of latter-day writers for words is clearer if we look back for a moment to another Faulkner novel where, with more savagery than sorrow or hope, Faulkner exposes the treachery of bodies *and* words.

As I Lay Dying is a novel obsessively concerned with embodiment, beginning with the punning title itself.[22] With an almost pitiless compression, the dying woman Addie Bundren marks the fatal connections between words and bodies in her single monologue. Words, like bodies, have no meaning until we fill them, and even then, "words dont ever fit even what they are trying to say at" because "words are just a shape to fill a lack; and that when the right time came, you wouldn't need a word for that anymore than for pride or fear" (157–8). Words, rather like women, are vessels, "a significant shape profoundly without life" that are used by bodies who don't even know they are dead but for the temporary fiction of meaning attached to flesh (159). So, Addie tests the word "sin" against the deed, the "doing that creeps along the earth" (160). In the light of the deed, her adultery with the minister Whitefield, the "high dead words seemed to lose even the significance of their dead sound" (161) and with the birth of Jewel, "the wild blood boiled away and the sound of it ceased" (162). Bereft of word, concluded in deed, Addie can get ready to "clean house" and die.

22 Eric J. Sundquist, *Faulkner: The House Divided* (Baltimore Md.: Johns Hopkins University Press, 1983), 29.

In contrast to Addie's passionate and bitter contention with the gap
between words and the thing itself, her lover is troubled by no such
discontinuity. As Whitefield heads toward Addie's deathbed, he rehearses
the words he will say to her husband in confession: "Anse, I have sinned,
Do with me as you will" (165). But Addie is dead by the time Whitefield
arrives and he decides that his good intentions will suffice for the deed;
the words he practiced will be enough. So, he abandons his confession
and enters the household with a fanfare of holy blabber and empty talk.
As Addie says of Cora Tull, "people to whom sin is just a matter of
words, to them salvation is just words too" (163). The comment is
Addie's last word, and then we move directly to Whitefield's monologue.
The swift, merciless juxtaposition of Addie and Whitefield's monologues
underscores the integrity of Addie's language. Words are disconnected
from the land and blood of fleshly life when people make them so, and
Addie dedicates her dying to plumb this truth. Like her crazy, lonely
son Darl, Addie sees too much about how people use each other through
words for their own "secret and selfish thought" (155). As her body
rots, barely lasting the trip to Jefferson in order to bury her, the words
attached to it become meaningless, just as she says they are. Her young
son Vardaman says, "My mother is a fish," flipping her into a familiar
metaphoric pool of reference while trying to make sense of her death
with the materials he has at hand – the fish he caught and ate for dinner
the evening of her death. "Then it wasn't and she was, and now it is
and she wasn't" (63), he says, trying to figure out how she once was
present, and her body still is, but she is not. Darl, slowly sinking into
the madness of disassociated identity, insists that "Jewel's mother is a
horse." He is naming Jewel's fractious horse as the tangible expression
of Addie's illegitimate passion, focusing not on the question of Jewel's
paternity, but on the question of Addie's identity. What relationship is
"mother" to Addie to Darl in light of her wordless deed?

What these contending descriptions of Addie all amount to is "My
mother is who I say she is," which in fact means "My mother is a reason
to go to Jefferson." None of these have much to do with the body called
Addie Bundren. Her family is intent upon transporting her rotting body
to Jefferson, not because she wanted to be buried there, although this is
the ostensible excuse, but because each one has a private reason for
wanting to get to town. Vardaman wants to eat bananas and look at a
toy train, Dewey Dell needs an abortion, Cash is interested in purchasing
a talking machine, and Anse is going to town to buy some new teeth
and get remarried. The body to which this language is attached survives
fire and water, rescued not because it was Addie but because it meant
so many things not–Addie. Like the words about it (mother, love, Addie,
horse, fish), it was emptied of meaning long ago, which is exactly what

she says. Dying happened in words, during lying, during living, the
dignity of corporeal form reduced to this grotesquerie of decayed language and body both.

Well, Addie is, after all, an adulterous wife, and it is not surprising
that the treachery of words and bodies both is enacted upon the body
of a woman, as if to make absolutely certain we have gotten the message
that the body of every symbol is absurd. Words and women's bodies –
we are to distrust them both, but each novelist would admit that this is
still all we have, and despite the polemic of androcentric fiction this is
as true for women as for men. The baby girl in *Rabbit, Run* drowns,
reappears in *Rabbit, Redux* as the teenager Jill, and is burned to death,
only to be reborn as Rabbit's granddaughter in *Rabbit Is Rich*. On one
level, this kind of sequence seems to confirm the eternal immensity of
women, and the monologue of the dead Addie can function as the same
kind of cosmic immortality, as does the absolute absence of Caddy in
The Sound and the Fury. Yet metaphor is always a doing and an undoing,
a giving and taking, a necessary vulnerability in fiction, refusing to let
us make absolute, unchanging statements about who we are. The language used by androcentric writers manages to convey an underlying
commonality between women and men that is not immediately apparent
in prior readings, and thus returning us all to water.

Elegy: From Water to Tears

According to Annie Burnham Cooper (Chapter 3), her flirtatious
minister kills himself by cutting his throat and jumping into a cistern.[23]
The guiding language for this chapter – the fox in the well – derives
from fiction, but it also comes from life. Fiction and life, words and
bodies, live within each other, have an immeasurable gravity that demands they be taken seriously together. Perhaps that is one reason why,
of any event in Updike's fiction, people usually remember that in *Rabbit,
Run* his drunken wife lets their baby daughter drown in the bathtub.
The horror and pity of that event is the "simple circle" around which
the subsequent Rabbit sagas revolve, and in congruence with the fox in
the well, it provides a paradigmatic circle for the androcentric fiction
discussed here.

Harry "Rabbit" Angstrom "was not a water animal," and John Updike
gives us abundant evidence to suppose that Rabbit is usually in danger
of drowning. A sexual stream of consciousness builds and flows through
the center of this novel, much as it does in *Omensetter's Luck* and *The
Sound and the Fury*. As Rabbit awaits the birth of his daughter, "he feels

23 Penelope Franklin, ed., *Private Pages: Diaries of American Women* (New York: Ballantine,
1986), 173.

underwater, caught in chains of transparent slime, ghosts of the urgent ejaculations he has spat into the mild bodies of women" (*Run:* 184). Prior to Janice's return home with the new baby, he is trying to sleep, but "like an unsteered boat, he keeps scraping into the same rocks," below him a "bottomless sea." He flounders in this half-sleep, jumbled sexual fantasies pressing upon him as presences in an underwater world. He finally masturbates, but falls asleep only fitfully, in a bed whose wrinkled sheet looks like a net. Shortly thereafter, Janice and the baby girl come home from the hospital, and she lies like Moses in a cradle of plaited rushes (215).

All is tranquil until Rabbit returns home from church one afternoon, urgent with the need to make love to Janice. But the baby cries persistently, "an infuriating noise of strain, . . . a persistent feeble scratching at some interior door," that prevents Rabbit from approaching his wife. His son Nelson is fretful and whiny, "as if, being closest to the dark gate from which the baby has recently emerged, he is most sensitive to the threat the infant is trying to warn them of" (224). The walls of the apartment "sweat like the walls of a prison," as the wild feeble warning wears on. Finally the baby weakens into silence as though "night itself had swept in and washed her away like a broken piece of rubbish" (227). Metaphors of walls and water converge, doubling the effect of enclosure and heightening the sense of danger and urgency. Inside the apartment awash with sexual waters, the baby floats in her fragile basket, her cries scratching at some interior door, warning of flooding flesh. Rabbit, sensing high water, flees the apartment and rides a bus away from the dangerous walls. He feels that there is "something better for him than listening to babies cry and cheating people in used car lots and it's this feeling he tries to kill, right there on the bus . . . he closes his eyes and tries to kill it" (250). While Rabbit sits on the bus trying to kill his own sense of uniqueness, Janice lets the baby girl drown in the bathtub. Updike allows the water metaphor to work out its literal significations, and the result is that words finally tell the truth about female beings.

A girl-child not only has to negotiate all the double prisons men must endure – spirits trapped inside bodies, bodies trapped in life – but she also must negotiate the fictions men have built around her. Those man-made fictions are the interior door. Since one of these fictions seems to be that women are all flesh – water creatures – the literal logic of the metaphor leads Updike to launch the baby girl in the bathwater. The walls of the interior prison, the waters women drown in, are the words men have written about them. Updike affirms this in allowing the child to drown. It is the only way he has to admit that the truth about embodiment is that it is everyone's condition, and not just something peculiar to the higher nature of spiritual male beings. For a moment, the old dualism vanishes and the humanity of women is acknowledged in a most unlikely place, and in a most ironic and tragic manner.

There are times, then, when Updike temporarily achieves an inclusive and compassionate look at the absurdity and anguish of mortality. Rabbit *and* Janice repair to a burrow at the end of the 1960s in *Rabbit Redux,* and even the mean-spirited Roger in *Roger's Version* says, "there is an odd erotic illumination that comes over us when for a moment we see women as simply the females of our animal species, another set of forked creatures condemned to a daily round of ingestion and defecation, of sleep and exertion. We are in this together. *In carnem*" (183). Finally, in *Rabbit Is Rich,* the flood water of language recedes, and drowning waters are replaced by rain and tears. Updike has always been conscious of the framing and limiting function of windows, and in this novel – unlike previous water and window language – we often see the aging Rabbit pressing his nose against a rain-streaked window, thinking of childhood, thinking of death. Rain seems to him "the last proof left to him that God exists" (116), perhaps because "our tears are always young, the saltwater stays the same from cradle . . . to grave." God may be the salt in tears and water, "in the universe in the way salt is in the ocean, giving it a taste" (422, 433).

Gass, despite the courage of words, arrives at the same sorrow and resignation. Furber says to God, "Why have You made us the saddest animal?" and then answers himself and the dead Henry Pimber, "He cannot do it, Henry, that is why. He can't continue us. All He can do is try to make us happy that we die. Really, He's a pretty good fellow" (*Luck:* 214). Despite this kindly assessment of God's limitations, the fact remains that there is no word that can alter the fate of our containment, nor do any of these novelists suggest that religious institutions have anything to offer for our bereavement. We are eternally unprepared for what we are, which, to circle back to the house and containment language that opened the discussion of women, is like being "lost in space. Like what souls must feel when they awaken in a baby's body so far from heaven: not only scared so they cry, but guilty, guilty. A huge hole to fill up" (*Rich:* 433).

Androcentric authors have constructed shelters within this unman-ageable emptiness, trapdoors to cover the well and guard against the ever-present threat that the earth could open any minute. Yet even the most vigilant fox (restless rabbit, stubborn mole) will stumble one day, find that leaping (running, digging) is always followed by falling, no matter how skillful the words used. Words are as tricky as bodies, for sometimes the words imposed between self and body (spirit and decay) are as confining as they are liberating.

Viewed from a distance, what we have is a grand cultural box within a box effect. Perhaps it is inevitable that the intersection of spirit and body produces fictions of infinite regress. Men write that they are spirits trapped in bodies, bodies subject to the undignified pleasures of sexual nature, which in turn is the symbol of all life contingency. Woman is the enclosing metaphor of that sexual nature. Men are trapped by women. But women cry out that they are trapped by these very words that men feel and write and think about women. They, too, are prisoners of disproportionate flesh, fictional flesh devised largely by men. Indeed, the androcentric imagination has made a prison from words, trapping women within words, and men within the words mistaken for women. Each spirit can point to the person of the other sex as the cause of the lethal containment.

The "heart of the heart of the country" is the question of how we got to such an incongruity of flesh and spirit, and how that incongruity is created or complicated by the intercession of language. But what begins as a question about sexual bodies and religious spirits becomes a question of female sexuality and male spirituality and the fictions we perpetuate about both. Despite our sophisticated intellections about language, however, the total impact of these androcentric narratives is that of physical presence. Knowledge is written in flesh, not simply in words, and despite all doctrinal protestation, the Word is not enough. Creation, fall, and death is the only believable and verifiable story we seem to have, not Incarnation, and certainly not Resurrection. The sheer intensity of the physical beyond words keeps bringing religion back to the sexual body, the sign of our mortality, yet the vehicle for any possibility we can dream of, including the realm of the not-physical. As the tormented Furber discovers, "you may call our soul our best, but this, our body, is our love. . . . How simply is our fondness for it guaranteed; we can't live outside of it, not as we are, not as we wish" (*Luck:* 214). Yes. How simply is our fondness for it guaranteed.

7

Fatal Abstractions: Metaphors of Embodiment in the Gynocentric Imagination

In a short story by Mary Gordon, a wife gives her husband a short story to read. The story makes him think of another woman from his past, and he weeps from the remembered loss. Although she comforts him, the wife feels betrayed by his revelation and his failure to protect her from this intrusive knowledge. After he has fallen asleep, she moves to a spare bed in another room. "She lies on top of the spread, stretching her limbs as far away from her body as she could. Her sex was open – utterly vulnerable, she thought."[1]

In this simple image we see a woman enacting a nonverbal gesture that would be known only to a woman in privacy with herself. There is no male gaze to prompt, validate, or claim her. She spreads her legs for herself, using her sexual body to express her feelings of vulnerability and betrayal. The gesture is potentially sexual, but not necessarily so. It just depends upon who is looking. A woman does not express herself apart from androcentric culture, but she is also not the same body for herself that she is when portrayed through the androcentric gaze. That is, there are always at least two stories to negotiate when reading women's fiction, the story about life in a patriarchy and the responsive female voice inside the story about patriarchy. Both stories are authentic to women's writing – living in relationship to androcentric norms and claiming distance at the same time.

In the outer narrative – Gordon's story itself – the woman acts as a loving wife should. She comforts her husband who thoughtlessly grieves out loud in response to the story he has read. The shared story to which he responds is one inner narrative, but the "heart of the heart" of the narrative is the unspoken gestural response through which the wife recapitulates in her own terms the loss evoked by the shared inner story.

---

1 "The Other Woman," *Temporary Shelter* (New York: Random House, 1987), 155. Subsequent page citations in the text appear in parentheses.

Her gesture is not subversive; it is a contrapuntal complicity with the "outer story" in which they both live. The world is governed by certain patriarchal expectations about women's bodies. He expects to pillow his head upon her body and be comforted; she allows him to do so without reproaching him because "she was a woman, her body had been bred to deceit" (156). That is, she does not betray his trust and her recognition of the order of things – that women's bodies are available for comfort and shelter. But by using her body – the tangible reassurance of the order of things – to express *her own* relationship to the order of things, she summarizes the doubled narrative of women's writing about embodiment. It is a story within a story.

In terms of the conventions of embodiment, male writers show themselves to be in ambiguous relationship to embodied life by depicting a conflictual relationship between themselves and women, who are, as we've seen, the living metaphors of embodied life. For the homiletic writers, the ambiguity of embodied life was expressed in terms of imprisonment, confinement, and suffering. Clearly, they were in combat with the heavy hand of patriarchal patronage, but at the same time, their translation of the female body into its spiritualized meaning indicates how much their struggle was also a self–civil war. The writing of twentieth-century women makes the doubled narrative boundaries of female writing even clearer. The subterfuge of nineteenth-century writing is no longer necessary, for many things can be said in the female voice that could not have been directly uttered in the century gone. Nonetheless, the problem of speaking two stories at the same time remains, for the meanings attached to women's bodies have not magically vanished just because we have been able to name them out loud. By living within this story about themselves, women can only write about embodiment as being in conflict with themselves and the female sexual body. It is as though there are three kinds of bodies in the world – men, the iconic female sexual body, and women. Men and women both stand in an uneasy relationship to the female sexual body.

Not only does a woman know her own body to be tricky and portentous, but she also knows that her comforting sexual body is part of the sustaining fiction between women and men, indeed, part of the sacred fiction of the universe. Sometimes the comforting sexuality of her body is a true story, not only for her partner, but for herself as well. But while acknowledging and exploring the reality of this position, women writers also insist that a woman is not just a symbolically charged female body in an androcentric universe, but "just" a body, subject to the same pleasure, risk, and inevitable loss that attends all physical life. Most women occupy both positions at the same time, and the ways in which women writers portray female characters reflect this doubled experience. In women's fiction, two stories are always being told, one inside the other, at the same time: the story of the female sexual body and the story of embodied life as a woman human being.[2]

I am not going to prove this claim as much as take it for granted in the fiction of the four contemporary writers I have chosen to represent women's voices on embodiment: Mary Gordon, Marilynne Robinson, Louise Erdrich, and Margaret Atwood.[3] The three novels of Mary Gordon form a trinity, all dealing with cerebral, self-aware female characters. *Final Payments* (1978) begins with the death of a dogmatic father whose only daughter, Isabel, has devoted her youth to caring for him during his long decay into death. *The Company of Women* (1981) concerns another extraordinary girl-child, Felicitas, who is raised by a dogmatic priest and the five women who attend his ministry. Father Cyprian instructs Felicitas as though she were a son, teaching her to cherish the cool, confident realms of intellect and spirit. But Felicitas, once proud of her messianic status in her religious family, violates those expectations. Instead of functioning as a junior Jesus, she becomes a pregnant Mary in the crucial years of her apprenticeship, not even knowing who is the father of her child. *Men and Angels* (1985) deals with the realm of the spirit, the refuge of those who find themselves without the shelter of ordinary, human

2 The relationship of women's writing to the larger sexist society is a vexing one for feminist readers and critics. Margaret Homans, in "'Her Very Own Howl': The Ambiguities of Representation in Recent Women's Fiction," *Signs* 9 (Winter 1983): 186–205, develops the idea of more than one kind of marginality. She draws on work by Rachel Blau duPlessis, who introduces the term "(ambiguously) nonhegemonic" to describe the "both/and vision" of women's writing. In "Feminist Criticism in the Wilderness," Elaine Showalter speaks of women's writing in terms of undercurrents (an apt description for the metaphoric direction of my chapter) rather than as inside/outside, suggesting that women are writing inside two traditions simultaneously. See Elizabeth Abel, ed., *Writing and Sexual Difference* (Chicago: University of Chicago Press, 1982), 9–35. Sandra M. Gilbert and Susan Gubar's study, *The Madwoman in the Attic: The Woman Writer and the Nineteenth Century Literary Imagination* (New Haven: Yale University Press, 1979), describes nineteenth-century women's writing as simultaneously conforming but subverting of dominant culture, what they call a "palimpsest" (73). Nancy K. Miller draws on this idea in discovering a revised iconography of desire found in women's writing. See "Arachnologies: The Woman, the Text, and the Critic," in *The Poetics of Gender* (New York: Columbia University Press, 1986) 270–95.

   Other interesting explorations of the question of the hidden text of women's speech and the art of reading and hearing silences appear in Mary Field Belenky et al., *Women's Ways of Knowing: The Development of Self, Voice and Mind* (New York: Basic Books, 1986); Susan Griffin, *Pornography and Silence: Culture's Revenge against Nature* (New York: Harper & Row, 1981); and Tillie Olsen, *Silences* (1965; reprint, New York: Laurel, Dell, 1978).

3 As a Canadian writer, Margaret Atwood is an outspoken champion of Canadian identity and culture and I owe her, if not my readers, some apology for including her in a study otherwise devoted to American writers. I hope my use of her will be understood as a tribute to her influence and importance to American feminism and American writers. It would have been difficult to conceive of this chapter without her.

love. Gordon's novels, then, are not nearly so conventionally shaped by institutional religion as they might seem: the father is dead, the son is an extraordinary girl-child, and the Spirit is powerless to supply the life-giving gift of love. Biological fathers are dead or absent, leaving mothers and daughters to work out the essential, framing question: How are we to be responsible for the miraculous, accidental, and risk-taking encounters of bodily love?[4] With Gordon, Margaret Atwood finds traditional body/spirit, male/female polarities highly troubling, and she offers no easy solution to the enigma of female reproductive sexuality and woman's mind. Atwood's heroines, only one of whom is situated within traditional religious boundaries, live in a problematic and destructive relationship to their bodies. Often they are women who have not yet managed to outwit or discard the religious romance of heroes, rescue, and seminal/verbal emissions; they are women for whom the traditional Christian symbolism about women (and the secular dispensations of that symbol system) is intensely alienating, but who have few resources for subverting or discarding the forcefield of that pervasive symbol system.

Atwood's several doubling devices – her use of mirrors is exemplary – underline the stacked story related by her female characters.[5] Marian, the anorexic narrator of The Edible Woman (1969), is so repulsed by her impending marriage and the reproductive female body that she refuses to feed hers, and speaks of herself in the third person throughout the long middle section of the novel. The nameless narrator of Surfacing (1972) goes looking for her father who has drowned, just as she has drowned the memory of her abortion. Both deaths are the products of fatal abstractions, and her healing is attainable only through a kind of furious, holy primitivism designed to give the voracious, undeniable body its due. In Lady Oracle (1972), fat girl Joan Foster escapes her inglorious life of substantial flesh by becoming a grown-up writer of Gothic romances, only to find that she needs an escape, not from "real" life, but from the escape itself. Finally, a female narrator known only by her master's name tells us in The Handmaid's Tale (1986) what it is like

4 I use the following hardcover editions of Gordon's novels: The Company of Women (New York: Random House, 1981); Final Payments (New York: Random House, 1978); and Men and Angels (New York: Random House, 1985). Page citations in the text appear in parentheses.
5 For example, Pamela S. Bromberg, "The Two Faces of the Mirror in The Edible Woman and Lady Oracle," in Margaret Atwood: Vision and Forms, ed. Kathryn VanSpanckeren and Jan Garden Castro (Carbondale: Southern Illinois University Press, 1988), 12–23; Roberta Rubenstein, "Escape Artists and Split Personalities: Margaret Atwood," in Boundaries of the Self: Gender, Culture, Fiction (Urbana: University of Illinois Press, 1987), 63–122. Sandra Gilbert and Susan Gubar discuss mirrors as an important metaphoric device for women in The Madwoman in the Attic, as does Jenijoy La Belle, Herself Beheld: The Literature of the Looking Glass (Ithaca, N.Y.: Cornell University Press, 1988).

to live in a religious universe in which body/spirit polarities have been conquered by eliminating a meaningful body altogether.[6]

Louise Erdrich's three novels about life on North Dakota Indian reservations take up body/spirit antimonies from a cultural perspective that is not available from within the institutions of white Christianity. Using both male and female narrators, Erdrich creates a poetic archaeology of contemporary Native American identity. In *Love Medicine* (1984), the loss and confusion of contemporary life on a reservation is reflected in the densely overlapped narratives of many survivors, each of whom tells a story about love and water. In *The Beet Queen* (1986), the intricate, floating web of narrative voices that characterizes *Love Medicine* becomes sky-borne, and the voices of women take over the telling of the tale, speaking of flight and falling and the resilience, solidity, and tragic fragility of bodily love. Two key metaphors that govern *Love Medicine* and *The Beet Queen*, water and flight, focus the simpler narrative structure of *Tracks* (1988), the third novel of this unfinished series about Native American life.[7] There are only two narrators in *Tracks*, Nanapush, the patriarch of one of the extensive families we see years later (in *Love Medicine* and *The Beet Queen*), and Pauline, who becomes Sister Leopolda. She, too, will figure prominently in subsequent narratives. Nanapush is telling his story to his beloved, willful granddaughter, Lulu, but he is also the voice for a third, powerful character, who, like the old gods she represents, does not speak for herself. This is Lulu's mother, Fleur Pillager, who belongs to the water world of the old spirits. Her spiritual opponent is the bird-like Pauline, whose best moments are spent hovering over the beds of the dying. Erdrich presents her people without condescension or polemic, and although there are moments of grace and ecstasy, we know with the characters that we are hearing a story of profound loss and bereavement.

This theme of loss, which takes more personal focus in Gordon and Atwood and then extends to cultural and racial dimensions in Erdrich, is given its most expansive articulation in Marilynne Robinson's *Housekeeping* (1981).[8] The title is one of several compassionate ironies, for this

6 I use the following editions of Atwood's novels: *Cat's Eye* (New York: Doubleday, 1988); *The Edible Woman* (1969; reprint, New York: Warner, 1989); *The Handmaid's Tale* (Boston: Houghton Mifflin, 1986); *Lady Oracle* (1976; reprint, New York: Fawcett Crest, 1987); and *Surfacing* (1972; reprint, New York: Fawcett Crest, Ballantine, 1987). Page citations appear in the text in parentheses.

7 I use the following editions of Erdrich's novels: *The Beet Queen* (New York: Bantam, 1987); *Love Medicine* (New York: Bantam, 1985); and *Tracks* (New York: Henry Holt, 1988). Page citations in the text appear in parentheses.

8 *Housekeeping* (New York: Bantam, 1987). Page citations in the text appear in parentheses. *Housekeeping* is Robinson's only novel, but it should become a literary classic. I inflect the novel toward its more sorrowful meanings, but other readings are quite possible. See Marcia Aldrich, "The Poetics of Transience: Marilynne Robinson's *Housekeeping*,"

intensely poetic novel is about the dissolution of housekeeping through the wearing away of time. From beginning to end, the novel is filled with water. Helen Stone leaves her two daughters Ruthie and Lucille with their grandmother and commits suicide by driving her car into Fingerbone Lake. When Grandmother dies, Aunt Sylvia Fisher arrives to preside over the dissolution of the fragile household. Lucille runs away to live with the Home Economics teacher, but Ruthie drifts with Sylvie, finally quitting school altogether in order to wander the lakeside with her abstracted aunt. Unmoored from all the usual human attachments and structures, they slip from the reality of the normal into the dreamwork of natural transience, living as water creatures in a vast "millennial present."

Shelter, loss, escape, accident, sanctuary, restoration, love: this is the language of embodiment in women's fiction. Although embodiment is still as much a question of sacred proportions for women writers as for men, the terms "religion" and "sexuality" have little currency in women's fiction. Perhaps this is because we are reading about what it means to have iconic significance from the perspective of the icon. Women writers both acknowledge the charged meaning of the female sexual body in the context of traditional language about embodiment and point through that meaning to a more universal human tongue about finitude and love.

Two key metaphors of flight and water express a central issue in women's writing about embodiment, that of boundaries – who determines them and what happens when they are crossed.[9] By violating or

---

Essays in Literature 16 (Spring 1989): 127–40; Joan Kirkby, "Is There Life after Art? The Metaphysics of Marilynne Robinson's *Housekeeping*," *Tulsa Studies in Women's Literature* 5 (Spring 1986): 91–109; Anne-Marie Mallon, "Sojourning Women: Homelessness and Transcendence in *Housekeeping*," *Critique* 30 (Winter 1989): 95–105; Elizabeth Meese, "A World of Women: Marilynne Robinson's *Housekeeping*," in *Crossing the Double-Cross: The Practice of Feminist Criticism* (Chapel Hill: University of North Carolina Press, 1986), 55–68; and Rubenstein, "Transformations of the Ordinary: Marilynne Robinson," in *Boundaries of the Self,* 211–30.

9 Contemporary criticism provides a helpful context for reflecting upon fluidity and boundaries in women's writing and experience. See, for example, Nancy Chodorow, who develops the idea of women's "permeable ego membrane" in *The Reproduction of Mothering: Psychoanalysis and the Sociology of Gender* (Berkeley: University of California Press, 1978); Helen Cixous, "Castration or Decapitation," *Signs* 7 (Autumn 1981): 41–5, and "The Laugh of the Medusa," *Signs* 1 (Summer 1976): 875–93; Luce Irigaray, "When Our Lips Speak Together," *Signs* 6 (Autumn 1980): 69–79; Betty Krasne, "Beware of Death by Water," *Anima* 6 (Fall 1979): 5–10; Marilee Lindemann, "This Woman Can Cross Any Line: Power and Authority in Contemporary Women's Fiction," in *Engendering the Word: Feminist Essays in Psychosexual Politics,* ed. Temma Berg et al. (Urbana: University of Ilinois Press, 1989): 105–24; and Dorothy Richardson, *Pointed Roofs, Backwater, Honeycomb, Pilgrimage,* vol. 1 (New York: Knopf, 1983). Susan Lanser discusses Richardson as the originator of stream of consciousness in *The Narrative Act: Point of*

rearranging traditionally recognized personal, social, and supernatural boundaries, women dislocate patriarchal ideas about embodiment without yet eliminating them altogether. As Myra Jehlen says, women's writing presents "a more fluid imagery of interacting juxtapositions. . . . Indeed, the female territory might well be envisioned as one long border and independence for women, not as a separate country but as open access to the sea."[10] The focus of women's writing is not upon men's bodies as a mirror image to men's writing about embodiment, nor a simple reversal of sexist perspectives. Like the male writer, women also seem to focus on women's bodies, but women write in an effort to understand the mortal humanity of women who may never escape the assigned meanings of the religiously loaded female sexual body.

Flight

Birds are a frequent resource in women's writing – predatory birds, fragile birds, caged birds, birds with perspective. In *Final Payments,* Isabel thinks of her father as a "great cruel bird" who seizes upon the compromising arguments of the modern world as a predatory hawk swoops upon prey (40). Anne Foster in *Men and Angels* thinks of her son as a "bird whose ardent heart seems nearly visible" (236) and turns into an avenging bird herself when her babysitter endangers the children (202). The narrator in *Surfacing* mourns her mother's failure to fly but in a visionary restoration sees her mother feeding the birds and then vanishing with the rustle of iconic wings (217). In Erdrich's *Tracks,* the religiously twisted Pauline also turns into a bird, both predator and scavenger, her transformation so well-suited to her being that she literally resembles what she symbolically represents. She screeches "as if she were a talking bird," and her fingers are "webbed and doubled over like a hatchling's claws" (52–3; 196). Pauline becomes the "crow of the reservation," living off scraps of stories and cast-off love. But unlike the human community that only tolerates her, she has perspective, she can see what lies below and she alone knows "death as a form of grace. . . . [she has] the merciful scavenger's heart" (68–9).

To be a bird is to be weightless and unencumbered, and "bird" often functions as a symbol of the mind-ful, transcendent spirit. We imagine that if our human eyes were winged, we would see, not what birds see, but what we would see of human meaning if only we could, just once, get a glimpse of the whole story. Somehow an aerial view would bring our lives to order. Flying, of course, is crucial to this longed-for per-

---

View in Prose Fiction (Princeton, N.J.: Princeton University Press, 1981). See Richardson's foreword for her remarks on the subject, pp. 9–12; and Rubenstein, *Boundaries of the Self.*
10 "Archimedes and the Paradox of Feminist Criticism," *Signs* 6 (Summer 1981): 582.

spective. There is something about imagined weightlessness that would at once free us and give us a knowledge we hardly have a name for when earthbound. When Anne Foster was alone, studying, "she was weightless . . . in some high territory, inaccessible. With the children there was never any flying off, flying up. A mother was encumbered and held down." But although Anne feels fortunate that she loves the "vivid body life the children lived and gave her" (*Men and Angels* 45), her babysitter, Laura, who also values weightlessness, sees that same body life only as death. Laura sees Anne's love for her children as a deadly, burning weight, so that "loving them as she did, [Anne] could not fly up to the Spirit, fly up from the flames" (118).

Helene Cixous argues in "The Laugh of the Medusa" that "flying is a woman's gesture – flying in language and making it fly." She goes on to describe the function of "flying" in French, which moves from flight to steal away, to steal:

> It's no accident: women take after birds and robbers just as robbers take after women and birds. They (*illes*) go by, fly the coop, take pleasure in jumbling the order of space, in disorienting it, in changing around the furniture, dislocating things and values, breaking them all up, emptying structures, turning propriety upside down.[11]

Drawing on Cixous's discussion, Susan Suleiman notes that a famous women's novel about flying, Erica Jong's *Fear of Flying,* turns propriety upside down by "stealing" most of its narrative tricks from androcentric language while exploiting all the other possible meanings of flight that are available – escape, perspective, weightlessness, falling. Women's writing – flying – is a deliberate transgression of accepted verbal and physical boundaries, and flying is not just a metaphor in women's writing, but a way of speaking about women's writing.[12] As Cixous says, "What woman hasn't flown/stolen?" and a little later on she refers to the writing woman as an "air-borne swimmer."[13] Cixous's exuberance for the craft of flying in this particular essay tends to mask the sorrow propelling women's words, however. Perhaps women imagine weightlessness and flight because we know what it means to be caged and wounded, trapped in alien territory, as the title of Maya Angelou's autobiography, *I Know Why the Caged Bird Sings* (1969), reminds us. Anne

11 "The Laugh of the Medusa," *Signs* 1 (Summer 1976): 887.
12 "(Re)writing the Body: The Politics and Poetics of Female Eroticism," in *The Female Body in Western Culture: Contemporary Perspectives*, ed. Susan Rubin Suleiman (Cambridge, Mass.: Harvard University Press, 1985), 9–10. Other uses of flight and falling appear in Mary Daly, *Gyn/Ecology: The Metaethics of Radical Feminism* (Boston: Beacon, 1978); Ann Beattie, *Falling in Place* (New York: Random House, 1980); and Toni Morrison, *Song of Solomon* (New York: Signet, NAL, 1977).
13 Cixous, "Laugh," 889.

Foster describes her father's voice as "heavy as a wounded bird, flapping, flying blind against the glass with his defeats and his apologies" (*Men and Angels:* 81). Offred in *The Handmaid's Tale* realizes that her predecessor did not escape, but committed suicide by hanging, and, with despair, Offred acknowledges the truth-making presence of her "ancestress, my double, turning midair under the chandelier, . . . a bird stopped in flight, a woman made into an angel, waiting to be found" (293).

Flight is one of the sustained metaphors of *The Beet Queen,* which begins when Adelaide Adare leaves her three children at a fairground, climbs into a stunt plane with the pilot, Omar, and disappears into the sky. Years later, however, we see the conclusion to her escape. She and Omar own a Birdorama in Florida, and she lives in the shadow of the giant cage, still trapped and flightless, screaming her life away like a bloodied, caged bird. Adelaide's niece, Sita, never sees this conclusion to Adelaide's flight, however, and dying, Sita romanticizes Adelaide's flight as effortless and eternal. "Her bones hollowed like a bird's. Her wings never made that terrible chicken sound, thrashing earth, but no sound at all. She didn't have to flap, but effortlessly swerved into the streams and the currents that flow invisible above us. So she flew off. That's what I should have done instead of transplanting phlox" (*Beet Queen:* 258–9) Sita decides, too late mourning her own earthbound conclusion. With Sita, we somehow imagine that there is something effortless that birds do, some attainable, graceful riding of currents that will give us perspective or peace.

But Adelaide's abandoned daughter, Mary Adare, turns this same longing against itself when she responds to Adelaide's flight. She sends her mother a postcard with an aerial view of Argus, North Dakota, and writes on the back, "All three of your children starved dead." Then she imagines the postcard alighting in Adelaide's hands, and her mother staring at each detail of the picture, but "she could not see her daughter who was too small to tell of, looking directly through her, not dead, but securely hidden in the aerial view" (*Beet Queen:* 52). In other words, women may never be allowed a clean take-off. Adelaide does not simply fly away to some free and weightless region, she steals her life away from her children, and she and they pay a lifetime price for her clip-winged freedom. Escape looks much different to those left behind, those without the luxury of romanticizing the heady possibility of the disembodied life represented by the flighty spirit.

Like Pauline of *Tracks,* Laura of *Men and Angels* represents the pity and terror of the religiously damaged person who never finds comfort in the simple presence of the loving body. The chilly austerity of a particular kind of Christian dualism torments each character, already victimized by the accidents of love, into her desperate, unlovable shape.

Laura tries to invoke the cool, detached love of the spirit against the hot, weighted life of the body and through a sheer act of will transcend what she is denied and so desperately needs. She imagines that she and Anne will fly up to the weightless realm of the Spirit, which is "cool and without body" (*Men and Angels:* 77); that she will rescue Anne from "drowning in flesh" (32). Tragically enough, Anne can feel Laura's yearning, "like a furnace left on in a summer house. She knew that Laura craved love. But the best Anne could do was to keep herself from being cruel" (158). Like Offred's ancestress in the house of Gilead, Laura, too, finally flees the pain of being no-body-at-all, and she slits her wrists in Anne's bathtub.

"The love of God means nothing to a heart starved of human love" (*Men and Angels:* 231). If there is a God or the remote, floating realm of spirit, it exists only because human love has preceded it, and the wings we imagine may not be as suited for flight as they are for shelter. Anne knows that while Laura was starving, she "let her husband's love feed her. Let the shade of its wing shelter her, cover her over. But no wing had ever covered Laura" (232). For Laura flight could only be a fatal exit, the imagined upward motion completed and resolved by its own inevitable downward motion. Flight, in other words, is the abstraction; falling – the inevitable downward pull of flesh – is the reality.

Women's fiction about embodiment carries a number of startling images of falling and fallen women, images that are directly related to flying or, a corresponding motion, jumping. After Adelaide flies off with Omar, her abandoned son, Karl, dreams that Omar suddenly pulls Adelaide out of her seat and drops her out of the airplane. "All night she fell through the awful cold. Her coat flapped open and her black dress wrapped tightly around her legs. Her red hair flowed straight upward like a flame. She was a candle that gave no warmth. My heart froze. I had no love for her. That is why, by morning, I allowed her to hit the earth" (*Beet Queen:* 15).

This image of a woman in a fatal fall is repeated in several places by Margaret Atwood. Elaine Risley of *Cat's Eye* dreams of a childhood nemesis, seeing her "falling, from a cliff or bridge . . . her arms outspread, her skirt open like a bell, making a snow angel in the empty air. She never hits or lands; she falls and falls, and I wake with my heart pounding and gravity cut out from under me, as in an elevator plummeting out of control" (378). The narrator of *Surfacing* describes her own position in marriage as a fatal fall, saying it was like "jumping off a cliff. That was the feeling I had all the time I was married; in the air, going down, waiting for the smash at the bottom" (51). Later she remembers how her mother also tried to fly when "she and her sister had made wings for themselves out of an old umbrella; they'd jumped off the barn roof, attempting to fly, and she broke both her ankles. She would laugh about this, but the story seemed to me then chilly and sad, the failure unbearable" (144).

In *Lady Oracle,* Joan Foster has an alter ego, a Fat Lady, who appears to her in pink tights, tiara, and a pink umbrella, the latter of which is a "substitute for the wings which I longed to pin on her" (111). Even when the adult Joan is no longer obese, she cannot shed her alter ego. Instead, and in defiance of all wisdom about fleshly immensity, the rebellious Fat Lady becomes airborne. In one daydream, "she'd be walking across her tightrope, in her pink tutu, and she'd fall, in slow motion, turning over and over on the way down" (279). In a later dream, however, as Joan gets closer to faking her own death in order to escape her life, the Fat Lady does not fall at all, but she floats. "Her secret was that although she was so very large, she was very light, she was hollow, like a helium balloon." Unfortunately, she hangs above the circus crowd helplessly, kicking her skates feebly, "her tights and the huge moon of her rump were visible," a whale of a female target, and although she even bursts into song from this amazing position, the authorities fail to appreciate her unique achievement and get a harpoon gun to shoot her down (304–5). In the image of the Fat Lady, the metaphor of flight is played for its literal absurdity. Here is what it means for women to be trapped by the female body, incarcerated by this embarrassing, symbolic immensity, and here is how ridiculous we look, longing for flesh to match a lightness of spirit. No one can fly, and especially not the humongous female body. All we can do is fall or get shot down in the flight.

Finally, Elaine Risley in *Cat's Eye* paints the story of "Falling Women," which is really about men, although you can't see them in the picture. The unseen men of the painting are like natural hazards, "like slippery rocks with jagged edges. You could walk with care along between the rocks, picking your steps, and if you slipped you'd fall and cut yourself, but it was no use blaming the rocks." Thus, "Falling Women" shows the women, "three of them, falling as if by accident off a bridge, their skirts opened into bells by the wind, their hair streaming upward. Down they fell, onto the men who were lying unseen, jagged and dark and without volition, far below" (282). According to this character – and this view is in line with most of Atwood's ironic and passive female narrators – the downward motion has no creator. Women fall against their will, but they are not pushed or pulled, nor do they jump. They are "merely fallen." This must be the meaning of the old sexual epithet, "fallen women," Elaine decides. "Fallen women were women who had fallen onto men and hurt themselves" (282). Contemplating her painting,

Elaine remarks, "Of course there was Eve and the Fall; but there was nothing about falling in that story, which was only about eating, like most children's stories" (282). Gravity, and in this instance, the specific gravity of the female body, is the natural sufficiency that pulls us earthward – the seriousness of flesh that inevitably concludes with the grave.

The metaphoric work of flight in these images of women plummeting to earth invites an interesting rereading of the Genesis account, which is, after all, a source for so much dualistic Christian misogyny. In the various images of flight and falling reviewed here, we can see that some motion prior to falling is missing from the biblical record and has been replaced by the earthbound activity of eating. But eating only maintains or adds to what already exists (the serious body), so eating the wrong food could not be the precipitating factor in human mortality. Women's version of "fall," our story within a story, corrects this grave error. Those blamed for the tragedy of mortality know that flight must have preceded the Fall. We did not stumble or trip. We deliberately grabbed umbrellas, fashioned wings, climbed onto tall buildings, leaped into airplanes, or knotted the rope to our only exit. We jumped, hoping to fly free and elude the heavy hand of God. This made God angry, and so he arranged for us to spend that lifelong moment before impact learning of the irresistible gravity of flesh, teaching us to fear the one thing that makes us different from him, and calling it love.

It can hardly be an accident, then, that we commonly refer to love as downward motion – falling in love – a phrase that anticipates its own despair. Offred of *The Handmaid's Tale* lives under a religious dictatorship in which every kind of body, male and female, is defined exclusively and literally by its reproductive potential. Living in a world stripped of all metaphor, she is in a peculiarly painful position from which to contemplate the pathway by which symbolic dualism has been made horrifyingly concrete. Reflecting on the time before Gilead, she says,

> *Falling in love,* we said; *I fell for him.* We were falling women. We believed in it, this downward motion: so lovely, like flying, and yet at the same time so dire, so extreme, so unlikely. *God is love,* they once said, but we reversed that, and love, like heaven, was always just around the corner. The more difficult it was to love the particular man beside us, the more we believed in Love, abstract and total. We were waiting, always, for the incarnation. That word, made flesh. (225–6)

The perfect word of love made into particular flesh is supposed to be the antidote for falling, and secularized as romantic love, we learn to believe that some kinds of falling are good and necessary, such as falling in love; such as falling under submission to male authority (Chapter 5). But like romantic love and its theological analogue, flight is a fatal abstraction, just like falling in love. It exists as possibility only in connection with the corresponding reality, the "smash at the bottom" (*Surfacing:* 51). Flight is to falling as word is to flesh – there is no rescue or escape from the downward motion of the body, certainly not for women, and probably not for men as well. Thus Offred moves from thinking about falling in love and loving as a perpetual act of falling to her last image of Luke trying to escape, "stopped dead in time, in midair, among the trees back there, in the act of falling" (227), because to fall is once to have attempted flight.

Fatal abstractions, these Christian ideas about bodily love, male spirits, female bodies, and women. By using flight, falling, and fleeing, women writers call attention to women's knowledge of the gravity and solidity of love. We see women in a variety of postures here, and by no means are they heroic or idealized. Adelaide Adare is fleeing her children; Elaine Risley records a woman's sense of fated and even helpless femaleness in patriarchal culture, naming what men mean for women without necessarily affixing blame; Pauline flies as the emblem of twisted Christian spirit, and her flight depends upon an increasing mutilation of her body; irrevocably trapped by the meaning of female in a literalized religious culture, Offred's ancestress becomes a "wrecked angel" by hanging herself in final flight from the female body.

In all these writers we can hear that love, like the body, has irresistible weight. Women are spirited creatures who need things to hold onto, for otherwise the spirit starves for the simple restoration of touch – reassuring weight and pressure of tangible love. We can imagine flying because we know that lifting, buoyant feeling of being "in" love, even as we are falling. But because we know love to be both buoyant and weighted, perhaps we were meant for swimming, not flying.

Water

When Laura says that Anne Foster is "drowning in flesh" (*Men and Angels:* 32), when Isabel Moore describes making love as "swimming over and under each other" (*Payments:* 151), or when Nector Kashpaw climbs through Lulu Lamartine's bedroom window, rising "like a flood that strained bridges" (*Love Medicine:* 100), we recognize water as a metaphoric resource that is not necessarily identifiable by a gender-determined usage. Water is a universal literary resource, and like their male counterparts, women use water as a metaphor for bodily life, sexual love, time, and memory. But although women and men share a literary and literal relationship to water, they do not necessarily have the same relationship to water. Thus, when we turn from metaphors of flight to metaphors of water, one of the most clarifying comments about the relationship of women to water involves a flight of sorts, a famous literary drowning: "I've always understood why Ophelia wanted to lie down in the water. . . . It was better than lying down with Hamlet. . . . And so much more private" (*Payments: 67*).

This shrewd and ironic comment could only have originated from a woman, for there are very few, if any, androcentric males who could conceive of the idea that a woman might choose death as preferable to drowning in the male/stream of consciousness that surrounds them. Furthermore, the comment also suggests we notice water is a resource for privacy and escape in women's fiction, even if, too often, water becomes a final privacy and a fatal escape. For example, there is Edna Pontellier's escape into water in *The Awakening,* Adrienne Rich's master metaphor for her 1972 volume of poems, *Diving into the Wreck,* Virginia Woolf's *To the Lighthouse* (and her own tragic death by drowning), the understanding water creature who provides a lonely housewife with an escape from the emotional poverty of her marriage in Rachel Ingalls's *Mrs. Caliban,* and the relentless blood and waters that return the drowned memory of slavery and infanticide to the anguished Sethe in Toni Morrison's *Beloved.* Given such company, we can see that Ophelia wasn't crazy, just realistic about her options. Perhaps when water is appealing to women as a refuge and source of power it is because, like flying, water allows a sense of weightlessness and freedom. The effortless circularity with which it closes around and upholds the body suspends the gravity of the female sexual body. Thus, women, who are so symbolically fat on cultural land, might well find this a congenial element. The character who knows why Ophelia prefers water to Hamlet is Isabel Moore of *Final Payments,* who is as sure of her body as a fish when swimming, but on land looks like "the hippopotamuses in ballet costumes in cartoons" (67, 101). She has a lot in common with Joan Foster of *Lady Oracle,* who stages her death by drowning in Lake Michigan for exactly the same reasons Ophelia lies down in the water.

As a metaphor for life and sexuality, time and memory, water is so ubiquitous in Atwood, Erdrich, and Robinson especially, that it would be impossible to rehearse all such usages, nor will I try to do so here. Rather, I will concentrate on the consequences opened by literal and metaphoric entrances into water as women writers understand the process. First, women often enter water as an expression of anger and loss, seeking escape, empowerment, and restoration of selfhood. Through water women exit, and in water women dissolve conventional notions of reality and religiosocial authority. Second, the result of crossing the margin of normality into water is that all gods, especially the Christian god, are dislocated, replaced, or redefined by this underwater perspective. The world we call "real" is flooded with the awesome, indifferent, finality of life promise, revealing the illusory solidity of all that we call real. The weightiness of the body is floated, in effect, upon a different set of meanings. Third, although such a crossing can produce moments of grace and power, the encounter with a world of no boundaries paradoxically teaches women about truly realistic limitations – we realize how little anyone can control water, the fragility of our protections, the certainty of our losses, the utter necessity of physical love to carry us through life water. In women's fiction, water is the metaphoric medium through which pass all conventional notions about reality and ultimate meaning, all of which are given back complete with the slippages, enlargements and distortions, foreshortening, depths, and buoyancy of water. Women's view of themselves as embodied beings in a patriarchal world, as women whose female bodies are encrusted with meanings like tenacious barnacles (which are, after all, part of the matter to which they are attached), comes from an underwater perspective.

In Margaret Atwood's *The Edible Woman,* Marian thinks of her life as a drift through an indifferent watery environment (85). Her roommate is like a "mermaid in a grubby green terrycloth robe," a lecherous boyfriend is a "giant squid," and the lonely office virgin trails herself "like a many-plumed fish-lure with glass beads and three spinners and seventeen hooks ... where the right kind of men might be expected to be lurking, ravenous as pike" (114). Even Marian's landlocked fiancé can get more adventuresome with water than she can. He suggests that they make love in the bathtub, which Marian immediately stocks with herself as an attractively drowned corpse in the bathtub-coffin (61).

In perfect simulation of androcentric perspective, she associates water specifically with the female sexual body, which she sees as a "fluidity sustained somewhere within by bones." She thinks of her female co-workers as large containers productive of an undifferentiated assortment of substances: "What peculiar creatures they were; and the continual flux between the outside and the inside, taking things in, giving them out, chewing, words, potato chips, burps, grease, hair, babies, milk, excrement" (171). Repelled by the idea that "she was one of them, her body the same," she feels suffocated by this "thick, sargasso-sea of femininity." She clenches her "body and her mind back into her self like some tactile sea-creature withdrawing its tentacles," and wishes for a man, so she can "hold onto him to keep from being sucked down" (171, 172). This example is an important reminder of the position of women within a larger narrative that is told about them, for sometimes it becomes the story that we, too, tell of ourselves. Marian's reaction to life water as the female body is just like any detached male's perspective on the uncontrollable messiness of reproductive life, all of which in an androcentric system is attributed to a negative female pole. Marian lives in a world awash with life water, and she struggles to secure some sort of self-authority against the horrifying fluidity of the female sexual body *and* the artificial boundaries imposed upon the female body by patriarchal society.

The persona of the abstracted Marian reappears in *Surfacing* as a female narrator who never tells us her name. All the issues are the same, although Marian is submerged in life water and the narrator in *Surfacing* has fled all water and lives in a world arid of emotional and physical connections. Marian expresses her sense of bodily and cultural alienation through her use of food and water. In *Surfacing,* the narrator's self and social detachment is expressed in her images of severed limbs and mutilation, as well as in her estrangement from her friends. But we also see more clearly in images of amputation and wound that the narrator's alienation is not simply the fault of cultural views of women, but a complicated product of her anger about those things combined with an arrogance so profound that she is at risk of self-destruction. Feeling barren of basic human emotion herself, she treats her body as a machine, while contemptuously evaluating her friends as shallow, mindless cartoon figures. For her, the lake is an entrance to self-knowledge and the beginning of dispersing that anger into appropriate channels as the water functions as both the sexual fluidity of life/death and her own memory. When she plunges into the lake, she finds her drowned father, but she surfaces as well with the memory of her own abortion. Her terrifying encounter with the drifting corpse of her fetus/father plunges her into a furious, renovating madness in which she seeks to repudiate in herself all aspects of what she calls human – that which objectifies and destroys natural life.

Immediately rejecting the powerless, "bland, oleo-tinted Jesus" of sentimental religious prints, she turns to the old gods for restoration, "the only ones who had ever given me anything I needed, and freely" (170). Then she reclaims life instinctively by allowing her lover, Joe, to impregnate her, and feeling "my lost child surfacing within me, forgiving me, rising from the lake where it has been imprisoned for so long" (193), she moves to protect her young as would any jealous mother animal. She hides from her human companions in order to attend to the gods, living according to the menacing natural powers of the wilderness, seeking restoration in raw body life. Her plunge into waterworld helps her challenge the limits of her father's rational, objectified world. "His were the gods of the head, antlers rooted in the brain" (180), gods insufficient against water, for she finds his body weighted underwater by his camera, the symbol of objectifying frame and domination. Now knowing "there were more gods than his," and that the lake is filled with death as well as with life, she enters the shifting, formless energy we usually keep at bay with what we call logic, rationality, reality – all ways of keeping the mind firmly clamped upon memory, bodily desire, and physical law. Upon finding his body, she imagines that, "after the failure of logic," her father indeed has entered a different place, which "would be like stepping through a usual door and finding yourself in a different galaxy, purple trees and red moons and a green sun" (170–1). And when her father returns to her in a vision, her sense of his chastened objectivism – his acceptance of water, which now corresponds with her understanding of things – is confirmed. She sees him

> in an orange haze, he wavers as if through water. He has realized he was an intruder; the cabin, the fences, the fires and paths were violations; now his own fence excludes him, as logic excludes love. He wanted it ended, the border, abolished, *he wants the forest to flow back into the places his mind cleared: reparation.* (223, my italics)

The lake is first the solution in which she recovers knowledge of her fetus/father's death, and then the solvent with which she strips away objectified and artificial identity as a socially acceptable white, middle-class woman. When she does so, she engages in a cleansing, but she also affirms the coextensiveness of the female sexual body with the organic world around her. She seeks to become porous, a corresponding fluidity to the life power from which she has been so alienated. By getting pregnant she takes the fluidity as part of herself. Like her father, she has understood that fences and paths were violations, borders that must be abolished, like the dispassionate logical processes of disembodied intellect. Marian of *The Edible Woman* is repulsed by the flow of things represented by the permeable female body, but her later incarnation in *Surfacing* seeks the transformative power of fluidity as restoration for her culturally dismembered body. By violating the boundaries that conventionally mark the limits between supernatural and organic experience and between the human body and the natural world, she redefines female embodiment in its own terms.

As has been well documented, Margaret Atwood's writing is indebted to her interest in Canadian folklore, fairy tales, myth, and the shamanistic traditions of various Indian tribes, hence the facility with which her female characters violate metaphysical boundaries. In *Surfacing,* Atwood plunges her narrator into an underwater world that is variously ruled by a "Mother of the Sea Beasts" or the Ojibwa water monster, Mis-shi-pi-zhiw.[14] Not surprisingly, then, the woman who refuses to acknowledge

14 See, for example, Elizabeth R. Baer, "Pilgrimage Inward: Quest and Fairy Tale Motifs in *Surfacing,*" 24–34, and Kathryn VanSpanckeren, "Shamanism in the Works of Margaret Atwood," 183–204, both in VanSpanckeren and Castro, eds., *Margaret Atwood;* and Marie-Francoise Guedon, "*Surfacing:* Amerindian Themes and Shamanism," in *Margaret Atwood: Language, Text and System,* ed. Sherrill E. Grace and Lorraine Weir (Vancouver: University of British Columbia Press, 1983), 91–111.

her given name in *Surfacing* has a relationship to water that is similar to Fleur Pillager's relationship to water in Louise Erdrich's *Tracks*. The world represented by Fleur Pillager is one narrative further away from us than the world spoken by the unnamed narrator in *Surfacing,* for Fleur does not tell her own story, and her narrative silence, like the absence of the narrator's name in *Surfacing*, is a sign of her circumscription by both cultural and gender barriers, as well as a sign of our distance from the alternative dimension to which she belongs.

From the beginning, Fleur belongs to water. She drowns twice in the Matchimanito, and each time, her male rescuers somehow take her place to propitiate the voracious Misshepeshu, the water man. With good reason, men feared her, "because it was clear that Misshepeshu, the water man, the monster, wanted her for himself. He's a devil, that one, love hungry with desire and maddened for the touch of young girls, the strong and daring especially, the ones like Fleur" (11). Pauline, who becomes Fleur's antagonist in a battle between religious worlds, says that Fleur "messed with evil, laughed at the old women's advice and dressed like a man. . . . She laid the heart of an owl on her tongue so she could see at night, and went out, hunting, not even in her own body" (12), and Nanapush confirms that "people said she ought to be harnessed." At the same time, Nanapush is glad when Fleur returns to the reservation after living in Argus, because "she kept the lake thing controlled" (35). Fleur returns to the shores of the Matchimanito to give birth to her child, and when she cries out in childbirth, "it was as if all the Manitous all through the woods spoke through Fleur" (59). There are various theories about the child Lulu, with her "green eyes and skin the color of an old penny," some being sure that she was fathered "by a man with brass scales, or by the lake." But the speculation is the idle gossip of those who are afraid and jealous of this woman of great power, so the story never gets straight. Apparently in the face of real water power, words have little value, for her story "comes up different every time and has no ending, no beginning. They get the middle wrong, too. They only know they don't know anything" (31).

Fleur Pillager is not just an elusive and powerful water witch, however. She is also closely associated with the land, likened in a variety of images to the tree of life. When Pauline stands in a leaky boat on the turbulent waters of the Matchimanito, she hurls her challenge not just to the thing with the gold eyes, but also to Fleur, who stands on the shore like a "rain-dark young tree" (200), a frail solidity who will fall with the loss of the land. Water is not only a source of empowerment, but is also the emblematic element of grief and change. Like so many of the other female characters mentioned here, then, Fleur enters water as a refuge expressive of her defiance, anger, and sorrow. When Eli betrays her with another woman, she returns to the embrace of the water man, and "Eli sees her dive into the lake at night, but she does not surface for hours after" (106). When it is clear she has lost the land, she weights her pockets with stones and tries to return to Misshepeshu. She "drowns" for a third and final time, for despite the fact that she is revived, she cuts herself loose from her dissolving world, her loss too great to sustain.

Sometimes women write as if they were water itself – in the extreme, Sylvie and Ruthie of *Housekeeping,* who become as vague and elusive to the containment of the "real world" as is water and time – sometimes as if they were the fragile, solitary outpost on the shores between life and death, poised on an exhilarating, terrifying margin, caught or uplifted between stories about the monumental female body and the ordinary, grinding contingencies of everyday embodied life. The narrator in *Surfacing* refers to herself as the entrance for her lover, "as the lake was the entrance for me" (172), and in the same vein feels her newly conceived child in the bowl of her belly, "undergoing its watery changes" (229). "I ferry it secure between life and death, I multiply" (200). Similarly, Pauline recognizes that Fleur "was the one who closed the door or swung it open. Between the people and the gold-eyed creature in the lake, the spirit which they said was neither good nor bad but simply had an appetite, Fleur was the hinge" (139). In a last display of her power before wandering the world, Fleur commends Eli's brother, Nector, to the water monster, a fate more worked out with exquisite metaphorical accuracy in *Love Medicine,* when Nector Kashpaw enters deep water by renewing his love affair with Lulu Lamartine, Fleur's daughter.

But Nector is married to Marie Lazarre, daughter of Pauline, and transfixed by the powerful daughters of Fleur and Pauline, he begins to feel more like Ahab than Ishmael, doomed to go down in the tidal forces he thought he could ride.[15] Fortunately for Nector, Marie is a water child, alive in defiance of Pauline's best efforts to contain her.[16] Marie is practical about water. While Nector is rushing into Lulu and reveling in raging water, Marie is hoping he'll get her a wringer washer, appurtenance of useful water to help care for the babies that seem to bob up in all corners of the house – life water in the flesh. She is also practical enough to allow him his plunge and still be willing to bring him home again. When Nector returns home from shooting the rapids with Lulu, Marie has just finished waxing the kitchen floor, which stretches between them like the terrible body of his betrayal:

15 See *Love Medicine,* esp. "The Plunge of the Brave," 89–129.
16 See the story of her birth in *Tracks,* 131–6, and then her entry into the convent in *Love Medicine,* where Pauline, now Sister Leopolda, recognizes her as a water creature and tries to scald the beast out of her (40–56).

He stood there looking at me over that long, shiny space. It rolled and gleamed like a fine lake between us. And it deepened. I saw he was about to take the first step, and I let him, but halfway into the room, his eyes went dark. He was afraid of how deep this was going to become. So I did for Nector Kashpaw what I learned from the nun. I put my hand through what scared him. I held it out there for him. And when he took it with all the strength of his arms, I pulled him in. (*Love Medicine*: 129)

In this image of Marie pulling in her sinking stone of a faithless husband, we see her in relation to her practical power with water. She is the shelter and savior against high water. Many years later, her position as shelter and practical container of water is confirmed in her dying. Nector's death is like one more fishing expedition. Says his grandson, Lipsha Morrissey: "Big thoughts was on his line and he had a half a case of beer in the boat. He waved at me, grinned, and then the bobber went under" (208). Lipsha is cradling his dying grandfather when Marie, frantic to get help for her stricken husband, falls "like a house you can't hardly believe has stood so long" (209). When that shelter falls, her grandson feels his known world come crashing about him, a disruption of earth and sky, "as though the banks gave way on the shores of Lake Turcot, and where Grandpa's passing was just the bobber swallowed under by his biggest thought, her fall was the house and the rock under it sliding after, sending half the lake splashing up to the clouds" (209).

Marie's mother Pauline was the withered, aerial foe of life water, but Marie claims the very thing her mother rejected by becoming shelter for those overwhelmed with deep water. For the doughty daughter of Pauline, for the narrator of *Surfacing,* and for Fleur and her female descendants, water functions as refuge and affirmation of the generative power of the female sexual body, and women who are confident of their affinity for water approach, enter, or command water as an elemental environment of escape, restoration, or power. In so doing, women also expose the perpetual slippage of Western ideas about embodiment and the boundaries between body/spirit, self/other, nature/culture, and male/female.

The image of Marie pulling her husband to shore and becoming a Christ figure in the process opens the second dimension to women's writing with water. Through women's eyes, we get a much different perspective on Christianity, Jesus, and triumphalist salvation schemes. Ironically, women are using one of the crucial elements of Christian symbolism, water, to challenge the received truths of Western Christianity about embodied life and women's bodies. By invoking a shamanistic kind of power, women in these novels transgress the culturally established boundaries between reality and metareality, physical and metaphysical, natural and supernatural, an activity that submerges the imprisoning conventions of Western Christian culture without necessarily establishing any alternative utopic promises. In these narratives, Christ and Christianity are not denied or erased but rather displaced and relocated by being washed clean of transcendent pretense so that Jesus can be seen as just one of the gods in a world of transience and uncertainty.

The narrator in *Surfacing* has always seen Christ as would a puzzled outsider, for having escaped from Christianity himself, her father "wished to protect us from its distortions" (59–60). For her, Christ is an "alien god," whom she associates with mutilation and severed body parts (26), a deity whose name is invoked as an expression of anger or disgust (48), or the "desperate beggar's whine" in the voice of a woman making love (95). Her school chums tell her that Christ is a "dead man in the sky watching everything I did," and her only defense against this terrifying paternal image is to invoke an equivalent horrible knowledge – "I retaliated by explaining where babies come from" (48).

But although Christ is an alien and incomprehensible image for her, when she enters the dark waters of mind and memory, she reworks Christ in the image of the heron who first appears in perfectly normal form flying above them like a "winged snake," and rather ingloriously croaking like a pterodactyl (69). After she finds a dead heron "strung up like a lynch victim" by its feet, however, she remembers the shape of that flight as a "blue gray cross" in the sky above them, and she decides that "whether it died willingly, consented, whether Christ died willingly, anything that suffers and dies instead of us is Christ" (164). The heron, then, functions as a Christ symbol, weaving together two old stories, one about the successive rhythms of natural life, the other about sacrificial death in the name of eternal life, both about how "human beings, men and women," have "turned against the gods," and ruthlessly use human power to invade and destroy the thing they fear and do not understand. At the same time, Christ is a fragile natural symbol – a heron symbol. He's just one of the gods, taking definition from the world that has given him birth, rather than the transcendent way around. In a sense, both the narrator and Christ are relocated together through the body of the water bird that did not rise from the water but died at the hands of men.

The clue to the narrator's and Jesus' mutual reconstitution is in this small image: in one of the narrator's Sunday school pictures, Jesus doesn't have a crown of thorns or the grotesque ribs of the crucifix, but is "alive and draped in a bedsheet, tired looking, surely incapable of miracles" (60), which is just about how the narrator looks as she is well into her transformation by water: "They'll mistake me for a human being, a naked woman wrapped in a blanket" she says, as she is hiding in the woods from her would-be rescuers. She goes on to associate herself with the slaughtered heron, saying, "They won't be able to tell what I really am. But if they guess my true form, identity, they will shoot me or bludgeon in my skull and hang me up by the feet from a tree" (219–20). In fact, she is a human being, a naked woman wrapped in a blanket, who has been driven to madness by the objectifying androcentric culture around her and by her own inability to accept the "average" of human life with its "needless cruelties and lies" (226). So, reading from this tenuous web of meaning, maybe Jesus, too, was just a tired human being wrapped in a bedsheet, confused and crazed by the inability of fleshly life to be perfect, tormented by the dying end to all bodies. The heron, the narrator, and Jesus know what it is like to be hunted by god-killers – the humans – but they are hunted not because they claim to be gods, but because they are not.

In *Surfacing,* Jesus appears as an alienating cultural symbol that gets reworked as a fragile natural symbol, just one more destructible and receding deity. In *Tracks,* Christ is a brutal trickster god who uses Pauline to combat the old gods, and especially the water man, "the devil in the land, the shadow in the water" (137). The "shadow in the water" is the embodied sexual life Pauline denies and fears, an alarming and majestic apparition of appalling "length and luxury" (195). Pauline's jealousy of Fleur leads her to shape her holy vocation around the goal of containing and destroying the creature with the gold eyes who lives at the bottom of the lake. Unfortunately, Pauline has difficulty distinguishing Christ from the devil, one of whom visits her at night, dressed as a peddler who jabs her with his scissors and needles. In spite of her confusion about which master she is serving (or if they are, perhaps, the same), Pauline is confident in her mission to "be His champion, His savior, too" (195). She returns to the lake to confront and conquer the water man, Nanapush, "the servant of the lake, the arranger of secrets" (196), and Fleur. But Fleur turns away from her, and Pauline's encounter with Misshepeshu turns into a land-bound wrestling match with her former lover Napoleon Morrissey, whom she strangles with her rosary. Then, having slain some demon of sexuality and earthly fluidity, Pauline returns to the mission, ready for confirmation in Christ, secure in her assurance that the erosion of tribal land by white developers "was the work of Christ's hand," brought about because she tamed the water monster (204). In a sense, she is right. Napoleon's relatives blame Fleur for his death, and they retaliate by targeting her land for speedy acquisition by the lumber company. Pauline's jealousy and antagonism toward sexual love become her weapon against her own culture; her bodily self-hatred translates as the energy that despoils the land.

Christianity takes some hard blows in this account of two cultural dissolutions. Displacing the old ways dissolves the patina of righteous piety surrounding Christianity; deliberate degradation of one culture turns into the irrevocable diminishment of the other. Pauline's god is no worse than the old gods, just allied with a different cultural power. Viewed from the losing culture, Pauline's god is, understandably enough, not especially appealing. Grampa Kashpaw yells the HAIL MARY in church because "God don't hear me otherwise," and his grandson, Lipsha Morrissey, know's he's right:

> God's been going deaf. Since the Old Testament, God's been deafening up on us. Now there's your God in the Old Testament and there is Chippewa Gods as well. Indian Gods, good and bad, like Lake Turcot. That water monster was the last God I ever heard to appear. It had a weakness for young girls. . . . Our Gods aren't perfect, is what I'm saying, but at least they come around. They'll do a favor if you ask them right. You don't have to yell. . . . I have to wonder if Higher Power turned its back, if we got to yell, or if we just don't speak its language. (*Love Medicine:* 195)

Nanapush enters a similar, practical objection. He tells Father Damien he doesn't like to come to church because the pews are too hard. Besides, he feels "no great presence either," and decides that "the old gods were better, the Anishinabe characters who were not exactly perfect but at least did not require sitting on hard planks." The priest says that "God sometimes enters the soul through the humblest parts of our anatomies, if they are sensitized to suffering," to which Nanapush responds, "A god who enters through the rear door . . . is no better than a thief" (*Tracks:* 110).

Viewing the Christian god as a sneaky sodomite is undoubtedly one of those tricks of underwater perspective – outrageous, distorted, or maybe just a different way of naming reality. Put differently, the flight offered through the disembodied promises of triumphalist Christianity contains no superior logic or truth, and viewed from a different cultural and gender perspective, the dualistic spirit of Christianity is as relentless, quixotic, and brutal as the action of water or the appetites of the water man. Being a fisher of men is not much different from being the water monster, for the love of Christ "is a hook sunk deep into our flesh, a question mark that pulls with every breath" (*Tracks:* 205). Thus, Pauline cannot escape water, she merely becomes a creature of boiling water (*Love Medicine*), hard water (*Beet Queen*), and her new name, Sister Leopolda, cracks in her ears "like a fist through ice" (*Tracks:* 205). Her new god is just like the old gods, part devil, part deity, culturally ascendent but still part of the elusive, shifting natural world.

When Mary Adare plunges, face first, down a slide into ice at the school playground, Leopolda thinks the image created is the face of Christ, although Mary thinks it looks just like her brother Karl, who is

a lonely, demonic presence in *The Beet Queen*. Later, the sun melts the
ice image, and "the face of Karl, or Christ, dispersed into little rivulets
that ran all through town. Echoing in gutters, disappearing, swelling
through culverts and collecting in basements, he made himself impossibly
everywhere and nowhere all at once. . . . I felt his presence in the whis-
pering and sighing of the streams" (37). Here, finally, Christ gets reworked as a fragile natural symbol – reworked, in fact, as the very element
from which Pauline seeks flight because, finally, there is no absolute
flight from embodied, natural life.

Perhaps the most poignant evocation of this last truth appears in *Housekeeping* when Ruthie reflects upon the meaning of Christ, water, and
loss. Here, with graceful, elegiac strokes, the abandoned child tells us
that "in the newness of the world, God was a young man" who had not
"realized the ramifications of his laws, for example, that every shock
will spend itself in waves." Troubled over the ever-widening sorrow of
the first creation, God purged the world with a flood, which was itself
yet another source of everlasting shock and loss. That is why "one cannot
cup one's hand and drink from the rim of any lake without remembering
that mothers have drowned in it, lifting their children toward the air,"
and although that was so long ago, there is still a certain flavor "in the
breath of creeks and lakes, which, however sad and wild, are clearly
human" (192–3). Water, then, is the element and emblem of eternal loss
and loneliness, and although this inexperienced god later came to earth,
"He is known to have walked upon water, but He was not born to
drown" (194). He may not have been meant to drown, but he did die
after all, and "the mourning would not be comforted until He was so
sharply lacked and so powerfully remembered that his friends felt Him
beside them as they walked on the road" (194). As Ruthie understands
it, then, what Christians might call Incarnation and Resurrection are not
promises of rescue from the fate of embodied life but simply a story
about bereavement, memories of the past, not prophecies for the future.
In her words:

> But every memory is turned over and over again, every word, however
> chance, written in the heart in the hope that memory will fulfill itself,
> and become flesh, and that the wanderers will find a way home, and
> the perished, whose lack we always feel, will step through the door
> finally and stroke our hair with dreaming, habitual fondness, not having
> meant to keep us waiting long. (195)

We share with god grief, not immortality. What we know and believe
of god comes from our knowledge of his absence and loss, our doctrines
all stamped by the flickering remembrance of eternal yearning, written
upon the heart, just as Harriet Beecher Stowe proclaimed over a century

ago. Thus, "the force behind the movement of time," that is to say, water, "is a mourning that will not be comforted. That is why the first event is known to have been an expulsion, and the last is hoped to be a reconciliation and return" (192).

The hypnotic rhythms of language in *Housekeeping* are so attuned to natural music – especially the action of water – it is easy to be bedazzled by the natural imagery in the novel as a counterbeat to conventional, religious, and social structures. Similarly, Erdrich and Atwood both make extensive use of ethnographic materials, traditional resources that are unusually porous to our own sentimental and utopic expectations. It would be a serious misreading, however, to find these treatments a call for a return to nature as the panacea to Christian dualism, and none of these novels discussed here in fact opposes "natural" against "Christian," in any dualistic sense of things. Pauline and Fleur both give flesh to the intricacy and logic of the religious systems they represent, each body life-shaped by the inextricable spirit, but Fleur is no more sentimental, fecund female body than Pauline is analytic, rational spirit. Fleur is a monumental creation, clearly a shamanistic figure of great power, but she is also a woman still susceptible to the same losses and mistakes as any mortal creature. She loses her power because "in her mind she was huge, she was endless. There was no room for the failures of anyone else" (178). She cannot accept her failure to save the land, the lake, her second child.

Fleur is much like the narrator in *Surfacing* who cannot tolerate the meaning of "human" with all its cruelty, risk, and inevitable loss. Both characters enter water in desperate grief and anger at the limitations of human, female power. But, as the narrator in *Surfacing* discovers, some sort of primeval naturalism driven by the arbitrary and brutal rituals of the old gods is not a sufficiently honest response to human pain any more than is blaming the "Americans," men, human beings, or Christianity for all the perplexities of embodied life. There is no easy choice, which is why the novel closes with her poised upon a critical, wavering margin, the wilderness at her back, the city of man before her. Waiting, watching, unsure, she knows only this:

> No gods to help me now, they're questionable once more, theoretical as Jesus. They've receded, back to the past, inside the skull, is it the same place. They'll never appear to me again, I can't afford it; from now on I'll have to live in the usual way, defining them by their absence and love by its failures, power by its loss, its renunciation. I regret them; but they give only one kind of truth, one hand.
>
> No total salvation, resurrection . . . their totalitarian innocence was my own. (227)

The challenge to Christianity, then, is complex and equivocal, for although water encourages an experience of connectedness and the fluidity of life, this has less to do with some sort of sentimental "being one with nature" and more to do with how little control we really have over the way our lives flow and spill from one thing to another. There is no salvation by natural immersion any more than there is salvation through Christianity's bloodshed and disembodiment. Christianity can't save us from water any more than nature worship can efface the appealing idea of transcendence and release from mortal loss. Water dissolves all pretensions, leaving only a series of temporal choices we would like to outwit: fly and fall with Christianity or swim, slip, and drown in the dreamwork of the natural world.

The consequence of entering water and dissolving the authority of accepted signs is the discovery that, behind the seeming substance of human construction, nothing remains forever but water. Even the natural world is in perpetual shift, and when female characters transgress the social, religious, and natural boundaries we normally observe against water, when the gods are realized in their true shape and perspective, we see how the world is opened to the (sexual) surge, slippage, and fluidity that ceaselessly wash under and around the margins of what we call solid and real. Challenging the conventional wisdom of Western Christianity about the "real" world and female bodies creates a crossing that opens the self and the "real" world to the watery natural rhythms of time counted out by sexual life, embodied love, and the memory of both.

In remarkably similar passages, Atwood, Erdrich, and Robinson identify water-induced boundary slippage as a pivotal revelatory event for their characters. In *Surfacing,* the narrator's search for her mother initiates a second, metaphorical entry into water that may be even more important than her introduction to her fetus/father.[17] Knowing her "father's intercession wasn't enough to protect" her, the narrator returns to the cabin and lies down next to her mother's jacket whose leather smell is that of "loss, irrecoverable." And as she tries not to think about this loss, the rain begins, "sound of an avalanche surrounding. I feel the lake rising, up over the shore and the hill, the trees toppling into it like sand collapsing, roots overturned, the house unmoored and floating like a boat, rocking and rocking" (204). This unwilling plunge into her grieving

17 The search for her mother is one way in which the muted interior discourse of woman living in patriarchy is woven into *Surfacing,* for the emerging urgency of her quest for her mother is modeled on the myth of Demeter and Persephone. See Sherrill E. Grace, "In Search of Demeter: The Lost, Silent Mother in *Surfacing,*" in *Margaret Atwood,* ed. VanSpanckeren and Castro, 35–47.

love for her mother is the entrance that confirms her passage from the
visible world of firm earth to the felt world of natural transience. A
similar passage into metaphysical fluidity occurs in *Tracks* when Fleur
Pillager expresses her grief and rage over the loss of her land by cutting
through the trunks of all the trees around her cabin. When the loggers
arrive, the trees begin falling about them, for "all substance was illusion.
Nothing was solid. Each green crown was held in the air by no more
than splinters of bark" (223). Having leveled the forest to the lake, Fleur
steps into the traces of a cart piled with her belongings and departs. Like
the narrator in *Surfacing,* she has become a wanderer in a world of eternal
drift, cut loose by unutterable loss and grief.

Sylvie Fisher of *Housekeeping,* of course, is the prototypical model for
drift who merely introduces Ruthie to the external environment corresponding to the element of Ruthie's own unmoored heart. "Sylvie in a
house was more or less like a mermaid in a ship's cabin. She preferred
it sunk in the very element it was meant to exclude" (99). Slowly the
house is opened to the elements, and when the lake actually floods the
town, Sylvie allows the water to run its course through the house. "The
pantry curtain rod was deeply bowed by the weight of water climbing
up the curtains. . . . The house flowed around us" (61–4). In this increasingly amorphous state of affairs, Ruthie drifts longingly from one memory of her mother to another, but her sister Lucille begins to "regard
other people with the calm, horizontal look of settled purpose with
which, from a slowly sinking boat, she might have regarded a not-too-
distant shore" (92). Lucille wants out of water and tries to take Ruthie
with her, but Ruthie is already "drifting in the dark," dreaming "that
Sylvie was teaching me to walk underwater" (174–5), and she can no
longer hear Lucille. When she and Sylvie are no longer on a margin
between water and cultural land, but clearly crossed into the regions of
eternal drift, she and Sylvie burn the house and give themselves over to
water. They cross the railroad trestle bridge by foot in the night. "It was
so dark there might have been no Sylvie ahead of me, and the bridge
might have created itself under my foot as I walked, and vanished again
behind me" (212). The bridge, "swaying with the slow rhythm that
moves things in water," vanishes behind Ruthie just as Ruthie and Sylvie
vanish from Fingerbone. They are presumed drowned in the lake, and
in a sense, they are. "Sylvie and I are not travelers," says Ruthie (216),
but just there, part of the inexplicable presence and motion of things
felt, but never quite seen, the water motion of time and lost love most
of us defend ourselves against with the ordinary protection of "housekeeping."

Here, then, in exactly the same terms we find in *Surfacing* and *Tracks,*
is the meaning of the world as water-shift:

The appearance of relative solidity in my grandmother's house was deceptive. It was an impression created by the piano, and the scrolled couch, and the bookcases full of almanacs and Kipling and Defoe. For all the appearance these things gave of substance and solidity, they might better be considered a dangerous weight on a frail structure. . . . (158–9)

Everything that falls upon the eye is apparition, a sheet dropped over the world's true workings. The nerves and the brain are tricked, and one is left with dreams that these specters lose their hands from ours and walk away, the curve of the back and the swing of the coat so familiar as to imply that they should be permanent fixtures of the world, when in fact nothing is more perishable. (116)

Entering water plunges us into a physical and metaphoric expression of anger and grief, for water dissolves all certainty or hope of rescue or glorious salvation, leaving only the sure knowledge of risk and bereavement and the relentless action of time upon the timed obsolescence of the body. No gods are perfect or absolute, and there is no rescue or final salvation from the uncertainty of embodied life; no final flight from water, not even with Jesus.

Airborne Swimmer, Fish in Skywater
"Well, that's no way to raise children," huffed one of the members of my reading group after finishing *Housekeeping,* but perhaps the novel is one of the more honest accounts of what we cannot control, not even women fully invested in the mythos of the infinitely productive, sheltering female body. This is the third outcome of entering water. We learn that although women have some affinity for water, this affinity is by no means absolute or certain in its consequences. As participants in the patriarchal story about women, we know we are expected to stave off the deadly certainty of water with the solidity and promise of the female sexual body, but as participants in the story of embodied life, women are trying to honor a promise we cannot even fulfill, even for ourselves. Like their male counterparts, women find the contingency and transience of human existence a daunting, unwelcome revelation, nor are all women magically reconciled or comfortable with life water. Although some female characters in these novels seek and accept water, no restoration is without sadness, and some characters simply find water a destructive and alienating element.

Sita Kozka in *The Beet Queen* spends her dying days living and sleeping on the pool table in her basement, ironic cue to no water at all, watching the sky-blue waters of the beer lamp next to her. As for real water, she has "never seen a waterfall or even heard a moving stream," but she does know the "punishments and torn banks" of the river, "a tongue of destruction that dwindles by summer to a foul mud rope." So Sita prefers her bathtub to real water, the "marvel of clean water from a spout, hot and wild," or the perpetually sky-blue waters of her beer lamp. Unable to fly, she does not know how to swim, and so she slowly dies, artificially buoyed for a time by pills and the comforting, unmovable surface of the pool table (258).

Furthermore, to understand water is not necessarily to control water, nor are we ever really prepared for the relentless certainty with which water returns everything in its most elemental form. A hilarious sequence about personal flood control in *Tracks* pits Nanapush against the dolorous Pauline, who walks like a duck because she wears her shoes backwards as penance and who has vowed to visit the privy only twice a day. Knowing she is tired and thirsty, Nanapush entices her to drink lots of tea, while entertaining her with a long story about a flood, a phallus, and a drowning maiden. "In the old language there are a hundred ways to describe water and he used them all – its direction, color, source and volume," Pauline reports, and "as the water in the story mounted, my feet jigged the harder" until finally she has to make a humiliating run for the outhouse, her hopes for eternal life seriously compromised by her unwilling posture as a water bird.

Joan Foster in *Lady Oracle* finds herself in a similar dire and comic condition relative to the unexpected returns of water. Joan has staged her own death by drowning in Lake Michigan in order to escape her husband Arthur, her lover, her public reputation as a writer of enigmatic verse about women, and her secret life as a writer of romance fiction. Unfortunately, her dramatic demise does not erase the past she flees, but so dramatizes and enlarges her own confusions that while she keeps trying to write her Gothic novels, the story lines twist and unravel on her. The beautiful but malevolent female character in her novel drowns, only to reappear as an enormous fat woman with "strands of red hair straggled down her bloated face like trickles of blood." Redmond, the appalled hero, notes that her "hair smelled of waterweed, of oil and decaying food and dead smelts," much as we might expect from someone who has drowned in Lake Michigan (355, cf. 338). Indeed, when she implores the hero to make love with her and calls him "Arthur," we know that Joan Foster has surfaced in her own Gothic novel, redeposited in her most elemental form on the shores of her own fantasy.

In *Men and Angels,* water returns to Anne Foster graphic knowledge of unrequited love. Anne can feel the terrible need of Laura to be loved, but she finds Laura vaguely repulsive, so the best Anne can do is reproduce gestures of regard that she hopes will satisfy her sense of responsibility to Laura. But when Laura carelessly allows Anne's children to play on thin ice, Anne is transformed into the lethal symbol of killing spirit ("she had become the wings, the beak; she could feel her body whirring . . . ready to swoop, ready to strike," 203) and orders her out of the house by evening. Anne returns with the children later that evening to find "water splashing down the stairwell," not icy water, but blood-stained water. Laura has killed herself in the overflowing bathtub. Against all her maternal strength, invading the exclusive shelter of Anne's love for her children, is a "dead girl lying in a tub of red water, one hand, the left, grazing the white tile floor" (212). Anne has not, after all, preserved her children from treacherous life streams. Through water, everything is returned and nothing is forgotten, and the girl who had no love becomes forever memorable through water. "I began to think of time as having a shape," says Elaine Risley at the opening of *Cat's Eye*, "something you could see, like a series of liquid transparencies, one laid on top of another. You don't look back along time but down through it, like water. Sometimes this comes to surface, sometimes that, some-times nothing. Nothing goes away" (1). Or, as Ruthie says, "If one is lost on the water, any hill is Ararat. And below is always the accumulated past, which vanishes but does not vanish, which perishes and remains" (*Housekeeping:* 172).

As with so many women encountering water, Anne finds her under-standing of Christian promise seriously dislocated. "How could Anne ever love a God who let a young girl bleed, who let her die thinking she should give her life to bring someone else to Him? . . . The only sane thing to say was that God was not within the Universe. Or it was God who held the razor to Laura's wrist" (*Men and Angels:* 224). When Anne identifies God as the killer, she is calling up an implicit subtext in women's fiction – the romance of the Word that governs our sociotheological universe. As demonstrated in Chapter 5, however, God's embrace may be a fatal one; the male/hero/God may be the killer, not the savior. Viewed through water, the certainty offered by romance wavers and shifts. Indeed, the narrative idiom of romance is a distinctive voice in women's writing perhaps because the formula for romance so well cap-tures the simultaneous complicity and defiance of our doubled story; perhaps because the rescue that is essential to romance is so universally appealing. "The sorrow," Ruthie points out, "is that every soul is put out of house," and like any town in the world, Fingerbone is haunted by transients who are "terrifying as ghosts are because they were not very different from us." She goes on to tell us exactly about the basis underlying religiosocial systems: "Pity and charity may be at root an attempt to propitiate the dark powers that have not touched us yet. . . . And so it was important to the town to believe that I should be rescued and that rescue was possible" (*Housekeeping:* 178–9). The religious ro-mance – rescue from "homelessness" – serves exactly the same function as the Gothic romance. Both hold the line against transience and loss. As Joan Foster says, "I longed for the simplicity of that world, where happiness was possible and wounds were only ritual ones. Why had I been . . . banished to this other place where everything changed and shifted?" (*Lady Oracle:* 316). Not surprisingly, then, Joan's attempts to escape her own fantasy worlds are not entirely successful and she finds herself "in the central plot" of her own gothic romance. But when she steps toward her true love, "the flesh fell away from his face, revealing the skull behind it" (377). The hero is her killer.

Celestine James measures her encounters with Karl Adare against her notions of proper courtship narrative, looking for "a burning sweetness on his lips," "the glances, the adoration," "the burning kiss, when the music roars," the "slow burning fuse in his loins" (114–19). But not only is Karl not much of a resource for romance, he is also the lonely devil figure who wanders *The Beet Queen,* shadowside of the disappearing god. Thus, in short order, we find the male-hero-god reported as a killer, the devil, a natural hazard (*Cat's Eye*), and a fatal abstraction (*Handmaid's Tale*), and through it all, women recording their simultaneous attraction and disillusionment, complicity and rebellion against this powerful paradigm for female-male-god relationships.

Not only has god been dissolved or dislocated, but the clear message from women is that neither "god" nor "man" – our name for ultimate protection and authority – is any real protection or comfort in the drowning times. Given the enlarged magnificence of the female sexual body, and given the absence and recession of god and fathers (as is clearly the case in all of these fictions), women are acutely aware of their task as protection and shelter. Women writers speak of the female body and women's activities as mothers and wives as part of a process of providing shelter against water through the "rituals of the ordinary as an act of faith," "as if reenacting the commonplace would make it merely commonplace again" and restore safety and love (*Housekeeping:* 16, 25). From her utter darkness the unloved Laura cries out, "Why could they never see, the mothers, that their houses were their sanctuaries? For the children to be safe in, to be happy" (*Men and Angels:* 208). Laura yearns for shelter *from* the messiness and ambiguity of bodily love (precisely that which mothers are least able to provide daughters), whereas on the other end of the spectrum, Isabel Moore (*Final Payments*), who has spent much of her young womanhood isolated by the spiritual life of her dogmatic father, is freed by his death *for* embodied love. For her, the intimacy and security of sexual love is protection: "I felt I had finally joined the company of other, ordinary humans. . . . I was saying over and over, I am the beloved; the beloved is mine" (140).

Loving in the body and tending shelter around the bodies we love all constitute the "ordinary," what Robinson has called "housekeeping." But what we require of our shelter is often quite contradictory, and like our relationship to water, choosing the "housekeeping" is by no means a simple or unambiguous decision. Are women shelter for the body or against the body? Given the enlarged symbolic function of the female sexual body, who gives protection against the exigencies of flesh to the ones whose bodies are supposed to be shelter and life for others? Who mothers the mother?

Although the portrait of women as the true stability of human life certainly has its self-serving moments, what is generally not present in women's writing is any of the exaggerated reverence for pregnancy and motherhood that infuses popular culture and informs the savagery of so much androcentric writing about women. Women are as busy dismantling the image of themselves as earth mothers as they are re-creating it. Margaret Atwood's alienated heroines speak of their productive bodies as angry gods in need of propitiation (*Edible, Surfacing*), or as traps – mindless, vegetative casings of suffocating dimensions. Marian in *The Edible Woman* views her pregnant friend as resembling "a boa constrictor that has swallowed a watermelon," "a pitcher plant in a swamp," "a strange vegetable growth" (30, 31). The dieting narrator of *Lady Oracle* who avoids the consequences of the female sexual body by being fat instead of pregnant, ridicules her former fleshly immensity as: "a beluga whale," "rubber raft," "nourishing blob," "slug covered with salt," "giant basketball," "giant popsicle" (78, 219, 236, 299, 156, 317), and the nothing-but-a-mother female trapped in the religious theocracy of Gilead knows herself as a "prize pig," "swamp," "ambulatory chalice," and a "melon on a stem" (*Handmaid's Tale:* 69, 73, 136, 154).

Mary Gordon's women are not nearly so self-loathing in their body images, but they are no less vocal about the uncertainty and anger of being female: "I understand mothers who want to take their babies' lives. It is life they must punish, for cheating them, for trapping them in the oldest trick in the world, the female body" (*Company:* 244). These words are from Felicitas, the unwilling "virgin" mother, but even a woman invested in her maternity knows the anguish of divided self represented by the female sexual body. Anne Foster is denied a job because in the public world she exists only as a category. Her prospective employer assures her that another woman was hired, as if that will satisfy her, "as if he believed she were applying for the job only as a gesture, as a member of a class, interchangeable with any other member, and so it didn't matter that she didn't get the job herself, since it existed for her only symbolically" (*Men and Angels:* 11–12). The dilemma for women living in an androcentric universe as the female sexual body is that "for a woman to have accomplished something, she had to get out of the way of her own body. . . . One wanted to believe that the price was not impossible for these accomplished women, that there were fathers, husbands, babies, beautifully flourishing beside the beautiful work. For there so rarely were" (50).

Here, then, is one narrative – women in conflict with the story told about them as iconic, female body. But virtually inseparable from that narrative thread is the story of children. As an embodied being, a woman can only write as both shelter and as one needing shelter, as the mother of children but also as the child herself. In story after story, women record their anger and anguish at being in need of the very shelter they are supposed to represent. Women clearly express their own embodied humanity, not in bearing children, which is unalterably bound with the patriarchal version, but in having been children. Those speaking as adult mothers once were the children they are pledged to protect, and the two-voiced story they tell from within the patriarchy is related by an adult dreaming of lost children, returning like a hungry ghost to the scene of childhood loss. Laura is the unloved child in *Men and Angels* who perishes in order to be remembered; Pauline who grows up to be the tormented spirit of cultural death is the bent girl of tin whom everyone tolerates but no one loves. Mary and Karl Adare are the abandoned children in *The Beet Queen*. Mary becomes the resident witch of the novel, while Karl is the drifting, promiscuous devil. He is disconnected from human affection, Satan understood as an abandoned child who tries to jump into flight, but realizes that "the place I'd landed on was only a flimsy ledge, and there was nothing else to stop me if I fell" (96).

The grandmother in *Housekeeping* dreams of such lost children: falling children, drowning children, children who were "sky black and stark naked and who danced with the cold and wiped their tears with the backs of their hands and the heels of their hands, furious with hunger" (25). Ruthie fears that she and Lucille resemble these ghostly children to her grandmother, who can only offer them "deep dish apple pie as a gesture of well-meaning and despair" (26), and when her grandmother dies, Ruthie becomes one of the "cold, solitary children" who belong to the evanescent permanence of lonely wind and water (154), forever searching for the parent "not perished, not perished." Finally, she takes her mother's place in waterworld, dreaming "that the bridge was the frame of a charred house, and that Sylvie and I were looking for the children who lived there, and though we heard them we could never find them" (175).

Sita Kozka has a similar dream about the Day of Judgment, when tiny, perfectly formed children will be resurrected and their bones gradually clothed with flesh. But what if they cannot find their parents, she wonders. "What if their parents have sinned themselves into hell. . . . Imagine the poor children left to wander, searching through the ranks of the dead for someone or something familiar" (260). All of the action of *Cat's Eye* is precipitated and determined by the memories of a cold, lonely child whose games of love and betrayal determine the configurations of adult life for Elaine Risley. Nearing age fifty, Elaine becomes suicidal, still tormented with the voice of that past, "the voice of a nine year old child" (394). Joan Foster never really outruns her own isolated and self-loathing childhood self, and many of the doubling devices Atwood uses in *Lady Oracle* work to draw us into the central doubled figure of the mirrored mother and daughter. The narrator in *Surfacing* clearly exemplifies the doubled tale of parent/child location, for although she goes back to her childhood landscape to reproach her dead parents for not giving her sufficient protection against the adult world of "human being," she is confronted by her aborted child with her own analogous failure to provide shelter.

"If you tell your children God doesn't exist they will be forced to believe you are the god, but what happens when they find out you are human after all, you have to grow old and die?" (122), she wonders, articulating one of the central questions of *Surfacing*. Her answer is her recognition that parents cannot be blamed for not being god, any more than god can be blamed for not being, period. This is what she means when she says the gods are as questionable as Jesus and when you grow up you allow them to "dwindle, grow, become what they were, human," referring both to her parents and to her ideas of god, who may after all, be the same thing. Eventually, the gods "walk ahead of us, and walk too fast, and forget us, they are so lost in thoughts of their own, and soon or late they disappear. The only mystery is that we expect it to be otherwise" (*Housekeeping*: 215).

Isabel Moore has incarcerated her body in penance for daring to love beyond the death of her father, so that "never again would I be found weeping, like Mary, at the tombstone at the break of dawn." But there is no guarantee against loss, and Isabel decides that Incarnation calls us to the present "luxury of our extravagant affections" (*Final Payments*: 243), not a disembodied, other-worldly future. A friend reminds Anne that Laura missed the point of the gospels – "that she was greatly beloved." But this is not enough, and the coldest lesson of water may be that in the absence of ordinary love, "the love of God means nothing to a heart that is starved of human love" (*Men and Angels*: 231). Christian mythos offers no more sanctuary than any other religious universe, but becomes just one more story among stories, all necessary but none complete enough to preserve us. There is no Word, or words that can substitute for the only real thing we put between ourselves and death – the real body of our own, halting love, not the idea or thought of body, not the signifier, signified, or symbol, but only the warm changeable flesh of ourselves. Even Father Cyprian who "wanted to live in unapproach-able light, the light of the pure spirit, . . . untouched by accident and preference and failure," cannot live without the "great richness of the ardent" and the "irresistible gravity of affection and regard" (*Company:* 284, 288).

Women's fiction challenges Christian dualism by affirming the life-giving pleasure of the sexual, loving body despite its menacing fertility and deadly obsolescence. No one will be saved by childbearing any more than by fleeing the body altogether. Reproducing life does not make the body sacred, loving with the body does. Isabel Moore is not particularly concerned with pregnancy, but rather, simply having permission to enjoy the love made possible through the flesh. She decides that "people loved God because their bodies had not done well by them, had not given them sufficient pleasure. Pleasure. I held the word in my mouth like a plum" (*Final Payments:* 142). Recognizing the pleasure of bodily love and accepting that pleasure for herself prove to be more difficult than she first imagines. Nonetheless, by the end of the novel, we know that she is ready to embrace her physical capacity for love when she recognizes that, like Christ, she has a body, and although we may eventually die, part of the promise of Incarnation is that the body "had been given to me for my pleasure, and the love of those whom loving was a pleasure" (247). In *Tracks,* Fleur Pillager and Eli Nanapush love so passionately that their voices are heard, "uncontained by the thick walls of the cabin. These cries were full of pleasure, strange and wonderful to hear, sweet as the taste of last summer's fruit," and the hungry people who are fishing on the frozen lake outside stand still to listen until they "heard the sat-isfaction of silence. Then they turned away and crept back with hope," faintly warmed by the bounty of Fleur and Eli (130).

Yet such affirmations are always set against an edge of uncertainty. Isabel knows there is no guarantee against death; Fleur and Eli cannot hold together the land and themselves around the daughter they love so much. Symbolically and metaphorically powerful, yet really only pos-sessed of human possibility, women record their own anguish at being divided against themselves, at being part of a promise they did not create, but that they nonetheless struggle to honor. We cannot simply abandon or destroy the female sexual body. There are husbands and lovers and relatives to consider, children to protect, life to cherish, including our own. And when there is no woman to use the female sexual body wisely, we are, like Ruthie and Sylvie in *Housekeeping,* set adrift without course or mediating compassion, unsheltered from the inexorable wear of mortal time, barely embodied, barely loved.

Between the two master metaphors of flight and water is created a res-onance through which women confirm the necessity of dreaming transcendence while living with water. The degrading and lethal dualisms of Christianity have been well documented by feminist scholars, and clearly this heritage is a continuing source of anger and frustration in women's fiction. For the most part, however, women's fiction does not replicate the understandable but too-simple polemic lofted against the Western heritage by some feminist thinkers. Rather, women's fiction suggests that whatever its role in sustaining the dualisms of Western culture, Christianity did not create the divide between body and spirit. Transcendence is as viable a dream as immanence; there are reasons why we separate body from spirit yet forever yearn to call two, one. Perhaps no matter what the system purporting answers, we would have arrived at the same conclusion, just from being and watching the world around us. Certainly this is what the logic of metaphor would teach us. "It was perhaps only from watching gulls fly like sparks up the face of clouds . . . that I imagined" such a thing as salvage or salvation, Ruthie says. "Ascension seemed at times such a natural law. If one added to it a law of completion – that everything must finally be made comprehensible – then some general rescue" might be possible (*Housekeeping:* 92).

More prosaically, here is another way of reading the resonances between metaphors as they arise from our bodily experience in the world. Most land birds are wary of water, which is why a bird bath must be shallow, with a gradual, rough slope. Otherwise the bird is afraid of slipping and won't drink or bathe in the container. Given the right depth and surrounding surface, however, birds plunge into water with an utterly charming enthusiasm of flap and blabble. First they dip their heads into the pool and then curve up, beating the water into a light struck spray around them. After bathing, the bird is soggy and weighted and more easily a target for predators, so most birds move promptly to an upper region after the bath.

If you have ever held a young bird and felt it hunch down for a second into its body, its thin, tense feet pressed against your palm in the moment before flight, that whole frail frame vibrant with the anticipated lift, then perhaps you know instinctively, body upon body, what many spend a lifetime dreaming: even water birds have need for flying. The experience that leads gynocentrist Helene Cixous to describe women's writing as creation by an "airborne swimmer" may be exactly the same experience that androcentrist William Gass describes as "fish in skywater."[18]

18 Cixous, "Laugh," 889; William Gass, *Omensetter's Luck* (1966; reprint, New York: NAL, 1972), 76.

8

Conclusion: Words Are Not the Thing Itself

At the conclusion of Ellen Glasgow's *Vein of Iron*, the dying philosopher, John Fincastle, is granted the same vision with which *Surfacing*'s narrator restores her dead father to organic humanity. Struggling homeward, Fincastle finds "the world had worn so thin he could see through it." What he sees are all the fragments of remembered reality, floating and rolling "like an ocean of space... all a part of the running waves.... The world and life were all one." Like the father in *Surfacing*, who, "after the failure of logic" wants the border abolished, "wants the forest to flow back into the places his mind cleared," Fincastle relinquishes his dedication to the rational, objectified view of the world, answering a "faculty deeper, stronger, wiser than the power he had called reason."[1]

Julia Bader notes the same kind of disruption of "reality" in the writing of Sarah Orne Jewett, Mary Wilkins Freeman, Charlotte Perkins Gilman, and other nineteenth-century American women writers. She says that in these writers, "the narrative pauses to suggest that an external reality hitherto objectively perceived and transparently visible can blur and dissolve, that the firm, knowable texture of the familiar world can be shaken and lost," and she goes on to suggest that this quality of writing – a quality that we have seen at a number of points in the works discussed in Chapters 4 and 7 – serves as a commentary on the "process and hazards of female perception and self-perception."[2] The dissolution, evasion, dislocation, and defiance of recognized social, sexual, and religious boundaries characterize gynocentric fiction by women whether we are

---

1 Ellen Glasgow, *Vein of Iron* (1935; reprint, New York: Harbrace Paperback Library, 1963), 388–400; and Margaret Atwood, *Surfacing* (1972; reprint, New York: Fawcett Crest, Ballantine, 1987), 170, 223.
2 Julia Bader, "The Dissolving Vision: Realism in Jewett, Freeman and Gilman," *American Realism: New Essays,* ed. Eric Sundquist (Baltimore, Md.: Johns Hopkins University Press, 1982), 176.

talking about Harriet Beecher Stowe's supernaturalized heroines, the iron-clad courage of Ellen Glasgow's Ada Fincastle, or the cerebral women of Mary Gordon's fiction.

What, however, does the fluidity or thinning of boundaries (between self and other; natural and supernatural; the loving body and the spirited, thinking mind) have to do with religion, sexuality, and embodiment? This book began with a question about religion and sexuality – about how writers of fiction have related physical, sexual intimacy to religious experience and institutions, and how the consequences of that meta-phoric, cultural transaction have shaped cultural ideas about male and female identity. In the preceding chapters, I have replicated metaphoric structure by sex-segregating the fiction under consideration, hoping to generate an implicit dialogue between the often polarized voices of men and women. When I arrived at reading gynocentric fiction, however, I found that the distinction between religion and sexuality that was so cogent to androcentric writing was not especially useful for thinking about women's fiction. At the same time, contemporary women's fiction also forced my question beyond the original defining boundaries of the institutional church. Thus, one disconcerting result of the women's fic-tion I have studied here is that the metaphoric patterns of representing female experience render my inaugural questions at least partly obsolete.

The similarity of religious and sexual passion is taken for granted by the nineteenth-century writer, who focuses instead on the consequences of mis-using or repressing the connection between religion and sexuality. Drawing on a sense of purifying passion, the homiletic writer imagines reprioritized boundaries – the heart over the head, the passion of the transfigured female body over the chilly doctrinal austerities of patriarchal Christianity. In these fictions, Christ himself is translated through the radiant model of the religious body of woman, while sexual passion is effaced in favor of its ecstatic translation as passionate religious speech.

Contemporary women writers proceed with the challenge to conven-tional boundaries by identifying the iconically weighted female body as the problematic pivot point for any number of traditional boundaries. As we have seen, there are several reasons why boundaries and the female sexual body are so problematic in women's writing. Woman's status as a marginal insider – ambiguously nonhegemonic, to recall Margaret Ho-mans's term – is one reason. As Annis Pratt describes it, women's fiction

> manifests alienation from normal concepts of time and space precisely because the presentation of time by persons on the margins of day to day life inevitably deviates from ordinary chronology and because those excluded from the *agora* are likely to perceive normal settings from phobic perspectives. Since women are alienated from time and space,

their plots take on cyclical, rather than linear, form and their houses and landscapes surreal properties.[3]

Another problem is that we are reading and writing in the gap between experience and an adequate language for that experience. Therefore, naming clearly what women are doing if they are not accepting traditionally recognized boundaries at face value is frustrating. The narratives of the ex-centric female voice use the authoritative structures of centrist culture to challenge and redescribe that culture as it is experienced by those who are both marginalized and circumscribed by the master narrative. Thus, women are always trapped inside someone else's story, always telling two stories at the same time. There is no clean second narrative, and no uncompromised defiance, for the story of being woman in a patriarchal context inevitably depends upon the symbolic structures of the "master" narrative.

Finally, women cannot escape or turn the tables on traditional boundaries because the androcentric narrative is no more absolutely false than an idealized feminist narrative can be absolutely true and righteous. Simply reversing the values placed on difference will not suffice to the complexity of embodied life. Indeed, some of the "master" language may be useful and true to some common experience beyond its engendered distortions. As suggested by the metaphors of flight and water, the immanence of body life is no more superior an idea than the transcendence of the spirit. Thus, the perpetually ambiguous and entangled cultural position of the writing woman relative to her own body and language does not lend itself to experiencing the world in terms of absolutes such as the traditional dualisms displayed by body/spirit and religion/sexuality. As the self-conscious possessor of a female sexual body in an androcentric world, we are continually in the process of crossing territories, violating expectations, searching for alternative descriptions. Moreover, given how much language relies upon its source in physical experience, it is not surprising to find women struggling with a partly alien tongue to express a different, but not absolutely different, kind of embodied experience.

For these reasons, then, distinguishing between "religion" and "sexuality" makes sense only if we are thinking about traditional, male-authored fiction that is invested in the absolute meaningfulness of the boundaries between domains of experience. In gynocentric writing, there is no pointing to "religion" and "sexuality" and no excessive interest in the transgression of one domain by the other. Rather, the shift to a gynocentric narrative shows us that when we speak of religion and sex-

3 Annis Pratt, *Archetypal Patterns in Women's Fiction* (Bloomington: Indiana University Press, 1981), 11.

uality, body and spirit, public or private, or even male or female –
whether those terms are honored, reinforced, effaced, or evaded – we
are speaking about issues of control, authority, and the function of different kinds of boundaries in maintaining an essential sense of self and
cultural identity. The dialogue, and all too often war, between women
and men about authority and control returns us to the importance of
recognizing how language shapes domains of experience and how language is shaped by that originating domain, the human body.

Narrative itself is commonly described in terms of shelter, boundary,
and control. From John Updike's burrowing Rabbit and marshy minister
(for whom encapsulation in any form short of a coffin has great charm)
to Walker Percy's falling, abstracted heroes, to William Gass's fox in the
well and his work in progress (which "returns us to Gass's predilection
for inner sanctums whose walls are made of language instead of earth"),
we are reminded of the architecture and boundary function of narrative.[4]
By telling a story, we build a structure and a frame around ourselves
through which we may enter and make sense of time and the loss of
time and ourselves in that flow. A story cuts into what would otherwise
look like one damn thing after another and establishes borders that we
patrol, resist, reinforce, or dismantle and try building again.

The metaphors that shape our narratives are significant structures built
upon a sense of boundary. Metaphor works by both confirming and
violating our notions about discrete domains of experience by putting
those domains into contact with each other, thereby creating new borders
of experience. The question of boundaries is crucial to women and men,
as we see in both sexes' concerns about enclosure, entrapment, shelter,
authority, fluidity of boundaries, and women's bodies. Indeed, one of
the most common metaphoric devices we use in fiction reiterates boundaries, the banal trope of in/out, so routine and necessary to our speech
that virtually any piece of writing can be said to assume an implicit in/
out orientation on the world. According to Lakoff and Johnson, "We
are physical beings, bounded and set off from the rest of the world by
the surface of our skins, and we experience the rest of the world as
outside us. Each of us is a container, with a bounding surface and an in-
out orientation. We project our own in–out orientation onto other physical objects that are bounded with an inside and an outside." Similarly,
we make or designate "containers" even when there is no literal, physical
geography to mark boundaries. Thus we can speak of being "out of his
mind," "falling in love," "keeping her in sight," being "in trouble" or
"out of danger," or simply feeling "out of it." We conceptualize events,

4 Arthur Salzman, *The Fiction of William Gass: The Consolation of Language* (Carbondale:
Southern Illinois University Press, 1986), 117.

actions, activities, ideas, and our bodies in terms of boundaries, for "there are few human instincts more basic than territoriality."[5] Thus, while controlling and patrolling the boundaries of our physical and psychic environment, we push on those "containers" in order to create new ones.

This is such a tidy, truthful description, it seems a shame to muddy it up, but for all their sophistication about embodied language, Lakoff and Johnson (and later Johnson, 1987) take no cognizance of the possible difference in the way in which men and women observe bodily boundaries and use language about those boundaries. Women's bodies are entered and exited in ways that men's bodies are not, and women do not always have a choice about how or whether passage will occur. Whether she likes it or not, a woman in a patriarchal culture comes to know how fragile the sovereignty of the body can be; for her, boundaries can never be absolute. Thus, when Luce Irigaray says, "Between us the movement from inside to outside, from outside to inside knows no limits. . . . Between us the house has no walls, the clearing no enclosure, language no circularity," is she simply launching a fancy piece of rhetoric, or has she described a portion of bodily/linguistic experience untouched and unobserved by the androcentric imagination?[6] As we can learn from reading gynocentric fiction, in/out may look much different from a woman's body, the phrase "falling in love" defined more by the "falling" than by the "in."

The critical difference we have so much trouble negotiating and expressing to our satisfaction is that we use the same language to express different kinds of relationships. Although water is a common metaphor in men and women's writing, women have an affinity for water not present in androcentric writing. Male characters in androcentric fiction struggle against water while railing against the imperturbable female body that seems to move so effortlessly in that same element. In some ways, women confirm that view of themselves, for male characters in gynocentric fiction are usually presented in an adversarial relationship with water in a way that women are not. Other metaphors of enclosure and imprisonment reveal much the same thing.[7] Women and men both write about entrapment or encounters with risky life water, but men seem to think they are entrapped and flooded by women and the consequences of uncontrolled female sexuality; women find themselves en-

5 George Lakoff and Mark Johnson, *Metaphors We Live By* (Chicago: University of Chicago Press, 1980), 29.

6 Luce Irigaray, "When Our Lips Speak Together," *Signs* 6 (Autumn 1980): 73.

7 Sandra Gilbert and Susan Gubar argue that "most male metaphors of imprisonment have obvious implications in common" with women's metaphors, but also some different "aesthetic functions and philosophical messages," in *The Madwoman in the Attic: The Woman Writer and the Nineteenth Century Literary Imagination* (New Haven, Conn.: Yale University Press, 1979), 85, 87.

trapped by what men have written and said about them, flooded by words and the consequences of being the real possessor of that awesome female sexuality.

There *is* something in common here, however, something that returns us again to the function of narrative boundary as shelter against the wearing of time and the accidents of love. Gynocentric authors still write, even if satirically, of the longing for romance in which men and women act in comfortingly predictable ways. Romance is a formulaic dream of rescue from ambiguity and uncertainty, a narrative island of clarity secured amidst the menacing hum of ordinary, but often devastating, existential risk. But the tradition of romance in women's fiction is not that much different from the longing of the male narrator in *Roger's Version* to think that women are conspiring to take care of him. The androcentric narrative about women is also a rescue story, a romance about the infinitely sheltering female body. The commonality is audible when we realize that as often as the androcentric narrative resounds with the cry of an angry, lost boy-child, it is echoed and answered by the equally poignant cry of the gynocentric narrative voice lamenting woman's loss as a mother, as a motherless girl-child. The tragedy is that the androcentric voice repeatedly blames women for the loss of embodied security. Women seem to have no one to blame but themselves as the owner of that iconic monument to certainty and security, the female sexual body.

Yet, the one secure common bodily fact we share, the ground beyond all the exigencies of difference sounds so simple-minded to just say: that love and life in the timed obsolescence of flesh is a risky business. The fox falls into the well and dies there; women plummet to the stony androcentric earth despite their effort at wings. Although the fall itself looks different to male and female writers, the conclusion is the same. We are destined by the same ultimate gravity, and no one has secret knowledge or preserve against that eventuality. There is no rescue and no permanent iconic refuge that will not imprison us as much as it shelters us. At best, what we all have is what must be a tenuous border against chaos, the "temporary shelter" of body language.

The relationship between speech and love, sex and text, constitutes an unavoidable engima, no matter what the location of the writer. The narrator in *Surfacing* tries to draw herself apart from language, which she sees as one of the destructive instruments of the human culture that "divides us into fragments." Her rejection of "alien words and failed pictures" by sinking herself into the nonverbal forcefield of the natural world is part of her effort to escape her own incriminating entanglement in what it means to be human. Yet, as she contemplates returning to the human world, she also recognizes her imminent return to language, saying "for us it's necessary, the intercession of words" (172, 230).

Comparing the use of metaphor in writing by women and men helps restore a sense of the healthy fluidity of the trope born from body. Women's writing affirms that there are vital connections made between the loving body and language, and that metaphor, with so many properties of love itself in its capacity to give and take away, connect and flee, is an essential portion of physical touch. The world of *The Handmaid's Tale* is a religious universe built upon the destruction of metaphor, a world of literalized body and literalized language, a world built upon absolute boundaries. In such a world, there are no meaningful connections we can take for granted through metaphor. Offred says: "I look at the one red smile. The red of the smile is the same as the red of the tulips in Serena Joy's garden, towards the base of the flowers where they are beginning to heal. The red is the same but there is no connection. The tulips are not tulips of blood, the red smiles are not flowers, neither thing makes a comment on the other." Or: "I sit in the chair and think about the word *chair*. It can also mean the leader of a meeting. It can also mean a mode of execution. It is the first syllable in *charity*. It is the French word for flesh. None of these facts has any connection with the others."[8]

Offred lives in the world created by the intersection of two terms driven to their extremes: religion become fundamentalism, sexuality become pornography. Fundamentalism, for which the gender-driven dualities of body and spirit, religion and sexuality are so essential, *is* pornographic. Pornography dismembers and disperses the body into its mechanical parts for pleasure and domination; fundamentalism dismembers the body into its mechanical parts for procreation and domination. Both create a contained, claustrophobic universe in which bodies are a means to a cannibalistic end, a world in which we find the security and tyranny of absolute relationship between the word and the thing itself replacing reciprocity. Absolutizing metaphor as traditional theology does relative to God language, as sexist writing does toward women, violates both the language and the thing to which it refers, making language and "thing" metonymic parodies of the complexity of human experience. The terrible irony of Offred's world is that because the tantalizing intercourse between speech and body-act has been violated by the repression of metaphor, meaningful language and meaningful body become black market commodities in Gilead. As Offred protests, "Can I be blamed for wanting a real body, to put my arms around? Without it I

8 Margaret Atwood, *The Handmaid's Tale* (Boston: Houghton Mifflin, 1986), 33, 110.

too am disembodied."[9] Understanding metaphor and its relationship to the speech-act of our physical selves is part of the process of knowing in what way words are *not* the thing itself.

Certainly, this confusion between words and the thing itself, obviously another expression of boundary issues, has led men to step with confidence past the portals of woman-being, only to retreat or lash out with dismay and bitterness when real women do not respond like the words used to contain them. And perhaps those with a more lively, literal, historical sense of physical endangerment (women, minorities) are those most likely to understand the ways in which words are so important, but not to be confused with the thing itself. In Toni Morrison's *Beloved,* yet another novel in which the action is precipitated by the fluidity of boundaries (present/past and natural/supernatural, to name but two) the unchurched preacher, Baby Suggs, seizes her own language of redemption to draw together the dismembered black body. She calls her people to love themselves by speaking in love each part of the battered body, affirming the precious power shared between body and speech. At the same time, saying things out loud may not be enough for restoration, and naming is an empty power if there is no touched, loved body to go with it, or if there is no one to listen. Finally, Baby Suggs stops preaching because there are no word, words, or Word that can free her from the evils of racism and sexism that have so violated the sustaining intimacy of connection between herself and self; herself and the loved ones lost. But Morrison offers another image in the lovemaking of Sethe and Paul D, which begins with the image of a tree. Sethe's tree is carved upon her back, "the decorative work of an ironsmith too passionate for display." Paul D puts his cheek upon her scarred back, and "learned that way her sorrow, the roots of it, its wide trunk and intricate branches, . . . and he would tolerate no peace until he had touched every ridge and leaf of it with his mouth."[10] In this intimate image, the ear of his mouth hears her story from the speech on her back, body language far more eloquent than any words that could be wrapped around it.

The pretense that there is no reality but that of language (and even it can be said to be only evasively present) is a product of the same kind of lingua-pomp engaged in by those who are in no danger of ever having been or even listened to the "other." In my own small subfield, religion and literature, there are few women writing, and even a casual survey of recent male productions indicates that white, male universalism has proceeded as usual. The future of religion and literature is the subject of

9 Ibid., 104.
10 Toni Morrison, *Beloved* (New York: Knopf, 1987), 17–18.

another book entirely, but as the present work certainly indicates, the current practice of religion and literature is deeply scarred by the fatal, exclusivistic abstractions of Western theological and literary traditions.[11]

There is a quality of imagination required of critic, reader, and writer that is best spoken of metaphorically, because metaphor is the essence of knowing embodied language and creating any notion of deity at all. Try this. While I was writing Chapter 7, my husband and I were raising three orphaned baby robins, and from that experience I learned something important about "otherness," metaphor, and the relationship of metaphor to the particularity of flesh. I use the term "particularity" advisedly, referring not to the scandal, which is the Christian misnomer, but the unexplainable, touching absurdity of the thing. I have had a young bird perch on my hand for feeding and when finished, lean over and wipe its beak on the palm of my hand, a motion of such simplicity and trust it took my breath away. Of course, I ascribe a significance to this gesture beyond all reason. The bird, after all, is only doing what comes naturally – I could have been a gutter edge or a fence top for all it cared. But when one of my young ones died, I wept in outrageous proportion to the actual loss, and I wondered: if I can so mourn the loss of one baby bird, is this what god's caring is supposed to be – is this the absurdity of particularity?

I understand the abstraction from experiencing my ridiculous bonding with a baby bird. The thought of particular love is nice, but comprehending the risky, miraculous accidents of love and affection only grows from the physical reality of flesh meeting flesh in the myriad ways possible to us. Knowing love's possibilities begins with using our moral, metaphoric imagination, and any ongoing notion of deity depends on our generosity of imagination on behalf of something or someone outside ourselves, and not on some abstracted commandment from a deity who may be going deaf. Presumably, we read and write in order to flesh out the connections we cannot have literally, and that is why the imaginative act of listening to and for the "other" is so important. Following the trope used by Morrison of the listening mouth pressed to the speech of the body, then, we might well think of metaphor as not simply essential body speech, but also as a kind of body hearing, an attentive language figure that, in its give and take between unlike domains, suggests something important about the art of hearing. Without listening to the clever configurations of sound and silence that we have created, we will continue to experience the deformities of polarized passion, given no legit-

11 For a discussion of women's fiction and the study of religion and literature, consult my "Margaret Atwood and Toni Morrison: Reflections on Postmodernism and the Study of Religion and Literature," *Journal of the American Academy of Religion*, forthcoming.

imate audience or outlet. Remember, the story of passion is also a tale of transgressed boundaries, a crossing and yet a not crossing. The paradoxical dialect of listening to and hearing the unspoken word also contains the craft for negotiating many of our perplexing, shifting boundaries.

In Updike's *A Month of Sundays,* Marshfield registers his fear of silence as a fear about the absence of God. If we stopped talking, would we hear anything (or would we hear something we don't want to hear)? But Marshfield is not just worried about the absence of an answer, he's worried about the absence of a listener, for without the listener (reader) is there a story to be heard? Compulsive (male) speech lofted against the suspected (female) absence is one way to avoid a negative answer. But another remedy is to create a listener somewhere as a narrative act of preservation. Marshfield's listener is Ms. Prynne/the reader (neither of whom gets to talk back). In the gender-skewed world of Marshfield, the ideal listener is the passive, receptive woman, waiting to be filled with his death-defying words.

In some sense, every author creates a listener by assuming a reader, and yet there is something about this internal textual activity that suggests an uneasiness about this assumption; Marshfield's anxiety to be heard is not just some weirdness belonging to the irredeemably androcentrist character. Women's writing also features a designated listener within the text: Janie telling her story to Phoebe in *Their Eyes Were Watching God* (1937), Nanapush telling Fleur's story to Lulu in *Tracks,* Celie in *The Color Purple* (1982) writing letters to a divine listener who never answers – never listens? – and then to Nellie (who listens, who answers in kind). In Carson McCullers's *The Heart Is a Lonely Hunter* (1940), the listener is a deaf-mute, an ideal receptacle for all those starved hearts yearning to be heard. And, of course, no one bothers to learn or to listen to his language because they are all too busy being heard to take time to hear. They fill his silence with themselves, and, having never listened to him, they are shocked and angry when he betrays their confidence in his boundless ear by revealing himself to be just another lonely human being. He kills himself for lack of a listener; their words about him were not sufficient to the thing itself.

Talking about the importance of story-telling and narrative is not enough, even recognizing the need of flesh upon flesh for human nur-turance is not enough, for a story told without the graciousness of hearing is only half born. Only in the saying and the hearing is preserved common ground and private territory both; only when we hear as easily as we speak and write will those other bound and polarized territories of human passion – religion and sexuality, body and spirit, male and female – become less painful and perplexing to us. By considering the stubborn density of desire in terms of male *and* female accounts, perhaps we can know, finally, that speaking cannot be without hearing, just as spirit cannot be without body, word without flesh, transcendence without immanence, religion without sexuality.

Appendix A:
The Homiletic Novels and Their Authors

ANON. *Prairie Missionary* (1853). The author wrestles with herself in accepting her call as a minister's wife, but her worst travails are not spiritual, but physical. Life as a frontier missionary is filled with poverty and sickness.

BEECHER, Eunice White Bullard (1812–97). *From Dawn to Daylight, or The Simple Story of a Western Home by a Minister's Wife* (1859). Wife of Henry Ward; her caustic portrayal of their Indiana frontier ministry was banned for many years in Indianapolis.

BROWN, Almedia Morton (n.d.). *Diary of a Minister's Wife* (1881). A minister and his wife visit, and are visited by, congregants and colleagues, which gives the author a chance to catalogue types of ministers. The *Supplement to Allibone's Critical Dictionary of English Literature* (1891) lists five other works by this author.

BRUCE, Mrs. E. M. (n.d.). *Thousand a Year* (1866). Dedicated to ministers and "their patient wives." A country parson moves to a city parish, but he and his wife are tyrannized by the expectation they will live fashionably on a meager income. The *Supplement to Allibone* lists two other series of writings by this author.

CHESBRO', Caroline (1825–73). *The Children of Light: A Theme for the Time* (1853). *Victoria, or the World Overcome* (1856). A confused plot featuring spiritually pure women, one of whom is executed for witchcraft. There is also an older puritanical minister with a sordid passionate past of unspecified proportions and a young, dull minister colleague involved in these dark doings.

DELAND, Margaret (1857–1945). *John Ward, Preacher* (1882). *Old Chester Tales* (1898).

EVANS, Augusta Jane. See WILSON.

GLASGOW, Ellen (1873–1945). *The Miller of Old Church* (1911). From a large cast of characters emerges the egotistical Reverend Mr. Mullen, who would have won success in any profession as "a shining light of mediocrity." *Vein of Iron* (1935).

HARRIS, Corra May White (1869–1935). *A Circuit Rider's Wife* (1910).

HUBBELL, Martha Stone (1814–56). *The Shady Side: or, Life in a Country Parsonage* (1853).

PARKER, Jane Marsh (1836–1913). *Barley Wood, or Building on the Rock* (1860).

247

In a girl's seminary, Episcopal virtue triumphs over Presbyterian tyranny in the characters of the saintly Agnes Ryland and her stern father. Dialogue involves extended pious debate about denominational differences. A side plot finds the high-spirited Molly Raymond being seduced by a sleezy professor who forever destroys her religious integrity. *The Midnight Cry* (1886) deals with the Millerites.

PHELPS, Elizabeth Stuart (1815–52; mother). *The Sunny Side, or, The Country Minister's Wife* (1851). The lives of minister Henry Edwards and his wife Emily are dominated by the constant struggle to feed and clothe their family on the parson's pittance. Much of the plot is concerned with the strategies for thrift employed by the ever-cheerful Emily, who also manages to record the constant criticism and demands to which the minister's family is subjected. [H. Trusta], *A Peep at Number Five, or a Chapter in the Life of a City Pastor* (1855). More of the same except in the city.

PHELPS [Ward], Elizabeth Stuart (1844–1911). *The Gates Ajar* (1868). *Beyond the Gates* (1883). *Sealed Orders* (1879). *The Gates Between* (1887). *Fourteen to One* (1891). *A Singular Life* (1895). *The Story of Jesus Christ. An Interpretation* (1897).

PRENTISS, Elizabeth Payson (1818–78). *Stepping Heavenward* (1869). The spiritual autobiography of heroine Katy Mortimer, who is a doctor's wife cultivating self-discipline, self-sacrifice, and Christian humility. Although this work is homiletic in its fervor for perfected womanhood, the realities of nineteenth-century life – frequent deaths, especially of children, the demands of extended family, and the never-ending duties of women – are vividly rendered.

SMITH, Elizabeth Oakes (1806–93). *Bertha and Lily. Or, The Parsonage of Beech Glen. A Romance* (1854).

SOUTHWORTH, E.D.E.N. (1819–99). *The Deserted Wife* (1850). Pure young Sophie Churchill is forced into marrying the sinister minister, John Huss. He is a lunatic, however, driven mad because his first wife was seduced by a famous man and went crazy. Sophie loves and nurtures him, he dies, and the story line turns to the next generation. As much a romance as a homiletic entry, and an atypical romance at that.

SPOFFORD, Harriet Prescott (1835–1921). "Her Story" (1872).

STOWE, Harriet Beecher (1811–96). *Uncle Tom's Cabin* (1852). *The Minister's Wooing* (1859). *The Pearl of Orr's Island: A Story of the Coast of Maine* (1862). *Oldtown Folks* (1869). *Pink and White Tyranny; A Society Novel* (1871).

TERHUNE, Mary Virginia Hawes [Marion Harland] (1831–1922). *Alone* (1854).

WARNER, Susan [Elizabeth Wetherell] (1819–85). *The Wide, Wide World* (1850).

WILLIAMS, Catherine Read Arnold (1787/1790–1872). *Fall River: An Authentic Narrative* (1834). An impassioned account of the trial of Rev. E. K. Avery for the murder of mill worker Sarah Maria Cornell. Although some commentators classify this as a novel, it is better described as documentary fiction.

WILSON, Augusta Jane Evans (1835–1909). *St. Elmo* (1867).

WOOLEY, Celia Parker (1848–1918). *Love and Theology: A Novel* (1887; title changed in the fifth edition to *Rachel Armstrong*). The *New York Times* (5 August 1894, 18) classed this novel with Deland's *John Ward*, then noted that Parker moved beyond her contemporaries in expressing her religious convictions by becoming a minister herself in Geneva, Illinois. The novel stages religious discussions through the activity of two ministers and their courtships and is much less a polemic in favor of superior womanhood than the other homiletic novels.

Appendix B:
The Parsonage Romances and Their Authors

ABBOTT, Jane Ludlow Drake (1888–1962). *Yours for the Asking* (1943). In a mountain ministry in Black Creek, Kentucky, marital problems develop between the stuffy minister and his kind, high-spirited wife. Jane Abbott was the author of more than twenty novels.

AUSTIN, Jane G. (1831–94). *The Desmond Hundred* (1891). A Christ-like minister cannot marry because it would interfere with his love for God.

BAILEY, Temple (1869–1953). *Enchanted Ground* (1933). The minister is not as important a character in this novel as the lovable Lucifer figure, Boone Musgrave, who redeems himself at the end by demonstrating that "a son's place is with his mother" (334). Irene Temple Bailey was, according to her biography in *American Women Writers: A Critical Reference Guide from Colonial Times to Present* (1979–82), "amazingly popular" and "one of the highest paid writers in the world" (93).

BARBER, Elsie Marion Oakes (1914–). *The Wall Between* (1946). *Hunt for Heaven* (1950). Utopian religious leader John Bliss and his devoted daughter, Rebecca, find establishing a commune rough going. Strange father–daughter material here. *Jenny Angel* (1954). Barber sold the movie rights to her first novel; a brief note in the *New York Times* (30 March 1947, II, 5) records her arrival in Hollywood to write the screenplay.

BEALS, Helen Abbott (1888–). *The River Rises* (1941). Boston-bred Hollice Meade is married to a neurotic minister but falls in love with an engineer whose work may threaten the valley community. Hollice is passionate and sexy, and Beals is sympathetic to her without making her sickly husband completely unpalatable. Beals wrote at least four novels, but the trail runs out after 1941.

BROWN, Alice (1857–1948). *The Willoughbys* (1935). Brown is usually classified as a local colorist.

CHESTER, George Randolph (1869–1924) and Lillian (1888–n.d.). *The Ball of Fire* (1914). George Randolph was a journalist and the creator of "Get Rich Quick Wallingford" (1908). Lillian (de Rimo) Chester was his second wife, whom he married before properly dispensing with the first, thereby causing great social commotion. This collaborative novel is the only fiction bearing her name.

250

COMSTOCK, Harriet Teresa (Smith) (1860–n.d.). *Terry* (1943). Comstock has some thirty-five novels to her credit. *Terry* seems to be the last novel published and would have appeared when she was eighty-three years old.

COOKE, Rose Terry (1827–92). *Steadfast: The Story of a Saint and a Sinner* (1889). Cooke is usually regarded as a local colorist.

DELAND, Margaret (1857–1945). *The Promises of Alice: The Romance of a New England Parsonage* (1919). *Promises* is not typical of Deland's writing, and she is better known for another novel about a minister, *John Ward, Preacher* (1882), which I have classified as homiletic fiction in Chapter 4. Deland's several volumes of Chester tales feature a kindly, older minister as a recurring character.

DOBSON, Ruth Lininger (n.d.). *Straw in the Wind* (1937), offers an excellent record of Amish speech and customs, and there are some powerfully drawn characters and events. A *New York Times Review* of *Straw* notes she lived in the Middlebury community for five years as a girl (16 May 1937, II, 10). *Today Is Enough* (1939) was her second, and apparently last, novel.

ELLIOTT, Sarah Barnwell (1848–1928). *A Simple Heart* (1887). An idealized minister and carpenter in Pecan, Texas, fades back into the prairie when his parishioners want a more modern fellow.

GREEN, Eleanor (1911–n.d.). *Ariadne Spinning* (1941). Strange and poetically written novel about a minister's wife whose dedicated husband falls in love with a young girl. Yet somehow Francesca is to blame for the death of the girl and must go into the world to do penance. According to Warfel, *American Novelists of Today* (1951), Green was a Guggenheim fellow in 1949.

HAUCK, Louise Platt (1883–1943). *If with All Your Hearts* (1935).

JENKINS, Sarah Lucille (1904–n.d.). *We Gather Together* (1948). All the Gordon daughters are married to ministers, but the story line belongs to the women. Contains some well-written material on race relations and children. *The Lost Lamp* (1950). Minister George Winfree is trying too hard to be perfect and has to take some lessons in humanity from his young daughter, Hannah. *Saddlebag Parson* (1956). A circuit rider in pre–Civil War Florida gets the fiery governess on the last page, the only one of these three novels to fit fully the category of "romance."

LEE, Mildred Scudder (1908–n.d.). *The Invisible Sun* (1946). Her first novel. Although she idealizes her country minister, the writing is gutsier than the conventional romance. Her depiction of parish dynamics in a small southern town and her handling of race relations anticipates Harper Lee's *To Kill a Mockingbird* (1960). Her last listed writing appeared in 1972.

MARTIN, Helen Reimensnyder (1868–1939). *The Church on the Avenue* (1923). *Whip Hand* (1934). The handsome minister falls in love with the girl for whom he is a guardian, but not before he is pursued by a predatory female with a dark past. *Whip Hand* is a disappointing entry for a writer who was a socialist and feminist.

MASON, Caroline Atwater (1853–1939). *A Minister of the World* (1895). Stephen Castle is captivated by a city woman and moves to her urban church, but this chastened country boy returns to his small town parish to marry his waiting sweetie and minister to the poor. *A Minister of Carthage* (1899). A minister decides to stay with his home parish and marries the girl next door. Both novels could also be classified by the social gospel flavor that guides the romance.

MONTROSS, Lois Seyster (1897–1961). *No Stranger to My Heart* (1937). A romance about a minister's daughter who moves to Chicago and learns about the evils of high society.

NEFF, Elizabeth (–1942). *Altars to Mammon* (1908). A wealthy society girl helps the handsome young minister realize his activities on behalf of the poor. Probably her only novel. She was an 1874 graduate of Ohio Wesleyan University.

NOBLE, Annette Lucille (1844–1932). *The Parsonage Secret* (1898).

NOBLE, Lucretia Gray (1836–1927). *The Reverend Idol* (1882). Possibly her only novel. Her obituary notes that she was a friend of William Dean Howells and James Russell Lowell, and that she also wrote verse and essays (*New York Times*, 29 December 1927, 23).

RICHMOND, Grace Smith (1866–1959). *Red and Black* (1919). A popular writer of light fiction in which all the men are manly and all the women womanly.

SCOTT, Winifred Mary (Pamela Wynne, pseud.; n.d.). *Penelope Finds Out* (1927). A British author with at least sixty titles to her credit.

SUCKOW, Ruth (1892–1960). *New Hope* (1942). The young minister is virile and loves carpentry; the story focuses on his daughter and her childhood love, however. Suckow is best known as a regionalist.

TURNBULL, Agnes Sligh (1888–1982). *The Bishop's Mantle* (1948). She has twenty-eight books to her credit.

WALWORTH, Dorothy (1900–1953). *Nicodemus* (1946). A best seller that year in which a large cast of characters search for truth and meaning in New York City. Tatum, honest minister of faith and doubt, provides plot center.

WHITE, Nelia Gardner (1894–1957). *The Fields of Gomorrah* (1935). Married to the saintly John McKinstry, Lucy turns out to be an unworthy minister's wife whose mother-in-law upstages her during her husband's final illness. *No Trumpet before Him* (1947). Winner of the Westminster Press Fiction contest in 1948.

WIDDEMER, Margaret (1880/1894/1897–1978). *A Minister of Grace* (1922). Author of more than forty novels, she shared the Poetry Society Prize with Carl Sandburg in 1919 for *The Old Road to Paradise*.

WILSON, Mary Badger (n.d.). *Canon Brett.* (1942). A flyleaf note identifies her as a writer of light fiction for the *Saturday Evening Post*.

Bibliography

Fiction
Prairie Missionary. Philadelphia: American Sunday School Union, 1853.
Abbott, Jane (Ludlow Drake). *Yours for the Asking*. Philadelphia: J. B. Lippincott, 1943.
Adams, Henry. *Esther*, in *Democracy and Esther: Two Novels by Henry Adams*. 1884 [Frances Snow Compton]. Reprint. New York: Doubleday, Anchor, 1961.
Anderson, Sherwood. *Winesburg, Ohio*. 1919. Reprint, Introduction by Malcolm Cowley. New York: Viking Compass, 1975.
Angelou, Maya. *I Know Why the Caged Bird Sings*. 1969. Reprint. New York: Random, Bantam, 1988.
Atwood, Margaret. *Cat's Eye*. New York: Doubleday, 1988.
  The Edible Woman. 1969. Reprint. New York: Warner, 1989.
  The Handmaid's Tale. Boston: Houghton Mifflin, 1986.
  Lady Oracle. 1976. Reprint. New York: Fawcett Crest, 1987.
  Surfacing. 1972. Reprint. New York: Fawcett Crest, Ballantine, 1987.
Austin, Jane G. *The Desmond Hundred*. Boston: Houghton, Mifflin, 1891.
Barber, Elsie Marion Oakes. *Jenny Angel*. New York: Macmillan, 1954.
  The Wall Between. New York: Macmillan, 1946.
Barth, John. *Chimera*. New York: Random House, 1972.
Barton, Bruce. *The Man Nobody Knows: A Discovery of the Real Jesus*. Indianapolis: Bobbs Merrill, 1924.
Beals, Helen Abott. *The River Rises*. New York: Macmillan, 1941.
Beattie, Ann. *Falling in Place*. New York: Random House, 1980.
Beecher, Eunice White Bullard. *From Dawn to Daylight, or The Simple Story of a Western Home by a Minister's Wife*. New York: Derby & Jackson, 1859.
Brown, Alice. *The Willoughbys*. New York: D. Appleton-Century, 1935.
Brown, Almedia. *Diary of a Minister's Wife*. New York: J. S. Ogilvie, 1881.
Bruce, Mrs. E. M. *Thousand a Year*. Boston: Lee & Shepard, 1866.
Brummit, Dan. *Shoddy*. Chicago: Willett, Clark & Colby, 1928.
Buechner, Frederick. *The Final Beast*. New York: Atheneum, 1965.

Cable, George Washington. *Bylow Hill*. New York: Charles Scribner's Sons, 1902.

Cable, Mary. *Avery's Knot*. New York: G. P. Putnam's Sons, 1981.

Chesebro', Caroline. *The Children of Light: A Theme for the Time*. New York: Redfield, 1853.

Victoria, Or, The World Overcome. New York: Derby & Jackson, 1856.

Chester, George Randolph, and Lillian Chester. *The Ball of Fire*. New York: Hearst, 1914.

Churchill, Winston. *The Inside of the Cup*. New York: Macmillan, 1913.

Comstock, Harriet Teresa Smith. *Terry*. New York: Doubleday, Doran, 1943.

Cooke, Rose Terry. *Steadfast: The Story of a Saint and a Sinner*. Boston: Ticknor, 1889.

Cozzens, James Gould. *Men and Brethren*. New York: Harcourt, Brace, 1936.

Deland, Margaret. *The Awakening of Helena Richie*. New York: Harper & Row, 1905.

The Iron Woman. New York: Harper & Brothers, 1911.

John Ward, Preacher. 1882. Reprint. Ridgewood, N.J.: Gregg Press, 1967.

Old Chester Tales. New York: Grosset & Dunlap, 1898.

The Promises of Alice: The Romance of a New England Parsonage. New York: Harper & Brothers, 1919.

DeVries, Peter. *The Mackeral Plaza*. 1958. Reprint. New York: Popular Library, 1977.

Dobson, Ruth Lininger. *Today Is Enough*. New York: Dodd, Mead, 1939.

Erdrich, Louise. *The Beet Queen*. New York: Bantam, 1987.

Love Medicine. New York: Bantam, 1985.

Tracks. New York: Henry Holt, 1988.

Faulkner, William. *Absalom, Absalom!* 1936. Reprint. The Corrected Text. New York: Vintage, 1987.

As I Lay Dying. 1930. Reprint. The Corrected Text. New York: Vintage, 1987.

Light in August. 1932. Reprint. The Corrected Text. New York: Vintage, 1987.

The Sound and the Fury. 1929. Reprint. The Corrected Text. New York: Vintage, 1987.

Frederic, Harold. *The Damnation of Theron Ware*. 1896. Reprint. Edited by Everett Carter. Cambridge, Mass.: Belknap, 1960.

Gardner, John. "Pastoral Care." In *The King's Indian*, 1972. Reprint. New York: Ballantine, 1976.

Gardner, Martin. *The Flight of Peter Fromm*. Los Altos, Calif.: Kaufman, 1973.

Gass, William. *Omensetter's Luck*. 1966. Reprint. New York: NAL, 1972.

"The Tunnel." *Salmagundi* 55 (Winter 1982): 3–60.

Willie Master's Lonesome Wife. New York: Alfred A. Knopf, 1971.

Glasgow, Ellen. *Vein of Iron*. 1935. Reprint. New York: Harbrace Paperback Library, 1963.

Gordon, Mary. *The Company of Women*. New York: Random House, 1981.

Final Payments. New York: Random House, 1978.

Men and Angels. New York: Random House, 1985.

"The Other Woman." In *Temporary Shelter*, 151–6. New York: Random House, 1987.

Harris, Corra May White. *A Circuit Rider's Wife*. Philadelphia: Henry Altemus, 1910.

Hauk, Louise Platt. *If with All Your Hearts*. New York: Grosset & Dunlap, 1935.

Hawthorne, Nathaniel. *The Scarlet Letter*. 1850. Reprint. 3d. ed. Edited by Seymour Gross, Sculley Bradley, Richmond Croom Beatty, and E. Hudson Long. New York and London: W. W. Norton & Co., 1988.

Holmes, Oliver Wendell. *The Writings of Oliver Wendell Holmes*. Vol. 5, *Elsie Venner: A Romance of Destiny*. Riverside ed. Boston: Houghton Mifflin, 1861.

The Guardian Angel. 1867. Reprint of 1888 edition. Upper Saddle River, N.J.: Gregg Press, 1970.

Howells, William Dean. *A Foregone Conclusion*. Reprint of 1875 edition. Upper Saddle River, N.J.: Gregg Press, 1970.

A Selected Edition of William Dean Howells. Edited by Edwin H. Cady. Vol. 27, *The Leatherwood God*. Introduction and Notes by Eugene Pattison. Bloomington: Indiana University Press, 1976.

Hubbell, Martha Stone. *The Shady Side; or, Life in a Country Parsonage*. Boston: John P. Jewett, 1853.

Keable, Robert. *Simon Called Peter*. New York: E. P. Dutton, 1921.

Lee, Mildred. *The Invisible Sun*. Philadelphia: Westminster Press, 1946.

Lewis, Sinclair. *Elmer Gantry*. 1927. Reprint. New York: Signet, NAL, 1970.

McCullers, Carson. *The Heart Is a Lonely Hunter*. 1940. Reprint. Boston: Bantam, 1970.

Martin, Helen Reimensnyder. *The Church on the Avenue*. New York: Dodd, Mead, 1923.

Whip Hand. New York: Grosset & Dunlap, 1934.

Mason, Caroline Atwater. *The Minister of Carthage*. Philadelphia: Curtis; New York: Doubleday & McClure, 1899.

A Minister of the World. N.p.: Curtis, 1895.

Morrison, Toni. *Beloved*. New York: Knopf, 1987.

Song of Solomon. New York: Signet, NAL, 1977.

Nathan, Robert. *The Bishop's Wife*. New York: Grosset & Dunlap, 1928.

Neff, Elizabeth. *Altars to Mammon*. New York: Frederick A. Stokes, 1908.

Noble, Annette Lucille. *The Parsonage Secret*. New York: J.B. Dunn in association with National Temperance Society and Tract House, 1898.

Noble, Lucretia Gray. *The Reverend Idol*. Boston: Osgood, 1882.

Oates, Joyce Carol. *Son of the Morning: A Novel*. New York: Vanguard, 1978.

O'Connor, Flannery. *The Violent Bear It Away*. 1960. Reprint. In *Three by Flannery O'Connor*. New York: NAL, n.d.

Wise Blood. 1962. Reprint. In *Three by Flannery O'Connor*. New York: NAL, n.d.

Paul, Raymond. *The Tragedy at Tiverton. An Historical Novel of Murder*. New York: Viking, 1984.

Percy, Walker. *Lancelot*. New York: Avon, 1978.

Love in the Ruins: The Adventures of a Bad Catholic at a Time Near the End of the World. 1971. Reprint. New York: Avon, 1978.

The Second Coming. New York: Pocket Books, 1981.

The Thanatos Syndrome. New York: Farrar, Straus, Giroux, 1987.

Phelps, Elizabeth Stuart [H. Trusta]. *A Peep at Number Five, or A Chapter in the Life of a City Pastor.* Boston: Phillips, Sampson, 1852.

Phelps, Elizabeth Stuart. *The Sunny Side or, The Country Minister's Wife.* Philadelphia: American Sunday School Union, 1851.

Phelps [Ward], Elizabeth Stuart. *Beyond the Gates.* 1883. Boston: Houghton, Mifflin, 1892.

Doctor Zay. Boston: Houghton, Mifflin, 1882.

Fourteen to One. Boston: Houghton, Mifflin, 1891.

The Gates Ajar. 1868. Reprint. Boston: Fields, Osgood, 1869.

The Gates Between. Boston and New York: Houghton, Mifflin, 1887.

Hedged In. Boston: Fields, Osgood, 1870.

Men, Women and Ghosts. Boston: Fields, Osgood, 1869.

Sealed Orders. Vol. 85 of The American Short Story Series. Reprint of 1879 ed. New York: Garrett Press, 1969.

The Silent Partner. 1871. Reprint. Ridgewood, N.J.: Gregg Press, 1967.

A Singular Life. 1895. Reprint. Boston: Houghton, Mifflin, 1896.

The Story of Jesus Christ: An Interpretation. Boston: Houghton, 1897.

Walled In. London: Harper & Brothers, 1907.

Prentiss, Elizabeth Payson. *Stepping Heavenward.* New York: Anson, D. F. Randolph, 1869.

Rader, Dotson. *Miracle.* New York: Random House, 1977.

Richardson, Dorothy. *Pointed Roofs, Backwater, Honeycomb. Pilgrimage.* Vol. 1. New York: Alfred A. Knopf, 1938.

Richmond, Grace. *Red and Black.* New York: Doubleday, Page, 1919.

Richter, Conrad. *A Simple Honorable Man.* New York: Alfred A. Knopf, 1962.

Robinson, Marilynne. *Housekeeping.* New York: Bantam, 1987.

Schaeffer, Susan Fromberg. *Falling.* New York: Macmillan, 1973.

Scott, Winifred Mary [Pamela Wynne]. *Penelope Finds Out.* New York: Macaulay, 1927.

Sheldon, Charles M. *In His Steps.* 1896. Reprint. Published with T. S. Arthur, *Ten Nights in a Barroom.* Edited by C. Hugh Holman. New York: Odyssey, 1966.

Smith, Elizabeth Oakes. *Bertha and Lily: Or, the Parsonage of Beech Glen. A Romance.* 1854. Reprint. New York: Derby & Jackson, 1858.

Southworth, E.D.E.N. *The Deserted Wife.* New York: D. Appleton, 1850.

Spofford, Harriet Prescott. "Her Story." In *Old Madame and Other Tragedies,* 205–49. Boston: Richard G. Badger & Co., 1900.

Stowe, Harriet Beecher. *The Minister's Wooing.* 1859. Reprint. Introduction by Sandra R. Duguid. Hartford, Conn.: The Stowe-Day Foundation, 1978.

Oldtown Folks. 1869. Reprint. Edited by Henry F. May. Cambridge, Mass.: Belknap, 1966.

The Pearl of Orr's Island: A Story of the Coast of Maine. 1862. Reprint. Boston: Houghton Mifflin Co., 1896.

Pink and White Tyranny: A Society Novel. Boston: Roberts Brothers, 1871.

Uncle Tom's Cabin. 1851–52. Reprint. Afterword by John William Ward. New York: Signet, NAL, 1966.

Street, James. *The Gauntlet*. New York: Doubleday, Doran, 1945.

Stribling, T. S. *Unfinished Cathedral*. Garden City, N.Y.: Doubleday, Doran, 1934.

Terhune, Mary Virginia Hawes [Marion Harland]. *Alone*. 5th ed. Richmond, Va.: A. Morris, 1854.

Turnbull, Agnes Sligh. *The Bishop's Mantle*. New York: Macmillan, 1948.

Updike, John. *A Month of Sundays*. New York: Fawcett Crest, 1975.

    Rabbit Is Rich. New York: Fawcett Crest, 1981.

    Rabbit Redux. New York: Fawcett Crest, 1971.

    Rabbit, Run. Greenwich, Conn.: Fawcett Crest, 1960.

    Roger's Version. New York: Alfred A. Knopf, 1986.

Warner, Susan [Elizabeth Wetherell]. *The Wide, Wide World*. 1850. Reprint. Afterword by Jane Tompkins. New York: Feminist Press, 1987.

Wellman, Paul. *The Chain*. Garden City, N.Y.: Doubleday, 1949.

White, Nelia Gardner. *No Trumpet before Him*. Philadelphia: Westminster, 1947.

Widdemer, Margaret. *A Minister of Grace*. New York: Harcourt, Brace, 1922.

Wilson, Augusta Jane (Evans). *St. Elmo*. 1867. Reprint. New York: Grosset & Dunlap, 1896.

Wilson, Gregory [pseud.]. *The Stained Glass Jungle*. New York: Doubleday, 1962.

Wilson, Mary Badger. *Canon Brett*. New York: Greystone Press, 1942.

Secondary Sources

"God and Money." *Newsweek*, 6 Apr. 1987: 16–22.

"Harold Frederic." *Book Buyer* 8 (May 1881): 151–2.

"Heaven Can Wait." *Newsweek*, 8 June 1987: 58–65.

"It Isn't the First Time." *Newsweek*, 6 Apr. 1987: 23.

"Ministerial Virility." *The Biblical World* 17 (Jan. 1901): 3–5.

"Now It's Jimmy's Turn." *Time*, 7 Mar. 1988. 46–8.

"A Pastor Claims Dancing." *Christianity Today* 30 (8 Aug. 1986): 32–3.

A Saunterer in the Labyrinth [Harold Frederic]. "Musings on the Question of the Hour." *Pall Mall Budget* 33 (13 Aug. 1885): 11–12.

"A Sex Scandal Breaks over Jimmy Swaggart." *Newsweek*, 29 Feb. 1988: 30ff.

"Shady Side Literature." *New Englander* 12 (Feb. 1854): 54–70.

"Their Pastor an Adulterer." *People*, 7 Feb. 1986, 99–100.

"Weeding Out Clergymen Who Go Astray." *U.S. News and World Report*, 2 Oct. 1978: 63–5.

Abbott, Lyman, and Rev. S. B. Halliday. *Henry Ward Beecher and a Sketch of His Career*. Hartford, Conn.: American Publishing, 1887.

Abel, Elizabeth, ed. *Writing and Sexual Difference*. Chicago: University of Chicago Press, 1982.

Abell, Troy D. *Better Felt Than Said: The Holiness Pentecostal Experience in Southern Appalachia*. Waco, Tex.: Markham, 1982.

Aldrich, Marcia. "The Poetics of Transience: Marilynne Robinson's *Housekeeping*." *Essays in Literature* 16 (Spring 1989): 127–40.

Allen, Carolyn. "Feminist Criticism and Postmodernism." In *Tracing Literary Theory,* edited by Joseph Natoli, 278–305. Urbana: University of Illinois Press, 1987.

Ammons, Elizabeth, ed. *Critical Essays on Harriet Beecher Stowe.* Boston: G. K. Hall, 1980.

Audsley, George Ashdown. *The Art of Organ Building.* 2 vols. 1905. Reprint (2 vols. in 1). New York: Dover, 1965.

Bader, Julia. "The Dissolving Vision: Realism in Jewett, Freeman, and Gilman." In *American Realism: New Essays,* edited by Eric Sundquist, 176–98. Baltimore: Johns Hopkins University Press, 1982.

Baer, Elizabeth. "Pilgrimage Inward: Quest and Fairy Tale Motifs in *Surfacing.*" In *Margaret Atwood: Visions and Forms,* edited by Kathryn VanSpanckeren and Jan Garden Castro, 24–34. Carbondale: Southern Illinois University Press, 1988.

Barrett, Deborah. "Discourse and Intercourse: The Conversion of the Priest in Percy's *Lancelot.*" *Critique: Studies in Modern Fiction* 23 (Winter 1981–2): 5–11.

Baym, Nina. *Novels, Readers and Reviewers: Responses to Fiction in Antebellum America.* Ithaca, N.Y.: Cornell University Press, 1984.

———. "Passion and Authority in *The Scarlet Letter.*" *New England Quarterly* 43 (June 1970): 209–30.

———. *Woman's Fiction: A Guide to Novels by and about Women in America, 1820–1870.* Ithaca, N.Y.: Cornell University Press, 1978.

Beecher, Catherine. *Truth Stranger than Fiction: A Narrative of Recent Transactions Involving Inquiries in Regard to the Principles of Honor, Truth, and Justice Which Obtain in a Distinguished American University.* Boston: Phillips, Sampson, 1850.

Belenky, Mary Field, Blythe McVicker Clinchy, Nancy Rule Goldberger, and Jill Mattuck Tarule. *Women's Ways of Knowing: The Development of Self, Voice and Mind.* New York: Basic Books, 1986.

Bennett, Ernest Eugene. *The Image of the Christian Clergyman in Modern Fiction and Drama.* Ph.D. diss., Vanderbilt University, 1970.

Berg, Temma, Anna Shannon Elfenbein, Jeanne Larsen, and Elisa Kay Sparks. *Engendering the Word: Feminist Essays in Psychosexual Poetics.* Urbana: University of Illinois Press, 1989.

Berryman, Charles. *From Wilderness to Wasteland: The Trial of the Puritan God in the American Imagination.* Port Washington, N.Y.: Kennikat, 1979.

Boisvert, Raymond. "Walker Percy's Postmodern Existentialism." *Soundings: An Interdisciplinary Journal* 71 (Winter 1988): 639–55.

Booth, Wayne C. *The Company We Keep: An Ethics of Fiction.* Berkeley: University of California Press, 1988.

———. *The Rhetoric of Fiction.* 2d ed. Chicago: University of Chicago Press, 1983.

Briffault, Robert. *Sin and Sex.* Introduction by Bertrand Russell. Reprint of 1931 edition. New York: Haskell House, 1973.

Bromberg, Pamela S. "The Two Faces of the Mirror in *The Edible Woman* and *Lady Oracle.*" In *Margaret Atwood: Visions and Forms,* edited by Kathryn

VanSpanckeren and Jan Garden Castro, 12–23. Carbondale: Southern Illinois University Press, 1988.

Buell, Lawrence. "Calvinism Romanticized: Harriet Beecher Stowe, Samuel Hopkins, and *The Minister's Wooing.*" In *Critical Essays on Harriet Beecher Stowe,* edited by Elizabeth Ammons, 259–75. Boston: G. K. Hall, 1980.

Bugge, John. "Merlin and the Movies in Walker Percy's *Lancelot.*" *Studies in Medievalism* 2 (Fall 1983): 39–55.

Bustanoby, Andre. "The Pastor and the Other Woman." *Christianity Today* 18 (30 Aug. 1974): 7–10.

Bynum, Caroline Walker. *Holy Feast and Holy Fast: The Religious Significance of Food to Medieval Women.* Berkeley: University of California Press, 1987.

Cawelti, John G. *Adventure, Mystery and Romance: Formula Stories as Art and Popular Culture.* Chicago: University of Chicago Press, 1976.

Chodorow, Nancy. *The Reproduction of Mothering: Psychoanalysis and the Sociology of Gender.* Berkeley: University of California, 1978.

Ciuba, Gary. "The Omega Factor: Apocalyptic Visions in Walker Percy's *Lancelot.*" *American Literature* 57 (Mar. 1985): 98–112.

Cixous, Helene. "Castration or Decapitation." *Signs* 7 (Autumn 1981): 41–55.
"The Laugh of the Medusa." *Signs* 1 (Summer 1976): 875–93.

Clayton, Joan [pseud.]. "My Minister Kept Making Passes at Me." *Ladies Home Journal,* July 1985, 16, 20.

Coale, Samuel. "Frederic and Hawthorne: The Romantic Roots of Naturalism." *American Literature* 48 (Mar. 1976): 29–45.

Cohen, Chapman. *Religion and Sex: Studies in the Pathology of Religious Development.* London: T. N. Foulis, 1919.

Cooey, Paula M., Sharon A. Farmer, and Mary Ellen Ross, eds. *Embodied Love: Sensuality and Relationship as Feminist Values.* San Fransisco: Harper & Row, 1987.

Cott, Nancy. "Passionlessness: An Interpretation of Victorian Sexual Ideology, 1790–1850." *Signs* 4 (1978): 219–36.

Coughlin, Anne. *A Unique Heathen: The Sexual Dogmatics of Theodore Schroeder.* Ph.D. diss., Fuller Theological Seminary, University Microfilms, 1986.

Crowley, John. "The Nude and the Madonna in *The Damnation of Theron Ware.*" *American Literature* 45 (Nov. 1973): 379–89.

Crowley, J. David, ed. *Hawthorne: The Critical Heritage.* New York: Barnes & Noble, 1970.

Crowley, Sue Mitchell. "John Updike and Kierkegaard's Negative Way: Irony and Indirect Communication in *A Month of Sundays.*" *Soundings: An Interdisciplinary Journal* 68 (Summer 1985): 212–28.

Crozier, Alice C. *The Novels of Harriet Beecher Stowe.* New York: Oxford, 1969.

Cutten, George Barton. *The Psychological Phenomena of Christianity.* New York: Scribner's, 1908.

Dale, Corrine. "*Lancelot* and the Medieval Quests of Sir Lancelot and Dante." *Southern Quarterly* 18 (Spring 1980): 99–106.

Daly, Mary. *Gyn/Ecology: The Metaethics of Radical Feminism.* Boston: Beacon, 1978.

Davies, Horton. *A Mirror of the Ministry in Modern Novels*. New York: Oxford University Press, 1959.

Davis, Ann [pseud.]. "A Single Woman Speaks Up about Ministers." *Pastoral Psychology* 18 (Dec. 1967): 39–44.

Davis, David Glenn. *The Image of the Minister in American Fiction*. Ph.D. Diss., University of Tulsa, 1978.

Desmond, John F. "Love, Sex and Knowledge in Walker Percy's *Lancelot:* A Metaphysical View." *Mississippi Quarterly: The Journal of Southern Culture* 38 (Spring 1986): 103–9.

Detweiler, Robert. *Breaking the Fall: Religious Readings of Contemporary Fiction*. San Francisco: Harper & Row, 1989.

"Updike's *A Month of Sundays* and the Language of the Unconscious." *Journal of the American Academy of Religion* 47 (Dec. 1979): 609–25.

Donaldson, Scott. "The Seduction of Theron Ware." *Nineteenth Century Fiction* 29 (Mar. 1975): 441–52.

Douglas, Ann. *The Feminization of American Culture*. New York: Alfred A. Knopf, 1977.

"Soft-Porn Culture." *New Republic,* 30 Aug. 1980: 25–9.

Driver, Tom, and Herb Richardson. "The Meaning of Orgasm: A Dialogue." In *God, Sex and the Social Project: The Glassboro Papers on Religion and Human Sexuality*, pp. 184–200. Edited by James H. Grace. New York: Edwin Mellen, 1978.

Edwards, Jonathan. *The Works of Jonathan Edwards*. Edited by John E. Smith. Vol. 4, *The Great Awakening*. Edited by C. C. Goen. New Haven, Conn.: Yale University Press, 1972.

The Works of Jonathan Edwards. Edited by Perry Miller. Vol. 2, *Religious Affections*. Edited by John E. Smith. New Haven, Conn.: Yale University Press, 1959.

Eisenstein, Hester, and Alice Jardine, eds. *The Future of Difference*. New Brunswick, N.J.: Rutgers University, 1985.

Farmer, John S., and W. E. Henley. *Dictionary of Slang and Its Analogues, Past and Present*. 1890. Reprint. Introduction by Lee Revens and G. Legman. Rev. ed., 1903, 1909. Vol. 1. New York: University Books, 1966.

Faust, Oliver C. *A Treatise on the Construction, Repairing and Tuning of the Organ, Including Also the Reed Organ, the Orchestrelle and the Player Piano*. Boston: Tuners Supply, 1949.

Fetterly, Judith. *The Resisting Reader: A Feminist Approach to American Fiction*. Bloomington: Indiana University Press, 1978.

Fishburn, Janet F. "Male Clergy Adultery as Vocational Confusion." *Christian Century* 99 (15–22 Sept. 1982): 922–5.

Flax, Jane. "Postmodernism and Gender Relations in Feminist Theory." *Signs* 12 (Summer 1987): 621–43.

Fleischmann, Fritz, ed. *American Novelists Revisited: Essays in Feminist Criticism*. Boston: G. K. Hall, 1982.

Foucault, Michel. *The History of Sexuality: An Introduction*. Vol. 1. Translated by Robert Hurley. New York: Pantheon, 1978.

Fortenberry, George E., Stanton Garner, and Robert H. Woodward, eds. *The*

Correspondence of Harold Frederic. Harold Frederic Edition. Vol. 1. Fort Worth, Tex: Texas Christian University, 1977.

Fortune, Marie. *Is Nothing Sacred? When Sex Invades the Pastoral Relationship.* San Francisco: Harper & Row, 1989.

Foster, Lawrence. *Religion and Sexuality: Three American Communal Experiments of the Nineteenth Century.* New York: Oxford University Press, 1981.

Fowler, Doreen, and Ann J. Abadie, eds. *Faulkner and Women: Faulkner and Yoknapatawpha, 1985.* Jackson: University Press of Mississippi, 1986.

Franklin, Penelope, ed. *Private Pages: Diaries of American Women, 1830's–1970's.* New York: Ballantine, 1986.

Friedan, Betty. *The Feminine Mystique.* New York: Dell, 1963.

Friedrich, Otto. *Clover.* New York: Simon & Schuster, 1979.

Frye, Northrop. *Anatomy of Criticism: Four Essays.* New York: Atheneum, 1966.

Gallop, Jane. *The Daughter's Seduction: Feminism and Psychoanalysis.* Ithaca, N.Y.: Cornell University Press, 1982.

Gamble, Richard H. *The Figure of the Protestant Clergyman in American Fiction.* Ph.D. diss., University of Pittsburgh, 1972.

Gardella, Peter. *Innocent Ecstasy: How Christianity Gave America an Ethic of Sexual Pleasure.* New York: Oxford University Press, 1985.

Garner, Stanton. *Harold Frederic.* University of Minnesota Pamphlets on American Writers, no. 83. Minneapolis: University of Minneapolis Press, 1969.

"History of the Text." In *The Damnation of Theron Ware or Illumination,* edited by Stanton Garner, 353–415. Harold Frederic edition. Vol. 3. Lincoln: University of Nebraska Press, 1985.

Gay, Peter. *The Bourgeois Experience: Victoria to Freud.* Vol. 1, *The Education of the Senses.* New York: Oxford University Press, 1984.

The Bourgeois Experience: Victoria to Freud. Vol. 2, *The Tender Passion.* New York: Oxford University Press, 1986.

Genthe, Charles V. "*The Damnation of Theron Ware* and *Elmer Gantry.*" *Research Studies* 32 (Sept. 1964): 334–43.

Gerson, Noel. *Harriet B. Stowe. A Biography.* New York: Praeger, 1976.

Gilbert, Sandra M., and Susan Gubar. *The Madwoman in the Attic: The Woman Writer and the Nineteenth-Century Literary Imagination.* New Haven, Conn.: Yale University Press, 1979.

No Man's Land: The Place of the Woman Writer in the Twentieth Century. Vol. 1, *The War of the Words.* New Haven, Conn.: Yale University Press, 1988.

Gilligan, Carol. *In a Different Voice: Psychological Theory and Woman's Development.* Cambridge, Mass.: Harvard University Press, 1982.

Goldberg, B. Z. *The Sacred Fire: The Story of Sex in Religion.* New York: Horace Liveright, 1930.

Goldfarb, Russell M. *Sexual Repression and Victorian Literature.* Lewisburg, Pa.: Bucknell University Press, 1970.

Grace, Sherrill E. "In Search of Demeter: The Lost Silent Mother in *Surfacing.*" In *Margaret Atwood: Visions and Forms,* edited by Kathryn VanSpanckeren and Jan Garden Casto, 35–47. Carbondale: Southern Illinois University Press, 1988.

Grace, Sherrill E., and Lorraine Weir, eds. *Margaret Atwood: Language, Text and System*. Vancouver: University of British Columbia Press, 1983.

Griffin, Susan. *Pornography and Silence: Culture's Revenge against Nature*. New York: Harper & Row, 1981.

Guedon, Marie-Francoise. "Surfacing: Amerindian Themes and Shamanism." In *Margaret Atwood: Language, Text, and System*, edited by Sherrill E. Grace and Lorraine Weir, 91–111. Vancouver: University of British Columbia Press. 1983.

Hale, Nathan G. *Freud and the Americans: The Beginnings of Psychoanalysis in the United States, 1876–1917*. Vol 1, *Freud in America*. New York: Oxford University Press, 1971.

Halttunen, Karen. *Confidence Men and Painted Women: A Study of Middle-Class Culture of America, 1830–1870*. New Haven, Conn.: Yale University Press, 1982.

Hamilton-Pennell, Christine. "Pastoral Sexual Abuse: One Congregation's Ordeal." *Daughters of Sarah* 13 (July–Aug. 1987): 20–4.

Harris, Susan K. *19th-Century American Women's Novels: Interpretive Strategies*. New York: Cambridge University Press, 1990.

Heilbrun, Carolyn. "Critical Response II: A Response to Writing and Sexual Difference." In *Writing and Sexual Difference*, edited by Elizabeth Abel, 291–7. Chicago: University of Chicago Press, 1982.

Homans, Margaret. "'Her Very Own Howl'": The Ambiguities of Representation in Recent Woman's Fiction." *Signs* 9 (Winter 1983): 186–205.

Hopkins, E. J., and E. F. Rimbault. *The Organ: Its History and Construction*. 1877. Reprint. Preface and corrections by W. L. Sumner. Hilversum, Neth.: Frits Knuf, 1965.

Horn, William. "The Image of the Protestant Minister." *Lutheran Quarterly* 13 (1961): 193–210.

Howells, William Dean. *Atlantic Monthly* 28 (1871): 255–6.

"My Favorite Novelist and His Best Book." *Munsey's Magazine* 17 (1898): 18–25.

Hutcheon, Linda. *A Poetics of Postmodernism: History, Theory, Fiction*. New York: Routledge, 1988.

Irigaray, Luce. "And One Doesn't Stir without the Other." Translated by Helen Vivienne Wenzel. *Signs* 7 (Autumn 1981): 60–7.

"When Our Lips Speak Together." Translated by Carolyn Burke. *Signs* 6 (Autumn 1980): 69–79.

Jakobson, Roman, and Morris Halle. *Fundamentals of Language*. The Hague: Mouton, 1956.

James, William. *The Varieties of Religious Experience. A Study in Human Nature*. New York: Modern Library, 1902.

Jamieson, W. F. *The Clergy: A Source of Danger to the American Republic*. Boston: Colby & Rich, 1874.

Jehlen, Myra. "Archimedes and the Paradox of Feminist Criticism." *Signs* 6 (Summer 1981): 575–601.

Johnson, Charles A. *The Frontier Camp Meeting: Religion's Harvest Time*. Dallas: Southern Methodist University Press, 1955.

Johnson, George. "Harold Frederic's Young Goodman Ware." *Modern Fiction Studies* 8 (Winter 1962–3): 361–74.

Johnson, Mark. *The Body in the Mind: The Bodily Basis of Meaning, Imagination, and Reason.* Chicago: University of Chicago Press, 1987.

Johnston, Johanna. *Runaway to Heaven: The Story of Harriet Beecher Stowe.* New York: Doubleday, 1963.

Jones, Ann Rosalind. "Writing the Body: Toward an Understanding of L'Ecriture Feminine." *Feminist Studies* 7 (Summer 1981): 247–63.

Kaledin, Eugenia. *The Education of Mrs. Henry Adams.* Philadelphia: Temple University Press, 1981.

Kasserman, David Richard. *Fall River Outrage: Life, Murder, and Justice in Early Industrial New England.* Philadelphia: University of Pennsylvania Press, 1986.

Kauffman, Linda. *Discourses of Desire: Gender, Genre and Epistolary Fictions.* Ithaca, N.Y.: Cornell University Press, 1986.

Kelley, Mary. *Private Woman, Public Stage: Literary Domesticity in Nineteenth Century America.* New York: Oxford University Press, 1984.

Kern, Louis J. *An Ordered Love: Sex Roles and Sexuality in Victorian Utopias – the Shakers, the Mormons, and the Oneida Community.* Chapel Hill: University of North Carolina Press, 1981.

Kessler, Carol Farley. *Elizabeth Stuart Phelps.* Boston: Twayne, 1982.

Kierkegaard, Søren. *Fear and Trembling* and *The Sickness unto Death.* Translation, introduction, and notes by Walter Lowrie. Princeton: Princeton University Press, 1973.

Kirkby, Joan. "Is There Life after Art? The Metaphysics of Marilynne Robinson's *Housekeeping.*" *Tulsa Studies in Women's Literature* 5 (Spring 1986): 91–109.

Kolodny, Annette. "Dancing between Left and Right: Feminism and the Academic Minefield in the 1980's." *Feminist Studies* 14 (Fall 1988): 453–66.

Krasne, Betty. "Beware of Death by Water." *Anima* 6 (Fall 1979): 5–10.

Kunkel, Francis. *Passion and the Passion: Sex and Religion in Modern Literature.* Philadelphia: Westminster, 1975.

La Belle, Jenijoy. *Herself Beheld: The Literature of the Looking Glass.* Ithaca, N.Y.: Cornell University Press, 1988.

Lakoff, George, and Mark Johnson. *Metaphors We Live By.* Chicago: University of Chicago Press, 1980.

Lanser, Susan Sniader. *The Narrative Act: Point of View in Prose Fiction.* Princeton N.J.: Princeton University Press, 1981.

Lawson, Lewis A., and Victor A. Kramer, eds. *Conversations with Walker Percy.* Jackson: University Press of Mississippi, 1985.

Leites, Edmund. *The Puritan Conscience and Modern Sexuality.* New Haven: Yale University Press, 1986.

Lindemann, Marilee. "This Woman Can Cross Any Line: Power and Authority in Contemporary Woman's Fiction." In *Engendering the Word: Feminist Essays in Psycho-Sexual Politics,* edited by Temma Berg, Anna Shannon Elfenbein, Jeanne Larsen, and Elisa Kay Sparks, 105–24. Urbana: University of Illinois Press, 1989.

Linker, Kate. "Representation and Sexuality." In *Art after Modernism: Rethinking Representation,* edited by Brian Wallis, 391–415. Boston: New Museum of Contemporary Art, 1984.

McCoy, Ralph, compiler. *Theodore Schroeder, A Cold Enthusiast. A Bibliography.* "Biographical Sketch" by Dennis L. Domayer. "Impressions" by Arnold Maddaloni. Carbondale: Southern Illinois University Press, 1973.

McFague, Sallie. *Metaphorical Theology: Models of God in Religious Language.* Philadelphia: Fortress, 1982.

Models of God: Theology for an Ecological, Nuclear Age. Philadelphia: Fortress, 1987.

McHale, Brian. *Postmodernist Fiction.* New York and London: Methuen, 1987.

McLoughlin, William G. *The Meaning of Henry Ward Beecher.* New York: Alfred A. Knopf, 1970.

Mallon, Anne-Marie. "Sojourning Women: Homelessness and Transcendence in *Housekeeping.*" *Critique* 30 (Winter 1989): 95–105.

Marcus, Steven. *The Other Victorians: A Study of Sexuality and Pornography in Mid-Nineteenth Century England.* New York: Basic Books, 1964.

Martin, Judith. *Miss Manners' Guide to Excruciatingly Correct Behavior.* New York: Atheneum, 1982.

Meese, Elizabeth. *Crossing the Double-Cross: The Practice of Feminist Criticism.* Chapel Hill: University of North Carolina Press, 1986.

Merrill, Dean. "The Sexual Hazards of Pastoral Care." *Christianity Today* 29 (8 Nov. 1985): 105.

Miller, Nancy K., ed. *The Poetics of Gender.* New York: Columbia University Press, 1986.

"Arachnologies: The Woman, The Text, and the Critic." In *The Poetics of Gender,* 270–95. New York: Columbia University Press, 1986.

Modleski, Tania. *Loving with a Vengeance: Mass Produced Fantasies for Women.* Hamden, Conn.: Archon, 1982.

Moers, Ellen. *Harriet Beecher Stowe and American Literature: With a Note on Mark Twain and Harriet Beecher Stowe.* Hartford, Conn.: Stowe-Day, 1978.

Moi, Toril. *Sexual/Textual Politics: Feminist Literary Theory.* London: Methuen, 1985.

Moore, John. *Sexuality and Spirituality: The Interplay of Masculine and Feminine in Human Development.* San Francisco: Harper & Row, 1980.

Morey, Ann-Janine. "American Myth and Biblical Interpretation in the Fiction of Harriet Beecher Stowe and Mary Wilkins Freeman." *Journal of the American Academy of Religion* 55 (Winter 1988): 741–63.

"Blaming Women for the Abusive Male Pastor." *Christian Century* 105 (5 Oct. 1988): 866–9.

"Lamentations for the Minister's Wife, by Herself." *Women's Studies* 19 (1991): 327–40.

"Margaret Atwood and Toni Morrison: Reflections on Postmodernism and the Study of Religion and Literature." *Journal of the American Academy of Religion,* forthcoming.

and Cedric Chatterley. "Gestures: I. Notes on Empowerment, Control and the Consolation of Suffering: Pentecostal Women Talk about the Spirit. II. Notes on Supplication, Sublimation and Surrender: A Photographic Essay on Pentecostal Experience." *Cross Currents* 37 (Winter 1987–8): 427–41.

Mueller, Walter Ernest. *Protestant Ministers in Modern American Novels, 1927–1958: The Search for a Role.* Ph.D. diss., University of Nebraska, 1961.

Mulvey, Laura. "Visual Pleasure and Narrative Cinema." In *Women and the Cinema: A Critical Anthology,* edited by Karyn Kay and Gerald Peary, 412–28. New York: E. P. Dutton, 1977.

Natoli, Joseph, ed. *Tracing Literary Theory.* Urbana: University of Illinois Press, 1987.

Nelson, James. *Embodiment: An Approach to Sexuality and Christian Theology.* Minneapolis: Augsburg, 1978.

"Reuniting Sexuality and Spirituality." *Christian Century* 104 (Feb. 25, 1987): 187–90.

Nicholl, Grier. "The Image of the Protestant Minister in the Christian Social Novel." *Church History* 37 (Sept. 1968): 319–34.

Niebuhr, H. Richard. *The Kingdom of God in America.* New York: Harper Torchbook, 1959.

Northcote, Hugh. *Christianity and Sex Problems.* 2d rev. enl. ed. Philadelphia: F. A. Davis, 1916.

Oberdorf, Clarence. *The Psychiatric Novels of Oliver Wendell Holmes.* New York: Columbia University Press, 1946.

Ochs, Carol, *Women and Spirituality.* Totowa, N.J.: Rowman & Allanheld, 1983.

Oliver, Leon. *The Great Sensation: A Full, Complete and Reliable History of the Beecher-Tilton-Woodhull Scandal with Biographical Sketches of the Principal Characters.* Chicago: Beverly, 1873.

Olsen, Tillie. *Silences.* 1965. Reprint. New York: Laurel, Dell, 1978.

Pagels, Elaine. *Adam, Eve, and the Serpent.* New York: Random House, 1988.

Papashvily, Helen Waite. *All the Happy Endings: A Study of the Domestic Novel in America, The Women Who Wrote It, The Women Who Read It, in the Nineteenth Century.* New York: Harper & Row, 1956.

Partridge, Eric. *A Dictionary of Slang and Unconventional English. Colloquialism and Catch-phrases, Solecisms and Catachreses, Nicknames and Vulgarisms.* Edited by Paul Beale. 8th ed. New York: Macmillan, 1984.

Pattison, Eugene. "Introduction and Notes" to *The Leatherwood God.* Vol. 27 of *A Selected Edition of William Dean Howells.* Edited by Edwin H. Cady. Bloomington: Indiana University Press, 1976. 32 vols.

Payne, William Morton. "Recent Fiction." *Dial* 20 (June 1, 1896): 335–9.

Pearsall, Robert. *The Worm in the Bud: The World of Victorian Sexuality.* London: Macmillian, 1969.

Pellauer, Mary. "Sex, Power, and the Family of God: Clergy and Sexual Abuse in Counseling." *Christianity and Crisis* 47 (Feb. 16, 1987): 47–50.

Percy, Walker. *Lost in the Cosmos: The Last Self Help Book.* New York: Farrar, Straus & Giroux, 1983.

Person, Leland. "Hawthorne's Love Letters: Writing and Relationship." *American Literature* 59 (May 1987): 211–27.

Phelps, Arthur Stevens. "The Minister in Fiction." *Publisher's Weekly* 121 (Feb. 20, 1932): 849–51.

Porterfield, Amanda. *Feminine Spirituality in America: From Sarah Edwards to Martha Graham.* Philadelphia: Temple, 1980.

Pratt, Annis. *Archetypal Patterns in Woman's Fiction*. Bloomington: Indiana University Press, 1981.

Prioleau, Elizabeth Stevens. *Circles of Eros: Sexuality in the Work of William Dean Howells*. Durham, N.C.: Duke University Press, 1983.

Radway, Janice. *Reading the Romance: Women, Patriarchy and Popular Literature*. Chapel Hill: University of North Carolina Press, 1984.

Raible, Peter S. "Images of Protestant Clergy in American Novels." In *The Right Time: The Best of Kairos,* edited by David B. Parke, 17–31. Boston: Skinner House, 1982.

Reineke, Martha. "Life Sentences: Kristeva and the Limits of Modernity." *Soundings: An Interdisciplinary Journal*. 71 (Winter 1988): 449.

Reynolds, David S. *Faith in Fiction: The Emergence of Religious Literature in America, 1785–1850*. Cambridge, Mass.: Harvard University Press, 1981.

Rosenberg, Charles E. "Sexuality, Class and Role in Nineteenth Century America." *American Quarterly* 25 (1973): 131–53.

Rubenstein, Roberta. *Boundaries of the Self: Gender, Culture, Fiction*. Urbana: University of Illinois Press, 1987.

Ruegg, Maria. "Metaphor and Metonymy in the Logic of Structuralist Rhetoric." *Glyph* 6 (1979): 141–57.

Sacks, Oliver. *The Man Who Mistook His Wife for a Hat and Other Clinical Tales*. New York: Harper & Row, 1985.

Saltzman, Arthur M. *The Fiction of William Gass: The Consolation of Language*. Carbondale: Southern Illinois University Press, 1986.

Schorer, Mark. *Sinclair Lewis: An American Life*. New York: McGraw-Hill, 1961.

Scott, Nathan. *The Broken Center: Studies in the Horizons of Modern Literature*. New Haven, Conn.: Yale University Press, 1965.

See, Fred. *Desire and the Sign: Nineteenth Century American Fiction*. Baton Rouge: Louisiana State University Press, 1987.

Schroeder, Theodore A. "Converting Sex into Religiosity." *Medical Review of Reviews* 39 (Sept. 1933): 407–15. Reprint. Special Collections, Morris Library, Southern Illinois University at Carbondale.

"Divinity in the Semen." *Journal of Nervous and Mental Disease* 76 (Aug. 1932): 110–27. Reprint. Special Collections, Morris Library, Southern Illinois University at Carbondale.

Erotogenesis of Religion. A Bibliography. Bruno Chap Books. Washington Square, N.Y.: Guido Bruno, 1916. Reprint. Special Collections, Morris Library, Southern Illinois University at Carbondale.

"The Erotogenesis of Religion: Developing a Working Hypothesis." *Alienist and Neurologist* 34 (Nov. 1913). Reprint. Special Collections, Morris Library, Southern Illinois University at Carbondale.

"The Erotogenetic Interpretation of Religion: Its Opponents Reviewed." *Journal of Religious Psychology* 7 (Jan. 1914): 23–44. Reprint. Special Collections, Morris Library, Southern Illinois University at Carbondale.

"A 'Living God' Incarnate." *Psychoanalytic Review* 19 (Jan. 1932): 36–45. Reprint. Special Collections, Morris Library, Southern Illinois University at Carbondale.

"Religion and Sensualism as Connected by Clergymen." *American Journal of Religious Psychology* 3 (May 1908): 16–28. Worcester, Mass.: G. S. Hall,

1908. Reprint. Special Collections, Morris Library, Southern Illinois University at Carbondale.

"Revivals, Sex and Holy Ghost: Being a Description of the Psychic Eroticism of a Negro Revival." *Journal of Abnormal Psychology* 14 (Apr.–July 1919): 34–47. Reprint. Special Collections, Morris Library, Southern Illinois University at Carbondale.

"Shaker Celibacy and Salacity Psychologically Interpreted." *New York Medical Journal* 113 (1 June 1921). N.p.: A.R. Elliott, 1921. Reprint. Special Collections, Morris Library, Southern Illinois University at Carbondale.

Showalter, Elaine. "Piecing and Writing." In *The Poetics of Gender,* edited by Nancy K. Miller, 222–47. New York: Columbia University Press, 1986.

"Feminist Criticism in the Wilderness." In *Writing and Sexual Difference,* edited by Elizabeth Abel, 9–35. Chicago: University of Chicago Press, 1982.

ed. *The New Feminist Criticism: Essays on Literature and Theory.* New York: Pantheon, 1985.

Shuck, Emerson. *Clergymen in Representative American Fiction, 1830–1930: A Study in Attitudes toward Religion.* Ph.D. diss., University of Wisconsin, 1943.

Siebers, Tobin. *The Ethics of Criticism.* Ithaca, N.Y.: Cornell University Press, 1988.

Sizer, Sandra S. *Gospel Hymns and Social Religion: The Rhetoric of Nineteenth Century Revivalism.* Philadelphia: Temple University Press, 1978.

Small, Miriam Rossiter. *Oliver Wendell Holmes.* New York: Twayne, 1962.

Smith, F. Lannom. *Man and Minister in Recent Fiction.* Ph.D. diss., University of Pennsylvania, 1968.

Snitow, Anne. "Mass Market Romance: Pornography for Women is Different." In *Powers of Desire: The Politics of Sexuality,* edited by Anne Snitow, Christine Stansell, and Sharon Thompson, 245–63. New York: Monthly Review Press, 1983.

Sontag, Susan. *Styles of Radical Will.* New York: Farrar, Straus & Giroux, 1966.

Spretnak, Charlene. *The Politics of Women's Spirituality: Essays on the Rise of Spiritual Power within the Feminist Movement.* New York: Anchor, Doubleday, 1982.

Steig, Michael. "The Intentional Phallus: Determining Verbal Meaning in Literature." *Journal of Aesthetics and Art Criticism* 36 (Fall 1977): 51–61.

Steinberg, Leo. *The Sexuality of Christ in Renaissance Art and in Modern Oblivion.* New York: Pantheon, 1983.

Stout, Leo. "Clergy Divorce Spills into the Aisle." *Christianity Today* 26 (Feb. 5, 1982): 20–3.

Sundquist, Eric J., ed. *American Realism: New Essays.* Baltimore, Md.: Johns Hopkins University Press, 1982.

Faulkner: The House Divided. Baltimore, Md.: Johns Hopkins University Press, 1983.

Sussman, Irving. *As Others See Us: A Look at the Rabbi, Priest and Minister through the Eyes of Literature.* New York: Sheed & Ward, 1971.

Sweet, Leonard I. *The Minister's Wife: Her Role in Nineteenth-Century American Evangelicalism.* Philadelphia: Temple University Press, 1983.

Taneyhill, Richard H. *The Leatherwood God.* Ohio Valley Historical Series, Miscellanies no.7: Cincinnati: 1871.

Theweleit, Klaus. *Male Fantasies.* Translated by Erica Carter and Chris Turner in collaboration with Stephen Conway. Foreword by Barbara Ehrenreich. Vol. 1, *Women, Floods, Bodies, History.* Minneapolis: University of Minnesota Press, 1987.

Thurston, Carol. *The Romance Revolution: Erotic Novels for Women and the Quest for a New Sexual Identity.* Urbana: University of Illinois Press, 1987.

Titon, Jeff Todd. *Powerhouse for God: Speech, Chant and Song in an Appalachian Baptist Church.* Austin: University of Texas Press, 1988.

Titus, Warren I. *Winston Churchill.* New York: Twayne, 1963.

Tompkins, Jane. *Sensational Designs: The Cultural Work of American Fiction, 1790–1860.* New York: Oxford University Press, 1985.

Tucker, Mary Orne. *Itinerant Preaching in the Early Days of Methodism, by a Pioneer Preacher's Wife.* Boston: B. B. Russell, 1872. In *The Nineteenth Century American Methodist Itinerant Preacher's Wife,* edited with an introduction by Carolyn De Swarte Gifford. New York: Garland, 1987.

VanSpanckeren, Kathryn. "Shamanism in the Works of Margaret Atwood." In *Margaret Atwood: Visions and Forms,* edited with Jan Garden Castro, 183–204. Carbondale: Southern Illinois University Press, 1988.

VanSpanckeren, Kathryn, and Jan Garden Castro, eds. *Margaret Atwood: Visions and Forms.* With an autobiographical foreword by Margaret Atwood. Carbondale: Southern Illinois University Press, 1988.

Vicinus, Martha, ed. *Suffer and Be Still: Women in the Victorian Age.* Bloomington: Indiana University Press, 1972.

Voight, Gilbert P. "The Protestant Minister in American Fiction." *Lutheran Quarterly* 11 (Feb. 1959): 3–13.

Waller, Altina L. *Reverend Beecher and Mrs. Tilton: Sex and Class in Victorian America.* Amherst: University of Massachusetts Press, 1982.

Weisberger, Bernard A. *They Gathered at the River: The Story of the Great Revivalists and Their Impact upon Religion in America.* Boston: Little, Brown, 1958.

Weir, James Jr. *Religion and Lust, or The Psychical Correlation of Religious Emotion and Sexual Desire.* 3d ed. Chicago: Chicago Medical, 1905.

Welter, Barbara. *Dimity Convictions: The American Woman in the Nineteenth Century.* Athens: Ohio University Press, 1976.

Williams, Catherine Read Arnold. *Fall River: An Authentic Narrative.* Boston: Marshall, Brown, 1834.

Wilson, Edmund. "Two Neglected American Novelists: II Harold Frederic, the Expanding Upstater." *New Yorker,* 6 June 1970: 112–34.

Wiltenburg, Joy. "Excerpts from the Diary of Elizabeth Oakes Smith." *Signs* 9 (Spring 1984): 536–48.

Woods, Ralph. *The Comedy of Redemption: Christian Faith and Comic Vision in Four American Novelists.* Notre Dame, Ind.: University of Notre Dame Press, 1988.

Woolf, Virginia. *A Room of One's Own.* 1929. Reprint. New York: Harcourt, Brace & World, 1957.

Wright, Robert. *The Social Christian Novel in the Gilded Age, 1865–1900.* Ph.D. diss., George Washington University, 1968.

Yarborough, Stephen R. "Walker Percy's *Lancelot* and the Critic's Original Sin." *Texas Studies in Literature and Language* 30 (Summer 1988): 272–94.

Ziff, Larzer. *The American 1890's: Life and Times of a Lost Generation.* New York: Viking, 1966.

Zlotnick, Joan. "*The Damnation of Theron Ware* with a Backward Glance at Hawthorne." *Markham Review* 2 (Feb. 1971): 90–2.

Index

276   INDEX

Cambridge Studies in American Literature and Culture

Continued from the front of the book